Medieval Persian Court Poetry

Poets in Discussion (British Library Ms. 132)

Medieval Persian Court Poetry

Julie Scott Meisami

Princeton University Press, Princeton, New Jersey

Published by Princeton University Press, 41 William Street,
Princeton, New Jersey 08540
In the United Kingdom: Princeton University Press, Guildford, Surrey

Library of Congress Cataloging in Publication Data will be found on
the last printed page of this book

ISBN 0-691-06598-5

Publication of this book has been aided by grants from
The Andrew W. Mellon Foundation and the Persian Heritage
Foundation

This book has been composed in Linotron Sabon

Clothbound editions of Princeton University Press books are printed
on acid-free paper, and binding materials are chosen for strength and
durability. Paperbacks, although satisfactory for personal collections,
are not usually suitable for library rebinding

Printed in the United States of America by Princeton University
Press, Princeton, New Jersey

Contents

Illustrations

Preface

THE poetry of medieval Persia came into being and developed to a high level of artistic excellence under the patronage of the local Iranian dynasties that began to emerge in the latter half of the tenth century. Despite subsequent changes in patterns of patronage (particularly in the mid-twelfth century and after), a significant amount of poetry continued to be produced in and for courtly circles up to the beginning of the modern age.[1] It is to be expected that this circumstance would exert a profound influence on the forms and genres most favored and the values depicted therein, but it is a lamentable fact of Persian studies that in general such influence has been evaluated negatively and court patronage has been judged as leading primarily to the composition of fulsome and insincere panegyric characterized stylistically by excessive ornamentation, artificiality, and rhetorical bombast. A typical view is that expressed in a recent survey of Islamic civilization:

> The re-emergence of Persian as a literary vehicle in about 900 took place in a particular political and social setting that gave it great force and at the same time set definite

[1] Medieval Persian poetry, also referred to as "neo-Persian," began its development some two centuries after the Islamic conquest of Iran. For discussions of the early stages of this development (particularly under the Samanids in the tenth century), see especially Jan Rypka, *History of Iranian Literature*, pp. 126–71, and G. Lazard, "The Rise of the New Persian Language," *Cambridge History of Iran (CHI)*, 4:611–22. A full understanding of the rise of other, noncourtly types of poetry (for example, mystical) will require, among other desiderata, a comprehensive study of shifting patterns of patronage, and in particular of the development of noncourtly centers of patronage (chiefly religious) and of the role of various social groupings and classes (for example the urban bourgeoisie) in contributing to changes in the popularity of specific genres, the decline of some and the appearance of others. While such questions have been touched upon (see, in particular, the works cited in note 5), no comprehensive study of the problem has as yet been undertaken; the value of such an undertaking in enhancing our perception of the total picture of the development of Persian literature would be inestimable.

> limits to its potentialities. . . . One social and economic fact, present from the beginning, could never be entirely shaken off: the overwhelming bulk of Persian literature, until modern times, was composed under dynastic or noble patronage, and this had two unfortunate consequences. In the first place, it led to much commissioned work, uninspired stuff deliberately designed to flatter the patron. Secondly, taste tended to be markedly "courtly"—artificial, lush, over-ingenious; and there was a natural disinclination in such an atmosphere for the writer to risk liberties and innovations, especially if these too obviously suggested the natural and the real. Nevertheless, Persian writers—at least the greatest of them—were marvelously successful in working within these constrictions, and from time to time they even managed to break or circumvent them—with varying consequences to themselves.[2]

Largely because of this negative view of court poetry, many critics have preferred to devote their attention to other types, especially to mystical poetry, in which they find (according to their particular ideological bent) either the record of a deep personal experience or a covert means of combating the pernicious influence of court patronage.[3]

While not denying that such patronage can produce bad writing as well as good (as can any other kind of patronage or, for that matter, none at all), the view that it is inevitably inimical to artistic creativity is grossly erroneous, as is the automatic equation of "courtly" taste with the "lush, artificial, and over-ingenious," as opposed to the "real" or "natural." Studies on medieval literature in the West have shown court patronage to be an essential factor in stimulating the composition of many of the outstanding works of the Western literary tradition.[4] No similar study, aimed at clarifying the interaction

[2] G. M. Wickens, "Persian Literature: An Affirmation of Identity," in *Introduction to Islamic Civilization*, ed. Roger M. Savory, p. 72.

[3] For further discussion of such views see chapters 1 and 6.

[4] Exemplary studies include, for English literature, Richard Firth Green,

between the poet and his courtly milieu, has yet been undertaken for Persian court poetry, although several studies of individual poets have made considerable headway in this respect.[5] This book represents an effort to reevaluate medieval Persian court poetry by placing it in its proper historical and literary perspective. It is by no means exhaustive, or even as comprehensive as one might wish; many poets worthy of inclusion have been omitted, others emphasized perhaps disproportionately; and the work as a whole, rather than attempting a general survey of the tradition, offers instead a series of interpretive essays on specific aspects of it, aims to provide insights into the whole, and suggests directions for further investigation.

Throughout these chapters, the terms *court* (or *courtly*) *poetry* and *courtly love* recur. These terms, and the manner in which they are used, will be discussed in more detail in chapter 1. Their application to any portion of the Persian poetic tradition has (not without justification) been questioned; but no alternatives have been suggested, and the terms—subject to proper definition—remain useful conceptual tools.[6] It is self-evident that love is the primary topic of medieval Persian poetry; it may be assumed that the manner in which it is treated

---

Poets and Princepleasers, and Daniel Javitch, *Poetry and Courtliness in Renaissance England*; and for French, Daniel Poirion, *Le poète et le prince* (see Bibliography).

[5] See especially Jerome W. Clinton, *The Dīvān of Manūchihrī Dāmghānī: A Critical Study*, and, more recently, J.T.P. de Bruijn's study of Sanā'ī, *Of Piety and Poetry (OPP)*, which raises many questions concerning the crucial issue of patronage as well as other aspects of the profession of poet in medieval Persia.

[6] Cf. R. Rehder, "Persian Poets and Modern Critics," *Edebiyat* 2 (1977), 111. Rehder's objections are made in the context of the use of the term by Michael Hillmann in his *Unity in the Ghazals of Hafez*; the point that Hillmann uses the term indiscriminately and without attempt at definition is well taken, but the generalization that any application of Western critical concepts or terms to non-Western literatures is inappropriate is, I think, exaggerated. The debate among Western scholars concerning the term's validity is too extensive and complex to discuss here; for useful references, see the essays in *The Meaning of Courtly Love*, ed. F. X. Newman, and the response by Jean Frappier, "Sur un procès fait à l'amour courtois," in *Amour courtois et Table Ronde*, pp. 61–96.

by court poets reflects the values and sensibilities of the courtly audience. However, in using the term *courtly* to describe the ideal of love depicted by these poets, I depart from the views both of those who (like C. S. Lewis) would limit *courtly love* to a specific historical period and geographical locus or relate it to a concrete "system" or "code" (either social or literary),[7] and of those who (like Peter Dronke) hold the opinion that " 'the new feeling' of *amour courtois* . . . might indeed occur at any time or place" and is "not confined to courtly or chivalric society."[8] I prefer the view of scholars who regard *courtly love* as an essentially literary phenomenon expressive of a mode of thought that has close ties with courtly values.[9]

Persian court poetry combines the ethics of courtly conduct with those of the conduct of love in a fashion designed to emphasize the former at least as much as the latter. Like the connection between poet and court in Persia, the courtly ethic that informs this poetry has its roots in antiquity; it influenced not only the Persian literature that developed in the Islamic period, but the Arabic tradition as well (through which it may even have extended its influence to medieval Europe).[10] The central

[7] C. S. Lewis asserts categorically that courtly love "appeared quite suddenly at the end of the eleventh century in Languedoc" and insists on "its *systematic coherence* throughout the love poetry of the troubadours *as a whole*" (*The Allegory of Love*, pp. 2, 3; my emphasis). Similarly, A. J. Denomy states, "Courtly love made its appearance in the Middle Ages, in a culture and civilization that were Christian" (*The Heresy of Courtly Love*, p. 19), a view that is modified somewhat in his "Courtly Love and Courtliness," *Speculum* 28 (1953), 44–45.

[8] Peter Dronke, *Medieval Latin and the Rise of European Love-Lyric*, 2d ed., 1:xvii.

[9] In their introduction to the collection *In Pursuit of Perfection*, Joan Ferrante and George Economou observe that "a distinction must be made between an established doctrine, a rigid system of rules of behavior, which did not exist, and a mode of thought, expressed in literary conventions, which can be traced through so much medieval literature" (p. 3). See also J. M. Steadman, "Courtly Love as a Problem of Style," in *Chaucer und seine Zeit*, ed. A. Esch, pp. 1–33. The problem is discussed more fully in chapter 1 of this book.

[10] On the influence of Iranian courtly ethics on the Arabic tradition, see de Bruijn, *OPP*, p. 157, and chapter 1 of this book.

virtues of this ethic, loyalty and service, are of equal importance in the context of love; and while Persian poets do not speak of courtly love any more than do their European counterparts, they do make explicit connections between love, courtesy (*murūvat*), chivalry (*javānmardī*, *futūvat*), and the virtues associated with all three.[11] An examination of the connections between these related value systems is a major preoccupation of this book.

A final observation: my approach in the essays that follow is broadly comparative. Since it is evident—regardless of the direction in which one may be traveling—that the medieval world does not stop at, say, the border between Christian Byzantium and the Islamic territories, it is also clear that valuable insights may be gained from comparing the various manifestations of what is, to a great extent, a unified tradition, which shares certain basic attitudes and assumptions despite the particular local coloring of the individual cultures that make up the whole.[12] Frequently an example from one area may throw

[11] The connection between love and *murūwah*, however, is made explicitly (albeit in a negative way) by the Hispano-Arabic poet Ibn Quzmān, when he declares, "Let others lay claim to courtly love" (*ʿIshq al-murūwah ghayrī yaddaʿīhi*) (quoted by A. Hamori, "Form and Logic in Some Medieval Arabic Poems," *Edebiyat* 2 [1977], 167). On the "courtliness" of courtly love and the question of medieval terms that suggest the concept, see Ferrante and Economou, *In Pursuit of Perfection*, p. 4; Denomy, " 'Courtly Love,' " 47–63; J. D. Burnley, "*Fine amor*: Its Meaning and Context," *Review of English Studies*, n.s., 31 (1980), 129–48; Jean Frappier, "Vues sur les conceptions courtoises dans les littératures d'oc et d'oïl au XIIe siècle," *CCM* 2 (1959) 135–37. The similarity between the terms *murūwah*/*murūvat* as used by Arabic and Persian poets, and the troubadours' *courtoisie* or *cortezia*, is often quite striking. The Islamic concept of *futūwah* (Persian *javānmardī*) is said to have been of Iranian origin; cf. Claude Cahen, "Tribes, Cities and Social Organization," *CHI*, 4:320–22, and L. Massignon, "La 'Futuwwa,' ou 'pacte d'honneur artisanal' entre les travailleurs musulmans au Moyen Age," *La Nouvelle Clio* 4 (1952), 171–98; see also *EI*², s.v. "Futuwwa." For discussions (pro and con) of the possible influence of Arabic *futūwah* on troubadour poetry, see Denomy, "*Jovens*: The Notion of Youth Among the Troubadours, Its Meaning and Source," *Medieval Studies* 11 (1949), 1–22; Erich Köhler, "Sens et fonction du terme 'jeunesse' dans la poésie des troubadours," in *Mélanges René Crozet*, 1:569–72.

[12] Compare the methodological problems and approach outlined by M.G.S.

unexpected light on a problem from another; I have therefore felt at liberty to draw parallels and inferences where they seemed appropriate. Further (and perhaps more important), the continuity between the Persian tradition of court poetry and that of Arabic, which developed several centuries earlier—a continuity all too often obscured by the fragmentation of literary studies along linguistic, geographical, or political lines—will be stressed throughout this book, in particular with respect to the development of panegyric poetry and of the love lyric.

The chapters that follow represent the results of both earlier research on medieval Persian court poetry and new work undertaken specifically in connection with this book. Any resulting unevenness will, I hope, be forgiven; my goal is to say, not the last word on the topic, but a much-needed first word in order to stimulate greater interest and more extensive research on the many and varied aspects of court poetry. I wish to express my sincere thanks to the many colleagues and friends who, through their unflagging support, have encouraged me in the completion of this work. While it is impossible to name all those who have been a source of encouragement, I must single out for special mention Jerome Clinton of Princeton University, James Monroe of the University of California at Berkeley, Daniel Javitch of New York University, and Joseph Snow of the University of Georgia, whose support and advice have been unstinting. The Comparative Literature Department at the University of California, Berkeley, provided the affiliation that made it possible to use library and other resources, while some

Hodgson in his invaluable study of Islamic culture and institutions, *The Venture of Islam*, in particular the methodological portion of the Introduction (1:22–67) and the chapter entitled "Cultural Patterning in Islamdom and the Occident" (2:329–68). Rehder comments on the utility of comparative literary studies ("Persian Poets," 98); but his periodization is too limited and his methodology hindered by his unwillingness to accept Western terminology as having a place in the conduct of such studies. See also James T. Monroe, *The Art of Badīʿ az-Zamān al-Hamadhānī as Picaresque Narrative*, pp. 98–100; and J. S. Meisami, "Norms and Conventions of the Classical Persian Lyric," *Proceedings of the Nineteenth Congress of the International Comparative Literature Association*, 1:203–207.

portions of the research on poetic structure were done during my tenure of a Fellowship for Independent Study from the National Endowment for the Humanities. Special appreciation must go to Peter Whigham for his invaluable assistance with the translations and to Marjorie Sherwood of Princeton University Press for her encouragement and advice. Finally, my deepest thanks to Esmail, Mona, and Ayda, whose patience during the various phases of this book has been monumental and whose support has been most precious.

The dating employed in this study is, for purposes of simplicity, in accordance with the Christian calendar; Islamic scholars will have no trouble making the necessary conversions to Hijri dates. Transliterations follow the system of the Library of Congress for Arabic and Persian. Bibliographic references are given in brief form in the footnotes; full citations, together with a list of abbreviations for works referred to frequently and for periodicals, will be found in the Bibliography. Unless otherwise noted, translations are my own; since some texts lent themselves more readily to rendering in English than did others, and since some of the translated excerpts form part of more extensive projects and have received more attention over a longer period of time, I apologize in advance for any unevenness. In general, in the interest of brevity, I have limited myself to quotations in translation only, except where certain features of their language made reference to the original obligatory; page references to the editions used will aid specialists who wish to consult the works in the original languages. The illustrations are reproduced with the permission of the British Library, London, and the John Rylands University Library, Manchester.

Medieval Persian Court Poetry

· I ·

Poet and Court in Persia

The Traditional Background

The close relationship between court and poet in Persia dates from pre-Islamic times, when the poet-minstrel enjoyed an important and influential position at the court of the Iranian emperors.[1] Ancient Iranian society centered around the person of the ruler, the king of kings, who ruled through an administration headed by his chief minister; traditionally, the ruler remained separate from his household, concealed from even the highest dignitaries by an intervening curtain, and transmitted his commands to the assembled court through a noble who bore the title Khurram-bāsh, "Be joyful."[2] The king showed himself in public only on such ritually important occasions as the equinoctial festivals of Naw Rūz, the New Year, in the spring, and Mihrigān, in the fall.[3] Court life

> was governed by a strict and elaborate etiquette. The courtiers were grouped in three classes according to their birth and office. Members of the royal family and the knights of the retinue had the highest standing. There were also jesters, jugglers, clowns, and musicians. The last played an important part in Court life and were likewise divided into three grades, according to their skill and the instruments on which they performed.[4]

[1] See Mary Boyce, "The Parthian *Gōsān* and Iranian Minstrel Tradition," *JRAS* (1947), 10–12; Clinton, *Manūchihrī*, pp. 1–2.

[2] The etymology of this term appears doubtful; its source seems to be the Arab historian al-Masʿūdī in his work *Murūj al-Dhahab*, who may be providing a translation for a corrupted term. Cf. *Les prairies d'or*, ed. and trans. Barbier de Meynard and Pavet de Courteille, 2:158.

[3] C. Huart, *Ancient Persia and Iranian Civilization*, pp. 145–47. See also R. Ghirshmann, *Iran: From the Earliest Times to the Islamic Conquest*, pp. 309–11; and especially M. G. Morony, *Iraq After the Muslim Conquest*, pp. 70–98.

[4] Ghirshmann, *Iran*, p. 312. For a detailed picture of Sassanian court eti-

It was to this latter group that poets, as practitioners of an oral art closely associated with music, belonged. The favor they enjoyed at court is attested to by references in ancient texts as well as by popular traditions. Mary Boyce describes the minstrel of Parthian times as "entertainer of king and commoner, privileged at court and popular with the people; present at graveside and at the feast; eulogist, satirist, storyteller, musician; recorder of past achievements, and commentator of his own times."[5] Under the Sassanians, poets enjoyed an even more privileged position:

> Musicians and singers of the first rank belonged to the highest class of courtiers, comprising nobles and princes of the royal blood, and were placed on a footing of equality with the greatest of them. The court-minstrels appear to have been in constant attendance in the king's audience-chamber, where they were called on at the discretion of the *xurrambāš*; and also at state-banquets and upon special occasions; and yearly they presented poems . . . as offerings to the king at the festivals of Mihrgān and Naurūz.[6]

The example of Bārbad, the renowned court minstrel of Khusraw II Parvīz, whose memory is enshrined in later Persian epic and romance, reflects the importance and influence of the poet at court.[7] Although the poetry of these court poets and minstrels has vanished almost completely—due both to its predominantly oral nature and to changes in Persian literary taste

quette, see further A. Christensen, *L'Iran sous les Sassanides*, pp. 388–410; and the anonymous Arabic *Kitāb al-Tāj*, ed. Aḥmad Zakī Bāshā.

[5] Boyce, "Parthian *Gōsān*," 17–18. Compare Morton Bloomfield's remarks on the Anglo-Saxon scop, in "Understanding Old English Poetry," *Essays and Explorations*, pp. 62–65.

[6] Boyce, "Parthian *Gōsān*," 22; cf. *Kitāb al-Tāj*, pp. 146–48.

[7] Cf. Boyce, "Parthian *Gōsān*," 23–25; Huart, *Ancient Persia*, pp. 145–46; E. G. Browne, *A Literary History of Persia (LHP)*, 1:14–16, and idem, "The Sources of Dawlatshāh; with . . . an Excursus on Bārbad and Rūdakī," *JRAS* (1899), 54–61; Rypka, *History*, pp. 55–57. Bārbad's importance is recalled both by Firdawsī in the *Shāhnāmah* and by Niẓāmī in *Khusraw u Shīrīn* and the *Haft Paykar*.

following the Islamic conquest[8]—the abundant reminiscences of it indicate an awareness of the tradition which led to a continuity of the close relationship between poet and court in Islamic times.

The emerging Arab caliphate, stimulated by the demands of the new, urban society that was rapidly displacing the old tribal one, drew heavily on Persian models of court conduct and etiquette. Arab contacts with Persian culture, which had always existed in some form or other, increased markedly, first under the Umayyads but especially with the early Abbasid rulers, whose court protocols (like their bureaucracy) derived in large part from Sassanian practice.[9] Models were provided through the translation and imitation of works of the "mirror for princes" type, manuals of statecraft which had formed an important genre of Sassanian prose literature, by secretaries and scribes who were themselves often of Persian origin, like ʿAbd al-Ḥamīd al-Kātib (d. 750) and Ibn al-Muqaffaʿ (d. 754).[10] Along with attempts to establish hereditary rule, the seclusion of kings in the Sassanian style came to be practiced. Iranian festivals such as Naw Rūz and Mihrigān were cele-

[8] Cf. Boyce, "Parthian *Gōsān*," 32–41; Clinton, *Manūchihrī*, pp. 2–3.

[9] Victor Danner, "Arabic Literature in Iran," *CHI*, 4:566–67, gives a brief account of early contacts. Persian influence on Umayyad court life increased sharply during the brief reign of Yazīd III (720), whose mother was Persian; see M. Sprengling, "From Persian to Arabic," *AJSLL* 56 (1939), 214–17 et passim. For the Abbasids, see Hodgson, *Venture*, 1:239, 280–84, and the references cited on 505–506; Morony, *Iraq*, especially pp. 27–98. For a valuable caveat against viewing such contacts either in terms of "influence" or of national self-assertion, see Hodgson, 1:40–45, and Morony, pp. 3–9. The view that assumes a recourse to Iranian models by the Abbasids has recently been challenged by Jacob Lassner; see *The Shaping of ʿAbbasid Rule*, pp. 3–4, 13–15 et passim.

[10] See A.K.S. Lambton, "Islamic Mirrors for Princes," *Quaderno dell'Accademia Nazionale dei Lincei* 160 (1971), 419–23. As Lambton notes, "The possibility that [Islamic mirrors] were influenced by Byzantine mirrors . . . cannot be ruled out, but whereas there were Arabic translations of Pahlavi *andarz-nāma*, I do not know of any similar translations of Byzantine mirrors" (421). See also C. E. Bosworth, "An Early Arabic Mirror for Princes: Ṭāhir Dhū l-Yamīnain's Epistle to His Son ʿAbdallāh (206/821)," *JNES* 29 (1970), 15, and Danner, "Arabic Literature," passim.

brated with great pomp in Baghdad. Poets were elevated from their earlier roles of tribal panegyrist-satirist or urban minstrel to a position comparable to that enjoyed by the Sassanian court minstrels; and panegyric became the major end of the Arabic *qaṣīdah*, presented to the ruler on ceremonial occasions as well as utilized for the praise of lesser notables.[11] Many poets became the familiars of royalty and aristocracy, some holding the much-coveted office of *nadīm*: boon companion to the ruler.[12]

This important and influential institution, of Iranian origin—the founder of the Sassanian dynasty, Ardashīr Bābakān, is said to have described it as "part of government (*siyāsah*), and the means of strengthening rulership"[13]—was regulated by a strict etiquette, and an abundant literature developed concerning the qualifications and proper conduct of the *nadīm*.[14] The following passage from the ninth-century mirror the *Kitāb al-Tāj* suggests both the significance of the position and the eminent suitability of the poet to occupy it.

> A courtier who accompanies the king (on a journey) must be familiar with the stages of the route and its dis-

[11] Cf. M. M. Badawi, "From Primary to Secondary Qaṣīdas: Thoughts on the Development of Classical Arabic Poetry," *JAL* 11 (1980); and see chapter 2 of this book.

[12] See Badawi, "Qaṣīdas," 10; and especially A. G. Chejne, "The Boon-Companion in Early ʿAbbasid Times," *JAOS* 85 (1965), 327–35. On the urban *majlis*, the "salon" or intimate gathering at which the caliph or vizier would sit with a small group of familiars and boon companions, see G. E. von Grunebaum, "Aspects of Arabic Urban Literature Mostly in Ninth and Tenth Centuries," *Islamic Studies* 8 (1969), 292–93.; J.-E. Bencheikh, "Le cénacle poétique du calife al-Mutawakkil (m. 247)," *BEO* 29 (1977), 39, and idem, "Les secrétaires poètes et animateurs de cénacles aux IIe et IIIe siècles de l'Hégire: contribution à l'analyse d'une production poétique," *JA* 263 (1975), 265–315.

[13] Chejne, "Boon-Companion," 330. Al-Masʿūdī states that the king's courtiers (*nudamāʾ*) occupied the first rank in the social hierarchy established by Ardashīr (*Les prairies d'or*, 1:217–18).

[14] On the Arabic and Persian literature concerning the *nadīm*, see the works cited by Chejne, "Boon-Companion," 328 et passim. For exemplary treatments see *Kitāb al-Tāj*, pp. 71–159, and the chapter on the *nadīm* in Kaykāvūs ibn Iskandar, *A Mirror for Princes: The Qābūs Nāma*, trans. R. Levy, pp. 196–200.

> tances, and be able to direct him as to the correct road, its landmarks and its watering-places. He should yawn and sleep but little, nor should he cough or sneeze. His disposition should be balanced, his constitution sound; he should (be able to) make amusing and pleasant conversation, and to make time (appear) short, both day and night. He must be knowledgeable concerning the battles of tribes and their noble deeds, and know both rare verses and current proverbs; he must be acquainted with every art, and be able to choose properly from good or bad: if (for example) he speaks of the Hereafter and the blessings of Paradise, he informs (the king) thereby of the rewards God has prepared for the pious and makes him eager to obtain them; and if he speaks of Hellfire, he warns him of that which leads thereto. Thus does he counsel abstention (from evil) at one time, and encourage him (to do good) at another. The king has the greatest need of one who possesses such qualities, and when he finds such a person, it is proper that he not part from him, unless some matter destroy his immunity and require punishment.[15]

From this passage it becomes clear that the *nadīm* is expected to function not only as boon companion and familiar, but also as a source of counsel and of moral guidance—a function the court poet who might hold this office would be especially qualified to discharge.[16] An understanding of this seldom-acknowledged aspect of the role of *nadīm* and poet alike throws new light on the careers of such famous Abbasid court poets as al-ʿAbbās ibn al-Aḥnaf (d. c. 808), Abū Nuwās (d. 813?), and Abū al-ʿAtāhiyah (d. 828), who served as boon companions to various rulers (Abū Nuwās, for example, was the *nadīm* of the caliph al-Amīn and before that had enjoyed

[15] *Kitāb al-Tāj*, pp. 71–2.

[16] Cf. Boyce, "Parthian *Gōsān*," passim; on the importance of the didactic element in pre-Islamic Persian court poetry, see ibid., 30–32. Moral edification as a duty of the courtier is emphasized in, e.g., Kaykāvūs, *Mirror for Princes*, p. 198, and Naṣīr al-Dīn Ṭūsī, *The Nasirean Ethics*, trans. G. M. Wickens, pp. 238–39; as an important aspect of the court poet's function, by Niẓāmī ʿArūẓī in his chapter on poetry, *The Chahár Maqála* ("*Four Discourses*"), trans. E. G. Browne, pp. 42–87.

the friendship and confidence of al-Amīn's father, the famed Hārūn al-Rashīd).[17] The position of intimacy enjoyed by such poets may account for their ability to specialize in the minor genres of erotic, bacchic, and gnomic poetry, without being obliged to compose panegyric (for which others were employed);[18] while the fact that their function was not limited to entertainment but incorporated an ethical dimension suggests that, on occasion at least, the personae of the distraught lover and the debauched libertine, so characteristic of Abbasid (and later of Persian) court poetry, may have served as vehicles for messages more profound than appear at first glance. With respect to the latter in particular, the principle, enunciated in the *Kitāb al-Tāj*, that the drunkard is immune from punishment for improprieties uttered while in a state of inebriation, is illuminating: "Drunkenness has limits; should his boon companion reach them, it is most becoming and fitting that the king not reproach him if he unwittingly commits an error, if a (careless) word gets the better of his tongue, or if some fancy causes him to offend."[19] The negative example set in such poetry as that of Abū Nuwās might serve as a forceful reminder of the correct path;[20] similarly, the complaints of the dis-

[17] Chejne, "Boon-Companion," 330. Under al-Rashīd the position was held by al-ʿAbbās ibn al-Aḥnaf and Abū al-ʿAtāhiyah (ibid., 333).

[18] On the problem of specialization see J.-E. Bencheikh, *Poétique arabe*, pp. 111–15, and N. Tomiche, "Réflexions sur la poésie de ʿAbbās b. al-Aḥnaf," *Arabica* 27 (1980), 275–77. Badawi's assertion that "no poet could afford to earn his living as a poet by his occasional poems: unless a poet had independent means of livelihood . . . he had no option but to compose panegyrics if he was to survive on his poetry," and the corollary assumption that, since panegyrics were written to please the patron, the *qiṭʿah*—the independent poem on love, wine, etc.—was composed by the poet "primarily to please himself, or to relieve his feelings" ("Qaṣīdas," 12), overlooks both the poet's dual identity as courtier and the essentially public nature of medieval Arabic poetry in general, whether composed for formal occasions or for more intimate gatherings. On the other hand, the possibilities offered by the various strategies for indirect discourse available ensured that the poet would to some extent at least be able to find expression for his own views.

[19] *Kitāb al-Tāj*, p. 45.

[20] This dimension of Abū Nuwās's poetry is suggested by Andras Hamori, who describes the poet's libertine persona as being the antithesis of the *wāʿiẓ*,

traught courtly lover in the poems of al-ʿAbbās might suggest to the ruler that his obligations toward his dependents are at least as pressing as those of the lady toward her devoted lover.[21]

With the development of neo-Persian poetry at the courts of local Iranian princes from the late tenth century onward, the close relationship between court and poet continued to prevail. It is important to remember—as Gilbert Lazard reminds us—that the development of Persian literature

---

the preacher of orthodox morality. Abū Nuwās preaches by negative example, which can be as potent a form of instruction as positive exhortation. See *On the Art of Medieval Arabic Literature*, pp. 50–71. The relations between Abū Nuwās and the Caliph al-Amīn are the subject of many anecdotes, which, though perhaps apocryphal (and undoubtedly politically motivated), are nevertheless representative of the potentials of such a connection; see, for example, Abū Hiffān al-Miḥzamī, *Akhbār Abī Nuwās*, ed. ʿA. A. Farrāj, pp. 23–26, 83–85, 122–23, 129–31, et passim. To Abū Nuwās are also attributed (probably apocryphally as well) some satirical verses on al-Amīn; see Adam Mez, *The Renaissance of Islam*, trans. S. Khuda Bukhsh and D. S. Margoliouth, p. 353. From the persona of Abū Nuwās derives that of ʿUmar Khayyām as well as the *rind* of later Persian poetry (especially *ghazal*, culminating in Ḥāfiẓ, who explicitly opposes *rind* and *vāʿiẓ*); cf. A. Christensen, *Recherches sur les Rubāʿiyāt de ʿOmar Ḫayyām*, p. 45, who asserts that Abū Nuwās (like his predecessor Bashshār ibn Burd) continued an Iranian poetic tradition dating from Sassanian times.

[21] An anecdote concerning al-ʿAbbās suggests such a function for the love poem: It is recounted that the Caliph al-Rashīd and his favorite, one Maria, had a falling out, and pride prevented their reconciliation, as neither was willing to lose face. The vizier Yaḥyā ibn Khālid al-Barmakī sought al-ʿAbbās's assistance in bringing the two back together. Al-ʿAbbās composed four verses, beginning with "Each of the lovers was angry, desirous [of the other], distressed" (*al-ʿĀshiqāni kilāhumā mutaghaḍḍibu / wa-kilāhumā mutashawwiqun mutaṭarribu*). Yaḥyā sent the verses to al-Rashīd, who commented on their aptness to his own situation and presented them to Maria, whereupon the two were reconciled, and the poet was richly rewarded by all parties. (Quoted from the *Aghānī* by Karam al-Bustānī in his introduction to the *Dīwān* of al-ʿAbbās, pp. 6–7; cf. also Tomiche, "Réflexions," 275–76). A. Guillaume has suggested that Abū al-ʿAtāhiyah's sudden "conversion" from a composer of erotic and bacchic verse to ascetic may have had political implications, coinciding as it did with his coming under the patronage of al-Faḍl ibn Rabīʿ; his ascetic stance and warnings of the transience of worldly glory may have provided a poetic weapon in that minister's intrigues against the Barmakids. See *EI*² s.v. "Abū 'l-ʿAtāhiya."

was neither a pure and simple resurgence of the ancient culture nor the expression of an entirely fresh culture of Arab-Islamic origin. The links with ancient Iran had been established partly perhaps by such of the Middle Persian writings as were still being read, but surely much more by what had been handed down to Arabic literature and what still remained, more or less modified and brought up to date, in the living oral tradition. It is in these two sources, Arabic literature and oral Iranian literature, that the origin of the forms and themes of Persian poetry must be sought.[22]

Histories, biographies of poets, and other sources attest to the importance of court poets throughout the medieval period. The famous chapter on poetry in the *Chahār Maqālah* (1155–57) of Niẓāmī ʿArūẓī describes the relationship of mutual benefit that existed between poet and patron; for, since the poet's chief official function was to spread the fame and repute of the ruler,

> so a king cannot dispense with a good poet, who shall conduce to the immortality of his name, and shall record his fame in *díwáns* and books. For when the king receives that command which none can escape [i.e. death], no trace will remain of his army, his treasure, and his store; but his name will endure forever by reason of the poet's verse.[23]

The same writer recounts numerous anecdotes testifying to the influence of poets in the political sphere; similarly, ʿAwfī and

[22] Lazard, "Rise," p. 612. The view that neo-Persian literature represents a reaffirmation of Iranian national identity is exemplified by Wickens, "Persian Literature"; see also Rypka, *History*, pp. 141–42 et passim. On the interpenetration of Arabic poetry into Persian court life, see Danner, "Arabic Literature"; C. E. Bosworth, "The Ṭâhirids and Persian Literature," *Iran* 7 (1969), 103–106; *EI²*, s.v. "al-ʿAbbās ibn al-Aḥnaf"; and see R. Blachère, *Un poète arabe du IVe siècle de l'Hégire . . . Abou ṭ-Ṭayyib al-Motanabbî*, pp. 271–84, on the popularity of that poet's verse at the Samanid court (al-Mutanabbī also spent a brief period as panegyrist of the Buyids in western Iran) and the numerous Persian commentaries on his *Dīwān*.

[23] Niẓāmī ʿArūẓī, *Chahár Maqála*, p. 45.

Dawlatshāh record in their biographical works the names of poets (many now only names) who occupied important positions at court. Maḥmūd of Ghaznah is said to have established the title of poet laureate (*malik al-shuʿarā*ʾ) to honor his chief panegyrist, ʿUnṣurī; the institution was preserved by his successors and adopted by his rivals, the Saljuqs.[24] Until the Mongol catastrophe, which altered patterns of patronage and literary taste as radically as it did other aspects of Iranian life, the court poet enjoyed considerable privilege and influence in return for ensuring his patron's repute by means of his eloquent verses; and though his prestige may have diminished somewhat after the establishment of Mongol hegemony, the careers of individual poets still attest to a degree of continued influence and esteem.[25]

In keeping with the ethical dimension of the court poet's function, panegyric preoccupations were never far removed from didactic ones. The ethical dimension of court poetry has received little serious attention from critics eager to associate court poetry in general, and panegyric in particular, with flattery and bombast, despite abundant evidence—provided in particular in philosophical discussions of poetry and in ethical writings, especially those of the mirror-for-princes variety—

[24] Cf. Lazard, "Rise," p. 618. Dawlatshāh provides abundant examples of poets who held the post of *nadīm*; cf. *The Tadhkiratu 'sh-Shuʿará*ʾ ("*Memoirs of the Poets*"), ed. E. G. Browne, pp. 9–10 (Amīr Muʿizzī), 44–5 (ʿUnṣurī), 72 (ʿAzraqī), etc. Bayhaqī's *History* testifies to the importance of poets at the Ghaznavid court; see *Tārīkh-i Bayhaqī*, ed. Q. Ghanī and ʿA. A. Fayyāẓ, pp. 273–74 (a description of poets receiving honors at the Mihrigān festival), 274–80 (on the state and importance of poetry in general, and a *qaṣīdah* on the same topic), 384–87 (on the importance of poets to kings, and in particular their obligation to impart good advice). See also Gītī Fallāḥ Rastgār, "Ādāb u rusūm u tashrīfāt-i darbār-i Ghaznah az khilāl-i *Tārīkh-i Bayhaqī*," in *Yādnāmah-i Abū al-Faẓl Bayhaqī*, pp. 424–65. Anvarī's poetic description of his duties as *nadīm* provides further illumination of this important function; see chapter 2, n. 53. On Maḥmūd's institution of the post of *malik al-shuʿarā*ʾ see Dawlatshāh, *Tadhkiratu 'sh-Shuʿará*ʾ, p. 45; on the requirements of the poetic profession in general during the Ghaznavid period, see de Bruijn, *OPP*, pp. 155–60.

[25] On the cultural changes that followed the Mongol invasion, see Rypka, *History*, pp. 248–49, and Hodgson, *Venture*, 2:437–500; see also chapter 6, n. 48.

for the view that an important function of poetry is moral instruction by example. To cite only one instance: al-Fārābī, in his discussion of poetry in the *Fuṣūl al-Madanī*, notes its effect on the imagination in moving the hearer to seek good and avoid evil,[26] in terms that both recall the passage from the *Ki-*

[26] Al-Fārābī, *Fuṣūl al-Madanī, Aphorisms of the Statesman*, ed. and trans. D. M. Dunlop, p. 49. In the same work, al-Fārābī defines poetry as follows: "All poetry has been invented to produce an excellent imaginative impression of the object. It is of six kinds, three of which are praised and three blamed. Of the three which are praised one is that by which are aimed at the improvement of the rational faculty, and that its actions and thought should be directed towards happiness, the production of an imaginative impression of divine matters and good deeds, excellence in producing an imaginative impression of the virtues and approving them, the reprobating of evil deeds and the vices, and holding them in scorn. The second kind is that by which are aimed at the improvement and correction of those accidents of the soul which are related to strength, and the breaking of them down till they become moderate and cease to be excessive. Such accidents are anger, pride, cruelty, effrontery, love of honour and domination, greed and the like. Those who possess these qualities are led (*sc.* by this kind of poetry) to employ them in good, not evil deeds. The third kind aims at the improvement and correction of the accidents of the soul related to weakness and softness, viz. desires, base pleasures, falseness and slackness of soul, pity, fear, anxiety, grief, shame, luxury, softness, and the like, that they may be broken down and cease to be excessive, till they become moderate, and (the possessor) is led to employ them in good, not evil deeds. The three kinds which are blamed are the opposites of the three which are praised. For the former ruin all that the latter correct, bringing it from the moderate state to excess" (pp. 49–50). See also al-Fārābī's observations on poetic discourse translated by Vicente Cantarino, *Arabic Poetics in the Golden Age*, pp. 116–17; and compare the views of Averroes (Ibn Rushd), discussed in ibid., pp. 180–81, and in idem, "Averroes on Poetry," in *Islam and Its Cultural Divergence*, ed. G. L. Tikku, pp. 10–26. The relevance of the views of the philosophers on poetry has been questioned by, among others, G.J.H. van Gelder, who objects that "they are not or hardly concerned at all with Arabic poetry and their direct influence on traditional Arabic theory and criticism is inappreciably slight" (*Beyond the Line: Classical Arabic Literary Critics on the Coherence and Unity of the Poem*, p. 166); however, what scholars generally term "criticism" is, in fact, rhetoric, the orientation of which is quite different, and for serious discussions of the function of poetry one must go to the philosophers, exegetes, ethical writers, and, often as not, the mystics. For analogous problems with respect to medieval European poetry, see Judson B. Allen, *The Ethical Poetic of the Later Middle Ages*, pp. xi–xii et passim. See also Allen's discussion of Averroes' conception of poetry (as transmitted to medi-

tāb al-Tāj concerning the courtier's duty to encourage his prince to pursue good and avoid evil and anticipate Niẓāmī ʿArūẓī's observation that the poet "by acting on the imagination . . . excites the faculties of anger and concupiscence in such a way that by his suggestion men's temperaments become affected with exultation or depression; whereby he conduces to the accomplishment of great things in the order of the world."[27] The thirteenth-century ethical writer Naṣīr al-Dīn Ṭūsī's reminder of the importance of the courtier's counsel in directing his prince toward the good—that, by following "the path of subtlety and manipulation," he show him "the way of best interest," so that "gradually, in moments of privacy and intimacy, he should be brought (by examples, by tales of past rulers, and by subtle devices) to see the ill-advised form of his own opinion"[28]—expands on a topic addressed by al-Ghazzālī (d. 1111) in his *Nasīḥat al-Mulūk*, where he enjoins the ruler to devote

> constant attention to the Biographies of the Kings and inquiry concerning the activities of the Kings of Old; because the present world is the continuation of the empire of the forerunners, who reigned and departed, each leaving a memory to his name and [acquiring] treasure in this life and the next. The treasure for the next life is righteous conduct, and the treasure in this life is a good name among the people.[29]

Who better equipped to provide such guidance than the poet, who, as the repository of tradition, has at his ready command ample material to employ toward this end, as well as the elo-

---

eval Europe via Hermann the German's Latin translation of his commentary on Aristotle), "Hermann the German's Averroistic Aristotle and Medieval Poetic Theory," *Mosaic* 9:3 (1976), 67–81.

[27] Niẓāmī ʿArūẓī, *Chahár Maqála*, p. 43; the essay is filled with concrete examples of the ethical (and political) effect of poetry.

[28] Naṣīr al-Dīn Ṭūsī, *Nasirean Ethics*, p. 238.

[29] Al-Ghazzālī, *Ghazālī's Book of Counsel for Kings (Nasīḥat al-Mulūk)*, tr. F.R.C. Bagley, p. 74. On the value for the ruler of reading history, compare R. F. Green, *Poets and Princepleasers*, pp. 138–45.

quence to produce the desired imaginative effect? I will examine various ways in which the medieval Persian court poet addressed himself, in general, to the ethical dimension of his task, and specifically in the major genres of court poetry, panegyric, romance, and love lyric; this introductory chapter is intended to provide a theoretical and critical background to the chapters that follow, together with a brief consideration of precedents in the related Arabic tradition, and of parallels in the Western.

Courtly Language, Courtly Love

The question arises as to the means to be employed in his task by the court poet, who, if he presumes to preach to his prince, is surely destined for a short career, if not for a swift journey to the next world. More particularly, how is the poet to impart moral guidance—whether generalized or directed to a specific issue or circumstance—in the major genres of court poetry, which (though they may incorporate a gnomic element) are not overtly didactic? Finally, since the poet-courtier is necessarily obliged to couch his advice (or his criticism, if the occasion demands) in oblique and indirect language, which will at once conceal and reveal and which will not offend his patron, how is he to develop a poetic style that will enable him to achieve these ends?

The *Kitāb al-Tāj* instructs the courtier on how to address the king:

> He who addresses the king should not employ base language or expressions, saying (for example), "Listen to me," or "Understand what I'm saying," or "You, there," or, "Don't you see?" Such (expressions show) the speaker's incapacity of expression; they are useless interpolations in his discourse, a deviation from pleasing eloquence, and a sign of dull wits and small substance. *Let*

his speech flow smoothly, his style be pleasant and coherent, and coarse expressions rarely used.[30]

This advocacy of subtle indirection recalls Renaissance rhetorician George Puttenham's advice to the court poet that, in pleading his suit, he speak only

> of pleasant & lovely causes and nothing perillous, such as be those [suits] for the triall of life, limme, or livelyhood; and before judges neither sower nor severe, but in the eare of princely dames, yong ladies, gentlewomen and courtiers . . . and that all his abuses tende but to dispose the hearers to mirth and sollace *by pleasant conveyance and efficacy of speach. . . .*[31]

On the close association between courtly manners and poetic style in the Renaissance, Daniel Javitch observes:

> Not only would the ornament, the feigning, and the play esteemed in court be exemplary for the poet, but by the very possibility of association these virtues of proper courtliness would help to justify the stylistic procedures that have permanently characterized poetic discourse. For poetry had always possessed and had been seen to possess the ornamental, deceptive, and playful properties that proper court conduct eventually shared with it. . . . The concurrence of the court's esteem for artistic conduct and the rise of poetic activity could not but enhance the value of such activity as well as encourage it. . . .
>
> But the poet's role was not just enhanced because his beautiful tactics corresponded to ones cultivated by courtiers. A code of conduct like Castiglione's [*The Courtier*, discussed earlier by Javitch] attests that beautiful play need not exclude didactic purposes. It reveals, moreover, that in the courtly milieu dominating society, didactic

[30] *Kitāb al-Tāj*, pp. 112–13 (my emphasis), and cf. also pp. 83–84, where the author criticizes the "poets of old" (i.e., the Arabṣ) for addressing kings and caliphs, and even the Prophet, by their *kunyah*.

[31] George Puttenham, *The Arte of Englishe Poesie*, quoted in Javitch, *Poetry and Courtliness*, p. 78 (my emphasis).

Poet Reading to His Young Patron (British Library Ms. 132)

purposes must assume recreative form. The Renaissance poet, believing as he did in the power of his art to improve society, may not have needed to be assured that his own recreative activity could bear profit. But because he could instruct while delighting, because his didactic strategies were so acceptable to the courtly milieu, he could present himself as an indispensable moral agent in a high society not disposed to be edified by more severe methods.[32]

That an analogous relationship between courtly manners and poetic diction existed in both the Arabic and the Persian traditions of court poetry may be inferred from the testimony

[32] Javitch, *Poetry and Courtliness* pp. 104–6; for a full discussion of Puttenham's work and its connections with the qualities required of a good courtier, see especially pp. 50–75. The didactic ends of Renaissance poetry are perhaps best expressed by Sidney's *Apology* (see ibid., pp. 93–104); many of Sidney's statements—such as that poetry instructs by *moving* rather than by *teaching* (p. 103)—bear a striking resemblance to statements on the effect of poetry in the writings of the medieval Islamic philosophers. Cf. Cantarino, *Arabic Poetics*, pp. 116–17; and see also Ismail Dahiyat's discussion of Avicenna's (Ibn Sīnā) views on poetry, *Avicenna's Commentary on the Poetics of Aristotle*, pp. 34–38.

of historical and written records that bear witness to the emphasis on manners and decorum, the delight in verbal play, and the general admiration for elegance of all sorts characteristic of their courtly milieus.[33] The brilliance of the Abbasid court is recorded in histories such as al-Masʿūdī's (d. 956) *Murūj al-Dhahab*, while the cultivation of a refined and luxurious lifestyle is reflected in *adab* literature. The *Kitāb al-Muwashshā* of al-Washshā' (d. 936), for example, describes the elite group known as the *ẓurafā'* (sing. *ẓarīf*), the "refined people" of Baghdad, and expounds on not only the manners, dress, and accouterments proper to this class, but the standards of discourse appropriate to them as well. Not surprisingly, eloquent speech (*faṣāḥah*) is considered one of the two indispensable constituents of the fundamental virtue of the *ẓarīf, murūwah* (chivalry), the other being the ability to lead (*riyāsah*).[34] Four qualities distinguish the *ẓarīf*: *faṣāḥah, balāghah, ʿiffah,* and *nizāḥah*—elegant speech, rhetorical eloquence, decency (chaste conduct), and probity; however, according to one authority, "Elegance (*ẓarf*) resides solely in the tongue, for to say 'so-and-so is a *ẓarīf*' means to say that he is eloquent, and of excellent speech (*balīgh jayyid al-manṭiq*)."[35] Significantly, elegance is also strongly associated with the proper conduct of love (a good third of the book is devoted to the topic); as we shall see, the decorum of love and that of discourse are closely related.

Such emphasis on decorum—both of discourse and of love—reflects to a great extent the exigencies of urban, courtly life and the tastes of the courtly audience. The delight of this

[33] Cf., for Arabic, the descriptions of court life in Mez, *Renaissance*, pp. 379–408 et passim, and the sources cited therein; von Grunebaum "Aspects," 293–94; M. M. Ahsan, *Social Life under the Abbasids*; and for Persian, Rastgār, "Ādāb va rusūm," and Hodgson, *Venture*, especially 2:487 (on the relation of literary language to courtliness).

[34] Muḥammad ibn Isḥāq al-Washshā', *Kitāb al-Muwaššā*, ed. R. E. Brunnow, p. 32; the two qualities recall the distinction between speech and action that recurs in ethical literature. For discussions of this work see Lois A. Giffen, *Theory of Profane Love among the Arabs*, pp. 13–15 et passim; J.-C. Vadet, *L'Esprit courtois en Orient dans les cinq premiers siècles de l'Hégire*, pp. 317–51.

[35] Al-Washshā', *al-Muwaššá*, p. 41.

audience in verbal elegance and play, coupled with the need for an oblique mode of expression that would make the moral lessons of poetry more palatable by "hiding them in such [things] as have a pleasant taste" (to quote Sir Philip Sidney),[36] were undoubtedly among the factors that contributed to the emergence, in the late eighth and early ninth centuries, of the *badīʿ* style, which came to dominate Abbasid poetry and exerted a pervasive influence on Persian. One of the acknowledged originators of this style was the court poet Bashshār ibn Burd (d. 784), who was of Persian descent and whose frequent criticisms of Arab culture and values, when not expressed directly in his satires, were voiced indirectly in *qaṣīdah*s and love poems, in a manner made possible only by the new style. Similarly, Abū Nuwās's flights of licentious bawdry rely to a great extent on the possibilities offered by this style, and their elegance of expression often acts as ironic commentary on their frequently obscene content.[37] The characteristics of the *badīʿ* style, the rhetorical devices subsumed under it, and the circumstances surrounding its appearance and development have been discussed extensively.[38] Two points, however, have re-

[36] In the *Apology for Poetry*; quoted by Javitch, *Poetry and Courtliness*, p. 98.

[37] I am indebted to James Monroe for pointing out this feature of Abū Nuwās's style; the humor that it engenders provides a safety valve, making the poet's implicit criticism more palatable than those more overtly expressed (e.g., in the satires of Bashshār, whose career ended ultimately in disaster).

[38] See, e.g., S. A. Bonebakker, "Reflections on the *Kitāb al-Badīʿ* of Ibn al-Muʿtazz," *Atti del 3. Congresso di Studi Arabi e Islamici*, pp. 191–209; Amjad Trabulsi, *La critique poétique des arabes*, pp. 136–63. On the role of Muʿtazilite speculative theology in the development of *badīʿ*, see S. P. Stetkevych, "Toward a Redefinition of 'Badīʿ' Poetry," *JAL* 12 (1981), 1–29. The prevailing view that *badīʿ*—which "may be defined as rhetorical embellishment which is consciously sought after by the poets and thus gradually evolves as a principle of art rather than a mere instrument of it"—arose because "the traditionalism of Arabic poetry with regard to its content . . . compelled the poets to give exclusive attention to the 'attire' of their products" (W. Heinrichs, "Literary Theory: The Problem of Its Efficiency," in *Arabic Poetry: Theory and Development*, ed. G. E. von Grunebaum, p. 25) is reiterated by Badawi, who laments that "there is hardly a single Abbasid poet who managed to escape altogether the influence of *badīʿ*" (Qaṣīdas, 22).

ceived relatively little attention: first, its effect on the overall organization of the poem;[39] and second, its relation to the emergence of allegory.[40] Both factors exerted a decisive influence on the development, not merely of court poetry, but of the entire medieval Arabo-Persian tradition; they are of particular importance with respect to that type of poetry which exploits

[39] On *badīʿ* as an organizational factor, see Bencheikh, *Poétique*, p. 127 n. 57 et passim; and see Hamori, *Art*, pp. 101–41, and "Form and Logic" on the use of figures as organizing strategies. On the dynamics of various figures (and to some extent of *badīʿ* in general) see also, for Arabic, John Wansbrough, "A Note on Arabic Rhetoric," in *Lebende Antike: Symposion für Rudolf Suhnel*, ed. H. Meller and H.-J. Zimmermann, pp. 55–63 (specifically on *al-madhhab al-kalāmī*), and idem, "Arabic Rhetoric and Qur'anic Exegesis," *BSOAS* 31 (1968), 469–85; and for Persian, J. C. Bürgel, "Remarques sur une relation entre la logique aristotélienne et la poésie arabo-persane," *Correspondence d'Orient* 11 (1970), 131–43, and Robert Rehder, "The Unity of the Ghazals of Ḥāfiẓ," *Der Islam* 51 (1974), 88–93.

[40] In this respect *badīʿ* itself is another manifestation of the general interest of the period in the potentials of discourse of all sorts for oblique statement and polysemy; the primary manifestation is of course the proliferation of various schools of *ta'wīl*, allegorical exegesis (Muʿtazilite, Shiʿite, mystical), on which see especially Paul Nwyia, *Exégèse coranique et langue mystique*. I have discussed some of the general problems relating to allegorical style in an earlier essay on Ḥāfiẓ (see "Allegorical Techniques in the *Ghazals* of Hāfez," *Edebiyat* 4 [1973], 1–40) and will not repeat them here, taking allegorical expression to be one of the givens of medieval literature and only cautioning (along with the usual caveats against equating "allegorical" with mystical [cf. chapter 6 of this book]) the importance of remembering that, as Judson B. Allen reminds us, "allegorical statements in the Middle Ages were not, in our terms, either referential or symbolic, even though the forms of the sentences in which they expressed their allegories are the same as those which we now understand as symbolic. Therefore the array of terms, usually religious, which tended frequently to appear on the right-hand side of their allegorical statements were not by their location endorsed as 'right meanings.' Much more than this, these statements were simple descriptions . . . the whole class of [which] depended, as descriptions, on the presumption of a relationship of analogous parallelism between the level of reality to which the left-hand term belonged and that to which the right-hand term belonged . . . [and which] were not as much referential, or even linguistic, as cosmological. They presumed and reflected and constituted by their existence a particular classification and relational arrangement of all that was" (J. B. Allen and Theresa Anne Moritz, *A Distinction of Stories*, pp. 64–65. The particular relevance of Allen's statement to this study will become apparent in the final portion of the present chapter.

to the greatest extent the potentials of oblique expression for a wide range of ethico-didactic purposes: the poetry of love.

The predominant topic of Arabo-Persian court poetry, in both major and minor genres, is, without question, love; and the type of love depicted is in most cases (barring the obvious exceptions of satire and parody) that which—as indicated in the Preface—deserves the term *courtly* by virtue of its representation of an ideal aspired to by the courtly milieu. Although traditional scholarship has linked the emergence of courtly love in the Islamic tradition with the ʿUdhrī poets—those distraught lovers who wandered in the deserts, burning with unrequited (and chaste) passion which they expressed in their verses[41]—the problems connected with this attribution are numerous; not least of these is the doubt surrounding the very existence of many of these poets. Moreover, it is clear that, what-

[41] The complex problem of the authenticity and attribution of ʿUdhrī poetry has been debated at length by various scholars; cf. Hamori, *Art*, pp. 39–47, and particularly pp. 45–46; Vadet, *Esprit courtois*, passim, especially pp. 353–73, 393–94. Vadet considers the ascription of "courtly" attitudes—in particular the devotion of the poet-lover to a single lady and his unconditional loyalty to her—to be the product of a later age, an age whose ideals are exemplified by the *Kitāb al-Muwashshā* and the poetry of al-ʿAbbās ibn al-Aḥnaf (see pp. 359–60, 393; and cf. also Tomiche, "Réflexions," 284 et passim). R. Blachère, in his discussion of the ʿUdhrī poets both as poets and in the context of the "romans d'amour" in which they figure as heroes, notes in particular that much of the poetry attributed to them—especially that in which the "esprit courtois" figures prominently—is undoubtedly posterior to the poets themselves (see *Histoire de la littérature arabe*, 3:649–60, 711–16 et passim). The "romans d'amour" that tend to make of poets like ʿUrwah ibn Ḥizām, Qays ibn al-Mulawwaḥ ("Majnūn"), and other obscure figures heroes of a courtly (and later of a mystical) conception of love are largely the creation of later anthologists and apologists for love and express a nostalgia for, and a search for origins in, an idealized "Beduinity" that never existed in reality. Analogous tendencies in Western scholarship define the "courtly love" of the troubadours as essentially Platonic and chaste; cf. in particular Denomy, "Courtly Love," and idem, "An Inquiry into the Origins of Courtly Love," *Medieval Studies* 6 (1944), especially 175–88. It is possible to see in the equation of *al-ḥubb al-ʿudhrī* with *amour courtois* a response to a terminological, rather than a conceptual, problem: as mentioned in the Preface, Arabic lacks an equivalent term for the concept most often designated in the West as *fin' amors*.

ever its ultimate sources, the image of love presented by the court poets of the late Umayyad and early Abbasid periods (to say nothing of their Persian successors) is that cultivated by a mannered and refined court culture and dependent both on courtly conventions and protocols and on the courtier's attachment to "play" for its existence. At the same time, the ideal itself transcends the specific limitations of "real life" to encompass an ethical dimension the full implications of which extend beyond itself. As the decorum of the language employed to depict this conception of love parallels its courtliness in being elegant, refined, and susceptible to varied interpretations, so the value systems implied involve a similar and related set of parallels.[42] In the Arabo-Persian tradition taken as a whole, the level of sophistication both of the concept of love and of the language in which it is depicted develops over the centuries; Ḥāfiẓ's love poems represent a considerable refinement over those of Jamīl, but many of the typical motifs of the fourteenth-century Persian *ghazal* may be found inchoate in the eighth-century Arab poet's *Dīwān*.

Central to this concept of love is the principle of the lover's unswerving devotion and fidelity to his lady, of loyalty and service, which parallel those expected of the courtier. The analogy between the relationships of lover and beloved and of poet and patron, the similitude perceived between the lover's stance and that of the courtier, constitute important features of court poetry, which will be explored in the chapters that follow. Here I wish only to suggest that many poems that are os-

[42] Some scholars consider courtly love as a primarily stylistic phenomenon; Steadman, for example, notes: "Like the ideals of 'courtoisie' and *gentillesse*, the problem of 'courtly love' cannot be divorced from the problem of literary decorum. All of these terms involved ideals of behavior proper to a particular social class. . . . The term 'courtly love' . . . denotes the type of behaviour suitable to persons of noble rank. As such it represents (essentially and specifically) the application of a rhetorical principle to the theme of *amor*" ("Courtly Love," p. 11). While I agree substantially with Steadman, J. B. Allen, Javitch, and others that earlier ages were more self-consciously and deliberately "rhetorical," this view ignores the important principle of analogous value systems that allowed the poetry of courtly love to be (to use a modern term) "relevant" in more than merely subjective terms.

tensibly about love are also about courtliness and courtly ethics, and, in particular, about the problematic issues of loyalty and justice. This specific aspect of Arabo-Persian love poetry further supports its designation as "courtly"; and it is interesting to speculate (though we can only speculate) that the parallelism perceived between love and courtliness may have been present in pre-Islamic Iranian literature. Certainly it is absent (or virtually so) from pre-Islamic Arabic poetry; for, however intense, love is doomed by the very nature of tribal life to be ephemeral, and this ephemerality constitutes the primary topic of love poetry.[43] We can only conjecture, on the basis of reminiscences in later works, about the nature of the love poetry composed by the court poets of pre-Islamic Iran; but it seems safe to assume that the close mixture of the erotic and the courtly, the use of matters of love to figure matters of state (as well as the sense of the participation of both in a larger ethical scheme) date from antiquity.[44]

Certainly there exists abundant evidence in early Arabic sources testifying to the Persian interest in matters of love; as an example, it suffices to recall al-Masʿūdī's description of a *majlis* (salon) of Yaḥyā ibn Khālid al-Barmakī devoted to a discussion of the topic, in which scholars and theologians of Persian origin figure prominently.[45] The importance of authorities of Persian descent in the development of love theory, and in general as reciters of stories and traditions concerning love

[43] Cf. Vadet, *Esprit courtois*, pp. 55–60.

[44] This mingling of the erotic and the courtly may have been a characteristic of the Parthian romance of Vis and Ramin, whose eleventh-century Persian treatment by Fakhr al-Dīn Gurgānī is discussed in Chapters 3, 4, and 5. On the "characteristically Persian" nature of the romantic tale as exemplified by *Vīs u Rāmīn*, see J. Rypka, "Poets and Prose Writers of the Late Saljuq and Mongol Periods," *CHI*, 5:558.

[45] Al-Masʿūdī, *Les prairies d'or*, 6:368–76; the whole spectrum of contemporary views on love is represented. The Barmakids themselves had been Buddhist, and not Zoroastrian, prior to their conversion to Islam (Hodgson, *Venture*, 1:295); thus it is not sufficient to examine Zoroastrian sources alone in an attempt to ascertain pre-Islamic Iranian views on love. On the importance of Buddhism in pre-Islamic and early Islamic Iran, see A. S. Melikian-Chirvani, "L'évocation littéraire du bouddhisme dans l'Iran musulman," in *Le monde iranien et l'Islam*. 2:1–72.

and lovers, has been noted.[46] Singers and musicians (many, again, of Persian origin, as were the famous father and son, Ibrāhīm and Isḥāq al-Mawṣilī) played an important role in the spread of courtly culture under the late Umayyads and early Abbasids,[47] while the Arabic poetry of courtly love itself developed largely at the hands of poets of Persian descent, such as Bashshār and Abū Nuwās.[48] Some scholars have stressed the influence of Islam in the creation of a new love ethic, particularly since this ethic incorporated an analogy between love and religion, expressed in such topics as that of the "religion of love" based on the idolatrous adoration of the beloved, and the hope for reunion in the afterlife, of which early manifestations are found in the poetry of Jamīl.[49] Such attitudes, however, are a nearly universal feature of courtly love poetry, and involve a further analogy: that between lover-beloved and worshipper-divinity. Thus it is probably futile (if not irrelevant) to attempt to pinpoint specific sources for such general motifs; it is, however, legitimate to conjecture—given the presence of courtly attitudes in pre-Islamic Iranian society and their virtual absence in Arabic—that a continuity exists between ancient Iranian culture and Islamic court poetry, which drew on that culture for many of its models: a continuity expressive of the assumption that the ethics of love and of courtly conduct, and the virtues characteristic of each, constitute parallel and analogous systems of value.[50]

[46] See the authorities discussed by Giffen, *Profane Love.*

[47] Cf. Vadet, *Esprit courtois*, pp. 71–102.

[48] Ibid., especially pp. 159–263. Johann Fück has called attention to innovations in the area of prosodic structure based on Persian forms (*maṣnavī, rubāʿī*) and techniques (internal rhyme) during the Abbasid period, as well as on the widespread bilingualism in Iraq in the early Islamic period; see *ʿArabīya*, trans. Claude Denizeau, pp. 82–85.

[49] Cf. Hamori, *Art*, pp. 36–46. George Morrison traces the motif of reunion in the afterlife to Zoroastrian sources (see his translation of Fakhr al-Dīn Gurgānī, *Vis and Ramin*, pp. xiii–xiv); the conjecture is problematical, however, in that it is not the souls of lovers that meet in the Zoroastrian afterlife, but the soul of the deceased and his *daēna* (religion), embodied in female form. Cf. M. Molé, "Daēna, le pont Činvāt et l'initiation dans le Mazdéisme," *Revue de l'histoire des religions* 67 (1960), 155–68.

[50] This is, of course, an oversimplification; the major exception, however, would be the court of the Lakhmids—the Arab clients of the Sassanians—at

A fundamental virtue linking love and courtliness, and central to both, is loyalty. The *Kitāb al-Tāj* extolls loyalty (*wafā'*) as the greatest virtue of kings, in a chapter perhaps intended to contrast Persian courtly with Arab tribal values:

> It is proper conduct for kings to honor those loyal to them, to treat them with respect, to rely upon them and place their confidence in them, and to prefer them over (all others), elite or common, present or absent.
>
> For there exists in men no greater virtue, one more precious in value or more noble in action, than loyalty.[51]

The relevance of this conception of loyalty, with its stress on recognition of service, fulfillment of promises or obligations undertaken, the treatment of those to whom one is bound by its ties as equals, and their defense against the bad opinion of others, and, finally, "gratitude (shown) in both words and deeds,"[52] to both courtly and love ethics is self-evident: both are systems based on mutual obligation; the lord's responsibilities to his dependents and the lady's to her devoted lover are analogous.

The parallelism of these systems is exploited by Bashshār in both his love poems and his panegyric *qaṣīdah*s; in particular, his modification of the traditional topics of the latter anticipates subsequent developments in both Arabic and Persian. Bashshār's chief innovation (which is not unique to him, but of which his poetry furnishes among the earliest examples) lies in his exploitation of the potentials for parallelism that exist between the *nasīb*, the *qaṣīdah*'s erotic exordium, and the *madīḥ*

Hira, which would have been heavily influenced by Persia. (Their counterparts the Ghassanids, clients of the Byzantines, remained more tribally oriented; cf. Blachère, *Histoire*, 1:45–49).

[51] *Kitāb al-Tāj* p. 104. In Zoroastrian belief, the breaking of contracts, swearing of false oaths, etc., were among the major sins, provoked by concupiscence, for which the soul of the dead person was judged. See M. Molé, "Le jugement des morts dans l'Iran pré-Islamique," in *Sources Orientales*, 4: *Le jugement des morts*, p. 168. On traditional Arab conceptions of honor, and ethical values in general, see Bichr Farès, *L'Honneur chez les Arabes avant l'Islam*.

[52] *Kitāb al-Tāj*, p. 105.

or panegyric proper, in a manner that stresses both the parallels and contrasts between the relevant value systems. Far from constituting (as is often assumed) a mere "erotic prelude" intended to put the patron in a receptive mood, the *nasīb* is, frequently, integrally linked with the topics of the *madīḥ*; moreover, it provides a means for the covert expression of views or criticisms that cannot be stated explicitly in the *madīḥ*, given its overt encomiastic purpose. This potential for parallelism thus proves of considerable utility to the court poet; increased awareness of it is a concomitant of the development of *badīʿ* and reflects a concern both for indirection and for the structural and thematic integration of the poem.

Bashshār's procedure is well illustrated by a *qaṣīdah* dedicated to ʿUqbah ibn Salm (governor of Bashshār's home city of Basrah under the Caliph al-Manṣūr),[53] in which the conflicting concepts of love expressed in the *nasīb* (involving a contrast between tribal and urban ethical values) provide a background against which the panegyric itself must be read in order to be fully understood. The *nasīb* is addressed to a lady designated as Umm al-ʿAlāʾ, a sobriquet suggesting high birth and social station; the poet recalls their former love and laments their present separation, complains that a slanderer has changed her good opinion of him into bad, and, apostrophizing his traveling companions, bids them not to blame her for her actions but to remind her of his claim on her, a claim based on their exchange of vows. He then recounts—in a passage crucial to the interpretation of the poem as a whole—the words spoken to the lady by her confidante, reminding her of her obligations and urging her to deal justly with her lover.

> . . . "Requite him with forebearance [*ḥilm*]; for false
> accusations are not a quality of the forbearing.
> "Act (then) as God enjoins towards a youth wasted away

[53] Bashshār ibn Burd, *Dīwān*, ed. Muḥammad al-Ṭāhir ibn ʿĀshūr, 1:107–13. This *qaṣīdah* is discussed at greater length in J. Meisami, "The Uses of the *Qaṣīda*: Thematic and Structural Patterns in a Poem of Bashshār," *JAL* 16 (1985), 40–60. On the relations between Bashshār and ʿUqbah, see *Aghānī*, 3:981 ff. passim, and *EI*[2] s.v. "Bashshār ibn Burd."

by love, and the slander of enemies, and long
estrangement.

. . . .

"Remember his pledge to you, and be generous; a pledge
is sufficient cause for your generosity.
"A youth may offend without breaking his promise; so
fulfill what you promised at al-Rawḥā'.
"The noble man's promise [*wa'du 'l-karīmi*] is an
obligation upon him; fulfill (yours), and help him
(the lover) to triumph over his enemies."

(lines 13–18)

The virtues evoked in the *nasīb*—*ḥilm, sharaf, karam*—are the traditional manly ones for which the *mamdūḥ* is customarily praised in pre-Islamic panegyric, although specifically Islamic overtones are suggested by the exhortation to act "as God has enjoined" (*fa-ttaqī 'llāha*), and the injunction "fulfill" (*awfī*) recalls the principle of loyalty (*wafā'*) discussed earlier;[54] the implied parallel between lady and patron is thus emphasized. Moreover, the final statement is put in the masculine, giving it the authority of a *sententia*, which is generally applicable and not restricted either to this particular instance or to the love relationship. Unmoved by this eloquence, however, the lady bids her confidante transmit her reply that "all things are destined to perish" (*Kullu shay'in masīruhu li-fanā'i* [line 21])—a message that curiously enough consoles the lover and reconciles him to their separation.

The introduction of such motifs in the *nasīb* ensures that they will be present in the minds of the audience during the subsequent *madīḥ*, in the course of which—embedded in a passage extolling the patron's generosity—the poet recalls 'Uqbah's promise to replace a favorite slave boy, who had died, with another. The earlier emphasis on the fulfillment of promises, and the added stress on the public nature of the patron's promise, made openly ("not in secret," in contrast to the lady's, made "under the cloak"), suggests that this promise,

[54] See Farès, *L'Honneur*, passim; and cf. Meisami, "Uses," 52–53.

like the lady's, was unfulfilled.[55] This topical aspect of the poem, however, is less important than the implicit comment (which the allusion makes possible) on the values underlying the parallel situations in *nasīb* and *madīḥ*, which are linked by the motif of (broken) promises. The contrast between the values advocated by the confidante (from which the poet is careful to distance himself by the device of indirect discourse) and those for which the patron is praised (extravagant generosity and fearless courage in war) suggests conflicting ethical systems, and a criticism of that system that produces injustice even on such a trivial occasion as that referred to in the *madīḥ*.

This point may be clarified by examining in more detail the parallelism between the lover-beloved and poet-patron relationships. Their similitude derives in the first instance from the status accorded to the lady, a status that would not be possible without the new, courtly conception of love, which is reflected in this poem. The lady's superiority, her power of life and death over the lover, is like that of the ruler over his subjects and of the patron over the poet, just as her ability to grant or refuse favors resembles theirs. Court poets of this period often address their lady as *sayyidah* (lady), *amīrah* (princess), or *mawlātī* (my mistress)—epithets not employed by the poets of the desert, either pre-Islamic or ʿUdhrī. The lover's devoted service, moreover, is closer to that of the courtier than of the obsessed ʿUdhrī lover; for it implies the obligation on the part of the person served to respond with favor, not only in the specific context of erotic passion, but in a larger ethical context that enjoins tolerance, forgiveness, paying no heed to unjust slander—in short, the very principles enunciated in the *Kitāb al-Tāj*. Love ethic and courtly ethic are parallel; and the latter, rather than merely providing a series of apt metaphors for the love relationship, is one term of a comparison that works both ways.

This parallelism sheds light on the nature of Bashshār's in-

[55] It may also have come late or fallen short of expectation. Bashshār's impatience with the late fulfillment of promises (and a specific instance involving ʿUqbah) is related in the *Aghānī* (3:1028).

tended criticism. Both lady and patron represent the Arab "establishment," still tied to the old, tribal values, while the confidante and the poet-lover represent the new *mawlā* class, for whom these values, while still expressed by the same terms, take on new meaning in relation to an ethic that combines the Islamic principle of equity with the Iranian virtue of loyalty. ʿUqbah's generosity is motivated not by principle but by caprice: "He gives neither from hope (of salvation) nor fear (of Hellfire), but because the flavor of giving pleases him," stresses the poet (line 35). The poet's consolation—ethical rather than emotional—is embodied in the lady's apparently heartless remark (which means more than she herself suspects) that all things are doomed to perish; not merely the relationships in which the poet put his hope, and which proved to be flawed, but the injustice that was the source of those flaws, will pass, and justice will ultimately prevail in the hereafter.[56]

Bashshār's *qaṣīdah* points to the direction in which the form would be developed at the hands of later Arabic poets and their Persian successors. It relies on a conception of love that is intimately linked with courtly society and courtly ideals and that contrasts with the obsessive but self-immolating love typical of the ʿUdhrī poets. In this poetry, it is not the lover's behavior—his suffering at his beloved's cruelty, his pleas for favor and reminders of past vows, his total dedication to his lady—that is the essential element; such motifs are, as Dronke has shown, to a greater or lesser extent characteristic of all love poetry.[57] It is, rather, the parallel between the lover's stance and that of the poet-courtier, between the lover's suit and his own, that defines the specifically "courtly" nature of this po-

[56] As we shall see, this topic recurs throughout the Arabo-Persian tradition. It may well represent another aspect of the continuity of Iranian values in Islamic literature, as some scholars consider the preoccupation with the afterlife and the belief in the transient nature of this world to be typical of Zoroastrian beliefs; cf. G. Lazard, "Deux poèmes persans de tradition pehlevie," in *Mémorial Jean de Menasce*, ed. P. Gignoux and A. Tafazzoli, p. 436. (Compare, however, J. Pedersen, "The Islamic Preacher," in *Ignace Goldziher Memorial Volume*, ed. S. Löwinger and J. Somogyi, 1:226–51.)

[57] Dronke, *Medieval Latin*, l:xvii.

etry. While the topic of love provides an attractive means of veiling the poet's didactic purposes under the portrayal of refined emotions, the understood analogies between the love ethic and the courtly make this poetry an effective vehicle for the expression of more general concerns.[58] Chapters 2 and 6 are devoted to a discussion of the courtly uses of love topics in the Persian *qaṣīdah* and *ghazal*, while the intervening chapters focus on the somewhat different treatment of love in the romance. Before embarking on these discussions, however, it is necessary to introduce a final preoccupation of this book,

[58] This is true also with respect to the independent love lyric, which, though devoted to the single topic of love, and thus even more to the depiction of the lover's state, can still exploit this potential parallelism when necessary. (Cf. the example cited in note 21.) A discussion of this problem with reference to the Arabic love poem is clearly beyond the scope of the present study; chapter 6 deals with it with respect to the *ghazal*. Compare T. R. Edwards's comment on Spenser's *Colin Clout's Come Home Again*: "For Spenser, I think, the conjunction of love and ambition shows that both prove the value of devotion. One learns to understand the Court, the world of power and policy, by investing its central figure of authority with some properties of a love-object . . . and one learns to cope with failure at court by associating it with failure in love. Each kind of failure makes available a role of devotion-despite-rejection that feels dignified and imaginatively fruitful" (*Imagination and Power*, p. 61). The potential for parallelism between the *nasīb* and the remainder of the *qaṣīdah* (whether *madīḥ* or otherwise) was not unknown even in pre-Islamic poetry, where the portions of the poem exhibit considerable thematic linkage in any case. Its particular utility for the court poet as a means for indirect ethical or topical commentary seems to date from the late Umayyad–early Abbasid period; Bashshār's *qaṣīdah* is therefore prototypical. This parallelism was exploited by later Arabic poets as well as by the Persian poets discussed in chapter 2. Some of the medieval rhetoricians, at least, seem to have been aware of the technique; cf. the remarks by Ibn al-Athīr and al-Kalāʿī (who observes of al-Mutanabbī that he frequently "used to turn towards the intended theme in the *ghazal* of his *qaṣidas*") quoted by van Gelder, *Beyond the Line*, p. 148. Van Gelder discounts the structural significance of the device on the basis of the fragmentary nature of the rhetoricians' approach. De Bruijn also comments (but does not expand) on the potential for symbolic relationships between the themes of the panegyric and its prologue (*OPP*, pp. 189–90). The availability and deliberate use of such strategies refute the widespread opinion that the panegyric poet totally suppressed his own beliefs, opinions, or wishes in favor of his encomiastic end; for he was able to express them through the potentials for indirection that are, so to speak, built into the genre.

namely, an important stylistic principle that is characteristic of Persian poetry and that has received little (if any) recognition.

Neo-Persian Poetry: The Poetics of Analogy

The exigencies of courtly discourse which were a formative factor in the development of *badīʿ*, the suitability of the poetry of love for expressing both general ethical issues and the more practical concerns of court life, and the parallelism between the ethics of love and of courtly conduct that we have considered in connection with the Arabic poetry of the Abbasid period were from the very beginning important features of neo-Persian poetry. The attention given to the Arabic tradition in the preceding section was intended to lay the groundwork for the ensuing discussion, as well as to demonstrate the continuity of the tradition of Arabo-Persian court poetry as a whole, beginning with the Abbasid poets (into whose work many older Iranian elements were absorbed—generally becoming thoroughly Islamicized in the process)[59] and continued by their successors, the court poets of Persia.

The fragmentation of Islamic literature into discrete entities defined by language, ethnicity, geography, or period has tended to obscure its continuity. The affinities of Arabic poetry with its pre-Islamic roots are often emphasized, while those with the earlier Iranian tradition are ignored or treated in terms of "influence" and those with later Persian poetry largely disregarded; histories of Persian poetry speak, similarly, of Arabic "influence" and Iranian continuity (if not of "national resurgence").[60] But just as the Arabs, heirs to the

[59] On the "Islamicization" of Iranian cultural elements see especially A. Bausani, "Muhammad or Darius? The Elements and Basis of Iranian Culture," in *Islam and Cultural Change in the Middle Ages*, ed. Speros Vryonis, Jr., pp. 43–57, and Christensen, *Recherches*, pp. 38 ff. On Muslim "exclusivity" with regard to inherited cultural elements, see Hodgson, *Venture*, 1:445–51.

[60] On the problems produced by this fragmentary approach, particularly by the identification of "Islamic" with "Arabic" and the opposition, to this arti-

Hellenistic-Byzantine and Iranian civilizations that preceded them, drew upon these traditions for both general knowledge and specific models, while transforming the elements thus acquired through the medium of their own developing culture, the Persians in turn were the continuators of this dynamic, feeling themselves its bearers rather than its opponents.[61]

The period from the tenth through the thirteenth centuries, when Persian court poetry flourished, saw major developments in all areas of intellectual life. It was an era of mobility and of dialogue between diverse intellectual currents which had by this time reached a stage of maturity, and of intense competition in the area of courtly patronage as well.[62] We may recall the efforts of Maḥmūd of Ghaznah to attract poets and scholars to his court, where their presence would testify to his own glory; similar policies were adopted by his Saljuq rivals. Such rivalries contributed to the flourishing of courtly letters, as did the generally dynamic intellectual atmosphere that characterized the period.[63] Court poetry was, needless to say, not unaffected by the general intellectual currents of the time; and one current in particular demands mention here, because it was especially influential in shaping the development of poetic style, and particularly of poetic imagery. This is the growth of what may be called the analogical habit of thought, which, from the tenth century onward, became an increasingly important mode of perception and conceptualization, and which was closely tied to a new understanding of the relationship between man and nature, and a new evaluation of the importance of man himself.

M.-D. Chenu has pointed out that in medieval European thought, through the successive stages of a dynamic that culminated in the twelfth century, the "supernaturalistic" view of

ficial entity, of an "Iranic" civilization, see Hodgson, *Venture*, especially 1:39–45, 2:293–4; see also J. C. Tavadia, "Iranistic and 'Islamic' Studies," *Indo-Iranian Studies*, 1:43–50.

[61] See, for example, S. D. Goitein, *Studies in Islamic History and Institutions*, pp. 55 ff., and Morony, *Iraq*, especially pp. 3–23, 507–27.

[62] See Hodgson, *Venture*, 2:293–97.

[63] Cf. ibid., 1:152 ff.; C. E. Bosworth, *The Ghaznavids*, pp. 129–41.

the universe as an uncontrollable and inexplicable mystery gave way to a perception of that universe as an entity in which "the whole penetrates each of its parts," an ordered *kosmos* in which the various "levels" of creation are parallel and analogous and exist in harmony with one another. In this ordered hierarchy, the continuity perceived as existing between man and the cosmos is expressed by the concept (previously extant as a commonplace without being philosophically adumbrated) of man as microcosm in whom all the potentials of the macrocosmic universe are contained.[64] A similar development can be traced in medieval Islamic thought, which in all its disciplines—from theology to literature—relied heavily on the principle of analogy (*qiyās*).[65] From its function as a tool of deductive reasoning, analogy became a more generalized cognitive and conceptualizing mode; as such, it dominates that monumental encyclopedic work of the late tenth century, the *Rasā'il* of the Ikhwān al-Ṣafā' of Basrah, of which G. P. Conger has observed:

> It is in the *Encyclopaedia* of the Brethren of Sincerity that the theory that man is a microcosm first becomes impos-

[64] M.-D. Chenu, *Nature, Man, and Society in the Twelfth Century*, ed. and trans. J. Taylor and L. K. Little, pp. 6 ff. On the macrocosm/microcosm see also G. P. Conger, *Theories of Macrocosms and Microcosms in the History of Philosophy*; and especially S. K. Heninger, Jr., *Touches of Sweet Harmony: Pythagorean Cosmology and Renaissance Poetics (TSH)*. Heninger notes the early association of this analogy with Pythagoras (p. 189); as we shall see, the poetics of analogy incorporates a number of essentially Pythagorean elements: not only the assumption of correspondences between the various levels of creation, but number symbolism, spatial form, and a general emphasis on structure and proportion. See especially chapters 3, 5, and 6 of this book.

[65] See J. van Ess, "The Logical Structure of Islamic Theology," in *Logic in Classical Islamic Culture*, ed. G. E. von Grunebaum, pp. 21–50; van Ess notes: "God has created hidden and manifest things, and the manifest ones are destined to be a 'sign' for the hidden ones. Man has to find out this connection (*ta'alluq*) between them, and he does it by *istidlāl* or *qiyās*. Both these terms seem to be used in the same sense. *Qiyās* is not only analogy as generally translated, it was, in that time, the common term for every form of intellectual endeavor and of speculation leading to a new result" (p. 34). On *qiyās* as a tool of exegesis, see J. Wansbrough, "Majāz al-Qur'ān: Periphrastic Exegesis," *BSOAS* 33 (1970), 247–66.

> ing. It is no longer fragmentary, but fundamental; and it is no longer isolated, but linked up with a comprehensive and correlated world-system. In particular, the *Encyclopaedia* is noted for its detailed parallelisms between the universe and man.

These include "detailed parallelisms between world processes and periods and bodily processes and periods"; further,

> the parallelisms are carried into social and ethical relationships when it is said that the regular course of the stars corresponds to good standing on the part of men, and retrograde motions to mistakes, and "stars standing still" to stagnation in men's work, and stars rising or passing toward the horizon to the success or failure of men. Agreements and harmonies among the stars are paralleled by human loves, conjunctions by union of the sexes, constellations by society, the breaking up of a star group by human separations.[66]

It is but a short step from this analogical mode of thought, "based in the belief that the universe formed an ordered structure of such a kind that the pattern of the whole was reproduced in the pattern of the parts, and that inferences from one category of phenomena to another were therefore valid methods of approach for the understanding of either,"[67] to an analogical mode of writing that derives its resonances from this same system of correspondences.

In the largest sense, analogical thinking simply presumes that full explanation of any given subject is accomplished

[66] Conger, *Macrocosms and Microcosms*, pp. 51, 49. See also S. H. Nasr, *An Introduction to Islamic Cosmological Doctrines*, pp. 25–104; on the concept of man as microcosm, see ibid., pp. 96–104; de Bruijn, *OPP*, p. 202; and the *Rasā'il Ikhwān al-Ṣafā' (RIS)*, especially chapters 22, 25 and 33. One of the goals of the *Rasā'il*, as is clear from various comments throughout the work, is to inculcate this type of thinking in those who pursue wisdom. Undoubtedly the growth of Sufism contributed to the spread of analogical thinking; but it should not be associated (as it often is) with mysticism per se. Cf. Hodgson, *Venture*, 2:222–27.

[67] Eugene Vinaver, *The Rise of Romance*, p. 100.

> in terms of an ordered array of parallel narratives and figures and propositions, each resonating in terms of all the others, and all properly dealt with and analyzed by a conscious elaboration of one-to-one parallels. Full explanation is achieved by assent to the asserted parallels.[68]

By the mid-twelfth century (and perhaps even earlier), an analogical style of composition appears and becomes increasingly widespread in Persian literature of all types, and not least among the poets of the court. Specific aspects of this compositional mode, affecting both imagery and structure, will be dealt with in the following chapters. Here, however, I would like to emphasize that a definite distinction must be made between analogical and metaphorical styles, and that failure to make this distinction has led to consistent misinterpretation of the stylistic strategies of many medieval Persian poets.[69]

Orientalists have traditionally assumed that Persian poetic style is based predominantly on metaphor (that is, comparison on the basis of similarity) and have repeatedly decried the Persian poet's fondness for exaggeration and hyperbole, excessive attachment to rhetorical embellishment, and use of highly complex figures. The judgment of H. H. Schaeder, while extreme, is not untypical:

> From countless examples could be shown what the exorbitance of these image[s] leads one to suppose: that this poetry is unaware of the correct relationship between the poetical ego and the world, mankind and itself, which is what constitutes the true character of great poetry.[70]

A similar understanding of "the correct relationship between the poetical ego and the world" was undoubtedly the basis for

[68] Allen and Moritz, *Distinction*, p. 73.

[69] Quoted in Rypka, *History*, pp. 100–101.

[70] As Heninger emphasizes in his study, "Every art work rests upon cosmological assumptions, and . . . we as critics must discover those assumptions before we presume to interpret the work. . . . Esthetic assumptions and the psychology behind them are conditioned largely by cosmological assumptions" (*TSH*, pp. 11, 14). It is hoped to show in another study the underlying cosmological bases of medieval Persian analogical poetics.

H. Ritter's comparison of Niẓāmī Ganjavī with Goethe—a comparison in which the Persian poet's imagery is judged artificial and fantastic.

> "[With Goethe] the effect of Nature on Man is as it were directly transmitted to the hearer. The poet transports us in the most vivid manner to the same situation in which he found himself, and now the same natural phenomena affect us as directly as they affected him, his metaphors suggest as it were to us only the special manner in which Nature has affected him and must affect us. If, for instance, the Persian analyses the Night into its separate physical phenomena, the important thing for him is not so much to suggest a certain immediate emotional effect to the reader as responsive subject, by seeking to transfer him to a certain situation. He achieves his object in a more round-about way. The physical phenomena are robbed of their immediate effect by this modified interpretation. It is only in metaphorical transformation that they again acquire this effect. Thus he is at liberty to invent afresh phenomena which have no equivalent in reality at all."[71]

In Ritter's view, Niẓāmī's style is based on metaphorical comparison: "the direct figurative mode of expression, the metaphor, *istiʿāra*, or the metaphorical simile," by means of which the poet juxtaposes "comparisons pregnant with emotion, which in their totality evoke the desired state of mind."[72] As Rypka summarizes:

> Whereas the European poet experiences and portrays Nature dynamically, his Persian counterpart senses and describes it purely visually, with at the same time a tendency towards the decorative. The spatial, temporal, and physiological connection gives way before an imaginary new interpretation and this new association of things has a

[71] H. Ritter, *Uber die bildersprache Niẓāmīs*, p. 55; quoted in Rypka, *History*, pp. 106–107.

[72] Ritter, *Bildersprache*, pp. 4, 56; quoted by Rypka, *History*, pp. 106–107.

stronger, more inevitable, more "matter-of-fact" effect than the natural one.[73]

Not only does this view tacitly assume that the medieval poet's conception of "reality" is (or should be) identical with that of the post-Romantic (a difficulty that is beyond the scope of this book), it also presupposes that the Persian poet is (like his Arabic precursors) making comparisons between things on the basis of some likeness, whether perceived or imagined, in their attributes or qualities. Bashshār's exploitation of the parallels in the stances of lover and poet was based on such an implicitly metaphorical technique: they resemble each other because they possess certain common characteristics, just as patron and lady share the attributes of nobility, social status, and so on. But for later Persian poets the procedure is often quite otherwise; for the assumption of continuity between man and nature makes likeness inconsequential but analogy essential.[74]

The distinction between analogy and similitude is explicitly

[73] Rypka, *History*, p. 107.

[74] "In . . . a scheme which posits various levels of creation with a common pattern persisting at each level, there is also the corollary assumption of an elaborate network of correspondences between the levels. An item holding a certain position on the horizontal scale within a given category will share an identity with an item holding a correspondent position within another category. Each item, in fact, must have its counterpart at each level in the hierarchy, else the common pattern would be violated . . . and cosmos destroyed" (Heninger, *TSH*, pp. 331–32). See also J. B. Allen's discussion of Averroes' *assimilatio*: "*Assimilatio* . . . is more than comparison, because comparisons, though made for the sake of the mutual illumination which the two terms involved can be expected to provide, are connected in too disparate and possibly arbitrary ways fully to define the strong relationship which syntax, at one level, and the elements of the cosmic song, at the other, imply. *Assimilationes* are indeed made, but they are conceptually verified, and are therefore true and invitable" ("Hermann the German," 79; see also 75–80). Cf. idem, *Ethical Poetic*, p. 36: "It is vitally important to notice that both assimilatio, and by implication representatio as well, suppress any distinction between those relationships which exist within the real world, or within the world of words, and those relationships which exist between words and things. In other words, they presume a kind of ontological continuity between language, thought, and fact—a continuity which is characteristic of medieval thought."

invoked by Jalāl al-Dīn Rūmī in his *Discourses*, as—in the course of describing his own parables—he differentiates between comparison (*misāl*) and likeness (*misl*):

> All that I say is a comparison, it is not a likeness. Comparison is one thing, and likeness is another. . . . When things appear unintelligible [*nā-maʿqūl*] and are enunciated by means of a comparison, then they become intelligible [*maʿqūl*], and when they become intelligible, they become sensible [*maḥsūs*].[75]

Rūmī's examples of this distinction are illuminating:

> Comparison does not resemble likeness. Thus, the gnostic gives the name "spring" to relaxation and happiness and expansion, and calls contraction and sorrow "autumn": what *formal resemblance [az rū-yi ṣūrat]* is there between happiness and the spring, sorrow and the autumn?[76]

Metaphorical comparison—where the metaphor is essentially an extended or amplified simile—presupposes a gap between man and the universe that contains him, a gap that can be crossed only by grasping at perceived or imagined resemblances. Analogical comparison presupposes a continuity in which similitudes are, so to speak, generic constituents of existence. In a mode of composition based on analogy, metaphor transcends the status of a trope to become "a consistent means for signifying the inner substance of things," in a world in which "everything is a figure," a sign testifying to the unified

[75] Jalāl al-Dīn Rūmī, *Discourses*, trans. A. J. Arberry, p. 174; *Kitāb-i Fīhi mā fīhi*, ed. Badīʿ al-Zamān Furūzānfar, pp. 165–66. Arberry's translation unfortunately obscures this important distinction. In the *RIS, mithāl* signifies most commonly "analogue"; see, for example, 2:457, where *mithāl* and *tashbīh* are used interchangeably in this sense. H. Corbin discusses *mithāl* in the philosophy of imagination of Ibn ʿArabī, where it signifies the "typification," in the sensible world, of "what exists in the world of spirits" (*Creative Imagination in the Ṣūfism of Ibn ʿArabī*, pp. 225–25).

[76] Rūmī, *Discourses*, p. 174 (my emphasis); *Fīhi mā fīhi*, p. 167.

and unifying order of creation.[77] The ultimate manifestation of this style is, of course, allegory, in the broadest sense: analogy also presupposes polysemy. In this book, however, I am less concerned with allegory per se than with the more general aspects of the development of analogical composition in Persian court poetry, the purposes for which it is employed, and the ways in which it affects both imagery and structure.

In concluding this introductory chapter, let me briefly recapitulate some of the basic points stressed in these preliminary remarks. A central assumption of this book is that court patronage, far from constituting an obstacle to poetic creativity, for a lengthy period provided the only conditions under which it could flourish and did not truly lose its importance until the modern age. The poetry composed at and for courts not only reflects the tastes, aspirations, and values of the courtly audience, but attempts to refine them through the use of poetry for didactic purposes, and specifically to guide the courtly audience (and in particular the ruler) toward the good. The primary topic of Persian court poetry (other than panegyric, with which it is often combined) is a love relationship that may be

[77] Chenu, *Man and Nature*, pp. 99, 119. Two important caveats must be added here. The first is that the analogical style does not replace the metaphorical but coexists with it, and the degree of importance given to each varies from poet to poet; the second is that the development appears not to be restricted to Persian poetry, but to occur in Arabic as well, as recent studies of the Arab rhetoricians' views on metaphor (and their increasing restriction of the term *istiʿāraḥ* to comparisons based on likeness) suggest. See, in particular, W. Heinrichs, *The Hand of the North Wind*; see also B. Reinert, "Probleme der vormongolischen arabisch-persischen Poesiegemeinschaft und ihr Reflex in der Poetik," in *Arabic Poetry: Theory and Development*, ed. G. E. von Grunebaum, pp. 71–105; Wansbrough, "Rhetoric," and idem, "Note." What is important is that a stylistic development of this sort does take place (the Arabo-Persian tradition is neither as static nor as monolithic as is generally supposed, and more than time—or even personal preference—separates Manūchihrī from Ḥāfiẓ), and that behind it lies a conceptual development that determines the reasons particular images (which may be the same in either style) are employed. For an illuminating discussion of the analogical style in medieval Europe, see especially Chenu, *Man and Nature*, pp. 103 ff.; and see also Poirion, *Le poète et le prince*, pp. 62–63, 94 et passim, on analogical imagery in medieval French court poetry.

termed courtly both because it reflects an ideal to which courtly society aspired and because it shares important parallels with the relationship of courtier (and poet) to prince. Stylistically, court poetry is characterized by indirection and rhetorical complexity, which reflect the exigencies of courtly discourse, by structural and thematic sophistication, and by the use of analogical compositional modes and a tendency to allegory. In the chapters that follow, it should become clear that medieval Persian court poets (like all poets worthy of the name) were neither naive thinkers nor haphazard craftsmen, neither ecstatic improvisors nor prisoners in the bonds of a restrictive and conventional formalism, but self-conscious artists practicing a respected and demanding craft.

· II ·

The Poetry of Praise: The Qasidah and Its Uses

THE panegryic *qaṣīdah*, the first major genre of Persian court poetry, was at first, necessarily, heavily influenced by Arabic models (poets were, moreover, expected to be able to compose fluently in both Arabic and Persian). These models were soon developed and modified to suit the specific needs of poets at Persian courts, in particular the more courtly image of the ruler they sought to project, an image that contrasted with the more heroic one, which increasingly dominated the Arabic *qaṣīdah*.[1] On the basis of these modifications, critics often make a distinction, in speaking of Persian poems, between "Arabic" and "Persian" *qaṣīdahs*, the latter characterized by the substitution, in the *nasīb*, of a lengthy descriptive passage (most commonly of a garden, but sometimes of a natural landscape, a hunting scene, or a building) or an erotic passage reflecting a more sophisticated, courtly relationship, for the desert-inspired topics of the Arabic model.[2] Such modifications, however, had little effect on the function of either the *qaṣīdah* as a whole or the *nasīb* in relation to the remainder of the

[1] On the contrasting "self-images" of Arab and Persian culture, see Hodgson, *Venture*, 2:154–57.

[2] Jerome Clinton defines the "Arabic" type as "based on the model of the classical Arabic qasidah, with its lament at parting, description of the poet's steed, and strenuous journey through the desert," while the "Persian" "contains no hint of desert origins, and both in its subject matter and its more extensive panegyrics reflects the situation and demands of the Ghaznavid court" (*Manūchihrī*, p. 74); but as Clinton's own analysis shows, these distinctions are not always valid, as "Arabic" *qaṣīdahs* may in fact lack the *nasīb* or substitute for it a descriptive or meditative passage. See also *EI*[2] s.v. "Ḳaṣīda." The innovations typical of the "Persian" *qaṣīdah* are not unknown to earlier Arab poets, as a perusal of the *dīwāns* of (for example) Abū Tammām or al-Mutanabbī will demonstrate. The relationship between the Persian and Arabic forms of the *qaṣīdah* requires more systematic study.

poem, and the potentials for indirect comment through implicit parallelism seen in the *qaṣīdah* by Bashshār (discussed in chapter 1) continued to be exploited by Persian panegyrists regardless of the specific model employed.

Although the *qaṣīdah*'s emergence dates from the time of the Samanid rulers of Bukhara, its most significant developments date from the eleventh century, after the eclipse of that dynasty.[3] Two major centers in particular encouraged the production of panegyric poetry of the highest quality (as well as in considerable quantity): the court of the Ghaznavids in the east and, slightly later, that of the Saljuqs in the west (and, following the breakup of the central Saljuq regime, the courts of the local princes who were its successors). To illustrate the patterns of continuity and change in the development of the *qaṣīdah*, particularly with respect to the function of the *nasīb*, I will focus on two very different poets, one from each of these centers, who are separated in time by some 150 years: Manūchihrī, panegyrist of Masʿūd of Ghaznah, and Anvarī, encomiast of a number of Saljuq princes as well as of a variety of other notables. Before discussing their contribution to the development of the *qaṣīdah*, however, I would like to address the more general topic of panegyric poetry itself, as this poetry has traditionally presented problems for both scholars and students of Persian literature.

It is often assumed that panegyric poets (and court poets in general) are either frustrated artists unable to cast off the restrictions of courtly protocol and write freely as they wish, or second-rate hacks who sell their inflated and insincere verses to the highest bidder. M.G.S. Hodgson has succintly evaluated the contemporary critic's discomfort when confronted with the very real fact of the abundance and high quality of such poetry and has pointed to some of the reasons for this discomfort.

> As in Arabic literature of the High Caliphal age, poetry was designed for public recitation, not (in the first instance) for private meditation; it was expected to adorn a

[3] On the poetry of the Samanid period (of which little remains), see Rypka, *History*, pp. 140–62; Danner, "Arabic Literature," pp. 617–19.

> courtier's life, almost like fine clothes. The consequences in Persian were comparable to those in Arabic literature: an emphasis on precision of form and familiarity of substance, so that no unexpected context will interfere with an appreciation of the virtuosity in handling received form and theme—and, incidentally, avoidance of any purely personal private reference that would detract from the common public decorum. . . . As in Arabic, in Persian also, of course, a great poet could rise above the limitations so imposed, could indeed make use of them to build the greatness of his poetry.
>
> Panegyric poetry was quite frankly praise of patrons, often of parvenus. If Modern Westerners are ill at ease with elaborate praise of living individuals—especially those dubiously worthy individuals who commonly are in a financial position to be patrons—it is in part because they are less given than their ancestors to formal courtesy even in everyday social intercourse. . . . We no longer pretend to be the most humble servants of persons we scarcely know, even in prose. We are ill at ease when the same sorts of courtesy are spelled out and elaborated in Persian verse.[4]

This unease has led to a general neglect, when not to outright condemnation, of many of the most brilliant poets of the age, who, because they composed panegyric, seem no longer to speak to modern audiences. While it is true that panegyric poetry is both highly formal and repetitious, these qualities should not be equated with monotony; they are, so to speak, generic characteristics of panegyric and were expected (or rather demanded) by its audience. Moreover, the existence of accepted formal and thematic conventions provided, not insurmountable restrictions, but a solid base on which the poet

[4] Hodgson, *Venture*, 2:297–99. Some of the Western critic's unease with panegyric may arise from linguistic usage; cf. the discussion by J. D. Garrison on the distinction, in English, between "panegyric" (with connotations of flattery) and "encomium" (a general term for praise), a distinction that does not appear to have a parallel in the Arabo-Persian tradition (*Dryden and the Tradition of Panegyric*, pp. 3–19, 101–19).

might build in an innovative manner and address questions of particular importance without departing from the decorum deemed appropriate to the genre.

The repetitious nature of panegyric reflects what some scholars have recognized as the ritual function of such poetry. The qualities for which a ruler (or other notable) might be praised are not merely (as Hodgson intimates) "conventions" analogous to those of polite conversation,[5] but point to the timeless nature of the virtues considered to inhere in the occupant of a given position. In a discussion of "royal" panegyrics, that is, poems addressed to the ruling monarch, Jerome Clinton, pointing to the futility of trying to gather accurate historical or biographical data from a panegyric *qaṣīdah*, and the equal futility of attempting to evaluate its several sections separately, stresses that the portrait of the sovereign presented therein must be considered, not "as a distorted portrait of a real monarch, and hence inaccurate and a failure, [but] as a successful presentation of an idealized monarch, for which the particular patron provides the occasion, but not the pattern." The panegyric poem, recited on ceremonial occasions in the presence of the assembled court, constitutes a ritual text that functions to affirm both the institution of the state (at the center of which was the monarch) and the membership of those present (i.e., the court) in that institution.[6] Clinton concludes:

> Seeing panegyric poems as texts for a ritual affirmation of the institution of Islamic monarchy has one immediate practical advantage in that it releases us of the discomfort

[5] Hodgson, *Venture*, 2:299. Unfortunately Hodgson is often prone to separate "literature" from other aspects of life, and consequently relegates much to the area of "convention," which is actually a reflection of broader attitudes; his discussion of both panegyric and romance suffers from this limitation, while the only genres he appears to consider seriously are the epic and didactic (or spiritual) *maṣnavī*.

[6] J. W. Clinton, "Myth and History" (Paper delivered at the Fifteenth Annual Meeting of the Middle East Studies Association, Seattle, Washington, November 1981), p. 3. I am indebted to Professor Clinton for permitting me to quote from this paper, which extends to Persian poetry some of the conclusions reached for Arabic in S. M. Sperl's earlier study, "Islamic Kingship and Arabic Panegyric Poetry in the Early Ninth Century," *JAL* 8 (1977), 20–35.

that arises when we read eulogy as the magnification and distortion of ordinary human character. Islamic monarchy is being praised, not an Islamic monarch. And panegyrics become hyperbolic assertions of truths that are presented in prose works on government in more moderate but no less emphatic terms. It also suggests a shift in our perception of the poet's role within the court, to one that does, in fact, have a greater measure of continuity with that of the pre-Islamic period than has been suggested before.[7]

This ritual aspect of panegyric is directly linked to the poet's role as moral preceptor. The composition of a panegyric ode affords the poet the opportunity to reaffirm this function by reaffirming the model of ideal monarchy accepted by the community to which the poem is directed, and by stressing his own ability to present that model verbally, to maintain it in the consciousness (and conscience) of the community, and to hold it up before the present monarch as an object of emulation. O. B. Hardison observes that the provision of such models was an important function of both classical and Renaissance panegyric.

> The efficacy of the poetry of praise [according to Plato] depends on its ability to arouse "emulation" or "imitation." The incentive that it offers is the prospect of immortality through verse. . . . The poetry of praise depends on an emotion—the hunger for fame—but it uses this emotion to strengthen the state by inculcating virtue. The idea that poets are the special custodians of fame is repeated by Horace, Cicero, and a host of other classical writers.[8]

[7] Clinton, "Myth and History," p. 5.

[8] O. B. Hardison, Jr., *The Enduring Monument*, p. 27; see also Garrison, *Dryden*, pp. 20–37. T. R. Edwards makes an illuminating comment on Aristotle's famous observation that epic (like tragedy) depicts men as "better than they are" in relation to the concept of that genre as a form of praise: "Not 'better' ethically or morally, I take it, but in their fuller representation of capacities that in other men remain undeveloped, unexpressed—in short, more *potent*"

We may recall Niẓāmī ʿArūẓī's assertion that "a king cannot dispense with a good poet, who shall conduce to the immortality of his name, and shall record his fame in *díwáns* and books," in support of which he cites the following verses:

From all the treasures hoarded by the houses
Of Sásán and of Sámán, in our days
Nothing survives except the song of Bárbad,
Nothing is left save Rúdagí's sweet lays.[9]

The fourteenth-century poet Ḥāfiẓ put the matter in somewhat plainer terms:

The poet exalts your noble deeds to the skies; do not
begrudge him his stipend and travelling provisions.
Since you seek good repute, let me say this: do not
begrudge silver and gold as the price of discourse.[10]
(QG 247)

Such verses serve as reminders both of the poet's importance in preserving the fame and reputation of his patron for posterity, and of the patron's obligation to reward the poet's efforts. What is at stake, however, is not merely the poet's livelihood, but his ability to offer to his patron the means of obtaining al-Ghazzālī's "double treasure": good repute in this life and salvation in the next. In this connection the patron's act of generosity provides tangible proof of his virtue, while his dependents furnish him with the means of demonstrating this virtue so that he may become an exemplar for all his subjects.[11]

(*Imagination and Power*, p. 8; author's emphasis). For the idea that praise is an incitement to nobility of morals, and therefore a beneficial type of discourse, see *RIS*, 1:139.

[9] Niẓāmī ʿArūẓī, *Chahár Maqála*, p. 45; the verses are by Sharīf Mujalladī.

[10] Ḥāfiẓ, *Dīvān*, ed. M. Qazvīnī and Qāsim Ghanī (QG); unless otherwise noted, citations of Ḥāfiẓ's *ghazal*s are designated by their numbering in this edition.

[11] On the importance of liberality see Naṣīr al-Dīn Ṭūsī, *Nasirean Ethics*, pp. 83–84 et passim. The *Kitāb al-Tāj* discusses how the economic arrangements of patronage should be ordered: "It is incumbent upon the king to take upon himself the payment, to his court and his familiars, of their rewards and stipends, either monthly or yearly. It befits the king to entrust someone with

By providing a model, panegyric combines encomiastic with didactic ends; its ultimate goal—the stimulation of virtue—makes the principle of decorum, which dictates that the subject be praised in terms appropriate to his position, more than a purely rhetorical consideration. The Ziyarid prince Kaykāvūs ibn Iskandar advised his son (should he choose to practice the poet's craft): "Your panegyrics . . . should be strong, bold and of lofty spirit; you yourself must know each man's worth, so that when you are composing a lauditory ode it shall be suited to the person to whom it is addressed."[12] "Suitability," however, is to be equated with neither verisimilitude nor biographical veracity, but with fidelity to the ideal pertaining to the category to which the subject belongs: king, minister, religious leader, and so on.[13] The poet does not merely record the noble deeds of his patron, but creates the motivation for them.

reminding him of these stipends, so that no one need submit (to him) a note, a reminder or a hint of any kind: such conduct would not be proper for a vigilant ruler (*Kitāb al-Tāj*, p. 145)." On the king as exemplar, al-Ghazzālī voices the traditional view: "You should understand that the piety of the people depends on the good conduct of the king. He must keep an eye on the activities of the subjects, small or great, and never connive at evil-doing on their part. He must honor the virtuous and reward good-doers, and he must restrain evil-doers from their wickedness and punish their evil-doing. . . . The people will then choose to act virtuously and refrain from evil. . . . Sages have said that the character of subjects springs from the character of kings; for the common people and the royal officials and troops become good or bad through the instrumentality of their kings inasmuch as they acquire their habits from them" (*Book of Counsel*, p. 60). Compare the verses of Claudian cited by Garrison: "The world shapes itself after its ruler's pattern, nor can edicts sway men's minds so much, as their monarch's life" (*Dryden*, p. 90).

[12] Kaykāvūs, *Mirror for Princes*, p. 184.

[13] The topic of panegyric decorum is discussed by the thirteenth-century Persian rhetorician Shams-i Qays Rāzī, who stresses that the qualities for which an individual is praised (preferably "spiritual" [*fazāyil-i nafsānī*] rather than merely physical) should correspond to the type (*jins*) represented, i.e., king, minister, etc. (*al-Muʿjam fí Maʿáyíri Ashʿári 'l-ʿAjam*, ed. M. M. Qazvīnī, pp. 328–30). Hardison (commenting on panegyric as a branch of epideictic rhetoric) notes: "[The encomium] involves much more than simple flattery. It is in some respects closer to biography than oratory. The body . . . is devoted to a summary of the life of the man being praised. It will usually begin with favorable notice of his nation, family, comeliness, and education. Such material should be secondary, however, to his noble deeds [which] need not be presented in the objective light of history [but] should be 'heightened' to make

In medieval Persia, as in the West at certain periods (most notably the classical and Renaissance), "the truest poetry is the poetry of praise . . . . [In the view of Scoliger] ʿGood fame is the reward of wise men. . . . Poets make others what they are themselves. Thus by the art which makes them immortal they confer immortality on those whom they celebrate.' "[14] This view of panegyric upgrades the poet's task from one of flattery to one of immortalization, and thus assumes its value. In rhetorical and philosophical treatises alike, panegyric, and specifically the *qaṣīdah*, is considered to be not only the most sublime form of poetry but virtually the only one worthy of discussion, and the standard for judging poetry in general.[15]

The panegyric *qaṣīdah*, however, does not consist merely of

---

the praise more emphatic. Since the encomium is quite long, it will be leavened by pleasant digressions and embellishments. . . . The most important innovation in epideictic theory after Aristotle was the idea that praise and blame should be didactic" (*The Enduring Monument*, p. 30).

[14] Ibid., p. 37. On the idea that poetry confers both present fame and future immortality, see also R. F. Green, *Poets and Princepleasers*, pp. 197–200.

[15] The fact that panegyric poems continued to be read and admired long after the sovereign and the occasion for which they were composed had become a memory—and so much so that they came to embody the standard of eloquence per se—testifies to the lasting importance of their dual function of portraying an ideal and inciting its achievement (cf. Garrison, *Dryden*, pp. 78–82). The esteem in which poetry was held in Islamic society has been the subject of controversy; some critics doubt that it was considered to be of worth at all. Far more important than the question of *whether* poetry was considered of value, or even permissible (as it clearly was), is the problem of *who* considered it to be unallowable or corrupt. It was primarily members of the conservative ranks of the religious class who found poetry of doubtful value and morality. The anonymous author of the twelfth-century Persian mirror the *Baḥr al-Favāʾid*, for example, considers poets (along with astronomers and physicians) among those who make light of religion; consequently, children and other impressionable persons should avoid their company. Neither should the child's reading material include poetry, particularly romance ("Persian books" such as *Vīs u Rāmīn*, *Jāmāsb u Luhrāsb*, and *Vāmiq u ʿAẕrā*), since it teaches lewdness and license; reading should be restricted to the Koran, *fiqh* and other religiously oriented works, and history (*Baḥr al-Favāʾid*, ed. M. T. Dānish-Pazhūh, p. 115). See S. A. Bonebakker, "Religious Prejudice against Poetry in Early Islam," *Medievalia et Humanistica* 7 (1976), 77–99; Bonebakker observes that speculation concerning the "allowability" of poetry accompanies the general movement toward speculation in all areas of intellectual life in the late Umayyad and early Abbasid periods (88–90).

an idealized portrait of a ruler or other patron. Although numerous examples exist of *qaṣīdah*s containing only encomium, equally numerous are those constructed on the polythematic model of *nasīb*, *raḥīl* (often eliminated by Persian poets), and *madīḥ*, as well as the concluding *duʿā* or prayer for the well-being of the patron, which often incorporates the poet's suit as well.[16] The polythematic *qaṣīdah* affords opportunities for greater subtlety and complexity, particularly in the potential furnished by parallelism between *nasīb* and *madīḥ* for the introduction, in the context of love, of motifs essential to understanding the panegyric proper. It is with this specific and seldom-discussed aspect of the *qaṣīdah* that I will be chiefly concerned in this chapter, and particularly with the various uses to which the *nasīb-madīḥ* parallelism may be put.

In his study of early Abbasid panegyric, S. M. Sperl divides the *qaṣīdah* thematically into two portions, linked by a set of contrasting relationships, which he terms *strophe* and *antistrophe*. The themes of the strophe are those that characterize *nasīb* and *raḥīl*: description of unhappy love or abandoned encampments, spring description, wine song, contemplation of old age or approaching death, and the desert journey of the poet to the patron. Those of the antistrophe (the panegyric proper) belong to one of two categories—themes of peace and themes of war—and are related to the strophe either by contrast or by congruence.[17]

This close thematic relationship makes it clear (as Clinton has observed) that the customary evaluation of the *nasīb* as a "pretty" opening that attracts the listener's attention and sympathy "is not really an explanation" of the function of this portion of the *qaṣīdah* in relation to the whole. He notes, "While the focus of the panegyric and the occasion for its composition and performance is the *madīḥ*, the meaning of the poem arguably is generated by the whole poem, not just the images of royal virtue and power in the *madīḥ*." To this general interpre-

[16] The *duʿā* is generally considered a Persian innovation (cf. *EI*² s.v. "Ḳaṣīda"); however, it was not unknown in earlier Arabic poetry, although the rhetoricians tend to consider it a defect (unless done on behalf of kings; cf. the view of Ibn Rashīq cited in van Gelder, *Beyond the Line*, p. 122).

[17] Sperl, "Islamic Kingship," 25–31.

tive principle he relates the divergence of themes in the Arabic and Persian *nasīb*.[18] These divergences themselves further support the notion that the function of the *nasīb* with relation to the poem as a whole remains constant, while the specific context or circumstances it seeks to reflect may change; and it is this notion of the *nasīb* as generating (in Clinton's term) the meaning of the entire poem that I will stress in my discussion of Manūchihrī and Anvarī.

The *qaṣīdah* by Bashshār discussed earlier provides a textbook example of the polythematic *qaṣīdah* as described some years later by Ibn Qutaybah in a passage that furnishes the locus classicus for description of the genre. While the passage is familiar enough, I will cite it here in order to elucidate some of its more salient points with respect to the subject of this chapter.

> I have heard men of letters say, that one who intends to compose a *qaṣīdah* begins by mentioning abandoned encampments, traces, and vestiges; he weeps, laments, apostrophizes the site, and begs his companion to stop, that he may make this an occasion to speak of those who have departed. For those who dwell in tents are (continually) alighting and departing—unlike those who dwell in towns—because of their migrations from well to well, their search for pasturage, and their pursuit of those places where the rain has fallen, wherever they may be. To this he joins the *nasīb*, and complains of the force of his passion, the pain of separation, and the excessiveness of his longing and desire, so as to incline hearts towards him and attract interest, and gain an attentive hearing. For the poetry of love [*tashbīb*] is close to the soul and insinuates itself into the heart, because of the love of amorous poetry and of the frequentation of women which God has placed in men's natures. . . . Once he is assured that he will be heard and heeded, he proceeds to the affirmation of his rights: thus he mounts up, in his poem, and complains of hardships and sleeplessness, night journeys, the midday

[18] Clinton, "Myth and History," p. 7.

heat, and the emaciation of his weary camels. When he is sure that he has convinced his addressee [*ṣāḥibihi*] of his right to hope for reward and to expect satisfaction, and has established the hardships encountered on his journey, he begins the *madīḥ*, in which he urges him to requite him and incites him to generosity, elevates him above his peers and diminishes their stature (as compared) to his noble station.

The excellent poet is he who follows these paths and observes a just balance between these parts, and does not make any one of them dominate the poem, nor make (one) so long that the listeners become bored, or cut it short while their souls still thirst for more.[19]

Several important points emerge from this passage. In linking the introductory portion of the *qaṣīdah* (the apostrophe of the *aṭlāl*) to the conditions in which its pre-Islamic originators lived, "continually alighting and departing," Ibn Qutaybah, apart from providing an early example of sociological criticism, reveals an understanding of the function of the *nasīb* in establishing the value system relative to which the poem as a whole must be interpreted. While he himself is famed for his strictures against departing from this convention—a conservatism said to reflect his anti-Shuʿūbī sentiments[20]—it is well known that many Abbasid poets either minimized this intro-

[19] Ibn Qutaybah, *Introduction au Livre de la poésie et des poètes*, ed. Gaudefroy-Demombynes, pp. 13–14. In *qaṣīdah*s where the *raḥīl* is omitted, the element of suffering is often included in the *nasib*. On the relevance of Ibn Qutaybah's description to *qaṣīdah*s of various periods, see R. Jacobi, "The Camel-Section of the Panegyric Ode," *JAL* 13 (1982), 1–22.

[20] This view is adduced, in particular, by G. Lecomte (*Ibn Qutayba*, p. 399, and *EI*² s.v. "Ibn Ḳutayba"); see also Trabulsi, *Critique*, pp. 70–73. For contrasting views, see S. A. Bonebakker, "Poets and Critics in the Third Century A. H.," in *Logic in Classical Islamic Culture*, ed. G. E. von Grunebaum, p. 96; Bencheikh, *Poétique*, pp. 117–19; van Gelder, *Beyond the Line*, pp. 42–45 et passim; and Jacobi, "The Camel-Section." The question of whether a *qaṣīdah* that incorporates such an introductory section is meant to appeal to tribal values, whereas those that begin in other ways invoke a more urban ethic, has to my knowledge not been investigated and would provide a stimulating topic for study.

ductory portion (as does Bashshār in his *qaṣīdah*), or modified it to suit the specific purpose of their poem, or dispensed with it altogether, even inveighing against it at times (as did Abū Nuwās), though rarely in the *qaṣīdah* itself.[21]

The view that the *nasīb* is intended to "obtain the attention of the auditors" seems illogical if one recalls the typically forceful language of the apostrophe, which should certainly have done so already. The problem is clarified by Ibn Qutaybah's insistence that the *nasīb*'s function is to "gain the hearts" of the audience—i.e., to arouse their sympathy, specifically with respect to the suit the poet will present—and by his distinction between the general audience to whom the *nasīb* is directed and before whom the poem is delivered (which might be the entire assembled court, a group of refined ladies, a gathering of notables, military leaders, etc.), and the individual to whom the *madīḥ*, and the suit it contains, is addressed. By establishing the context of this suit before the general audience, the poet creates strong moral support for its favorable reception by the patron; this clarification can be best and most subtly accomplished through the *nasīb*'s conventional emphasis on love, although other topics may also serve this purpose. Moreover, the fact that the poem's intended audience is not single but dual further opens the way for the presentation of a dual meaning, for which the *nasīb-madīḥ* parallelism provides a convenient strategy.[22]

[21] Cf. Bonebakker, "Poets and Critics," p. 96.

[22] This aspect of panegyric is discussed by Garrison, who comments that (in the view of classical and Renaissance poets) although the ruler may be divinely sanctioned, he is also limited by the restraints of law: "Central to the tradition of panegyric . . . is the attempt to reconcile . . . the themes of restoration and limitation" (*Dryden*, p. 58; and see pp. 53–63). He goes on to observe that this duality encompasses not only the themes, but the audience, of panegryric: to the monarch, the poem's subject and primary addressee, is opposed a wider audience. "By celebrating the current monarch in relation to a historical pattern that is made to seem inevitable or providential, the [poet] solicits the obedience of the people. The theme of limitation, on the other hand, is directed towards the king" (ibid., p. 59). This duality of the audience was, as indicated, noted by Ibn Qutaybah; with respect to the Arabo-Persian tradition, however (and presumably to the pre-Renaissance European), the reservation must be

This view of the *nasīb*'s function is borne out by Ibn Qutaybah's designation of the *raḥīl*—the description of the poet's arduous journey to his patron (often condensed, modified, or omitted by later poets employing different means of transportation to destinations less remote, and parodied by Abū Nuwās's descriptions of his wanderings, with his friends, in the desert wastes in search of a hospitable tavern)—as that portion of the poem in which the poet turns, explicitly, to "the affirmation of his rights" (*ḥuqūq*) vis-à-vis the patron. By calling attention to the physical hardships of the journey, he urges the patron to reward him and "incites him to generosity"—an action (more properly, a performance, before the assembled audience) designed to ensure that good repute which the patron desires, and which the poet's verses will immortalize.[23]

Seen in this light, Ibn Qutaybah's final remarks on the necessity to "observe a just balance" (or proportion) between the parts of the poem appear to reflect his recognition of the complementary functions of the several portions of the *qaṣīdah*—each of which must do its part in establishing the ethical context, the occasion, and the suasive medium that will predispose one toward a favorable reception of the poet's suit—and of the decorum necessary to each. The *nasīb* deals with love; if it is too short, the audience will not be aware of the wider issues against which the encomium itself must be seen: if it is too long, it will take on an independence, a self-sufficiency that will mitigate against effective fulfillment of its function. Similarly, the *raḥīl*, while encompassing the proper motifs evoking the poet's hardship and need (and it is in this context that the strictures against change become clarified: a desert journey involves more hardships, thus is more conducive to persuading the patron to generosity, than does passage through a land-

---

made that, given its aristocratic nature, the second audience for panegyric is not the people, but the court at large.

[23] Sperl comments on the caliphal *qaṣīdah*: "Its recitation amounts to a public renewal of faith in the state while reminding the sovereign of the duties of his high office. The sumptuous reward of the court poet is part of the ceremony: it is a public demonstration of generosity and symbolizes the life-giving function of the king" ("Islamic Kingship," 34).

scape of gardens or city streets), must not carry them to extremes, or, again, it will become independent of the remainder of the poem. (Bashshār's *qaṣīdah* exemplifies these principles; its *raḥīl* summarizes all the essential desert topics, passing over them with great rapidity in a single syntactic unit of ten lines, all effectively without caesura, and creating an impression of breathlessness and of the poet's haste to reach the patron.) Finally, the encomium itself (which Ibn Qutaybah seems to find the least interesting portion of the *qaṣīdah*, perhaps because its function is self-evident and its decorum largely predetermined) must be seen against the background of both *nasīb* and *raḥīl* in order to be properly understood.

It is of interest to compare Ibn Qutaybah's remarks on the divisions of the *qaṣīdah* with Roger Dragonetti's observations on the function of the exordium in medieval Western poetry and its relation to the subject of love. The ideal order of the parts of a poem, according to the rhetoricians, was exordium, argument (*narratio*), refutation, and epilogue (an order corresponding closely enough to that of the parts of the *qaṣīdah*). This ideal scheme imposed itself for centuries on all genres of composition, including lyric.

> The principal goal of the exordium, or prologue, is to move by means of its language, because first and foremost the speaker must concern himself with making his audience sympathetic to him. His words—as Brunet Latin writes—must put him in the listeners' good graces. The exordium thus demands subtle precautions with respect to its language, that is, as Brunet Latin continues, "plenty of fine word and sentiments; and it must be adorned throughout with pleasing language [*garni d'avenableté*], so that everything is suited to express that which will put you in the listeners' good graces [*à la grace des oïans*]."
>
> Treatises on courtly rhetoric observe the same principles: to become admitted to the rites of love, the lover must be able to employ its rhetoric; and since, according to Ovid, love is an art success at which depends in part upon the beauty of its discourse, the courtly lover's act is

like any other act of eloquence: he must persuade according to certain rules. . . .

Thus in the exordium the orator must select and develop those topics which are intended to win the audience's favor. Cicero calls this action *captatio benevolentiae*, an action which he views as entirely enchanting and appealing.[24]

Cicero's *captatio benevolentiae* echoes Ibn Qutaybah's description of the *nasīb* as a means to "gain the hearts" of the audience; the emphasis on gaining the sympathy of the public, the gathering before whom the poem is delivered, is as important for classical and medieval Western rhetoricians as it is for Ibn Qutaybah. The selection of "topics intended to win the audience's favor" (specifically, topics related to love), whether for exordium or *nasīb*, is not primarily determined by their attractiveness but by their relevance, their suitability to the overall situation of panegyric and of suit, as is implicit in Dragonetti's recognition of the parallelism between the lover's stance and language with those of the courtier, the importance of the topic of the irresistible power of eloquent language (paralleled by the Arabo-Persian commonplace of poetry as *siḥr ḥalāl*, "licit magic"),[25] and the analogy between the codes of conduct that inform both lover-beloved and poet-patron relationships. It is with these points in mind that I will now turn to a discussion of the ways in which two different poets manipulate the *nasīb* to generate the meanings of their poems.

Manūchihrī Dāmghānī (d. about 1040 or 41), panegyrist to Masʿūd (I) of Ghaznah (the son and successor of Maḥmūd),

[24] R. Dragonetti, *La technique poétique des trouvères dans la chanson courtoise*, pp. 400–401. On the topics of *captatio benevolentiae* see E. R. Curtius, *European Literature and the Latin Middle Ages*, trans. W. R. Trask, p. 70; on the ordering of parts of the poem, cf. O. B. Hardison, Jr., "The Place of Averroes' Commentary on the *Poetics* in the History of Medieval Criticism," in *Medieval and Renaissance Studies*, ed. J. L. Lievsay, p. 71.

[25] The source of the commonplace that likens poetry to licit (or white) magic is the Ḥadīth *Inna min al-bayāni la-siḥran wa-inna min al-shiʿri la-ḥikmatan*. See V. al-Kīk, *Ta's̱īr-i farhang-i ʿArab dar ashʿār-i Manūchihrī Dāmghānī*, p. 100.

The Court of Sulṭān Maḥmūd (John Rylands Library Ms. Pers. 932)

has been viewed as a transitional figure noted for his composition of both "Arabic" and "Persian" *qaṣīdah*s, and particularly noteworthy for his development of the latter type. As mentioned above, in the "Arabic" *qaṣīdah* the *nasīb* employs the topoi and conventions of the poetry of the desert, and the *raḥīl* is frequently retained as well; while the Persian *qaṣīdah* is introduced by a descriptive or erotic prelude that reflects the contemporary courtly environment. The distinction has little significance for our discussion, since the function of the *nasīb* (and often of the *raḥīl*) in both types is essentially the same, as can be illustrated by comparing examples of each. We may begin by considering one of Manūchihrī's most famous "Arabic" *qaṣīdah*s, that which begins (in Browne's translation) thus:

> O tentsman, haste, and strike the tent I pray!
> The caravan's already under way,

and which (states Clinton) "Browne included in his *Literary History* because he thought it 'typical of the classical qaṣīdah.' "[26] Typical it may well be, but for reasons that surely eluded Browne. While the historical context of the poem cannot, unfortunately, be identified, the poem *qua* poem is frustratingly allusive and suggestive.

The *qaṣīdah* is dedicated to Masʿud's vizier Aḥmad ibn ʿAbd al-Ṣamad—his second vizier (the first was Abū al-Ḥasan Maymandī, to whom Manūchihrī appears to have dedicated no poems), who survived Masʿūd's death and served his son and successor Mawdūd for two years before being executed by the latter.[27] Manūchihrī draws on the conventional desert imagery of the *nasīb* in a way that suggests both grief at the loss

[26] Clinton, *Manūchihrī*, p. 74. The poem is *qaṣīdah* no. 28 in the poet's *Dīvān*, ed. M. Dabīr-Siyāqī, 2nd ed., and no. 29 in the edition of Kazimirski (*Ménoutchehri*, pp. 73–76 [text]; see also pp. 207–10 [translation] and 362–64 [notes]). For Browne's (partial) English translation, see *LHP*, 2:31–34. On the basis of its "Arabic" style, Clinton considers the poem an early one; one should be cautious in making such assumptions, however, since the style of a particular poem is often dictated by the taste of the person(s) to whom it is addressed.

[27] Clinton, *Manūchihrī*, p. 27; cf. Bosworth, *The Ghaznavids*, pp. 61–62.

of a patron (unidentified) and a plea for the minister's protection, as well as other, vaguer possibilities.

> O tentsman, strike your tent; for the leader of the
>   caravan has already departed!
> The drummer has struck the first drum; the camel-
>   drivers are loading on the burdens.
> The time for evening prayer is near; and tonight I see
>   moon and sun opposite each other;
> But the moon is moving upwards, while the sun has
>   fallen behind the mountains of Bābil.
> Even so are the two silvery pans of a scale: the one
>   inclines below the other.
>
> (lines 1–5)

This suggestive opening, for all its "conventionality," presents some difficulty when it comes to interpretation, for the very nature of the imagery makes it obvious that it is not to be taken at face value. Questions of identity arise: Who is the leader of the caravan, who has already departed? (The image suggests either a military expedition or a funeral procession; on a literal level, if the caravan's leader has already departed, the tentsman is surely going to lag behind.) The reference to moon and sun opposed to each other calls to mind the commonplace comparison of these planets in conjunction to "a vizier whispering secrets to a king"; in the present instance, it is the moon that is rising while the sun descends, resembling a scale one pan of which is forced to incline before the other's greater weight.[28] Does the image refer to the elevation of a subordi-

[28] The quotation is from Fakhr al-Dīn Gurgānī's *Vis and Ramin*, trans. George Morrison, p. 58; see chapter 3 for a discussion of the passage in which it appears. The conjunction can, under certain conditions, produce a solar eclipse; see Paul Kunitzsch, "The 'Description of the Night' in Gurgānī's *Vīs u Rāmīn*," *Der Islam* 59 (1982), 107. The king is the sun's analogue in the system of the state; that of the moon can be either the vizier or the heir apparent (or even rebels who repudiate the king; see *RIS*, 3:13–14; Nasr, *Introduction*, p. 102). For a discussion of these and other analogical correspondence between the cosmos and human society, see *RIS*, 1:150–52. The reference to Bābil (identified by Kazimirski, *Ménoutchehri*, p. 362, n. 2, as simply west of Ghaznah ["au couchant"]) may be an intentional allusion to the area west of

nate over a superior? or (as seems possible) the replacement of the former vizier by a new one? Or does it simply signify the replacement of one patron by another?

The matter is hardly clarified as the poet continues, apostrophizing his departing beloved:

> I knew not, my silvery cypress, that the day would pass
> away so swiftly.
> You and I are heedless, but moon and sun are not
> heedless of this turning sphere.
> Oh my love, turn back, and do not weep; for the affairs
> of lovers are fruitless.
> Time is pregnant with separation; and whatever is
> pregnant must one day deliver its burden.
>
> (lines 6–9)

That both sun and moon are not "heedless of this turning sphere"—i.e., of the changing circumstances of life—while the lovers are, suggests not only an allusion to the topic of transience but a political allegory; this suggestion is increased by the poet's description, in the *raḥīl* (which is of some length), of his journeys, following separation from his love, across a desert covered with snow and ice:

> A desert so harsh and so cold that no one who enters it
> can escape.
> Its wind makes blood congeal in the body, for its wind
> is like a fatal poison.
>
> (lines 34–35)

The blackness of night eventually gives way to the light of dawn, and the snow that blankets the desert is finally melted by the sun, enabling the poet to make his way to the vizier, whom he praises in extravagant terms before making his suit:

---

the Tigris known as *arḍ Bābil*, which was ruled by the Lakhmids of Hira, and which incorporated the city of Mada'in (Ctesiphon) built by Khusraw Parvīz (see Morony, *Iraq*, p. 143), a possibility that seems likely in view of other, related allusions throughout the poem (see notes 30 and 32).

O eternally blazing sun, foundation of sovereignty, torch
of the tribes:
You are the shadow of God, and pure light; who in the
world has heard of such qualities.
. . . .
To you have I come, O lord, in hope of you[r favor] and
your benificence.

(lines 61–62, 67)

While these may seem extravagant terms of praise for a vizier, they are not unprecedented with Manūchihrī, who elsewhere refers to Aḥmad ibn ʿAbd al-Ṣamad as the "Sun of Viziers" and indeed "the sun of all men."[29] However, such hyperbolic expressions do not make the operation of interpretation any easier. Several tempting readings suggest themselves, but they are purely speculative and largely beyond the scope of this discussion, and will be referred to only briefly.

What cannot be questioned is that Manūchihrī has manipulated the conventions of the "Arabic" *qaṣīdah* to serve his own ends; for whatever interpretation we wish to place on the images he employs, it is evident that they stand for more, or other, than themselves. Specifically, they suggest both a state of political turmoil and the poet's personal circumstances of desolation and helplessness. The motif of worldly transience evoked by such images as those of the scales, the rising moon and declining sun, and the turning sphere provides a means by which Manūchihrī reinforces the immediate pathos of his own situation, while at the same time generalizing it as typical (especially for a court poet dependent on patronage). While there is no direct reference to specific political or personal circumstances, both the imagery and numerous allusions throughout the poem reinforce this impression. The poet compares himself, not once but twice, to the pre-Islamic Arab poet Aʿshā Qays (lines 51, 69), said to have been a panegyrist of the Sassanian ruler Khusraw II Parvīz; he threatens, if deprived of the privilege of serving the vizier (and, by implication, of his protection), to burn his pen and break his fingers (line 70)—an act

[29] Cf. *qaṣīdah* no. 7, discussed by Clinton, *Manūchihrī*, p. 142.

reminiscent of that performed by another servant of Khusraw Parvīz, the minstrel Bārbad, who, on hearing of his lord's imprisonment, broke his fingers and smashed his lute to bits.[30] In this context the *madīḥ* takes on new significance: the comparison of the vizier to the sun that provides light and warmth after the darkness and cold of winter has implications, not only for the poet's own situation, but for that of the state (restoration of political order is typically conveyed through the figure of the return of spring),[31] while at the same time the ideal of government presented is given more pressing relevance by the reminder, in the *nasīb*, that time plays no favorites, and that power, like beauty, is transient.[32]

Manūchihrī was also a master of the "Persian" *qaṣīdah*, a good example of which—and particularly of the typical "Persian" erotic exordium—is provided by a poem described by Clinton as "a unique variation upon the Persian model . . . composed of two qasidahs of the Persian pattern which are joined together to form a single poem."[33] In fact, the *qaṣīdah* is based on the rhetorical technique known as *ilmām*, expanded to apply to the entire poem;[34] its thematic unity derives

[30] Khusraw II Parvīz was deposed and later murdered in prison, presumably at the instigation of his son Shīruyah; see chapter 3 of this book. On Aʿshā Qays, see *EI*[2] s.v. "al-Aʿshā." The story of Bārbad is recounted by Firdawsī (*Shāhnāmah*, ed. M. Dabīr-Siyāqī, 5:2531–32) and alluded to by Niẓāmī (*Khusraw u Shīrīn*, ed. V. Dastgirdī [*KS*], p. 421).

[31] See Sperl, "Islamic Kingship," especially 27–31; Clinton, "Myth and History," p. 8. See also Garrison, *Dryden*, pp. 70–72 et passim.

[32] The consistent pattern of allusions to places and figures associated with Khusraw II Parvīz (Bābil, with its connection with Hira and, more important Khusraw's city of Madaʾin, al-Aʿshā and Bārbad, etc.) suggests that events in that ruler's life are being evoked as analogues or types of the specific topical circumstances of the poem.

[33] Clinton, *Manūchihrī*, pp. 82–90. See Manūchihrī, *Dīvān*, *qaṣīdah* no. 40.

[34] Cf. the passage on this technique in Ibn Rashīq al-Qayrawānī's *Kitāb al-ʿUmdah*: "Something of this kind [that is, movement forward and backward between topics] may occur when in the middle of the *nasīb* part of the panegyric is inserted, devoted to the person whom the poet intends to honour in his *qaṣīdah*; after which he returns to the *nasīb* and only then goes back to the panegyric. . . . This type is called *ilmām*" (quoted by van Gelder, *Beyond the Line*, p. 119). Al-Ḥātimī in his *Ḥilyat al-muḥāḍarah* refers to substantially the

from the use of the *nasīb* to present, as it were, a preview of the poem's central topic. It begins (I quote Clinton's translation):

> O idol of Hisar! you have nothing else to do—
> Why don't you have a party, why don't you serve wine?
> Since I spend my days in mirth,
> I want you to spend your days in mirth.
> If you are my lover, O handsome Turk,
> You must court me more than this.
> Show your love, increase your courting;
> You know that courting should arise from love.
> You are a tyrant Turk, I a patient lover;
> Tyranny is ugly, patience is good.
> If you become a tyrant bravo with me also,
> You will make yourself contemptible to me.
> I entrusted my heart to you, that you might divert me;
> I entrusted my heart to you for this, that you perform what is due me.
> Although I have committed a crime, in that I entrusted this heart to you,
> I wish you in pity to return it back to me.
> Return my heart in good condition, or else, from the court of the Shah,
> Tomorrow I will bring you a Tartar Turkish trooper.
>
> (lines 1–9)

This *nasīb*

> both provides . . . illustration of how groups of two or more bayts are joined into units, and . . . shows that the sequence of images in a nasib is not haphazard. . . . There is a quite natural movement from the invitation to share

same technique in his discussion of *iltifāt* and *iʿtirāḍ*, "when a poet starts a *maʿnā*, leaves it for another before the first is completed, and then returns to it in order to complete it" (quoted in ibid., p. 87). Both sources deal with the problem in their discussion of *takhalluṣ*, or transition to the panegyric proper (Persian *gurīzgāh*).

> the pleasures of wine and companionship in the first two bayts, to a complaint of neglect in the next two, and to the expression of resentment of bullying mistreatment in five and six. The last three bayts contain a threat of retribution if the obligations of lover are not fulfilled, which, with its introduction of the image of a legal court, neatly carries us into the gurizgah, since in this context legal court and royal court were one and the same.[35]

This reference to the court, with the implication that justice will be sought, anticipates the central topic of the poem; the specific meaning of this topic is, as we shall see, generated by the *nasīb*, which presents the motif of devoted service repaid by neglect and abuse—the subject of the lover's suit to his cruel beloved, for whom the heartless Turk becomes, from Ghaznavid times onward, a conventional figure who is more likely to be male than female.[36]

From the *nasīb* Manūchihrī moves to praise of his royal patron, Masʿūd (lines 10–15), whom he extolls for his magnificence and for the universal concurrence in his election:[37]

Him the army chose, him the peasants chose,
Him fortune chose, him God chose.
(line 12)

This is followed by three lines that "appear to be a *duʿa*,"[38] that is, a prayer for the ruler's continued prosperity, with which the "Persian" *qaṣīdah* normally concludes:

O, monarch of the world! You have hunted for a while,
Now for a time you should drink wine.
Take a goblet of wine, choose the gentle life;
Seek lawful riches, plant the branch of perfection.
O Shah! From compassion you made me, a slave, great;

[35] Clinton, *Manūchihrī*, p. 84.

[36] Ibid., p. 122; see the discussion in this chapter, and n. 41.

[37] On this "processional" topos of panegyric, which functions both to establish its ideal audience and to express the theme of national reconciliation and the unity of prince and subjects, see Garrison, *Dryden*, pp. 87–88.

[38] Clinton, *Manūchihrī*, p. 85.

May your fortune be eternal, and you eternally fortunate.

(lines 16–18)

This passage, and the lines that follow, recapitulate, in essentially the same order, the first three topics of the *nasīb*. The invitation to drink wine—here addressed directly to the ruler, rather than to the cruel Turk—is followed by an exhortation to live a pleasant life, while mention of the ruler's compassion (*raḥmat*) recalls (through verbal similarity) the plea for the beloved's pity (*ra'fat*) in the *nasīb* (line 8) and suggests parallel obligations. This, together with the somewhat curious mention of "lawful riches" (*māl-i ḥalāl*), which suggests an antithesis even though nothing specific along these lines has been mentioned, recalls the earlier motif of redress of grievance in the royal court and makes us realize that the only element not yet recapitulated in these three lines is the complaint and the suit itself, which, we may expect, will follow.

It is, in fact, this carefully prepared expectation of a suit yet to come that determines that the poem does not end here. Rather, it continues into its "second movement"—in actuality, the main portion of the poem—in which the lover's complaint of his beloved's cruelty finds a parallel in the poet's complaint about the attacks of the rivals. That this is the most important segment of the poem is indicated by its length: some thirty-odd lines, as opposed to ten for the *nasīb* (considered as concluding with the *gurīzgāh* at line 10), and ten for the *madīḥ* (concluding with lines 19 and 20, which combine praise of the ruler and of the poet himself, providing a transition to the poet's complaint, which begins at line 21).

The poetry which you have heard is lawful enchantment,
It is sweet measure, it is flowing utterance.
Speaking ill . . . of anyone who is your eulogizer
Would be a disgrace, would be a foul stain.[39]

(lines 21–22)

[39] Emending Clinton's reading, which has "Speaking ill *in it*" (ibid., p. 86); *andar ān* in the line in question must be read with the following *kas*, i.e., "about the person" (the eulogizer) rather than as referring to the poetry mentioned in the preceding line.

This paves the way for Manūchihrī's specific complaint: that he has been slandered by a poetic rival. This topic is the true subject of the *qaṣīdah*; and lines 18–25 are not a "new nasib" but introduce the poet's suit before the royal court by alluding to other famous (and irreproachable) individuals who suffered unjust slander—the Prophet Muhammad, Jesus, Mary, and an Apostle—in a list that is capped by the poet himself.[40]

Who am I that it is not possible for lies to be spoken of
  me?
  I am not the disc of the sun, nor the full moon.
(line 25)

Having thus established legal precedent (so to speak) for his case, Manūchihrī addresses his rival directly:

O shallow-minded poet! What have you against me?
  I thought you had more wit, were more
  intelligent.
You say that the praise of Khusraw is a lie.
  Woe upon you! It is a brave man who spoke thus
  [even] to a friend!
(lines 26–27)

His accusation continues through various stages until its conclusion at line 50; it moves from complaints of the rival's perfidy and hypocrisy ("When you see my face you behave most courteously. . . . But where I am not, you speak of my faults" [lines 29–30]) to boasts of his own prowess and the recognition, by other master poets, of his skill—poets who serve as "witnesses," who have examined him (*tajārub kardand*), and who, should the rival care to make a "trial" (*tajrubat*), would certainly judge in Manūchihrī's favor (lines 35–37). From these "witnesses" he moves to cause:

Because the Shah saw my poetry and was pleased,
  Contention was aroused in you, complaint was
  aroused in you.
(line 38)

[40] The poet alludes to Koran 4:106; cf. al-Kīk, *Ta'ṣīr*, pp. 94–95.

The ruler is thus designated as both the ultimate witness appealed to by the poet and as the provoker (however well intentioned) of the slander. The poet then turns to the topic of his devoted service, incorporating a brief *raḥīl* as he recalls his coming to Masʿūd's court:

I crossed these deserts and mountains on foot,
Both feet wounded, both eyes darkened.
In the hope that the king would read my verses,
That my fortune would prosper, and my days become Spring.
(lines 45–46)

Line 47 is almost a verbal recapitulation of 18, with its repetitions of *bandah* and *raḥmat*:

Now that the Shah of Shahs has been merciful to this slave,
You strive to turn the Shah's mercy from me.

The summary *raḥīl* and the recapitulation of the motifs of service and royal compassion announce the impending conclusion of this section, which is accomplished with a *sententia*, a frequent device for ending a poem or a portion of a poem:

Where envy is greater, fortune runs better.
Where there is more wind, a barque runs swifter.
(line 50)

The last four lines encompass the poet's suit (briefly put), which is followed by the *duʿa*.

Oh Shah! to spite the envier, I would that you commission me
To service, as you have other poets.
(line 51)

While it is true enough that courtly protocol requires brevity in putting one's suit, to avoid annoying or tiring the patron, Manūchihrī can afford to be brief in putting this explicit request; for not only has he already made his case at length, but he has established (through the *nasīb*'s emphasis on the obligation of reward for love service) the moral grounds for the granting of favor, as well as having predisposed the audience ("won their hearts") to look upon his plea with sympathy. Seen against the background of the complaint, the *nasīb* itself takes on a new dimension: the poet's claim to enjoy "mirth" every day is belied, not only by his beloved's cruelty, but by the slander of a rival; while the final and most serious implication of all this parallelism is that it is the ruler himself (rather than the beloved or rival) who is the true addressee throughout the complaint, and who is both responsible for the poet's distress and the sole source of his relief.

The implication that the ruler is in fact the alter ego of the cruel beloved is reinforced by the designation of the latter as a Turk. As Clinton points out,

> The figure of the poet as lover, singing his beloved's praises and suing her for the gift of love, has a striking similarity to that of the poet as eulogizer, singing the virtues of his patron and hoping thereby to win a generous gift of money. The similarity is enhanced by the fact that both the most desirable young slaves and the Sultans of the Ghaznavid line were Turks, and the attractiveness of the former made "Turk" a synonym in poetry for "beloved." . . .
>
> The resemblance of eulogizer to lover is one to which no poet of Manuchihri's day ever alluded. To have done so might have been considered an extraordinary impertinence and a punishable presumption. A poet reciting before his patron was figured not as a lover before his beloved, but as a bird singing before a rose bush in the garden. Or rather, the opposite: the birds of the garden were depicted as practicing the poet's art. . . . But the birds and flowers also re-enact the scene of lover and beloved, and one feels the further, unarticulated comparison is fairly panting to express itself. Or, since the position of all members of the court was that of absolute dependence on the Sultan, and this abject servitude was the chief factor of their existence, perhaps one should say rather that

an overt delineation of the relationship was unnecessary.[41]

The latter is, I think, the more reasonable view: the analogy between poet and lover, patron and beloved was so clearly understood that overt articulation (as well as being unsubtle and uncourtly) was, simply, unnecessary. This unspoken parallel becomes an informing principle of both the *qaṣīdah* and the courtly *ghazal*. In view of its importance, it is difficult to agree with Clinton that the *nasīb*s of different *qaṣīdah*s appear to be interchangeable, since this view emphasizes differences in subject matter in the various parts of the *qaṣīdah* rather than the complementary nature of their function;[42] further, if it is indeed the case that the *nasīb* can generate the meaning of the entire poem, then we may suspect that the type of *nasīb* selected depends on what the poet wishes his poem to convey not only on the surface level (what it says), but at a deeper level as well (what it implies). It is therefore likely that the closeness of the *nasīb-madīḥ* relationship ranges from neutral (when encomium is the primary goal), through the provision of conventionally parallel thematic elements (such as were pointed out by Sperl), to a point where the *nasīb* supplies the "true" (or covert) meaning, which is the poet's primary intent.[43]

In the light of these remarks, we may refer to Dragonetti's enumeration of the ideal order of the poem's parts: exordium, argument, refutation, and epilogue. This order is displayed to advantage in Manūchihrī's *qaṣīdah*: its exordium (the *nasīb*) is

[41] Clinton, *Manūchihrī*, pp. 122–23; on the "Turk" as an image of beauty, see Melikian-Chirvani, "Bouddhisme," p. 62 et passim.

[42] Clinton, *Manūchihrī*, p. 93.

[43] Obviously not every *qaṣīdah* demonstrates such a closely integrated relationship of parts. Often the *nasīb* functions merely as introductory material, although, expecially in those that include descriptions, there may be a definite congruence between the imagery of the several parts. The type of *qaṣīdah* discussed in this study occurs frequently enough to make it of some importance; it has been neglected by critics even though numerous examples can be found throughout the Arabo-Persian poetic tradition. There is a pressing need for a comparative typology of the *qaṣīdah*, a goal toward which a number of critics (among them M. M. Badawi and R. Jacobi) have been working independently, and to which the present study hopes to make a further contribution.

followed by argument (the poet's complaint against his rival), refutation (the declaration of his devotion and sincerity), and epilogue (suit and *duʿā*). Moreover, the *nasīb* itself first introduces—in miniature, as it were—this ideal order, which is then taken up and expanded (through the equivalent of *amplificatio*) in the main body of the poem.[44] Rather than suggesting any influence of post-Aristotelian rhetoric on Arabo-Persian poetics, such similarities indicate that parallel literary and cultural situations tend to generate parallel compositional strategies (a point that is even more striking with respect to the development of romance).[45] In East and West alike, the premodern world was more profoundly "rhetorical" in its attitude toward both poetry and life than are more recent ages.[46] Manūchihrī's *qaṣīdahs* reveal this rhetorical stance, in which the organization of the several parts of the poem and its verbal and thematic resonances (both infra- and extratexual) contribute perhaps more than does direct statement to conveying the poem's total meaning. This is equally apparent in the poems of a later and very different poet, Anvarī, whose work illustrates the twin principles of continuity and change within a literary tradition.

A contemporary of the great romance writer Niẓāmī, Awḥad al-Dīn Anvarī (d. 1189–90?) composed panegyrics for the later Saljuq princes, their ministers, and other notables.[47] His *qaṣīdahs* are frequently marked by a somewhat lighthearted use of the *nasīb*, in which, although the "beloved" carries the same implicit association with the patron, the context in which she (or he) is introduced and the vein in which she is treated show a decidedly humorous approach (a humor that

[44] Amplification (*basṭ-i sukhan*) is discussed at length by Shams-i Qays (*al-Muʿjam*, pp. 347–49). On the parts of the encomiastic oration see also Garrison, *Dryden*, p. 41.

[45] The question of Greek (or Hellenistic) influence on Arabic poetics has been much debated; see, for example, Cantarino, *Arabic Poetics*, pp. 63–69, and W. Heinrichs, *Arabische Dichtung und Griechische Poetik*, and, from the viewpoint of a Western medievalist, Allen, "Hermann the German."

[46] Allen, "Hermann the German," 67.

[47] See Browne, *LHP*, 2:346–91; Rypka, *History*, pp. 197–99.

must have been shared by the patrons to whom such *qaṣīdah*s were addressed). In particular, Anvarī rings changes on the time-honored topos of the beloved (and, by analogy, the patron) as the source of the poet's inspiration; for while the majority of poets treat this topic figuratively, Anvarī often gives it a disconcertingly literal twist.

One *qaṣīdah* in which this type of *nasīb* is employed begins, conventionally enough, with the poet, in his persona of distracted lover, writing a letter of complaint to his beloved:[48]

> I took a sheet of paper, picked up the pen,
> and dipped the reed's end in finest musk.
> Commencing, I told of my sad state;
> I uttered a thousand chapters, and stayed at no section.
> Now apologizing, now blaming, here coquetry, there need;
> now peace-seeking, now interceding; here warlike and there reproachful.
> "O you whose soul-refreshing draught is like the blessing of life;
> whose entrancing union is like the fortune of youth:
> "Do not imprison my body in the house of separation;
> do not roast my heart on the flame of patient suffering."
>
> (lines 5–9)

This outpouring is interrupted by a knock at the poet's door; it is none other than his "moonfaced beloved, the sun's envy," in person. He rushes to greet her, takes her in his arms, removes her veil, seats her beside him, and covers her hand with kisses, all the while marveling at his good fortune:

> How amazed I was: for such a guest
> had never in my life come to me, (even) in sleep.

[48] For the text of the *qaṣīdah* see Anvarī, *Dīvān-i Anvarī*, ed. Saʿīd Nafisī, pp. 19–20.

I am not so hesistant that I perform service
conditionally;
no, nor so rich that my wallet is bursting.
(lines 18–19)

Having thus (in the parenthetical statement of line 19, which stresses the unconditional nature of his love service) introduced the topics of service and the state of his own finances, he describes his tearful apologies. His beloved explains her unexpected visit: she has brought him a poem of her own composition, "pure magic, like your own creations," for him to present on the morrow at the private gathering of the minister who is his patron (*andar ḥarīm-i majlis-i dastūr-i kāmyāb* [line 23]). It is, of course, the very *madīḥ* that constitutes the remainder of the poem.

Is this *nasīb* merely a humorous twist on an old commonplace, or does it perform another function? *Nasīb* and *madīḥ* are disproportionate, the former some twenty-four lines, the latter only nine—a disproportion that suggests that the true subject of the poem is contained in its exordium. The motif of the poet's inability to produce a poem when the occasion demands recurs frequently in Anvarī's *qaṣīdah*s, and the volume of his panegyric production and variety of its dedicatees suggest that he was obliged to seek constantly for patronage, as do his frequent references to his impecunious state. In this poem, his beloved—that "illustrious guest"—gets him off the hook, so to speak, by providing the *madīḥ*, in which the patron's justice and generosity are, however briefly, stressed. (The brevity of the *madīḥ* further suggests the relatively "informal" nature of the gathering for which the poem was composed, implied by the expression *ḥarīm-i majlis*.) Does the poem, perhaps, constitute an apology for neglect of duty? The poet's excuse is that he is incapacitated by the pangs of love; but is he, perhaps, out of favor, and, desirous of restoration, using this means of flattering his patron—who may by convention be equated with the illustrious visitor who favors him so unexpectedly—as the "author" (i.e., the inspiration) of his verses? A few more examples may help to determine whether it is simply humor that is at work here, or whether the humor itself masks a subtler and possibly more pragmatic purpose.

Another *nasīb* begins with a description of the poet lying in bed, drunken, when suddenly, once again, the beloved knocks at the door.[49]

> Last night, in evening drunkenness, I had fallen
> senseless on my bed, when my beloved knocked at
> the door.
>
> . . . .
>
> As is my custom, I shouted, "Who is it?" She answered,
> "She whom you cannot do without, in grief or
> joy."
>
> . . . .
>
> She opened the door, kissed my hands, and drew me
> close as a heap of roses or a pitcher of sugar to her
> breast.
>
> (lines 1, 3, 5)

The night visit is, of course, a commonplace of the erotic poem, whether it is the *ṭayf al-khiyāl* of the early Arabic poets or the disheveled beloved typical of Persian *ghazal*; but this lady's visit has a purpose beyond that of mere consolation. She reproaches the poet for his drunken idleness:

> "Either you sleep, hung over, from dawn to dusk, or
> you are in your cups from dusk to dawn."
>
> (line 8)

She chides and admonishes him: "If you must drink, at least do so at the patron's feast"—the brilliance of which she proceeds to extoll. She then urges him to sit down that very night (since he has nothing better to do) and compose a *qaṣīdah* to present to the patron on the following day—the *madīḥ*, in fact, which forms the second portion (the *maṭlaʿ-i s̱ānī*) of the poem in hand (which, in contrast to the preceding example, is a lengthy encomium).

Similar examples can be multiplied. Another *qaṣīdah* in

[49] Ibid., pp. 118–19.

which the beloved is presented as the actual author of the *madīḥ* begins with the poet describing a ride in the countryside one holiday morning—when, as he puts it, the horse, "not content that I should dismount from him, attempted to mount me." Returning home, he is reproached by the lady for wasting his time in such pursuits: what will his patron, who expects a poem from him, have to say to him on the morrow? As in the preceding example, he confesses that, out of lovesickness, he has not been able to write a line for a week, as he is drunk by night and stupefied by day. She then recites to him a poem of her own composition, which he will present to the patron, thereby saving his reputation.[50]

In a *nasīb* that parodies the desert convention of departing lady and grieving lover who remains behind, the poet himself prepares to depart on a journey. His lady comes out of the house, weeping and reproaching: "Did you not swear that you would never swerve from loving me? Have you tired of me? Where are you going?" He embraces her and explains that he is leaving not because his love has changed, but because travel is the source of profit and success; it is of no avail to stay in a place where one is of little importance or worth. "If a tree could move from place to place, it would never suffer the cruelty of the saw or the tyranny of the axe," the poet observes; he has determined to improve his fortune by seeking the protection of a patron who will appreciate him and by entering into his service.[51]

In these examples we can begin to make out several recurrent motifs. Particularly prominent are the poet's complaints of lovesickness or of a particular instance of disappointed love, culminating in his resolve to put his complaint before the patron, in the hope of sympathy or aid. (In one variation on this motif, lacking the money to buy a Hindu slave girl with whom he has fallen in love, he is urged by her to ask his patron for the price; but when, after great trepidation, he puts his suit successfully, he finds that the entire episode has been a dream.)[52]

[50] Ibid., pp. 135–37.

[51] Ibid., pp. 121–23.

[52] Ibid., pp. 144–46. The fact that it turns out to be a dream presumably absolves the patron of complicity in this somewhat disreputable transaction.

These motifs can be characterized generally as compromising, on the one hand, repeated allusions to the poet's suffering either in the service of his beloved or from her protracted absence, and on the other, confessions of inability: not merely in respect to obtaining his beloved's favor, but inability to write the poem expected of him by his patron (though always for a good reason), inadequacy in the poem's style or diction, and not least the inadequacy of his own purse. In his *nasīb*s of this type, Anvarī establishes a distinct and consistent poetic persona: that of the self-deprecating *eiron*, victim of his own passions, unable to overcome his all-too-human weaknesses, which not infrequently cause him to fall short of his duty and which also bring him (not surprisingly) to the brink both of financial disaster and of disgrace. The *nasīb* thus functions to predispose the patron to be sympathetic and generous, to smile benignly on the poet, forgive his peccadilloes, and help him out of his predicament. Essential to this function, of course, is the analogy between patron and beloved: if the poet must depend on his lady, time and time again, to get him out of trouble, save his reputation, push him into the service of the patron, and remind him of his obligations, the implication is clear that the patron should certainly be no less helpful; conversely, when his lady lets him down, the patron must compensate for the poet's emotional deprivation through material favor. Further, by attributing the panegyrics he presents to the pen of his beloved, Anvarī is perhaps able to distance himself from them—both from their fulsome praise (which, one suspects, is frequently his own judgment of them), and from any inadequacies the patron might perceive in them (if, for example, he should fail to be amused).[53]

Compare two similar *qaṣīdah*s of Sanā'ī (mentioned by de Bruijn, *OPP*, p. 44), in his *Dīvān*, ed. M. T. Mudarris Raẕavī: no. 44 (pp. 68–71), where the beloved is an Arab slave boy, and the *nasīb* includes a macaronic dialogue between him and the poet; and no. 285 (pp. 641–47), where, as in Anvarī's poem, the beloved is a "Hindu."

[53] This self-deprecating persona is, needless to say, not typical of all of Anvarī's *qaṣīdah*s. On other occasions he is as fond of self-laudatory verses as the next poet, and he is also capable of direct and serious comment, as in the famous "Tears of Khurasan" *qaṣīdah* (see his *Dīvān*, pp. 105–108, and Browne, *LHP*, 2:384–89). The twin topics of boasting and self-deprecation are conven-

In this type of *qaṣīdah* Anvarī employs the *nasīb* as a means of preparing the way for the *madīḥ* in quite a different manner than does Manūchihrī, more often to counterbalance the encomium than to anticipate or clarify its topics; yet, in its broader aspects, the *nasīb*'s function is essentially identical in the examples by both poets. The love situation evokes unspoken parallels on the level of courtly conduct, while implicitly subjecting this conduct to examination or criticism; it also provides a means of alluding to the poet's specific circumstances in an effective but veiled manner. With Anvarī we see fewer direct parallels between *nasīb* and *madīḥ* than in the *qaṣīdah*s of Manūchihrī discussed earlier; Anvarī's ironic self-deprecation, which in appearance gives a more intimate tone to his *nasīb*, in fact distances him from his poem in a manner that contrasts with Manūchihrī's characteristic emphasis on himself as the speaker of his poem. Anvarī's self-deprecating stance is often maintained in the *madīḥ* itself.

The mind is at a loss to praise you with its own powers,
even though miracles can happen in any affair;

---

tional means by which the panegyric poet calls attention to his own needs and interests and are "complementary rather than contradictory. Within the framework of his praise to the patron, it is quite natural that [the poet] should begin by presenting himself as a humble and indigent person whose condition can only be improved by the grace of the protector. On the other hand, the poet has to stress the fact that he in turn can be of great value to the patron and fully deserves to become the object of the latter's liberality" (de Bruijn, *OPP*, p. 37). On the humility topos, see also Curtius, *European Literature*, pp. 159–62. Anvarī is also a master of the poetic complaint. His verses on his duties as *nadīm*, while incorporating an element of self-praise with respect to his varied talents, also reflect the multifaceted nature of the post and the poet's subservience to the patron's whim: "The status of *nadīm* becomes me, for, as you know, I know its manners well. // If a letter is to be written, I write with pen and fingertips a kingly brocade. // If you wish me to recite poetry I do so, from my own compositions or those of the ancients. // If you wish me to play backgammon or chess, I play it like a worthy opponent, as if by white magic. // If you wish jokes, I am light-spirited. . . . my service is without hope of profit" (*Dīvān*, p. 318). More explicit are his famous verses on the thanklessness of the poet's occupation (*Dīvān*, pp. 297–98; compare the complaint of Martin le Franc quoted by R. F. Green, *Poets and Princepleasers*, pp. 206–207).

> I too fall short of your praise in a few verses; I have [thus] apologized in a brief manner,[54]

he states in one poem, reiterating the humility topos that recurs in many of his *qaṣīdah*s; the conventionality of the topic does not preclude a suggestion of irony in such a line (particularly when it has been preceded by a lengthy passage of extravagant praise).

A prolific composer of panegyric (as well as of lesser forms), Anvarī finds many ways to vary his *qaṣīdah*s when he can, chiefly by means of diverse types of *nasīb*.[55] Such variations, however, are not merely embellishments or means of amusing his patrons, but function to convey an ethical message, and in particular to criticize the artificiality of courtly conventions and the difficulties of the panegyrist's profession. The juxtaposition of a light-hearted *nasīb*, in which the poet's chief concern is his inability to write a poem, with a lengthy piece of ornate panegyric reflects the contradictions inherent in the courtly society of the time, not least those that surround the court poet's dual role, as fool and as immortalizer of his patron's virtues. In Anvarī's *qaṣīdah*s the didactic element is not neglected, even though it is often conveyed in playful tones.

Manūchihrī is an outstanding practitioner of the panegyric *qaṣīdah* in its early stages, Anvarī in its late. For all the varia-

[54] Anvarī, *Dīvān*, p. 169.

[55] Other variations include a *nasīb* consisting of a poetic contest between the poet and his beloved (ibid., pp. 131–33) a three-way conversation with the moon and the beloved concerning the patron's virtues (pp. 176–78), and a *qaṣīdah* that begins with a description (of Baghdad) and concludes with a *nasīb* (pp. 111–15) that conveys an implicit criticism of the ruler, who is so preoccupied with matters of war that he neglects his dependents. On Anvarī's innovations in the *qaṣīdah* Rypka observes: "Though appreciating the masters of this style, he was well aware that it was static and inflexible in both form and expression, and he set about taking it apart and reshaping it. He did not regard its traditional sequence as sacrosanct, and was fond of beginning with praise . . . and then passing on to another subject. The customary types of exordium vanish, their lyrical qualities being allowed to appear wherever they like. He does not attach any particular value to romantic feelings . . . amorousness is . . . not identical with passion, it conceals something else: it is directed at the person eulogized" ("Poets and Prose Writers,"p. 565).

tion in their styles, their poems demonstrate that both poets conceived of the *qaṣīdah* as a whole composed of different but complementary parts, and of the *nasīb* as more than a diverting prelude, and that, although the uses to which the form's potentials are put may vary according to the particular occasion or circumstance, its informing principle—the analogy between poet and lover, patron and beloved—remains the same. One may conclude that the very choice of the polythematic type of *qaṣīdah* (as opposed to panegyric without preamble) is frequently a signal that the ultimate purpose of the poem is not purely or exclusively encomiastic, but involves more complex ends, among which the didactic and ethical are of particular importance.

· III ·

Romance: The Language of Experience

WHILE panegyric was, quite naturally, the first major poetic genre to appear and flourish in courtly circles where composition in Persian was encouraged, other genres did not lag behind. With Fakhr al-Dīn Gurgānī's *Vīs u Rāmīn*, composed around 1050 (only a decade after the death of Manūchihrī), the courtly verse romance emerged as a full-fledged genre with distinctive conventions of its own. Prior to this work (with the exception of several early efforts to be discussed later), the epic held pride of place in narrative verse, particularly in the unparalleled achievement of Firdawsī's *Shāhnāmah*, in which the ancient history of Iran, from its lengendary origins down to the Arab conquest, was recorded.[1] The emergence of romance only a few decades after the completion of this work reflects broader cultural developments the full dimensions of which, given the present state of knowledge, we can only surmise. This chapter and the two that follow will be devoted to an exploration of the characteristics of Persian courtly verse romance and will attempt to elucidate its major features and to

[1] The epic, particularly as represented by Firdawsī's *Shāhnāmah*, is less a courtly genre of the sort encouraged at the courts of rulers of non-Iranian origin like the Ghaznavids and the Saljuqs than it is the continuation of an older Iranian tradition patronized in Islamic times by the remnants of the former landed aristocracy, the *dihqān* class, whose importance diminished with the fall of the Samanids of Bukhara; thus it falls outside the scope of the present study. See Lazard, "Rise," pp. 624-28; M. Molé, "L'épopée iranienne après Firdōsī," *La Nouvelle Clio* 5 (1953), 377-93; Rypka, *History*, pp. 151-66. See also C. E. Bosworth, "The Development of Persian Culture under the Early Ghaznavids," *Iran* 6 (1968), 40-41, on the change from heroic to romantic epic. For an extensive catalogue of the fragments (often only single lines) remaining from pre-Saljuq heroic and romantic *maṣnavī*s, see M. J. Maḥjūb, "Maṣnavī-sarā'ī dar zabān-i Fārsī tā pāyān-i qarn-i panjum-i Hijrī," *Nashrīyah-i Dānishkadah-i Adabīyāt-i Tabrīz* 15 (1342/1963), 188-213.

correlate them with the courtly milieu in which it flourished and with the social and literary circumstances that attended its development.

A number of important and mutually illuminating parallels exist between the appearance of romance, at nearly the same period, in the courtly literature of both East and West. Discussing the rise of courtly verse romance in the West in the twelfth century, R. W. Southern observes that this literary phenomenon is "a reflection of a more general change of attitude":

> Briefly, we find less talk of life as an exercise in endurance, and of death in a hopeless cause; we hear more of life as a seeking and a journeying. Men begin to order their experience more consciously in accordance with a plan; they think of themselves less as stationary objects of attack by spiritual foes, and more as pilgrims and seekers.[2]

The factors involved in this change included an increased emphasis on the individual and on the importance of self-knowledge, together with a corresponding interest in personal relationships; a decline of reliance on traditional authority and a growing feeling that "it was necessary for men to take the initiative in solving problems for which they were given no real guidance in their texts";[3] and a social dynamic that gave rise

[2] R. W. Southern, *The Making of the Middle Ages*, pp. 221-22.

[3] Colin Morris, *The Discovery of the Individual*, p. 58. Compare M.G.S. Hodgson: "As urbanity and cosmopolitan mingling increased in society on the citied agrarianate level, the reliance was steadily eroded that an individual could place on inherited status or authority to guide his choices in life. It could seem that the individual, with his private interests, might have to face a society in which almost anything might seem as legitimate, or illegitimate, as anything else, and where he must make his way at every moment anew by his wits and by such resources as he could assure himself personally. . . . In the mid-Arid Zone . . . the pressures toward a cosmopolitan dissolution of local legitimations could be unusually strong. Perhaps on this account, in that region the compensating institutions proved to be the least tightly structured. They were highly flexible . . . but they also . . . did tend to leave the individual relatively insecure in status, and face to face with society at large—as his religion left him face to face with the supreme God—with a minimum of buffering intermediaries. . . . Practically all that is distinctive in the Islamicate social order . . . can

to conflicting codes of conduct and necessitated the discussion and evaluation of their relative merits. Philosophical developments also played an important role, in particular the evolution of a concept of the created universe as an ordered whole and humanity as a microcosmic embodiment of that larger order, while changes in literary taste that accompanied these more general changes were reflected in the evolution of new generic, stylistic, and structural modes.[4]

Similar changes in attitude marked medieval Islamic civilization and are reflected in literary developments, specifically the appearance of verse romance in the mid-eleventh century and the development of the *ghazal* somewhat later. M.G.S. Hodgson describes the intellectual climate of the time:

> In the tenth and eleventh centuries, all the different intellectual traditions were well matured—that of the adîbs, that of the Sharʿî ʿulamâʾ, and also that of the Hellenic-Syriac philosophic and scientific tradition which had so long depended on an active work of translation and adaptation. Each tradition was ready to look beyond its own roots. . . .
>
> Out of these dialogues among mature traditions, with their assumption of a minimal Sharʿî pattern as already given, and out of the relatively decentralized and emancipated social context generally, grew two forms of intellectual independence that were, though not unparalleled in other times, yet specially distinctive of the period. On the level of imaginative literature, we find the expression of a human image that was relatively secular. . . . Then in more explicit speculation, where the assumption of Sharʿî dominance was more pressing, we find a growing pattern of free esoteric expression of truths.[5]

be interpreted in terms of the relative openness of the social structure and the mobility, or insecurity, of the individual within it" (*Venture*, 2:63-64).

[4] Cf. Morton Bloomfield, "Episodic Motivation and Marvels in Epic and Romance," *Essays and Explorations*, pp. 97-128; Vinaver, *Rise of Romance*, especially pp. 15-52, 99-122; Chenu, *Man and Nature*, passim.

[5] Hodgson, *Venture*, 2:153.

It is this development of a new human image, set in the context of a dialogue examining the given truths—intellectual, social, religious—that gives rise to the genre of romance, the vehicle for the literary expression of this dialogue in courtly society.

Significantly, it was the reign of Maḥmūd of Ghaznah that saw both the culmination of attempts to versify the ancient Iranian epic tradition in Firdawsī's *Shāhnāmah*, and the appearance of the earliest verse romances. Under the Ghaznavids, Persian became the standard language of the court and of literary expression, in preference to Arabic, which under the earlier Samanids of Khurasan had been, if not favored, at least equal in importance. Ghaznah and the region it ruled was an area of great cultural diversity, unified by Maḥmūd under the banner of Islam but still characterized by varied languages and traditions. And while Maḥmūd had great repute as a military leader, he was not to be outdone with respect to the sophistication of his court by either his Samanid predecessors or by the court at Baghdad, and was at pains to attract the best minds and talents of the age to Ghaznah. His capital became a major center for the type of intellectual dialogue described by Hodgson, and the changing values embodied in romance could already be felt at the Ghaznavid court.[6]

The rise of romance reflects a growing disaffection with the social values embodied in epic. Perhaps the very favoring of "foreign" settings or stories by poets such as ʿUnṣurī (whose *Vāmiq u ʿAẕrāʾ* derives from a Hellenistic romance) and ʿAyyūqī (who based his *Varqah u Gulshāh* on the Arab legend of ʿUrwah ibn Ḥizām) points to an attempt to replace these values—as well as the Zoroastrian ambience of epic—with others.[7] For in fact, the heroic values embodied in the *Shāh-*

[6] On the literary and intellectual culture of the Samanid court, and the continuity of administration and patronage alike under the Ghaznavids, see Bosworth, "Development," 37. The orthodoxy of the Ghaznavids at times put limitations on the scope of intellectual dialogue at their court (witness, for example, their persecution of Avicenna [Ibn Sīnā] for his "heretical" views; see Bosworth, *Ghaznavids*, pp. 74, 234); nevertheless, as the first important dynasty to patronize Persian letters, their contribution to the development of Persian culture can scarcely be overestimated.

[7] On the sources of these romances, see the introductions to the editions cited in the Bibliography. Bosworth notes that ʿUnṣurī's poem was "based on

nāmah were essentially those of the old Iranian *dihqāns*, agrarian landowners descended from the lesser nobility of Sassanian times; and the waning of their fortunes was as much an effect as a cause of the waning of their system of values. Two major currents replaced the earlier heroic epic: the chivalric geste, based on tales of heroic exploits but taking on a romantic and fantastic tinge, and the "romantic" epic, "the poem or tale treating of romantic love and suffused with a lyrical strain."[8] The numerous minor epics that followed the *Shāhnāmah* were primarily of the first type; of them, Maryan Molé observes:

> The noble ideal which had inspired Firdawsī was disappearing. People no longer extolled the past grandeur of the Iranian empire, but were entertained by listening to the *gestes* of heroes. . . . And as the poetic value of these epics decreased, their heroes achieved their victories with increasing ease.[9]

The second type, the courtly verse romance, the primary subject of which is not heroism and valor but love, became a major genre of courtly poetry.

A central problem in the development of romance is the need for a style that can convey the inner experience of its pro-

---

a much earlier Persian romance allegedly dedicated to the Sāsānid Khusrau Anūshīrvān" and speculates that there may have been Turkish influence as well on the development of romance under the Ghaznavids ("Development," 43-44; cf. A. S. Melikian-Chirvani, *Le roman de Varqe et Golšâh*, pp. 29-30). An earlier Pahlavi version of *Vāmiq u ʿAẕrā'* is said to have been destroyed (the story seems to originate with Dawlatshāh) by the Tahirid governor of Khurasan, ʿAbd Allāh ibn Ṭāhir (828-44), "who not only ordered that the work be destroyed but ordered the destruction of all Persian and Zoroastrian works" (Mawlavi Mohammed Shafi, introduction to ʿUnṣurī, *Vāmiq u ʿAẕrā'*, p. 1). The sources of ʿUnṣurī's and ʿAyyūqī's romances are explicitly designated as non-Iranian by their authors. On possible Hellenistic influence on pre-Islamic Persian romance, see Mary Boyce, "Zariadres and Zarēr," BSOAS 17 (1955), 463-77; William L. Hanaway, Jr., introduction to Bīghāmī's *Love and War*, pp. 5-7. For parallel problems with respect to authorial attribution of sources in Old French romance, see M.-L Ollier, "Demande sociale et constitution d'un 'genre,' " *Mosaic* 8:4 (1965), 212-15.

[8] Bosworth, "Development," 43, and see in general 40-44.

[9] Molé, "Épopée," 386; cf. Bosworth, "Development," 41-43, and see also Rypka, *History*, pp. 162-66.

tagonists: a style at once expressive of emotion and capable of commenting on the significance of the actions and events depicted. Such a style is afforded neither by the elevated and conventionalized diction of the *qaṣīdah* nor by the straightforward narrative style of epic. The earliest romances, fragmentary as they are, provide evidence of efforts to achieve such a style. One of the first of which more than a few scattered verses survive, ʿUnṣurī's *Vāmiq u ʿAẕrā*, composed at the court of Maḥmūd of Ghaznah, employs a narrative style that differs little from that of epic (as well as retaining the *mutaqārib* meter characteristic of that genre); the difficulties of such a style, more suited to the narrative exposition of action than to expressing the characters' inner states (in other words, externally rather than internally oriented) are illustrated by ʿUnṣurī's account of the lovers' first chance meeting, outside the temple of Hera at Samos.

When Vāmiq reached the temple, he glanced inside it.
It chanced that ʿAẕrā' suddenly came out of the door;
  and the whole world was filled with light.
Vāmiq stared so long at that face that the fair temple-
  adorner became confused.
. . . .
ʿAẕrā' too looked at Vāmiq, and saw a prince worthy of
  crown and throne.
The hearts of both young people began to boil; you
  would say their minds had become emptied of sense.
It is from sight that confusion always stems, and the hot
  flame of love mounts to the brain.[10]

(lines 83–89)

In this passage, the emotions are described from without, while the concluding *sententia* acts as a gloss to explain and generalize the action. All in all, there is little difference between this scene and similar ones in epic. Even more stilted is the attempt to describe the lovers' inner turmoil as, following

[10] ʿUnṣurī, *Vāmiq u ʿAẕrā*, ed. Mawlavi Mohammed Shafi; all page references are to this edition.

the encounter, ʿAẕrāʾ returns home, attempting to hide her feelings, while Vāmiq soliloquizes on his state.

ʿAẕrāʾ followed a twisting course, and showed her
mother naught (of what she felt).
So that she would not know that she had lost her heart,
she brushed a floured feather over her blushing face.
Meanwhile Vāmiq said to himself: "My evil fortune still
does not leave me.
"It has brought such a beauty before me as to make my
heart grieve and melt.
"Who knows now who this beauty was? was she an
angel, or the moon (walking) on earth?"
So spoke that heart, dark as ebony; so he poured amber
(tears) over juniper gum (his cheeks).
(lines 102–107)

Again, the lovers' feelings and thoughts are externalized by means of comparisons based on simile, and the workings of their emotions are narrated in essentially the same tone as are their actions. Dialogue and monologue are minimal; character and motivation are subordinated to episode.

ʿUnṣurī's contemporary ʿAyyūqī experimented somewhat more successfully with respect to style in his *Varqah u Gulshāh*, chiefly by mingling passages of narration with others designated as "poetry" (*shiʿr*), in which the characters voice their private thoughts and feelings. Such passages resemble brief *ghazal*s before the fact; while they are closely connected semantically and grammatically with the narrative passages that precede and follow (and employ the same *mutaqārib* meter), their rhyme scheme departs from the *masnavī* of narrative verse to follow a pattern that later becomes customary for the *ghazal*, including the characteristic rhymed *maṭlaʿ*.[11] They in-

[11] Rypka terms these interpolations "love-songs in the form of *ghazals*" (*History*, p. 177); but they are not all love songs; neither does the *ghazal* yet exist as a form. It is tempting to speculate that they were performed to musical accompaniment contrasting with the rhythm of the narrative passages, but there is no evidence for such a practice. For a stylistic analysis of the poem, see Melikian-Chirvani, *Varqe et Golšâh*. pp. 26-50.

clude, not only love poems, but poems of boasting and self-praise, elegy, and so on; in the following example, the heroine, Gulshāh, mourns the death of her lover Varqah:

> Her soul spoke its secrets to Death; in grief she began a poem.
> That lovely idol recited to herself an Arabic poem, in bitter grief,
>
> [Gulshāh's poem]
>
> Saying: "Henceforth, my heart, boast not of the world, for its glory is torment, and its love, bitter need.
> "Two supple cypresses in one garden it raised in contentment and love;
> "Without either committing a sin, it separated them from each other once more.
> "O Varqah, your separation from your beloved had made my long life, without you, short.
> "You told me: 'I shall return to you'; you left me, never to return.
> "When Fate opened the door to your death, I could not resist (opening) the door of grief.
> "Now I will come to you; make a place for me beside you."[12]
>
> (p. 112)

In such passages ʿAyyūqī comes considerably closer than did ʿUnṣurī to creating a style suitable for conveying passion and emotion; but his is still far from an adequate presentation of the inner life of his characters. Like ʿUnṣurī, his emphasis is on action (although he exhibits a greater attention to psychology); he is a master of suspense, and his poem is a "cliff-hanger" dividing naturally into segments that typically conclude at a moment of great excitement or uncertainty (a feature that undoubtedly reflects the work's composition for oral delivery, as do the poet's frequent direct addresses to his audience, his

[12] ʿAyyūqī, *Varqah u Gulshāh*, ed. Ẕabīḥ Allāh Ṣafā; all page references are to this edition.

interjections and comments).[13] In keeping with this oral style is the poet's final comment on the story he has related:

> Such is the way of the world throughout; and so it will
> ever be—to put it briefly.
> Two sweethearts with such love passed from the world
> with longing and grief.
> They saw nothing but faithfulness from one another, nor
> did they follow the path of error and cruelty.
> They gave their lives for each other; even such is faith
> [*āyīn*], nobility [*aṣl*], and lineage [*guhar*].
> Alas! that the unkind sphere of this world ever shows
> fidelity to none.
>
> (pp. 115–16).

While this conclusion voices the complaint of mutability, which is a universal commonplace of the medieval Persian tradition (and, indeed, of medieval literature in general), the story itself shows plainly that the lovers are less the victims of fate than of the covetousness and aggression of others, as well as of a system of values that, though it may be the object of nostalgic admiration, is also perceived to be outmoded.[14] But ʿAyyūqī's style is still unequal to presenting the issues in all their complexity; they are seen mainly from the outside, on the level of the action. The psychological depth that both these early ro-

[13] Cf., for example, ibid., p. 11, where ʿAyyūqī addresses his audience in the style of an epic narrator: "Now hear from me the circumstances of that attack [the raid of Rabīʿ ibn ʿAdnān on Gulshāh's tribe, in which she is kidnapped] which was carried out in anger." Melikian-Chirvani comments on the emphasis on action in this romance, contrasting it with Gurgānī's interest in detailing the emotional and psychological states of his protagonists (see *Varqe et Golšâh*, pp. 21-25).

[14] As Melikian-Chirvani notes, an important motivating factor in the romance is material wealth: "The possession of money is implicitly designated as a virtue. . . . For ʿAyyūqī, a suitor must be wealthy. The hero with whom the reader is asked to sympathize no longer dares seek the hand of Gulshāh once he is ruined. . . . Money motivates the action of the romance, because it is a necessity of life" (ibid., p. 33). I suggest, however, that ʿAyyūqī does not support such values, but holds them up for criticism, through the example of his lovers' fate.

mances lack is not achieved until a few decades later, with *Vīs u Rāmīn*, in which Fakhr al-Dīn Gurgānī at last succeeds in creating another dimension, which coexists with that of the narrated action: a dimension encompassing the innermost thoughts and feelings of the characters, as they (and we) ponder the meaning of their experience.

Vīs u Rāmīn, composed around 1054 at the court of the Saljuq governor of Isfahan, has acquired international repute as the Persian analogue of the story of Tristan and Yseut. The love triangle is substantially the same (an aging king, his young bride, and her lover—here, the king's brother); but Gurgānī's treatment of the triangle leads to an outcome radically different from that of any of the Tristan romances. With this work, the Iranian heritage becomes the primary matter of romance.[15]

[15] A problem that has received little attention is why romance, which first appeared at the Ghaznavid court, failed to flourish there and saw its major development under the Saljuqs, while by contrast, the *ghazal* made its greatest early progress at the hands of Ghaznavid poets (see chapter 6). Circumstantial evidence suggests an antipathy on the part of the Ghaznavids for the Zoroastrian cultural heritage, a sentiment that may also have political roots in their opposition to the Samanids and that may explain Maḥmūd of Ghaznah's ambivalent if not hostile attitude to the *Shāhnāmah* (Rypka, *History* pp. 161-62). Al-Bīrūnī's statement that the Persian language is most suited "to perpetuate historical epics dealing with the kings of yesteryear and to provide stories for evening social gatherings" (Bausani, "Muhammad or Darius?" p. 56) may reflect the view that such material was noncourtly (a view that perhaps provoked early romance poets to claim non-Iranian sources for their poems; see n. 7 here). The major successor to the *Shāhnāmah*, Asadī Ṭūsī's *Garshāsbnāmah*, written around 1054-56 (and thus contemporary with *Vīs u Rāmīn*), was composed not in the author's native Khurasan (nor yet in Ghaznah), but for Abū Dulaf, a prince of Transcaucasian Nakhjavan (Rypka, *History*, p. 164; see also Molé, "Épopée," 381-83). Perhaps the Saljuqs—who, unlike the Ghaznavids, "had not spent a formative period within the military slave institution or the cultural ambience of an indigenous Iranian dynasty" (C. E. Bosworth, "The Heritage of Rulership in Early Islamic Iran and the Search for Dynastic Connections with the Past," *Iran* 9 [1973], 61)—felt less uncomfortable with such Zoroastrian materials; it is also possible that materials reputed to have been destroyed in the east still survived in the west of Iran. Another factor may be the increasing cultural isolation of Ghaznah following the Saljuq defeat of Masʿūd I (1040): "The great days of the early Ghaznavid court, graced by the presence of the best Persian poets and some of the greatest scholars, were gone for ever. The loss of Khurasan with its rich cultural traditions had put Ghazna

More important, this is the first Persian romance in which stylistic features so characteristic of the genre both East and West are deliberately and skillfully employed; Gurgānī's poem thus parallels the achievement of the anonymous Latin poet who, in the mid-eleventh century in southern Germany, composed what Peter Dronke terms "the first medieval verse romance," *Ruodlieb*.[16] Despite certain obvious differences, both poets show sufficient similarity in their departure from the heroic values of epic and *chanson de geste*, in their emphasis on love, and in their efforts to convey a broad spectrum of human experience, to cause their works to stand as milestones in their respective traditions, pointing forward to what is to come.

In contrast to the heroic poem, in romance the emphasis is on word rather than on deed, on the exploration, through discourse and dialogue, of the moral complexities of experience; the action, rather than constituting its own raison d'être or functioning to demonstrate a hero's prowess, typically points to values beyond itself.[17] Romance is an interpretive (one might almost say an exegetical) genre, rather than an expository one. The romance writer conceives of his task as being the revelation, through the use of the rhetorical techniques available to him, of the meaning implicit in his material (usually a received source or sources, which he adapts or reworks): "What a good romance writer is expected to do . . . is to reveal the *meaning* of the story . . . adding to it such embellishing thoughts as he considers appropriate . . . [so as to] raise his work to a level of distinction which no straight-forward nar-

---

into a more isolated position than ever before. . . . This contrasts sharply with the bloom of Islamic scholarship in the same period under the Saljuqs. . . . Poetry was . . . the only branch of literary activity which was able to thrive in the later Ghaznavid period, although even poetry had to struggle to regain some of its earlier importance" (de Bruijn, *OPP*, p. 34). Many poets migrated either west, to the Saljuq territories, or east to India, in search of patronage (ibid., pp. 150-51). De Bruijn notes the greater influence of Arabic poetry on the later Ghaznavid poets, as well as the difficulty—owing to the numerous gaps in documentary evidence—of tracing the development of poetry at this period (ibid., p. 148).

[16] Peter Dronke, *Poetic Individuality in the Middle Ages*, p. 35.

[17] Cf. Vinaver, *Rise of Romance*, especially pp. 19-32.

ration could ever reach."[18] Vinaver's appraisal of the European romancer's attitude is equally applicable to Gurgānī, whose prologue to *Vīs u Rāmīn* reveals precisely the same understanding of, and approach to, his task.

Recounting the circumstances that led to the composition of the poem, Gurgānī relates being asked by his patron,

> "What do you say about the tale of Vīs and Rāmīn? They say it is a thing of rare excellence; in this country all are devoted to it." I replied, "It is a very beautiful story, collected by six scholars. I have never seen a better; it resembles nothing so much as a blossoming garden. However, its language is Pahlavī, and by no means everyone who reads it is aware of its purport; not everyone reads that language well, or even if he reads it, knows its meaning. It contains numerous descriptions of all manner of things, but when you read it over it has no great meaning. For at that time poetry was not an art; there was no scholar of quick wit; if only those scholars could see how diction is produced nowadays, meanings unraveled, meter and rhyme superimposed! . . . When a work has meter and rhyme it is better than when it is arranged haphazardly, particularly when one may find therein sentiments which, when one reads them, will one day stand one in good stead. However dainty and sweet a tale may be, it becomes refurbished by meter and rhyme.
>
> "There should be numerous sentiments and expressions scattered here and there in the story, like a royal pearl set in gold, shining out from its midst like stars. Then the nobles and intelligensia may read it to learn many sentiments from it, whilst the populace and ordinary folk merely read it for the sake of the story. A dis-

[18] Ibid., p. 17. On the relationship of *sen* and *matière*—which might be well rendered by the Persian *maʿnā* and *dāstān*—see ibid., pp. 16-23; see also Douglas Kelly, "*Matière* and *genera dicendi* in Medieval Romance," in *Approaches to Medieval Romance*, ed. Peter Haidu, pp. 147-59, and idem, "*Translatio Studii*: Translation, Adaptation, and Allegory in Medieval French Literature," *PQ* 37 (1978), 302-304; M.-L. Ollier, "The Author in the Text," in *Approaches to Medieval Romance*, pp. 26-41.

course should be such that when it issues from the poet's mouth it should travel the wide world, not merely stay at home, declaimed by none but its author!

"Now, those authorities of the past composed the tale of Vīs and Rāmīn. . . . They composed a story with strange expressions in it from every language. They took no pains over sentiments and proverbs, nor embellished it with these two. If a scholar were to apply himself to it, it would become as pretty as a treasure full of gems; for this is a famous story, whose incidents contain numberless marvels."

When the Lord heard my words, he placed a crown of pride upon my head. He thus requested me, "Beautify this story as April the garden." I shall tell it as best I can, and purge it of those meaningless expressions. . . . Now I must begin a tale which the perceptive will term no less than sage advice.[19] (*VR*, pp. 17–19; 7:29–72)

[19] Page references in the text are to *Vis and Ramin*, trans. George Morrison; section and line numbers refer to *Vīs u Rāmīn*, ed. M. J. Maḥjūb. The passage is also translated by Minorsky ("Vīs u Rāmīn: A Parthian Romance," *BSOAS* 11 [1943-46], 742-43); 7:36 (which Morrison renders "for then poetry was no art") should read, rather, "there was no professional poet" (to take the matter in hand; *shāʿirī-pīshah* should be taken as a parallel construction to *ḥakīmī chābuk-andīshah*). In 7:44, *naw-āyīn* gives a somewhat stronger meaning than Morrison's "refurbished" and conveys perfectly the sense of "making new" the traditional *matière* by revealing its deeper signification. In 7:48, *kām*, "mouth," has the additional meaning of "intention," strengthening the motif of the poet's self-awareness. Gurgānī's remark that the original was not versified may reflect the practice of Sassanian copyists of recording verse as if it were prose (in paragraphs), as well as inserting glosses and commentary—a practice that led to the later disparagement of such works, which were not recognized as poetry. See E. Benveniste, "Le *Mémorial de Zarēr*," *JA* 220 (1932), 282-86. For contrasting views on Gurgānī's model see Minorsky, ibid., and "Vīs u Rāmīn . . . (Conclusion)," *BSOAS* 12 (1947-48), 20-35; compare the brief review in Rypka, *History*, p. 178, and the preface to the edition by M. A. Todua and A. K. Gwakharia, pp. xix–xxvi. M. Molé has argued (somewhat convincingly) that the poem reflects contemporary circumstances surrounding the establishment of the Saljuq dynasty (" 'Vīs u Rāmīn' et l'histoire Seldjoukide," *AION* 8 [1958], 1-30); certainly it is not unlikely that an analogy to current political events was intended by the poet, this being a frequent medieval strategy. Prior to Gurgānī, ʿAyyūqī wrote, in a passage in

That Gurgānī regards his poem as "sage advice" indicates that he is concerned with more than merely "dressing up" a well-known story with rhetorical embellishments. His insistence that the function of style is to reveal meaning recalls Chrétien de Troyes' *bele conjointure*, defined by Vinaver as "the art of *composition* in the etymological sense of the term," an art that transforms "a mere tale of adventure into a romance" and "which only a learned man can practise properly."[20] *Conjointure*, or composition, used in this sense involves the integration of a variety of elements into the poem in order to create complexity of meaning; it includes both the selection and arrangement of the basic *matière*, or source material, of the poem and the utilization of structural and rhetorical strategies to reveal the significance of this matter. Central to this process is the creation of a style sufficiently complex to convey the complexities of the matter itself: a style that will present the action from a variety of perspectives rather than from the single perspective

---

praise of discourse (a standard topic of epic and later of romance): "Discourse is better than luxury and desire; it is better than a richly adorned treasure. // Discourse is sufficient wealth for its speaker; it is sufficient adornment for a man. // Listen to the discourse of the wise, and pay heed; for nothing less than discourse came from Heaven. // Discourse can elevate man to the sphere; it can draw the mountain down to the plain. // Discourse can turn your ugly deeds to good; it can show you the way to Paradise. // I have told this tale [*samar*] in pleasing discourse, as no-one else has told it before. // No-one, of the elite or the populace, has ever told such a tale in this meter and style. // I had opted for solitude, repented of poetry; but an adjudicator interfered. // For the sake of that kingly crown, I shall tell my story in Persian [*Darī*]. // Discourse should, without doubt, be colored by verse; the bride is made beautiful by the tiring-woman. // I shall adorn my discourse throughout, constantly seeking beauty from wisdom. // I shall versify an amazing tale from Arabic legends [*akhbār*] and books" (*Varqah u Gulshāh*, pp. 4-5).

[20] Vinaver, *Rise of Romance*, p. 37 (author's emphasis); and see pp. 34-38. The term suggests "that it is the degree of the poet's skill to combine words that distinguishes poetic originality worthy of imitation from mediocre attempts at verse. The components of word patterns, of images, of narrative events, extracted from the familiar and associated in a new ordering, make for other visions, other meanings" (Michelle Freeman, *The Poetics of Translatio Studii and Conjointure*, p. 66; and see pp. 65-73). See also Ollier, "Author." Niẓāmī refers to his *Haft Paykar* as a *tarkīb*, a term analogous to *conjointure* (see chapter 5, n. 30).

that characterizes epic narrative and that is still apparent in the romances of Gurgānī's predecessors discussed earlier.[21]

One means of conveying the complexity of experience is through the alternation of narrated action with monologue or dialogue, which acts as a sort of "interlinear commentary" on the narrative. Vinaver describes this "marriage of matter and meaning, of narrative and commentary," exemplified by Chrétien's characteristic technique of constructing his story so that it "develops simultaneously on two levels: that of feeling and that of action, one constantly motivating the other, even when by realistic standards no such motivation is required"; the technique functions to make the work structurally complete, to interpret the action of the narrative by providing a commentary that will illuminate the issues embodied in that action.[22] It contributes to the establishment of varied perspectives, which is a characteristic feature of romance—and which accounts for much of the "disjunction" commonly associated with it—and specifically serves to elaborate the nature and implications of the love relationship that is the central focus of the genre. The juxtaposition of contrasting ideas or images typical of medieval literature in general is given dramatic immediacy by this presentation of "multiple perspectives on reality," through which the poet is able to assert that "the 'meaning' of events is finally collective or cumulative, the sum total of partial (in both senses of the term) impressions."[23] It is effectively employed in Persian romance for the first time by Gurgānī.

[21] On multiple perspectives as an organizing principle in romance, see Robert Hanning, *The Individual in Twelfth-Century Romance*, especially pp. 171-93; see also Frederick Goldin, "The Array of Perspectives in the Early Courtly Love Lyric," in *In Pursuit of Perfection*, ed. J. Ferrante and G. Economou, pp. 51-52.

[22] See Vinaver, *Rise of Romance*, pp. 19-32.

[23] Hanning, *Individual*, pp. 171-72; cf. E. Vinaver, "Landmarks in Arthurian Romance," in *The Expansion and Transformation of Courtly Literature*, ed. N. B. Smith and J. T. Snow, p. 18. On the juxtaposition of thematic and structural elements as a medieval compositional principle, see in particular Robert M. Jordan, *Chaucer and the Shape of Creation*, especially pp. 10-60; Norris G. Lacy, "Spatial Form in Medieval Romance," in *Approaches to Medieval Romance*, ed. Peter Haidu, pp. 160-69.

In *Vīs u Rāmīn*, Gurgānī anticipates by some hundred years what Vinaver has termed one of the first "interior monolgues" on record—Fénice's pondering (in Chrétien's *Cligès*) the meaning of Cligès' statement, on his departure for King Arthur's court, that he is "altogether hers"[24]—as he shows Vīs debating "in her heart" whether to respond to Rāmīn's love:

> When Vīs set eyes on Rāmīn, it was as if she beheld her own dear soul. When she looked closely at Rāmīn's face, she laid waste her loyalty and love toward Vīrū. Then thoughtfully she said in her heart, "How, indeed, if Rāmīn became my mate? What, say, shall I suffer at the hands of this heart-ravisher who has thus dissipated the stock of Vīrū? Now that I am separated from mother and glorious brother, why should I burn in fire? Why should I sit so long in loneliness? How long am I to suffer tribulation? I am not made of iron! I shall find no heart's treasure better than this; I shall not turn my head from his covenant and command."
>
> Then she thought to herself and regretted the days gone by. But she did not reveal her love to the Nurse, although she was crazed with love. (*VR*, p. 103; 43:21–28)

Vīs's soul-searching bears little resemblance to the same topic as treated by ʿUnṣurī; for Gurgānī excels in depicting the internal conflicts of his characters, and a comparison of this passage with that from *Vāmiq u ʿAẕrāʾ* cited earlier reveals the distance between the two styles. Morever, such a monologue can serve to present, not merely the specific viewpoint of the speaker, but the alternatives with which he is faced and between which he must decide.

> The monologue is often a form of dialogue, in which the personality of the protagonist appears to be split: he makes a statement, questions it (usually by repeating and analysing the key terms), and then attempts to respond to

[24] Of Fénice's monologue Vinaver observes, "Nothing like it is to be found in the literature of medieval Europe before the middle of the twelfth century" (*Rise of Romance*, p. 27).

> this questioning as if it were a real question put by another person. Such a dramatic monologue corresponds to a real debate in which both parties reside in the protagonist.[25]

Rāmīn's distraught outpouring, after falling in love with Vīs, exemplifies this type of "inner dialogue," in which the speaker alternately argues for the adoption of conflicting courses (*VR*, pp. 161–62; 32:39–57).

Complementary to such monologues, which record the conflicting emotions and mental debates of their speakers, are passages of dialogue that juxtapose shifting or contrasting points of view. In *Vīs u Rāmīn* the figure of the Nurse, who serves as intermediary between the lovers, as a sounding board for their emotions, and as a buffer against the jealous king, increases the complexity of the viewpoints presented. The Nurse's attitude (like that of her counterpart in the Tristan romances) represents an aspect of the courtly view of love that is held up for comment, if not for criticism, as her advice to Vīs, that "only love matters," suggests:

> "Of no avail are wisdom, chivalry, wit, abstemiousness, rage, brawn, riches, jewels, fame, greatness, counsel, talent, kingship, fasting, mettle, or saintliness, neither sight of Shahrū nor of your relatives and kin, neither good advice nor true counsel. Once love has come, one must manage willy-nilly; suffer at the hands of others what may or may not be one's desire. My words will be revealed to you soon, for you have as yet seen but smoke from this fire. When you experience love farther than this you will then praise my words; you will see clearly and I too whether I am moved by love for you or spite; whether pretext came from Fortune or not, whether Fate be gentle to you or otherwise." (*VR*, p. 92; 41:170–78)

The presentation of conflicting points of view, of course, is central in passages that recount debates between the protago-

[25] Peter Dembowski, "Monologue, Author's Monologue and Related Problems in the Romances of Chrétien de Troyes," in *Approaches to Medieval Romance*, ed. Peter Haidu, p. 106.

nists—for example, that between Vīs, on the roof of her palace, and Rāmīn, who stands before the palace in the snow but is denied admittance—which I will discuss later in this chapter. In such passages, the lengthy detailing of opposing arguments, complaints, and reproaches typically reveals the participants to be at cross-purposes; lack of communication, rather than reasoned argumentation, is the chief issue in such scenes. (The technique is exploited to particular effect by Niẓāmī in *Khusraw u Shīrīn* and will be discussed later in this and the following chapter.)

Narratorial commentary adds yet another perspective on the events related; for an important generic feature of romance is that the author is present not merely as an ostensibly objective narrator, but in various other personae as well (a point to be examined in the following chapter).

> In [romance] the author (in his variously assumed *personae* of a narrator, orator, lyric poet, commentator, sage, etc.) appears and disappears according to the exigencies of his art. He is "present" in straight-forward narration or description, and he can be present in other modes of presentation of the story. His "presence" is not always direct.[26]

Once this principle is recognized, the pseudoproblem of assumed inconsistencies in the author's point of view will be re-

[26] Dembowski, "Monologue," p. 103; he observes further: "The real importance of the monologue must be sought in its function, and this function is determined by a universal human characteristic. The monologue is an expression of an old, common sense, psychologically well observed fact: a man does not talk to himself under normal circumstances, and conversely, if he does so, he is in an extraordinary psychological state. Thus functionally, the monologue . . . is an extensive, massive interruption of the narrative progression of the romance by an introspective, speculative, most often generalizing statement made by a protagonist under the immediate impulse of his apparent extraordinary state. Such an interruption of the 'horizontal' axis of the tale by a 'vertical' interjection of an analytic commentary—commentary, like the generalizing *sententiae*, very often both profound and trite—is something which almost always verges on the artificial. The different degrees of authorial 'presence' are, of course, to be expected in such a mode of presentation. The monologue offers a very rich field of study of the author's intervention in the work that he creates" (ibid., p. 108).

moved, and the too-frequent mistake of interpreting any and all statements (including those of specific characters) as a direct expression of the poet's personal beliefs will be avoided.[27] With respect to *Vīs u Rāmīn*, this principle resolves the difficulty of reconciling Gurgānī's apparently contradictory statements on love as both a joy and an affliction, which has hitherto troubled critics: both are recognized attitudes toward love that require expression in a poem dedicated to that topic; neither should be taken as the expression of a conviction that excludes the other. Such seeming inconsistencies are yet another means by which the poet presents his matter from a variety of perspectives.

Yet other perspectives, as well as stylistic variation, are provided by interpolated passages of song, sung either by Rāmīn (who, like Tristan, is a minstrel of repute), who uses them to express his plight, or by the court minstrel (as in the ballad of the tree, which alerts Mawbad to the lovers' continued relationship).[28] Such passages are not distinguished prosodically from the narrative, as was the case with ʿAyyūqī, but they are characterized by a marked lyrical tone and employ thematic motifs and images typical of the love lyric, as seen in this song sung by Rāmīn:

> "I saw a blossoming spring garden, worthy to have love planted in it. I saw a gliding garden cypress, I saw a talking heavenly moon, I saw there an April rose, its scent and color both of Paradise; fit to be a comforter in the hour of grief, a joy in the hour of happiness; I surrendered my heart to its love forever and preferred the gardener's trade to all else. I ever stray among its tulip beds and gaze on its blossoming spring glory. Day and night I am a denizen of the garden, while my enemy is left like a knocker on its gate. Why should the jealous bear envy? "God gives

[27] See, for example, ʿA. A. Shihābī's interpretation of Majnūn's prayer before the Kaʿbah, in Niẓāmī's *Laylī u Majnūn*, as an expression of the poet's concept of love (*Niẓāmī, Shāʿir-i Dāstānsarā*, pp. 232-33); see also chapter 4 of this book.

[28] See *VR*, p. 203; *Vīs u Rāmīn*, 67:17-24. The passage is explicitly designated a *masal*.

everyone his due." The wheeling sphere is worthy of the moon, thus it is that God has vouchsafed the moon to it."[29] (*VR*, pp. 146–47; 59:19–27)

A final means of providing varied perspectives on the love relationship is provided by the series of letters written for Vīs by a scribe (a device that implies yet another voice, and yet another viewpoint—this one explicitly rhetorical—heard therein) in which she reproaches Rāmīn for his infidelity and injustice and describes in detail her own inner turmoil.

All these techniques—monologue and dialogue, song and letter, and narratorial interjections—serve as commentary on the action, a commentary embodying acts of interpretation made from the viewpoints of the various actors and revealing the conflicting values that underlie their attitudes. More will be said on this question in the following chapter, which deals specifically with the presentation of character. The remainder of this chapter will focus on yet another method of providing commentary on the action of the poem and on its agents, namely, the manner in which these are described. In romance, the straightforward narrative style typical of epic, where the emphasis is on the action, and which still dominates the early efforts of ʿUnṣurī and ʿAyyūqī, is replaced by a style in which

[29] Such lyric passages may reflect an indigenous popular tradition of love poetry later incorporated into the *ghazal*, which develops into an independent form about a half-century later; they recall the parallel device used by many European romance writers of alluding to contemporary courtly lyrics (as, notably, does Gottfried's Tristan, who like Rāmīn, soothes his heart by composing love songs, which he sings in public, but whose true meaning is known only to himself). In their depiction of the love relationship Rāmīn's songs closely resemble the love poems of al-ʿAbbās ibn al-Aḥnaf and his imitators, a resemblance made even stronger by the association of both with music: al-ʿAbbās was the favorite composer of Ibrāhīm al-Mawṣilī (Tomiche, "Réflexions," 275). Pizzi's view that *Vīs u Rāmīn* derived from folk ballads has been discounted, notably by Gabrieli ("Note sul *Vīs u Rāmīn* di Faḥr ad-Dīn Gurgānī," *Rendiconti dell'Accademia Nazionale dei Lincei, Classe di scienzi morale, storichi e filologiche*, ser. 6, 15 [1939], 168-72); however, it seems not unlikely that such material may have been among Gurgānī's sources, deliberately manipulated and given some legitimation by being incorporated in his courtly poem.

narration is accompanied by extensive passages of description. Such passages, and particularly the details of the imagery chosen to describe the events in question, furnish a means for comment, especially as regards the moral dimension of the events. The function of imagery in Persian poetry has seldom been considered; thus it is of particular interest to study its use in romance to provide, not objective description, but interpretation.

Scenes of battle often afford an occasion for extended descriptive passages. Gurgānī's account of the battle between Mawbad and Vīrū, Vīs's brother and first husband, from whom Mawbad attempts to take her by force, begins, in true epic fashion, at dawn, with the two armies arrayed. The wardrum sounds, a "demon of wrath," while the fife screams like the Last Trump. "As blossoms scatter from the boughs at the sound of spring thunder, so at the roll of the wardrum the blossom of war spilled from the camp (*VR*, p. 41; 20:5)": thus the poet introduces, as the battle commences, a motif that will pervade the imagery used to describe it: that of the garden.

The early stages of the battle are described in a hyperbolic style, which gradually appears increasingly incongruous to its subject.

> When the armies faced each other at close quarters the heroes attacked each other furiously; you would have sworn two steel mountains clashed on that field. Messengers plied from one army to another; the javelin with four feathers, the black-feathered arrow; emissaries who found their way into the heart and settled in heart or eye. In every house where they took up their abode they turned out the master of the house.
>
> The ranks of battle and the fear of death were so formidable that the Resurrection materialized before the warriors' eyes. Brother was estranged from brother: none had any friend other than their own prowess. They found no ally other than their right arm; no judge but the dagger; whosoever was aided by his right arm, the dagger gave judgment in his favor. You would have sworn the

warriors had become sowers, but sowing steel in eye and heart! Speech makers fell silent, as men of sense were all senseless: no one heard any sound there but the roll of the drum and the shrilling of the fife.

Now the sword slipped into armor like water; now the arrow slid into the eyes like sleep; now the spearpoint glided into the heart like love; now the axe cracked the head like wit. You would have sworn the blood-thirsty sword knew where the Creator had disposed the soul in the body! The soul escaped from men by the same road as the sword had entered. The Indian blade was like a lily; a flood the hue of Judas blossom raining from it; like a myrtle branch with pomegranate petals hanging from it; like pomegranate petals with seeds upon them. The javelin was like a tailor in the battle; it kept on sewing warriors into the saddle! When Fate triumphed over the lives of the warriors, one became a fleeing wild ass, the other a lion. As Fortune closed on the ranks of the warriors, one became a scuttling mountain sheep, the other a cheetah. (*VR*, p. 43; 20:30–50)

In the melee Vīs's father, Qārin, is slain, his dead supporters piled round him: "You would have sworn the heavens rained golden hail, and round it tulip petals" (*VR*, p. 44; 20:55).

M. Shafīʿī Kadkanī has criticized Gurgānī's battle scenes (and specifically this passage) for their "inappropriate" imagery, which he considers more suitable for epic;[30] but such elaborate hyperbole far exceeds anything seen in the *Shāhnāmah*, where the attention is more on strategic detail and the recounting of deeds of prowess. Stylistically, this passage is much closer to the celebrational diction of victory *qaṣīdah*s

[30] "Fakhr al-Dīn Asʿad has a special mastery in the depiction of love and the states of loving, and in this area his images are mostly efficient and successful in transmitting the sense. But sometimes, when he departs from the area of lyrical matters and wishes to make his fancy soar in the fields of battle, his poetic images are inefficient and inappropriate to the subject. . . . [A passage such as that cited] shows that he has no experience in describing scenes of battle; while his hyperbole in this area . . . is suitable for epic" (M. Shafīʿī Kadkanī, *Ṣuvar-i khiyāl dar shiʿr-i Fārsī*, pp. 453-54).

that extoll the ruler's martial prowess, such as those composed by the panegyrists of the Ghaznavids, or by such Arabic poets as Abū Tammām and al-Mutanabbī, in which (in further contrast to epic) the devices of *badīʿ* figure prominently.[31] The allusiveness is deliberate and ironic; for Gurgānī's intent is quite other than the celebration of heroic actions, as becomes clear from the description of the battle's conclusion.

On Qārin's death, Vīrū harangues his nobles, who fall in fury upon Mawbad's army. The hyperbole that characterized the preceding passage is intensified.

> Speech was then carried on with sword and axe; the game the champions played was with heads! Son had no mercy at all on father, nor warriors on relatives and kin; brother was in feud against brother; in feud friend was worse than enemy! A darkness came up from the world, so that night came on before nightfall. At that moment men became blind as bats; the fount of light of the sun was choked with dust. Once eyes had been clogged up with dust, brother wounded brother: father failed to recognize son, and severed his head with the sword. You would have sworn the spearpoint was a spit, the bird upon it a

[31] Compare, for example, Abū Tammām's famous ode on the conquest of Amorium, noted for its likening of the captured city to a woman, and boasting such lines as "Many a moon's resplendence was gained under its [the war's] glare, and many a white tooth under its cloud. // Many were the ways to sequestered virgins through cutting necks like so many strings. // The Indian swords that quivered unsheathed won many a branch quivering on a sandhill [a woman with a narrow waist and substantial foundations to it]. // When the white swords that have been drawn from their sheaths return, they have a better claim to the women with white-bodied playmates than veils have" (quoted by Hamori, *Art*, pp. 129-30; author's emphases omitted). Compare also Farrukhī's *qaṣīdah* celebrating Maḥmūd of Ghaznah's military prowess: "The eye cannot see the well of light [the sun] for the black dust; the ear cannot hear the thunder for the tumult of drums and cymbals. // From the white-poplar arrows in the hands of warlike men mail-coats have become full of holes, like the paper of the king's target-butts. // The torrent of blood has passed through their midst; and bubbles have risen upon the blood like beads of amber. // The sword-blades are like the Judas-flower, the faces like *shanbalīd* [a white flower]: the one from men's blood, the other from the fear of plunder and hardship" (*Dīvān*, ed. ʿA. ʿAbd al-Rasūlī, p. 7).

spitted champion! Four-feathered arrows sprouted like trees from the eyes of the luckless. The tree of life sprouted from the body, over it the screen of helmet and mail; once the dagger ripped the screen, it cut the tree of life. The sky had become like a reedbed from spears; the earth like a winepress from men's blood. So much dust was there, so many swords dripping blood, that the whole world was full of smoke and fire. You would have sworn death had become a rushing wind, scattering the warriors' heads like so many leaves. The heads of the warriors were like polo balls, the legs of their horses like polo sticks. Death laid the warriors low on the soil, like a garden cypress cut off by the root. When the heavenly sun sank in the west, it became gold like the faces of lovers. You would have sworn the sun was the fortune of Moubad, and that the world was giving up hope of his glory. On the one hand the sun in distress in the heaven because of night, on the other Moubad in distress because of the enemy; the one disappearing from the sight of the eyes, the other deserting the striving warriors. When the King abandoned the field of battle, the world had fallen about the ears of his host. (*VR*, pp. 44–45; 20:76–90)

Decorative hyperbole has given way to grotesque, just as Mawbad's apparent victory has given way to flight. The image of the garden evoked at the beginning of the battle, and amplified in the first descriptive passage, has become perverted and ruinous: "Things rank and foul in nature / Possess it merely." The unifying topos of the passage is that of the world upside down: the "messengers" who ply between the armies carry, not suits for peace, but death; the "sowers" of the land bring, not its fertility, but its ruin; the sprouting of the tree of life is a sign of death, in this confusion where son knows not father, and friend turns to enemy. Irony is at work here; as Mawbad's unjust war was introduced by a passage employing the celebrational diction of praise, now his just defeat is described in the rhetoric of blame, and glorification gives way, in rhetorical and moral terms alike, to censure. The final stroke of irony lies in the comparison of Mawbad's declining fortune to the declining sun, whose face is yellow like that of the wasting lover; for while the cause of this battle was Mawbad's passion for Vīs, the means used in his attempt to obtain her is not that of the lover, but of the warrior. We are reminded, moreover, of the image that introduced this section: the rising sun, likened to the monarch of the sky and driving before it two horses, one black, one white (*VR* p. 41).[32]

Such a passage illustrates the complexity in the medieval poet's use of imagery. Gurgānī's imagery is still essentially metaphorical, as evidenced by the frequency of expressions such as "it seemed as if" and "you would swear that" and is based on perceived similitudes of attributes or qualities: severed heads like polo balls, the earth dripping blood like a winepress; but the choice of images is based, not on their decorative, but on their associative, aptness: polo balls suggest a grim game indeed (the metaphor is continued in another passage to be discussed later), while the fallen "tulip petals," pomegranate petals clinging to sword blades, and so on are the flora of a garden that is wholly corrupt.

Descriptions also provide metaphorical figures for qualities associated with character. In the passages cited (and throughout the poem), warfare provides a metaphor for Mawbad's conduct of love; elsewhere, the game of polo becomes another figure for the game of love in which Vīs, Vīrū, Mawbad, and Rāmīn are involved. Vīrū has just left Vīs in anger on hearing her declare her unswerving devotion to Rāmīn: "Rāmīn has so fettered us in love that I can never any more escape from his bonds. If you tell me, 'Choose one of these two: eternal Paradise or the face of Rāmīn,' I swear that I choose Rāmīn, for I see his face as my Paradise" (*VR*, p. 115; 47:90–92). On the morrow, Vīrū and Rāmīn compete on the polo field:

> When the sun of the world ascended in the revolving heaven like a golden ball on the polo field, the King played

[32] The lines are not in Maḥjūb's edition of *Vīs u Rāmīn*, or in those of Mīnūvī or of Todua and Gwakharia; they are presumably in the Istanbul manuscript on which Morrison based his translation.

> polo with his nobles; horsemen swarmed onto the field. On one side King Moubad was captain, having chosen twenty teammates from the champions [of whom Rāmīn is one]: on the other side King Vīrū, having picked twenty colleagues from their number. . . . Then they threw the ball on the field, hit it up to Saturn with the stick. Vīrū and Rāmīn showed prowess that day; sometimes one took possession of the ball from the other, sometimes the other way round. Of all the famed champions none struck the ball better than Rāmīn and Vīrū. (*VR*, pp. 115–61; 47:95–103)

Vīs—the stake of the metaphorical game—watches this contest from the roof of the pleasure dome (providing the occasion for a dialogue between her and the Nurse concerning her unhappy state). In the game below, both Rāmīn and Vīrū perform skillfully; but no mention is made of Mawbad's prowess: he is clearly a nonparticipant in the true game, the contest for Vīs. The polo game parodies the earlier battle between Mawbad and Vīrū, in which Mawbad was defeated; in this contest, however, Vīru and Rāmīn are equals, and Mawbad of no consequence.

Through the careful choice of descriptive imagery, the battle scene conveys a moral judgment on the combatants, as well as a general indictment of the use of violence to achieve personal ends, while the polo game suggests the equivalence of Vīrū and Rāmīn as claimants of Vīs, and the invalidity of Mawbad's claim. A particularly telling instance of such descriptive commentary follows Rāmīn's renunciation of Vīs to take up a career of knight-errantry, in the course of which he meets and weds the princess Gul. Vīs sends the Nurse to tell Rāmīn of her distress; the scene in which she encounters Rāmīn figures his moral state at this point in the tale and graphically conveys the association between his pursuit of prowess and his infidelity.

> [As the Nurse] took the road in the early morning, Marv became a bow and the Nurse the arrow shot from it . . . an arrow which went its whizzing way from Marv the royal abode to the march of Gurāb; when she came along

> the road to the march of Gurāb the faithless prince came before her on the plain; hunting wild ass, stag, and boar like a furious lion; his retinue on the plain like a castle; its rampart every kind of game; some with necks broken, some with fore- and hindlegs snapped asunder, so many arrows stuck in their hides that you would have sworn the game was winged! The air was full of falcons, the plain of hounds, both speeding in flight and coursing. The one had emptied the air of birds, the other the ground of wild beasts. The mountains were dyed with the blood of the mountain goat; as the rocky crag was made into a narrow defile for the deer. (*VR*, p. 235; 77:191, 78:1–8)

This description—with the anticipatory comparison of the Nurse to an arrow shot from a bow (reiterated in the statement that "her heart was filled with arrows by [Rāmīn's] cruelty" [*VR*, p. 235; 78:9])—prepares the way for Rāmīn's ruthless and insulting rejection of the Nurse and his curses on both her and Vīs. The "castle-like" disposition of his retinue on the plain, its ramparts formed of broken and disfigured game, constitutes a corollary motif to that of the "garden of the state," which recurs throughout the poem and which was evoked in the description of the battle between Mawbad and Vīrū. Here, castle and garden—the one fortified by man, the other a manifestation of nature's native harmony—are mutually opposed, the one threatening to destroy the other.

A high point of Gurgānī's use of description—one that points the way toward the eventual shift from metaphorical to analogical imagery, as well as establishing the precedent for what becomes a standard topos (a "set piece," as it were) of Persian romance—is the passage describing the heavens on the night that Mawbad carries Vīs off to Marv. The elaborate depiction of planets and constellations—corresponding to no known configuration of the heavens at that or any other time[33]—conveys in graphic terms the inauspicious nature of

[33] This has caused some consternation on the part of critics; Kunitzsch, for example, concludes that "the author—Gurgānī, or his anonymous historical predecessors—inserted this horoscope, which in itself is correct as to astro-

the occasion and anticipates the events that are to follow. As the passage is a lengthy one, I will attempt to select from it the most significant details. The poet begins by describing the utter blackness of the night:

> When the Sphere loosed the fetters of the demon of night, then roused the gleaming moon with the news, up in the castle Shahrū did likewise, and took a lesson from what the signs of the Zodiac had done; for she opened the hall of the castle to the King, then roused the gleaming moon [Vīs] with the tidings. It was a night dark and thick with pitch, black and dreadful like the day of separation . . . black as sorrow, blotted out like hope; let down like a curtain in front of the sun; you would have sworn that night had dug a pit in the west and that the sun had suddenly fallen from the sky into the pit; that the sky had put on black garments in mourning for it, and the heaven mustered armies from every quarter; it ever wheeled its armies to the west, for there the general lay fallen in the pit; the armies of the sky were on the march, the night serene as the will of a monarch. (*VR*, p. 56; 28:22-25, 29:1-7)

The military metaphor recalls Mawbad's battle with Vīrū and its inauspicious outcome, while anticipating further battles that will take place before the tale is done. In this black night, "Moon and sun had both hidden their faces, sleeping like lover and beloved" (*VR*, p. 56; 28:10), while the signs of the Zodiac exhibit unnatural conjunctions,

---

logical principles but which is kept void of astronomical elements pointing to fixed dates, as *a literary element only*, obviously with the intention of not giving the reader a hint towards a historical identification of the story told in the poem" (" 'Description,' " 109; my emphasis); while Minorsky concedes, "The poet displays his knowledge of the stars and their forebodings but it would hardly be possible to interpret his poetic images as astronomical observations forming part of the original tale" ("Vīs u Rāmīn [IV]," *BSOAS* 25 [1962], 282-83). I submit that for the Persian poet (if not for his critics), the historical veracity of such details was less important than their exemplary signification.

> the Ram facing the Bull, scenting the Lion of the sky; both stopped in their tracks from fear of the Lion, strength drained from fore and hind legs; the Twins like two lovers asleep, twined together like buckets on a water-wheel; the Crab lying at their feet; you would have sworn it had become lifeless and pincerless; the Lion standing before the Crab, arching its tail to its head like a bow; its eyes bloodshot like a lover's; its mouth open like a split pomegranate; a Virgin with two bunches of vines in her hands, rooted to the spot like one drunk; a Scales with all its connections severed, the two pans left but the beam broken; the Scorpion with head and tail brought together; languid as men afflicted with a chill; the Archer with the bow stuck in his hands, his legs frail and his hands *hors de combat*, the Lamb sleeping secure from him, hidden in grass and tulips; the Lamb, on an arrow being suddenly shot at it, falling wounded thereby; the Water Carrier's bucket fallen down the well, the Water Carrier left astonished like a lost soul; the Fish stuck motionless against its will; you would have sworn it was a fish fallen in the net. (*VR*, pp. 56-7; 29:13–16)

The strange nature of these conjunctions is stressed by the poet's comparison of the sphere itself to a magician, a juggler indulging in sleight of hand: "So many shapes did the heaven create and display that you would have sworn it was a magician" (*VR*, p. 57; 29:30). The patterns of the stars themselves are disrupted by such tricks: the northern hemisphere shows such configurations as the Dragon with its tail round the North Pole, a "woman bound with a chain, a man kneeling before her [Andromeda and Hercules]; opposite them an Eagle with spread wings, its feet grasping an arrow [Aquila]; a Youth standing like a guard [Bootes], in his hands a goblet and tray of gold [Corona Borealis] . . . a man without horse but still holding reins [Auriga] . . . a man [*sic*] sitting on a silver throne [Cassiopeia],[34] before him a horse broken from its hal-

[34] Kunitzsch identifies this constellation as Cassiopeia, necessitating that the

ter [Pegasus]; a man with a demon's head in his palm, a crown-bearer standing before him [Perseus and Cepheus]" (*VR*, p. 57; 29:31–39). The southern hemisphere is no less confused; and finally:

> From the east was stretched a sinister ascendant, so that Moubad's marriage might be inauspicious; the sun was in conjunction with the moon, like a vizier whispering secrets to a king. Old Saturn accompanied them, the fourth house of the ascendant was their position. Opposite the ascendant in the seventh house Deneb was the companion of aggressive Bahrām; Venus left between them, desperate of propitious advent. None of the influences militating for justice, whose conjunction might have been propitious for that enterprise, were favorable.
>
> It was under this ascendent that the King saw Vīs and did not experience of his mate the lot he fancied in his heart! (*VR*, p. 58; 29:51–58)

The confusion that reigns in the heavens on this night anticipates the disasters that will follow Mawbad's forcible marriage to Vīs. Astrological symbolism is a commonplace of medieval imagery; its role in Persian poetry has frequently been misunderstood and will be discussed further in connection with Niẓāmī. Gurgānī's use of such symbolism is essentially allegorical; many of the figures he depicts evoke the poem's dramatis personae and the relationships that exist between them. The initial image of the sphere loosing the fetters of night's demon, and its parallel on the human plane, Shahrū's surrender of Vīs to Mawbad, suggests that Mawbad's obsessive pursuit of Vīs has unleashed the forces of evil. Ram and Bull in confrontation with the Lion suggest Vīrū and Mawbad, past and present husbands of Vīs and both rivals of Rāmīn, who is repeatedly likened to a lion throughout the poem; here, moreover, the lion displays all the symptoms of a lover as he stands before the Crab, figuring Rāmīn's outpouring of his sor-

indefinite *yakī . . . nishastah* be translated as "a figure" rather than "a man" (" 'Description,' " 103).

rows to the nurse (who sleeps at the feet of the two lovers as does the Crab, in Gurgānī's depiction of the heavens, at the feet of the Twins). The Virgin with two vines is Vīs, who must finally choose one or the other; but for the moment Vīs is in the aspect of the woman bound with the chain, before whom kneels a suppliant lover.[35] There are many other parallels too numerous to list; the whole conveys an impression of conflict and confusion, and the cosmic disharmony evoked provides a fitting figure for the human disharmony manifested in the action of the poem.[36]

[35] Kunitzsch asserts that *du khūshah* must be translated as "two ears of corn" (corresponding to the traditional figure of Virgo) and not "two bunches of vines" (ibid., 101). Since, however, the Georgian version (composed in the twelfth century) supports the latter reading, and since the equation of wine with love (and more specifically with physical passion) recurs throughout the poem, it would seem that Gurgani's intent is at best (and perhaps intentionally) ambiguous. Kunitzsch also comments on the distance between the constellations Andromeda and Hercules, which suggests that the latter represents Mawbad, who conducts his pursuit of Vīs more as a warrior than a lover. Morrison mistakes *al-dhanab*, the Moon's descending node, for the star Deneb (ibid., 107, n. 54; see chapter 5, n. 44). The opposition of Ram, Bull, and Lion recalls the ancient symbolic motif of the Lion-Bull combat that was carried over into Islamic symbolism; see W. Hartner and R. Ettinghausen, "The Conquering Lion, the Life Cycle of a Symbol," *Oriens* 17 (1964), 161-71.

[36] As Kunitzsch observes, Gurgānī's catalogue of the constellations closely resembles that of al-Bīrūnī in the *Kitāb al-Tafhīm* (" 'Description,' " 96). Even the two constellations omitted by Gurgānī are symbolically significant: they are Lyra, the lyre, evocative of cosmic harmony, and the Triangle, which would suggest equivalent relationships between the parties involved rather than the unbalanced ones evoked by the image of the Scales with the broken crossbeam. (Cf. Conger's remarks on the parallelism between the actions of the stars and human actions in the beliefs of the Ikhwān al-Ṣafā' quoted in chapter 1.) De Bruijn comments on this passage: "Gurgānī treats his theme according to the conventions of descriptive poetry by providing an almost complete catalogue of constellations including all the signs of the zodiac. Each item is artfully elaborated by the use of rhetorical devices and poetical fancies. The section as a whole tends to become a goal in itself. Nevertheless, there can be no doubt that the contemporary reader, who was familiar with these stylistic modes, must have caught the connection with the essential elements of the episode to which the description belonged: the dark emotions of the mother and the king, the secrecy of the act and its fateful nature. All these elements are among the main motifs of this romantic epic. It is quite understandable that

A final aspect of Gurgānī's imagery that must be mentioned here, not least because it becomes a characteristic device of many later poets (and not only in romance, but in lyric as well), is the use of recurrent patterns of imagery. In *Vīs u Rāmīn* one of the most important of such image patterns is that of the garden, which is first seen in the prologue, in the description of Isfahan under Saljuq rule:

> Isfahān laughs with delight, for she has become full of bounty because of his [the Saljuq's governor's] justice. Isfahān was like a broken limb; what was broken has now become mended by his glory. It is hardly surprising that this year the very trees bear praise of the minister as fruit, or that from the security of his justice the winter wind scatters not a single petal from the garden. (*VR*, p. 15; 6:25–30)

This passage anticipates the many recurring references to gardens throughout the poem, and especially the frequent juxtapositions of the garden of the state and the garden of love. The latter provides the central metaphor of Rāmīn's song (quoted above), as it does for other such songs, sung by both Rāmīn and the court minstrel. With the flourishing garden described above is contrasted the ruined one pictured in the battle between Mawbad and Vīrū, with its sowers of death and its unnatural flowers: swords like lilies draped with the blossoms of the flowering Judas, like myrtle branches hung with pomegranate petals, and the final perverse image of the tree of life sprouting from the corpses of the dead. In such a context the garden becomes the concrete manifestation of the world upside down. Similarly, Rāmīn's complaint to Vīs (during the famous debate in the storm) describes the ruin of the garden of

---

Gurgānī resorted to this spectacular piece of descriptive art in order to emphasize a dramatic turning point in his story" (*OPP*, p. 190). Gurgānī's strategy, however, is more than a manifestation of the pathetic fallacy; his attention to detail is aimed neither at astronomical accuracy nor at finding in nature a parallel for human moods but is intended to demonstrate the significance of the actions to follow with respect to both the individuals involved and their consequences on the wider plane of social order and the harmony of the state.

love in imagery that evokes the parallel concept of a neglected state.

> "Alas for that affection and hope which my soul expended on the culture of love! I sowed love in the garden of my youth, made my soul gardener; it worked my garden with happy heart and watered it with the tears of its eyes. It neither slept one single night nor rested one single day but wore itself away in constant gardening; when the spring of bright union arrived, tulips, mallow flowers, and lilies came up; there were masses of blooms in a hundred corners through its length and breadth; its perfume spread abroad like rubbed musk. Its planes and willows became shady; its myrtle and cypress spread their grateful boughs. . . . Loyalty spread a wall around; no, not a wall, rather a renowned mountain. At the foot of the mountain ran a sweet stream, at the side of the stream a golden meadow. . . . Now the winter of separation has come: and with it the clouds and wind of disloyalty. The time of drought has come, in which every river has run dry. . . . Neither wall nor garden has survived, neither mountain nor river nor upland meadow. Vandals have uprooted its trees and knocked down its gate and wall . . . Alas for all those cypresses, roses, and willows! Alas for the days of pain and hope! . . . Now our ill-counselor has reached his heart's desire; may he be of ill fate and fortune like ourselves! (*VR*, p. 286; 87:65–86)

Elsewhere, Mawbad is likened to December desiring to wed Spring—"a hard matter indeed to unite the two!" (p. 52; 26:28)—while Vīs herself is repeatedly compared to a garden and associated with fertility.[37]

[37] Not least in the famous song of the minstrel which causes Mawbad to fly into a rage as he realizes the lovers still pursue their love: "I saw a tree growing on top of a mountain, such as scours the corrosion of care from the heart; a tree stretching its head to Saturn, its shadow falling over the whole world. In beauty it is like the sun, the world fixes its hopes on its leaves and fruit; beneath it, a bright tulip and rose bloom, violets and mallow flower and hyacinth grow; a bull of Gīlān grazes by its bank, now drinking its water, now cropping

The parallelism between the garden of love and the garden of the state is repeated and deliberate; their close connection, and the fact that the one cannot flourish unless the other is properly maintained and cared for, is directly related to the poem's political signification (discussed in chapter 5). The culmination of this image pattern is the comparison of Marv, on the occasion of Rāmīn's triumphal entry into that city to take his place on the royal throne, to Paradise (*VR*, pp. 345–46; 102:42-50); this is paralleled, in the epilogue, by a second likening of the flourishing state of Isfahan to a spring garden (pp. 352–56; 105:1–98). Just rule ensures prosperity.[38] Finally, the poem itself, in both prologue and epilogue, is referred to as a richly blooming garden.[39]

Imagery thus provides an interpretive commentary on character and action throughout the poem, a commentary that appears to be that of forces greater than the poet himself, rendered by the very cosmic order evoked by such descriptive passages. It is the poet's role to construct the proper *conjointure* of word, image, and concept, which will reveal the pro-

---

its verdure. May the tree be ever shady, may its shadow be more grateful than the heaven! May the water of the spring ever flow, and the bull of Gīlān ever graze by it!" (*VR*, p. 203; 69:17-24). Gurgānī's use of imagery based on the garden motif is discussed by George Morrison, "Flowers and Witchcraft in the 'Vīs o Rāmīn' of Fakhr ud-Dīn Gurgānī," *Acta Iranica* 3 (1974), 249-59.

[38] Gurgānī's recourse to the commonplace equation of monarchic restoration with spring recalls the use of this motif in the *qaṣīdah* (see chapter 2) and anticipates Niẓāmī's treatment of the motif in the *Haft Paykar* (see chapter 5).

[39] In the epilogue, Gurgānī tells his patron: "I have brought you a Mihragān present, fluent as the water of the spring of life. At this festival no subject has brought a present better than your servant's; by your order I have composed a romance [*dāstān*] beautiful as a blossoming garden; it is graced by proverbs of wisdom like fruit, sweet ghazals like spring basil; you are prince of the nobles of the age, so I have prefixed your name to this story; I began the work with your name and have set the seal of your name on its end. See how fortunate this story is; the spring splendor of your name is its crown and throne! . . . Through the glory of your name your servant's work will be on every tongue till the Resurrection" (*VR*, p. 356; 105:102-112). Gurgānī of course uses *ghazal* in its generic sense of "love poem," rather than in reference to its technical form; the term is not employed by rhetoricians in the technical sense even after the development of the independent *ghazal*.

found connection between event and underlying truth. This use of description supports the view that "under medieval presumptions, descriptions are not mere signs of an empirical reality, but rather [they] shape particulars in part according to what language presumes as itself."[40] In this act of shaping, imagery constitutes yet another, crucial perspective that complements and completes those already mentioned.

Although, rhetorically speaking, Gurgānī's imagery relies chiefly on similitude, as evidenced by his abundant use of explicit similes, it already shows movement toward a more analogical style of which perhaps the most representative examples, in romance, are found in the poems of Niẓāmī a century later. In his romances (and especially in the earlier poems, *Khusraw u Shīrīn* and *Laylī u Majnūn*), Niẓāmī relies even more than Gurgānī on the use of discourse and imagery; the straightforward narration of action is thus correspondingly minimized. *Khusraw u Shīrīn*, completed around 1185, focuses (to borrow a phrase from Jean Frappier) on "the analysis of emotion, the casuistry of love."[41] In it, the action episodes, which are kept to a minimum, furnish brief interludes between lengthy passages of discourse accompanied by extensive description.

Khusraw u Shīrīn is of special interest because of its close relation to *Vīs u Rāmīn*, which renders comparison between the two particularly relevant to the demonstration of the Persian romance writer's approach to composition. Not only does Niẓāmī employ the same *hazaj* meter, but he deliberately models many characters and scenes on the earlier work, as well as making both explicit and veiled allusions to it on the levels of language and imagery. Such parallels provide an intertextual perspective on both romances of a sort of which medieval writers were especially fond; this intertextual dimension at once in-

[40] Allen, *Ethical Poetic*, pp. 181-82.

[41] Jean Frappier (referring to Chrétien's *Cligès*), "Chrétien de Troyes," in *Arthurian Literature in the Middle Ages*, ed. R. S. Loomis, p. 171. Pierre Gallais describes *Khusraw u Shīrīn* as an "*anti-néo-super-Wîs et Râmîn*" in the style of *Cligès* and paralleling that poem's relation to the Tristan romances (*Genèse du roman occidental*, p. 156, and see pp. 153-57).

creases the complexity of Niẓāmī's romance and suggests that he views his poem as a commentary on (or, properly, an interpretation of) that of his predecessor.[42]

The "influence" of *Vīs u Rāmīn* on *Khusraw u Shīrīn* has generally been viewed as a case of one poet's imitation (conscious or unconscious) of the work of another.[43] It is, however, a standard medieval technique to rework the basic elements employed by a predecessor into a new poem, which may or may not serve as commentary on, or criticism of, the earlier work. The prologue to *Vīs u Rāmīn* makes clear that Gurgānī held such an attitude toward his model, which he was concerned to make meaningful; as for Niẓāmī, while he does not allude to Gurgānī's poem as a source, it is no less important to him than the one he does mention: Firdawsī's *Shāhnāmah*. Moreover, the contrast between Niẓāmī's approach to the story of the Sassanian king Khusraw Parvīz and that of the epic poet is not confined to his emphasis on the love of the monarch for Shīrīn (the only part of Khusraw's story left untold, as Niẓāmī modestly apologizes in his prologue) and his virtual indifference to the king's heroic and military exploits, recounted in detail by Firdawsī; it depends, both thematically and stylistically, on the intervening poem of Gurgānī, which is the true point of departure for Niẓāmī.

Like Gurgānī, Niẓāmī uses monologue, dialogue, song, and letter to present internal conflicts and contrasting attitudes. The poem is dominated by lengthy monologues delivered by the protagonists, as well as extensive dialogues in which Khus-

[42] On the subject of medieval intertextuality as it relates specifically to the composition and reading of romance, see M. A. Freeman, "Structural Transpositions and Intertextuality: Chrétien's *Cligès*," *Medievalia et Humanistica* 11 (1982), 149-63; see also *Intertextualités médiévales, Littérature* 41 (February 1981; special number), in which a translation of Freeman's essay is reprinted.

[43] See the discussion by M. J. Maḥjūb in his introduction to *Vīs u Rāmīn*, pp. 91-95. Although Maḥjūb rejects the view of Vaḥīd Dastgirdī that Niẓāmī intended to oppose his own vision of chaste love to the immorality of Gurgānī's poem, he considers the many parallels between the two works as representing either imitation for its own sake, or unavoidable resemblances resulting from the use of the same meter.

raw and Shīrīn declaim both their declarations of love and their mutual reproaches. (A most notable example, modeled on a crucial scene in *Vīs u Rāmīn*, will be discussed shortly.) Interspersed with such passages of discourse are songs sung by minstrels (culminating in the competition between the court poets Bārbad and Nakīsā), tales told by handmaidens and boon companions, philosophical discussions, and so on, which function as further commentary, as do the frequent narratorial interjections. In this chapter, however, I wish to focus on Niẓāmī's use of descriptive imagery; for while lengthy descriptions are a hallmark of his style, the precise nature and function of his imagery have often been misunderstood. Moreover, it is here that Niẓāmī's departure from epic style, as well as the differences between his style and that of Gurgānī, becomes apparent.

Khusraw u Shīrīn contains only one battle scene: the account of Khusraw's final and decisive engagement with Bahrām Chūbīn. Khusraw's wars against the usurping general, of central importance to the history of his reign, are dealt with at length by Firdawsī; the final battle and Bahrām's flight is the climax of events which began their course long before and which involve complex issues that Firdawsī details extensively.[44] In Niẓāmī's poem, Bahrām's rebellion is treated as a clear act of usurpation motivated by his desire for power; only the final battle is described, in less than a hundred lines. Khusraw himself is a somewhat less than willing participant in this engagement; forced by Bahrām to flee his kingdom shortly after his accession, he had been content to remain in Armenia, where he had taken refuge, and to spend his time courting Shīrīn and devoting himself to sport and pleasure. It is Shīrīn who recalls him to the duty of wresting the kingdom from the usurper and restoring order. Angered by this reminder, Khusraw leaves Shīrīn and travels to Byzantium, where the emperor

[44] Firdawsī, *Shāhnāmah*, 5:2235-2444. The *geste* of Bahrām Chūbīn was incorporated by Firdawsī into his epic; on the Middle Persian original and its early Arabic translation, see Franz Altheim, "The Most Ancient Romance of Chivalry," *East and West* 9 (1958), 129-44.

Heraclius gives him his daughter Maryam in marriage and helps him vanquish Bahrām Chūbīn.

Thus the war in question is pursued, not for the sake of honor or justice, but in anger; and Khusraw's actions, while appearing to bring him glory, in fact sow the seeds of his own destruction. The description of the battle—like Gurgānī's account of that between Mawbad and Vīrū—conveys its unheroic nature through a similar use of hyperbole and exaggerated imagery.

The armies, swords unsheathed to join the fray,
their wings and center formed into array.
The arrows' whizz, the sword's sharp clash like thunder
lions' livers, elephants' brain-pans rent asunder.
The roar of drums lent ears unto the dead,
while from the living brains all sense had sped.
The charging horses' hooves with gold were shod,
their armor decked with rubies from the blood.
The neigh of Arab steeds, a boiling roar,
into Earth's ears hot quicksilver did pour.
The horsemen drew their blades—bright lightning flared:
the lions their deadly fangs in grimace bared.
Death had for Life a mortal ambush laid:
of Resurrection's clamor sport had made.
Spearheads on men's breastbones to sharpness honed
had Armageddon on the field enthroned.
So many spears from bushes bristled forth
that their onrush had closed the way to thought.
No onager escaped, in that wild wood,
from lion, nor lion from the bite of sword.
. . . .

White arrow-eagles on their wings inscribed,
in blood, safe-conducts for the vulture tribe.
Mail-piercing barbs, in lethal poison steeped,
put those in hatred's armor fast asleep.
The bloody waves which rose in surging flood
star-wards, filled cup-like banner-knobs with blood.
In mourning for the spear-heads fallen low,

the Zephyr loosed the banners' locks to flow.
As fell with severed head each warrior chief,
both earth and sky did rend their robes in grief.
. . . .

The crimson silk of unfurled oriflammes
a bristling reedbed seemed, awash with flames.
More sharp blades hastened forth hot blood to taste
than stones and pebbles lie in desert waste.
More arrows on the warriors' helms rained down
than falling leaves in autumn fall to ground.[45]

(*KS*, pp. 161–63)

In the midst of the battle Khusraw attacks Bahrām; the latter, his defeat total and his troops in disarray, is forced (like Mawbad) to flee.

Such raging streams of blood there were, that heads
like polo balls upon the current sped.
The lassoes of the Byzantines, like chains,
were knotted like the curls of Africans.
With Hindu blades, like Hindu locks they sheared
away the heads of any who came near.
Of all the warrior horde, not one went free,
save Bahrām and a weary company.
. . . .

When from Khusraw proud Bahrām turned in flight,
his lost hopes proved his enemies' delight.
So doth the world man's harvest e'er consume:
to teach a juggler tricks, do not presume.
To what fair cypress has it stature lent
that in the end with suffering it's not bent?
What red rose has it nourished, that it's not,
at last, the hue of faded flower brought?
Not every mouthful's sugar, never think:
sometimes pure wine, sometimes the dregs you'll drink.
. . . .

[45] All page references are to Niẓāmī, *Khusraw u Shīrīn (KS)*, ed. Vaḥīd Dastgirdī.

The world doth sit a piebald steed; beware
lest nought but kicks shall come to be your share.
The world a swift bay charger doth bestride;
let Reason from its path quick draw aside.
Let none in traitor Time his trust display,
for it in harmony with none doth play.[46]

(*KS*, pp. 164-65)

The elaborate hyperbole and complex word play of this passage are a far cry from Firdawsī's straightforward narrative style. The resemblance to the battle scene in *Vīs u Rāmīn* is closer; but Niẓāmī has minimalized the action, both by his exaggerated use of the celebrational diction already seen in Gurgānī, and by the fact that what action there is, is conducted not by human agents, but by metaphorical substitutes for them (the "arrows' whizz" and the "swords' clash" rent the brains of elephants and the livers of lions), or by personified forces more powerful than they (death "laid an ambush" for life). Both devices accentuate the ironic contrast between the events themselves and the manner in which they are described. Where Gurgānī employed a high proportion of explicit comparisons, Niẓāmī typically suppresses direct statements of similitude, constructing a complex of figures based not only on similitude but on analogy as well. Thus, while the likening of warriors to lions exploits the negative potentials inherent in the comparison—lions are rapacious as well as brave—not only do the white-poplar arrows resemble eagles (a comparison based on the shared element, feathers) but those eagles are likened to messengers (an analogy based on function) bearing safe-conduct passes for the vultures. The fallen banners, stained crimson with blood, are a blazing reedbed—no mere decorative image, but one suggesting universal destruction, the ruin of man and nature alike, and anticipating the "burnt harvest" alluded to in the narrator's concluding comment. The passage illustrates the blending of metaphorical and analogical comparisons typical of Niẓāmī's early style; examples of his use of a

[46] For the final line I have preferred the variant reading (*KS*, p. 165, n. 3).

more fully analogical style will be seen shortly.[47] The strong authorial presence manifested in the final moralizing comments adds another dimension to the irony, since the generalizations that apparently refer to the Bahrām's fate will prove ultimately to apply to Khusraw.

A number of episodes in *Khusraw u Shīrīn* are explicitly modeled on *Vīs u Rāmīn*. Perhaps the most famous is the winter scene in which Shīrīn reproaches Khusraw from the roof of her castle. In *Vīs u Rāmīn*, the climax of the lovers' stormy affair is marked by the debate, filled with mutual accusations and blame, that takes place when Rāmīn visits Vīs in her castle at Marv. Pleading for Vīs to accept him, Rāmīn describes his lamentable condition as he stands outside the castle in the storm:

> "The world is full of smoke from the vapor of my sighs; my world has become as black as my fortune. The world is ever thus weeping for me; that is why tonight there is all this snow and rain. My heart is like a fire temple though my exterior is like a mountain of snow. . . . Love had reduced my body to this state—half burnt and half frozen. It is ignoble to kill in the snow someone whose very soul is compounded of loyalty itself! I thought that you would rescue me from the fire; I did not know that you would cast me into the snow! I am your guest, Moon of two

[47] The passage as a whole provides an excellent example of what Bürgel (discussing Ḥāfiẓ's imagery) describes as the "poetic syllogism" based on imaginary premises, in which "the natural relationship is replaced by a fantastic one, and natural behavior is justified by imaginary motivations. But these motivations, and these fantastic relationships . . . are themselves very real, if one ignores the fact that they are based on naturalized metaphors" ("Remarques," p. 142). Niẓāmī's treatment of conventional figures such as the "brave man/lion" comparison reminds us (as does Gurgānī's use of garden imagery in the battle scenes discussed earlier) of the negative potential inherent in such comparisons. This potential of comparisons for positive or negative meaning (i.e., for praise or for blame) is discussed by Averroes under the rubric *muṭābaqah*; see his *Talkhīṣ kitāb Arisṭūṭālīs fī al-shi ʿr*, in Aristotle, *Fann al-shiʿr*, ed. and trans. ʿAbd al-Raḥmān Badawī, pp. 205-206. Cf. also *RIS* 4:379, where the lion is used as a figure for tyrannical and ignorant rulers who seize what they can by force and whose subjects are filled with fear and misery.

> weeks; I have traveled a two months' journey in two weeks. People deem kind treatment meet for guests; they do not bury them thus in the snow! If putting me to death has become a light matter in your eyes, at least forbear to murder me thus in the snow!" (*VR*, pp. 288–89; 87:125-36)

Vīs, however, refuses to admit him, and he remains outside, suffering from both the pains of love and the inclement elements.

> The brave Rāmīn thus spoke to himself, his mount up to his knees in mud. The horse had been drenched all night with rain, and the rider was in worse case than his horse from snow. All night Rāmīn's eyes shed tears, the sky dropping camphor upon his soul. All night Rāmīn's head was wrapped in weeping clouds; all night the wind swirled round his breast. On his body cloak, boots, and leggings were frozen stiff as iron from the cold. (*VR*, p. 291; 87:191–95)

Despite her love for Rāmīn and pity for his state, Vīs steadfastly resists his pleadings, and eventually he departs in anger; although she soon repents her hardheartedness and follows him, they are not reunited until Rāmīn admits the injustice of his conduct toward her and resolves to dedicate himself to her service. Again, the setting is a snowstorm.

> When charming Vīs was separated from Rāmīn, the air became like a raging dragon. Its snow was indistinguishable from fatal poison, for the heart froze instantly at its touch. A black cloud came, disposed its ranks, and blocked both breath and sight of the beholder; flung snow in eye and face, so that even an elephant would have been crazed by it.
>
> It mercilessly blocked Rāmīn's road as the waves of the sea block the course of a ship. His body was in the snow, his heart in fire as he reproached himself for his anger and pride toward his sweetheart. He repented of his unpre-

> meditated words and shed a flood of coral upon his breast.
>
> Suddenly a shout escaped from him; you would have sworn his soul was riven from his body! Like the wind he twisted the reins of his horse, and found the jasmine-bosomed Vīs upon the road. He leapt from his steed senseless as one drunk and gave a cry like a soul forlorn; he said, "My idol, have mercy on me; do not heap distress upon my distress; my sin has become twofold through my folly, for evil appeared good in my eyes. . . . Now I have repented of my action; henceforth obedience on my part, command on yours!" (*VR*, pp. 319–20; 91:11–30)

Niẓāmī's adaptation of this segment displays a number of significant departures from his model.[48] Khusraw, who has been hunting, leaves his party (having consumed a considerable amount of wine beforehand) with a few companions to visit Shīrin in her castle. When he arrives, Shīrīn, like Vīs, bars her doors to him, but she considerately has a canopy erected outside the walls, so that he and his party will be protected from the snow. Thus Khusraw (unlike Rāmīn) can voice his complaints in relative comfort, without suffering from the inclement weather. The winter scene and the snowstorm are described in a far different manner:

> Night o'er the world its tent of black had cast;
> 'twas winter, and the chill wind raised its blast.
> The earth, whose breast did icy fire conceal,
> tempered the water's silk to sword of steel.
> Even that place which warmth of clime enjoys
> should not, vaingloriously, the cold oppose.
> (*KS*, pp. 299-300)

[48] That Niẓāmī "indisputedly copied" this scene from *Vīs u Rāmīn* is clear (in the view of M. J. Maḥjūb) from its lack of "verisimilitude": snow may be expected in Marv, but not in the warm climate of Qasr-i Shirin (*Vīs u Rāmīn*, pp. 92-93; the objection was presumably foreseen by Niẓāmī, who emphasizes the winter season and the bitter cold). This violation of realistic accuracy (if indeed it is that) may well serve to accentuate the parallels and contrasts between the two scenes.

Understatement is the keynote of this passage. The night's black canopy anticipates the canopy to be erected for Khusraw, while the conflict between heat and cold foreshadows the confrontation between Khusraw and Shīrīn. Their debate is, like that of Vīs and Rāmīn, a lengthy one, in which there are many close parallels with the model. One of these is Khusraw's appeal to the code of hospitality:

"But why your door upon me fasten tight?
Do *you*, yourself, thus wrong me, or my sight?
"Abandoning me, like earth, beneath your feet,
you mount, sky-like, on high to take your seat.
"All mention of my rank I leave aside:
for such a speech would bear the taint of pride.
"But am I not your guest? why then, before
a guest do you thus fasten up the door?
"Against a guest who has no life, no care,
save you, you should not thus your door secure.
"When noble folk their guests do entertain,
their needs they meet in somewhat better strain."

(*KS*, p. 306)

Unlike Rāmīn, Khusraw is in no danger of perishing in the storm; it is clear that what has suffered is not his person but his dignity. The weather is ignored during the ensuing colloquy; nature is not, as in *Vīs u Rāmīn*, the external reflection of the lovers' inner turmoil, and it is only with Khusraw's departure—in anger at Shīrīn's refusal to be swayed—that we are once again reminded of the storm.

At night, when that far-journeying gazelle
her musk-sac to her belly bound up well,
A thousand gazelle fawns lay down to sleep,
lips wet with milk, in that green meadow steep.
Like a gazelle bereft of musk, the king
from his beloved's reproaches felt the sting.
From every side great drops of rain and snow
descended, like the spring cloud's stormy flow.
The mighty hills did melt like mud; the snow

like molten lead upon the heart did flow.
The snow rained down like dirhams, and did veil
Shabdīz, beneath the king, in silver pale.

(*KS*, p. 344)

Here is no raging dragon, no evil force that torments the lover from without as does his evil demon from within, but a somewhat prosaic downpour—inconvenient, but scarcely malicious. The continuity perceived as existing between man and nature is of a different sort than was seen in Gurgānī's poem, where nature acted as commentator on events and as the reflection of human emotions. Here, nature and man are at once more explicitly fused and possess a greater potential for separation: a separation that is not a natural state but stems from man's own willful acts, and in particular from their often mistaken interpretation of the significance of the natural scene. The lines describing Khusraw's return to his camp make this point clear. As he draws near, the snowstorm abates.

As he, in hopeless state, the camp drew nigh,
within his heart the sunlike flames burned high.
The black clouds parted from before the green
rose-garden, and the moonlight brightly beamed.
The king had had his royal tent pitched high;
he left its tent-flap open to the sky.
No heart to look upon the world, from pain,
in garment's stead, he rent his heart in twain.
Nor laid he down his head in restful ease,
nor raised it from ungoverned Longing's knees.

(*KS*, p. 345)

Khusraw's "sun"—the heat of his desire—is compared, unfavorably, to the moon, which emerges from a rent in the clouds. Preoccupied with his own frustrated passion, he has "no heart to look at nature": unable to feel in harmony with it, or to take heart at the appearance of the moon or the calm that now possesses the sphere—auguries of future illumination and tranquillity—his thoughts are directed inward, and he mentally rends, not his garment (after the manner of the courtly lover), but his heart, in a bleak parody of the moon rending the black storm cloud.

In his study of Niẓāmī's imagery Hellmut Ritter commented on the "pictorial quality" of the poet's style and observed with respect to *Khusraw u Shīrīn* that one could eliminate a third of the poem's verses without obscuring the action.[49] Ritter's judgment overlooks both the quality of the imagery—which is not "descriptive" in the same manner as in Gurgānī's—and its function. Niẓāmī is concerned not with the description of reality (or even with adducing fanciful relationships between concrete objects) but with evoking, through the construction of a pattern of *visibilia*, a corresponding pattern that relates to the ethical signification of what is being described. Rather than "replacing" (as Ritter puts it) a "real" connection between levels of creation with a "poetic-fantastic" one that figures the "spiritual context" of a passage,[50] Niẓāmī's use of imagery reveals a conviction that there is no real distinction between this context and the "reality" on the level of which the action occurs. The relation between these levels, however, is not formal but analogical; thus the basis for comparison shifts from one of perceived or imagined likeness to one of assumed correspondence, and the operation becomes not merely rhetorical, but ethical.[51] The descriptive passages that Ritter found so fatiguing cannot be dispensed with if the poem is to retain its coherence and convey its meaning.

Essential to both of these is the assumption of continuity between nature and man, between macrocosm and microcosm—a belief that informs, for example, the description of the pleasance in which Khusraw courts Shīrīn by night.[52]

[49] Ritter, *Bildersprache*, p. 61.

[50] Ibid., p. 66.

[51] Cf. the passage on "likening" from Rūmī's *Discourses* cited in chapter 1; and see also notes 71 and 76 to that chapter. The true level of the action's meaning is the tropological, i.e., that pertaining to moral conduct; cf. Allen and Moritz, *Distinction*, pp. 70-74 et passim, and see chapter 6 of this book for a discussion of the tropological dimension of the *ghazal*.

[52] Ritter treats this passage as an example of nature reflecting the lovers' mood, after the manner of the Romantic poets (*Bildersprache*, pp. 47-50). Ritter's approach generally illustrates the inadvisability, with respect to medieval

It was a night whose light the day outshone,
the world illumed by the night-shining moon.
A night whose breeze, like Jesus' breath, gave life:
not one whose wind with lamps would come to strife.
The darkness' presence but one sign revealed:
the Fount of Life was in its shades concealed.
No black before that night-black palace stood
save Purity, the harem-chamber's guard.
. . . .

It was a night to seek the heart's desire:
pregnant with all to which one might aspire.
Here Venus in the earth's mines scattered jewels,
and there, the moon poured pearls in oyster-shells.
. . . .

The harmonies of Venus filled the night;
the week-old moon a full wine-cup clasped tight.
The Pleiads, fair familiars, all entranced;
and Mercury on the horizon danced.
. . . .

Each bird and beast, his provender assured,
his joyful music from the nest made heard.
Although the song of each was quite his own,
all with the night's sweet music were in tune.

(*KS*, pp. 131-32)

As a piece of pictorial description, however decorative or fanciful, this passage leaves much to be desired. Concrete objects are likened to abstractions, abstractions treated as if they were concrete, while allusive references abound; it would be difficult to reconstruct a visual image of this garden. The terms in which it is described relate to value rather than to physical characteristics: the breeze is life-restoring (*masīḥ-nafas*, "Je-

---

literature, of making an automatic association between descriptive imagery and "nature" (in the modern sense of "landscape"). Cf. the definition of description in Gervaise of Melkley's *Ars poetica*: "Description is demonstration of the property of some thing, such as a man, a place, time, or something of this sort. Description ought to be made of no material, unless it be such that an author may elicit from it some evidence" (quoted by Allen, *Ethical Poetic*, p. 196).

sus-breath'd"); the only indication of the darkness of night is the presence of the Water of Life; darkness itself, paradoxically perhaps, is likened to purity (*ʿiṣmat*), which in turn is compared to a black slave guarding the *ḥarīm*, the women's chambers. Many of these descriptive figures are identical with those conventionally employed in praise of the beloved, who is as beautiful as the moon, a source of light and of life to the lover. More specifically, chastity, purity, illumination, and life giving are all qualities associated throughout the poem with Shīrīn. The natural harmony between the various levels of creation is suggested by the musical metaphors: the feast of the heavens, at which Venus plays, Mercury dances, and the Pleiades are boon companions, is paralleled by the birds singing in their nests, each its own song, but all in accord with the music of the night. The only note of discord is produced by the human participants in the scene, each of whom, on this "night for seeking the heart's desire," interprets the scene differently, in accord with his or her perception of the wished-for goal.

The description of the lovers themselves begins by recapitulating the principal elements of the natural scene.

> The prince sat on the throne of Farīdūn,
> his heart on Jamshīd's *qiblah* ever turned.[53]
> Shīrīn's fair face to his mind shone so bright,
> he had no need of lamp or candlelight.
> The meadow breeze, laden with basil's scent,
> a message from the prince to Shīrīn sent:
> "A lovelier night than this one was there e'er?
> a fresher scent of flowers in the air?
> "Why should we watch such union from afar?
> let's see ourselves in light, if light we are.

[53] Dastgirdī glosses "the *qiblah* of Jamshīd" as a figure (*kināyah*) either for wine or for the sunlike face of Shīrīn, either of which would be an acceptable reading (*KS*, p. 32, n. 4); however, since Shīrīn is more commonly associated with the moon, and since Khusraw's passion for wine drinking is referred to throughout the poem, the former seems a more likely choice. The figure is, in any case, ironic: by Niẓāmī's time (and in his poetry), Jamshīd is an emblem of the transience of royal power (cf. Ḥāfiẓ's use of this exemplum in QG 81 and 486, discussed in chapter 6).

Lovers in a Walled Garden (British Library Ms. 138)

"If we're of blood, why does your blood not boil?
and if it does, how long your state conceal?
"Why should we not rejoice in weather fair?
The oven's hot: why not the bread prepare?
"Sweet spring does not renew itself each day,
nor is the trap sprung always by the prey."

(*KS*, pp. 132-33)

The summary of the imagery of the preceding passage—light, the refreshing breeze, perfume—forms an ironic introduction to Khusraw's message: that the lovers seize the moment nature has so generously provided. Khusraw seeks to manipulate the natural circumstances, seeing in them a justification for his message of *carpe florem*. But Niẓāmī's imagery—and particularly his technique of introducing a scene of human action with a descriptive passage that both anticipates that action and establishes its symbolic parameters—has prepared us against making such an easy equation: of embracing, as it were, the pathetic fallacy. The juxtaposition of such passages alerts us to the fact that nature, though seemingly in sympathy with man's desires, is neutral or, at best ambivalent; it is man who performs the act of interpreting nature based on his own ends.[54]

This principle is conveyed explicitly in the remainder of this episode, in which the poet establishes an even greater range of perspectives on the action, as well as employing recurrent image patterns that relate to the revelation of character. To pass the time, the king commands that Shīrīn's ladies tell diverting stories; they respond with brief parables in which are recapitulated—in miniature, as it were—a number of fundamental motifs that recur throughout the poem. The first tells of a king who discovered a treasure buried in the ground; on the surface this is a figure for Khusraw's falling in love with Shīrīn, but it

[54] A central belief of the Ikhwān al-Ṣafā' was that nature is the instigator of all physical events (see Nasr, *Introduction*, pp. 60-61). Niẓāmī perhaps intends a commentary on this belief through his emphasis on man's role as the interpreter of nature, a recurrent motif in all his romances and one closely linked to that of the deceptive nature of appearances.

also suggests an ironic allusion to their first encounter, when neither recognized the other.[55] The second tells of a pheasant playing beneath a tree, who is suddenly seized by a royal falcon. Throughout the poem allusions to the hunt abound; Khusraw's first meeting with Shīrīn (that is, when he first recognizes her) occurs while she is out hunting. (In the rooftop scene, Shīrīn tells Khusraw that he has come, not as a guest, but like a falcon in pursuit of a mountain quail [*KS*, p. 305].) The third maiden tells of a sweet-scented rose blooming in a garden which is carried off by a bird of paradise (or perhaps a lyrebird; the dictionaries are not clear)—a variation on the preceding motif which also involves an allusion to those archetypal lovers: the rose and the nightingale. Khusraw's princely splendor and overbearing manner are contrasted with the humble appearance and self-sacrificing demeanor of the nightingale. The fourth responds with a saw about two eyes seeing better than one, suggesting the motif of the need for informed perception and the deceptive nature of *visibilia*.

The fifth maiden tells of a bright stream running through a meadow, from which a thirsting lion suddenly drinks, again alluding to the first encounter of Khusraw and Shīrīn and to her consistent association with the water of life. The sixth speaks of a ruby hidden deep in a mine which was taken by a king and placed in his crown, the seventh of a resplendent pearl set alongside a ruby in a kingly necklace. The story told by the eighth again relates to the second meeting of Khusraw and Shīrīn: a moon is taking her pleasure in a hunting ground; suddenly, a sun descends from the heavens and encloses her in his own sphere. (The poet plays on the word *chanbar*, which can mean either a necklace or a collar of slavery, as well as, metaphorically, the heavenly sphere.) The ninth tells of a lonely boxtree joined by a lofty cypress, "for cypress and box flourish together." The tenth tells a story, modeled on the previous one, of Venus, who once wandered the sky alone until she came into auspicious conjunction with Jupiter, auguring good fortune (*KS*, pp. 134-35).

[55] The bathing scene is described in detail in chapter 4.

These brief parables function to comment on past events in the poem and to anticipate future ones; the final two, in particular, appear to foreshadow the happy union of Khusraw and Shīrīn and are a verbalization of the desire of all concerned for this auspicious event. The forecast is ironic, however, as the specific nature of this union is conceived of by each of the lovers in a way that puts them at cross-purposes (Khusraw wishing immediate gratification, Shīrīn insisting on marriage, since anything less will dishonor her); the resulting conflict between will and principle ensures many delays before their union is finally achieved. The problem in communication experienced by the lovers as the result of their disparate goals is reflected in the double-sided nature of the parables themselves, which may be interpreted positively, as pointing toward the lovers' eventual happiness, or negatively, as revealing the differences in character that will ultimately lead to their tragic end. This is particularly true in the case of both the recurrent hunt motif (in which Shīrīn is in reality the prey) and the sun-moon imagery used to refer to the two lovers.[56]

[56] The storytelling device used here with such concision becomes a central feature of the *Haft Paykar*; see chapter 5. An ironic twist to the hunt metaphor is found in the advice of the Armenian queen Mahīn Bānū to her niece Shīrīn (in which several of the basic motifs recur): "Your treasure bears a yet unbroken seal; / of this world you know not the woe nor weal. // This world knows how to cast its magic spell: / with stolen pearls, and rubies pierced so well. // This conquering lord, I see, has some design / to make you his; 'tis quite clear to my mind. // If this great lord loves you both true and fair, / a noble prey has fallen to your snare; // but if you find impatience be his style, / let me not see you heedful of his wiles. // That he, with sugared tongue, should freely taste / of Shīrīn's sweetness, must not come to pass" (*KS*, pp. 119-20). The passage is clearly meant to contrast with the Nurse's worldly-wise advice to Vis; Mahīn Bānū herself makes the connection when she tells Shīrīn, "While pure in essence you remain, to him // an antidote you'll be, not poison grim; // But should his love against your sense prevail, / he'll find you negligent and drunk withal. // Like Vīs, you'll bid farewell to your good name: / the world will your immoral love proclaim" (ibid., p. 20). A further ironic note is struck by the mention of Khusraw's "sugared tongue," not only referring to his blandishments, but anticipating as well his infatuation with, and marriage to, the courtesan Shakar, which becomes another obstacle to his union with Shīrīn (see chapter 4).

The significance of this particular image pattern is generally ignored, and most commentators take the repeated association of Khusraw with sun and Shīrīn with moon as a conventional hyperbolic comparison and let it go at that.[57] Certainly it is not uncommon to compare a king to the sun and a beautiful woman to the moon; but Niẓāmī's comparison, based as it is on analogy and not on similitude, transcends the conventional cliché and takes on, if not a new, at least a deepened meaning. Khusraw, of course, is sunlike because he occupies the same central position in human society as does the sun in the pre-Copernican cosmos; but Shīrīn is the moon's analogue not merely because of her beauty, or by virtue of her social status vis-à-vis Khusraw, but because she shares the moon's function of providing guidance through illumination.[58] Moreover, with his customary irony Niẓāmī rings subtle changes on this fundamental analogy: Khusraw's sunlike qualities have negative connotations (his arrogance and the destructive potential of his passion), while Shīrīn, formally his inferior, is morally his superior as she attempts, like the moon guiding the wanderer, to lead him toward the pursuit of wisdom and justice. The tragic conclusion of their story stems from the dominance, in this conjuction of sun and moon, of the sun's passionate recklessness; and their conjunction produces, not the auspicious outcome augured, but the eclipse of the sun's human analogue, the king Khusraw.

It is imperative to the reading of romance that the poet's use of imagery be analyzed with respect to its function and not viewed merely as the mechanical deployment of rhetorical figures that can be dismissed by being named. Niẓāmī's analogical imagery is an important means of conveying the deeper sig-

[57] Cf. Ritter, *Bildersprache*, especially pp. 26, 32, 39, et passim.

[58] The conjunction of sun and moon embodied in the projected union of the two lovers suggests an event of cosmic significance, which will produce great consequences in the world; such consequences, however, may be negative as well as positive, since under certain conditions the conjunction produces a solar eclipse (see Kunitzsch, " 'Description,' " 107-108). Similar sun-moon imagery is used in the *Haft Paykar* in the same context of the guidance exerted by the female principle over the royal male.

nificance of his poem; moreover, it is qualitatively different from that of Gurgānī and demonstrates a perceptible development in poetic style, which has generally been overlooked. Both poets, however, in keeping with the demands of their chosen genre, employ descriptive techniques, not for purposes of decoration, but much as they do the more obvious devices of discourse: to present multiple perspectives on human action and to convey, and comment on, the complexities of human experience. Once the function of such strategies is understood, it is no longer possible to dismiss either the lengthy passages of discourse or the complex descriptive imagery that characterize romance as disproportionate to the action and tedious to the reader attempting to follow the story; for "story" is not viewed by the romancer as an end, but as a means to a goal beyond itself: the presentation of an exemplary narrative of profound ethical significance.[59] The next two chapters will be devoted to an examination of crucial aspects of this ethical dimension of romance.

[59] I have already commented on Ritter's remarks on Niẓāmī's imagery; similarly, Gabrieli finds in *Vīs u Rāmīn* a disproportion of "rhetorical elements" (dialogue, monologue, sermons, and epistles) to narrative and observes that "the primary quality of epic poetry, the *Lust zu fabulieren* of Firdūsī and Niẓāmī, is lacking in Faḫr ad-Dīn" ("Note," 174)—a judgment that ignores the exemplary aspect of epic as well as of romance. He finds the work notable only for poet's "lyric qualities," exemplified in "effusions [that] take the external form of songs which the poet puts in the mouth of his characters," and concludes: "Whoever seeks in this work some realistic or individual trait, will not find it in the development of the plot nor in the characterization of the personages, but, here and there, appearing in the reflections and confessions of the author [specifically, meditations on delusive love]" (ibid., 178, 182-84).

· IV ·

Romance: Character as Moral Emblem

THE genre of romance is distinguished by the importance it gives to the inner life of its protagonists. As the devices of monologue, dialogue, and description are used to establish character and to comment on the action, that action itself further reveals the moral qualities of its agents. In contrast to epic and *chanson de geste*, where the action is characteristically organized with reference to a larger, external design (such as the fate of a people), the romance plot is organized around the protagonist and his biography—a type of organization that allows the romance writer

> to place in special relief the idea that the development of self-consciousness is the keystone of the individual's quest for happiness and self-perfection. The generic form of chivalric romance is closely linked to its quasi-didactic interest in presenting to the courtly audience an image of life in which individual aspiration has pride of place—whether it succeeds or fails, is serious or comic—and in which recognition of its priority is the necessary precondition to truly rewarding human activity.[1]

These remarks by Robert Hanning concerning twelfth-century European romance are equally applicable to Persian courtly romance, which shares with its Western counterpart the generic characteristics of the biographically organized plot, the emphasis on inner experience as revealed through monologue and dialogue, and the stress on personal aspiration and its frequent conflicts with public values. The major difference (and it is primarily one of degree and not of kind) is that

[1] Hanning, *Individual*, p. 196.

in Persian romance the love relationship is the dominant element (adventure is less emphasized), and the protagonist is seen as lover more often than in any other role. Thus the hero's "quest for happiness and self-perfection" is typically depicted through his quest for fulfillment in love and for union with the beloved. This emphasis on love has tended to obscure the ethical and didactic intentions of the Persian romancers; this chapter examines the love quests of a number of heroes of romance as a means of elucidating the more general implications of the love relationships in which they are involved.

The existence of "heroes," and even the depiction of character, in Islamic literature has been questioned by various scholars,[2] and most notably by G. E. von Grunebaum, who has

[2] In particular by G. E. von Grunebaum; see especially "The Hero in Medieval Arabic Prose," in *Concepts of the Hero in the Middle Ages and the Renaissance*, ed. Norman T. Burns and Christopher Regan, pp. 83–100 (discussed in this chapter); idem, "The Aesthetic Foundation of Arabic Literature," *CL* 4 (1952) 332–33; idem, "Literature," where he states: "Where man's choice is unimportant it cannot become a literary theme. Human conflict is strangely absent from Muslim and especially Arab-Muslim literature. . . . 'Standard' Islam has not known the drama nor the narrative depicting the conflicting claims on man of opposing moral laws; and its literature has refused to be concerned with conflicts that contrasting obligations toward his own fate in the Hereafter and toward his community on earth have imposed on many a hero of the faith" (11). Compare Gabrieli's remarks on *Vīs u Rāmīn* ("Note," 176–78). Marshall Hodgson follows the lead of such scholars in emphasizing the "conventions" of romance, stating that its heroes "normally . . . had to behave in orthodox fashion, both in love and in war; a personal response to the moral or sentimental question that might rise was out of the question" (*Venture*, 2:302, and see 301–303)—this despite his own observation elsewhere that a central theme of Islamic thought in general is "the demand for *personal responsibility for the moral ordering of the natural world*" (2:337; author's emphasis). On the importance of individual perfection and the treatment of this topic in literature (in particular by Sanā'ī) de Bruijn observes: "No subject was more important to [the Persian poets] than the development of human nature. They were first and foremost moral teachers, not only in their specifically didactic writings, but also in lyrical or epical forms of literature" (*OPP*, p. 217). Romance, like *ghazal*, reflects a growing interest in the individual (particularly in the twelfth century), expressed formally by self-naming in the former genre and the *takhalluṣ* in the latter, as it is in other arts by the increasing incidence of signatures on works of various sorts (see Rypka, "Poets and Prose Writers," p. 552; R. Ettinghausen, "The Flowering of Seljuq Art," *Metropol-*

stated categorically that medieval Islamic writers avoided depicting "heroic" figures in their works because their religion "feels that man, being prone to vanity, self-adulation, and many another misconception of himself, should restrain this temptation to pride and arrogance, and shy away from giving space in literature to the unobjective, the transitory—in short—to the individual."[3] While granting that the protago-

itan Museum Journal 3 [1970], 119; and see n. 47 to this chapter). A further aspect of the problem is that of defining what *personal* meant for the medieval writer; for illuminating comments on this topic, see Leo Spitzer, "Note on the Poetic and the Empirical 'I' in Medieval Authors," *Traditio* 4 (1946), 414–22.

[3] Von Grunebaum, "Hero," p. 85. Although von Grunebaum's investigation was severely limited, he generalized from his restricted findings on the inhibitions of the "medieval Islamic writer" as a species. Limiting his study first of all to Arabic (ignoring the Persian epic and romance traditions), then to prose (thus avoiding any investigation of the personae of either the *qaṣīdah* or the lyric—for example, in the poems of Abū Nuwās or al-ʿAbbās ibn al-Aḥnaf), and finally dismissing (largely on stylistic grounds) both the prose *sīrah* and the *maqāmah* as possible loci for "heroes," he ended up (*faute de mieux*) with hagiography and depictions of the Perfect Man as the only sources of "Islamic" heroes. On the danger of reductionist views of Islamic culture, see Hodgson, *Venture*, 1:88–95; on the specific limitations of von Grunebaum's approach to the study of Islamic culture, Hodgson observes: "The most brilliant interpretation of Islamicate culture as resulting from a closed circle of concepts is that of Gustave von Grunebaum . . . [who] exemplifies at his best what I call . . . the Westernistic commitment or outlook. . . . In his analysis, the formative assumptions of Islamdom . . . are derived at least in part negatively, by way of contrast (what Islam *lacks*), from certain contrary formative assumptions he ascribes . . . at once to the West and to Modernity. This method almost assures in advance that 'Eastern' cultures, as lacking what he finds unique to the West, will turn out to be essentially alike, but will be separated from each other just by what they have in common—that is . . . by a dogmatic claim to completeness, which has also suppressed their occasional glimpses of a Western-type or (preferably) Western-inspired rationally open humanism. The formative assumptions he sees in the West, on the contrary, turn out to be central to what is most distinctly human. . . . [His conception of 'man' turns out to be] identical with that primary figure of Westernistic myth, 'Western Man,' whose cultural traits as finally unfolded are held to be the highest and most human yet achieved" (2:362, n. 6). As Hodgson observes elsewhere, "The prime norms of a society must not be confused with the multiple actuality of the various standards and expectations actually effective in its cultural life. . . . It is doubtful if one should say of any major society . . . that such and such practical alternatives were closed to it because of such and such

nist in an Arabic work may function as "the entity through which the author as spokesman for himself or for the community conveys whatever wisdom, warning, or propaganda he has made it his task to convey," von Grunebaum asserts that such a figure exists as "a means and nothing but a means," whose function "as a tool not being relieved or enriched . . . by deliberate individualization, deprives him of much of the human interest we have come to expect in the protagonists of any narrative whatever"; he concludes:

> The concern for the individual by the medieval Arab author is considerably more restrained than it would be in [Renaissance] Europe. By this I do not mean to say these authors do nothing but repeat patterns and clichés, but I do mean that as a rule they do not use carefully worked out personages whose fate it is to serve as a model, a *mathal, exemplum*, or whose words and actions would symbolize some kind of doctrine or counsel.[4]

In point of fact, it is in precisely this manner that the protagonists of medieval Islamic literature function: as models or exempla of conduct to be emulated or avoided. We may recall al-Fārābī's dictum that poetry aims "at the improvement of the rational faculty, and . . . the production of an imaginative impression of divine matters and good deeds, excellence in producing an imaginative impression of the virtues and approving them, the reprobating of evil deeds and the vices, and holding them in scorn," and that it accomplishes this function not discursively but by example.[5] However, this exemplary function of literature does not reflect a reductionary process by which the individual is deprived of value, but precisely the op-

---

unalterable culture traits" (2:339). Hodgson's caveat must be extended to literature (which he seems to except): medieval Islamic literature is neither monolithic, nor static, nor the deterministic product of an assumed "mentality" specific to Islam.

[4] Von Grunebaum, "Hero," pp. 85–86.

[5] Al-Fārābī, *Fuṣūl al-Madanī*, p. 49; cf. the views of Averroës (Ibn Rushd) cited by Cantarino, "Averroës," pp. 17–18 et passim, and idem, *Arabic Poetics*, pp. 180, 186–88. (See also chapter 1, n. 26.)

posite: a conviction that the individual example validates the general principle, and, further, a belief in the human potential for both creativity and perfectability.

In marked contrast to von Grunebaum, Franz Rosenthal has emphasized this important aspect of Islamic thought:

> Muslim civilization was strongly dedicated to the belief in the supremacy of the individual. It was man for whom the world was created, and it was man who by virtue of his intellect and knowledge directed the world as God's representative. History was made by men. Their names and circumstances of their lives were considered the only available key to a satisfactory knowledge and understanding of historical developments. . . . The Muslim preoccupation with personalities is most visibly evidenced in the vast biographical literature developed in Islam far beyond anything that existed earlier in the Western half of the world as it was then known. For the Muslims, history was indeed biography, and the number of individuals who were subjects of biographical notices is truly tremendous. The considerable flourishing of autobiographical writing further accentuates the significance attributed to the uniqueness of human beings and the need felt for knowing about persons in order to know about ideas. It is true that from our point of view there was little in-depth probing of psychology and emotions. The data that were collected and thought worthy of attention and preservation are by and large restricted to certain types of routine surface phenomena. This, however, in a way serves to point up the intimate concern with the labeling of ideas and achievements and with providing them with the flesh and blood of individuals identifiable at least by name.[6]

Rosenthal contrasts this "philonymous" tendency with another which, "in view of the assumed availability of eternal truths . . . , [tended] to think of the real power in human ac-

[6] Franz Rosenthal, "Plotinus in Islam: The Power of Anonymity," *Quaderno dell'Accademia Nazionale dei Lincei* 198 (174), 444–45.

complishment as something essentially anonymous" and relied on devices such as pseudonymity and anonymity to avoid a clash with the first.[7] Both tendencies can be observed in literature: the first in the use of specific figures (kings, legendary characters, etc.) to exemplify types of conduct, the second by the presentation of characters who function also as personifications of abstract concepts or values. The two approaches may on occasion overlap and are often combined in a single work.

Detailed individualization of the sort we have come to expect in the modern novel is not a characteristic feature of medieval literature, where the writer's purpose in introducing characters is not "to make them behave like 'real people': everything they do is related to a problem and its elaboration within the work," and in keeping with this principle the author depicts only those traits relevant to the problem(s) treated.[8] Within these limitations, however, the character depicted may be of considerable complexity. Leaving aside the generically typical personae of lyric (to be discussed in connection with the *ghazal*), the "historic" heroes of *sīrah* and epic, the ironic "antiheroes" of the *maqāmah*, and the wealth of characters of all sorts in the *Thousand and One Nights*, when we reach romance we find that emphasis on contrast in character becomes a further means of conveying the complex nature of the human condition, and specifically of the variety of possible responses to that universal human experience, love.[9]

As already indicated, the dominant subject of Persian romance is love; it is, however, a subject through which are presented a variety of other issues.

> Love plays a special role in the attainment of self-awareness . . . in sophisticated romance. It fills the hero with

[7] Ibid., 445.

[8] Vinaver, *Rise of Romance*, p. 31. See also Warren Ginsberg, *The Cast of Character*, pp. 71–97.

[9] On the *maqāmah*, see James T. Monroe, *The Art of Badīʿ az-Zamān al-Hamadhānī as Picaresque Narrative*; on the Nights, see F. J. Ghazoul, *The Arabian Nights*, especially pp. 41–44.

> yearning for the lost or not yet won beloved, and it simultaneously prompts him to act to bridge the gap across which desire reaches out towards its object. Since the end of love is to make a new, inviolable relationship, a new "person" out of two previously separated selves, the outer adventures of the love quest function concurrently as metaphor for the self's great inner adventure: its quest to become the image it has generated of its own triumphant perfection.[10]

This self-image generated by the lover's passion is not (more properly, cannot be), for the Persian poet, confined to the limitations of individual subjectivity; for love itself, conceived of as that cosmic force that maintains harmony among the varied levels of creation, transcends interpersonal relationships to encompass the entire range of human experience. Love is the power that integrates macrocosm and microcosm; correspondingly, in romance the individual's personal experience of love, his quest for fulfillment, reflects at once his own moral qualities and his place in the larger order of things.

In his chapter on love in the *Akhlāq-i Nāṣirī*, Naṣīr al-Dīn Ṭūsī defines that virtue as the "yearning for synthesis" that arises from man's "natural direction towards perfection" and from his awareness that he cannot achieve this goal in isolation.

> Since the true nature of Love is the quest for union with that thing with which the seeker conceives it perfection to be united . . . therefore, Love is the quest for nobility and virtue and perfection, and the more one is moved by this quest the greater one's yearning for perfection, and the easier it is for such a one to attain thereto.[11]

A second look at *Vīs u Rāmīn* may shed light on specific aspects of the quest for perfection, which is associated, both by Naṣīr al-Dīn and by the writers of romance, with the pursuit of love. *Vīs u Rāmīn* has puzzled and disturbed commentators,

[10] Hanning, *Individual*, p. 204.
[11] Naṣīr al-Dīn Ṭūsī, *Nasirean Ethics*, p. 196.

many of whom have censured its "immorality"; certainly the poet's choice of this tale of flagrant, and successful, adultery may seem an odd one in view of his description of the poem as "a piece of sage advice."[12] As Gurgānī himself noted in his prologue, "It is a pleasing story, but few who read it understand its meaning."

The love of Vīs and Rāmīn is predicated upon their eminent suitability for each other. The aging king Mawbad—"December seeking to wed Spring"—is an inappropriate (not to say unnatural) partner for Vīs; it is in recognition of his unsuitability that Shahrū violates her contract with Mawbad and weds Vīs to Vīrū, who by virtue of both kinship and station is her most worthy partner. (The marriage, however, is never consummated.) Later, the same argument of suitability enables the nurse to persuade Vīs—married against her will to Mawbad, and desolate at her loss of Vīrū—to agree to meet with the lovestruck Rāmīn, a meeting that marks the beginning of their reciprocal passion. Rāmīn and Vīs are, in every way,

[12] A reading of the critical literature (especially in Persian) might produce the fanciful conclusion that *Vīs u Rāmīn* exists primarily to provide material for invidious comparisons with *Khusraw u Shīrīn*. For example, Shihābī states that "in *Vīs u Rāmīn* . . . the first stage of love, which has an animal and sensual aspect [*janbah-i ḥayvānī va shahvānī*], is described. . . . In this poem the primary goal of love is the lover's gratification [*kām giriftan*] by the beloved. . . . In this poem . . . in contrast to Niẓāmī's *Khusraw u Shīrīn*, neither lover nor beloved possesses either true love [*ʿishq-i ḥaqīqī*] or praiseworthy human virtues. For this reason, Niẓāmī in much of his story, where he speaks of Shīrīn's chastity and abstinence, means to reproach Vīsah" (*Niẓāmī*, p. 203). M. J. Maḥjūb describes Gurgānī's treatment of love as that proper to a "romantic novel in the modern sense [*rumān-i ʿāshiqānah bi-mafhūm-i imrūzī*]" which celebrates the carnal passion of two lovers who "had no accurate comprehension of philosophical subtleties" (*Vīs u Rāmīn*, p. 83), while the poem's French translator, Henri Massé, found in it a testament to Islamic fatalism: the lovers may be forgiven because their passion was preordained, hence inescapable (*Le roman de Wîs et Râmîn*, pp. 11–12, 15–18). Commentators tend to focus on the love story to the exclusion of other elements; Gabrieli, for example, clearly considers the poem's climax to be the consummation of the adulterous love relationship approximately one-fourth of the way through the work; the remaining three-quarters constitute merely a series of adventures that provides "variations" on the basic situation and produces an effect of repetition and monotony ("Note," 174–75).

peers, in age and station as well as in their devotion to each other; it is in this sense that their love is "fated." And it is this equality that gives the greatest validity, among the oaths and contracts that figure throughout the poem, to their lovers' oath, sworn upon this first meeting.

Mawbad, in his insistence that Shahrū's promise be fulfilled, disregards the marriage contract between Vīs and Vīrū and initiates the war in which Qārin is killed. It is not by might that Vīs is obtained, however, but by guile: defeated in battle, Mawbad succeeds, with bribes, threats, and flattery, in persuading Shahrū to deliver Vīs to him. As he is bringing her to Marv, Rāmīn sees her and falls instantly in love, and sets out on his own course—at once parallel, and diametrically opposed, to that of Mawbad—toward a goal they hold in common: possession of Vīs. Mawbad is fated never to achieve this goal, for a talisman prepared by the Nurse renders him forever impotent with Vīs (by accident, not by design).[13] Unlike her Western counterpart Yseut, Vīs does not share her body between two men; neither does she conceal her love, but when confronted by her suspicious husband declares it frankly and vows that only Rāmīn shall possess her. Mawbad's frustrated passion only renders more intolerable the damage done to his honor and his name; his efforts to win Vīs are characterized by violent rages, repudiations, and reconciliations, and by numerous acts of injustice committed not only against the lovers, but against others as well, of which the war against Vīrū is exemplary. His physical impotence becomes a figure for his moral incapacity and serves to underline the precise nature of his goal: undisputed physical possession of Vīs.

The affair between Vīs and Rāmīn is punctuated by quarrels, separations, and reunions that stem as much from the lovers' own troubled inner states as from Mawbad's hostility. A crisis is reached when Rāmīn, believing himself dishonored by this stormy affair, renounces Vīs to embark on a career of knight-errantry as his brother's general (*marzbān*), plunging himself into warfare and the hunt. That his preference of

[13] On the talisman, see Morrison, "Flowers and Witchcraft," 255.

prowess over love violates his lover's oath is demonstrated by the concrete infidelity of his marriage to the princess Gul, of whom he soon tires, longing for his old love.

This portion of the poem, which marks the low point of the love story, throws into sharp relief the contrast in character upon which the action hinges. If Vīs is taken as the pivot of this action, and Mawbad and Rāmīn as two opposing contestants for her who follow two different trajectories in their course toward this goal, it is here that these trajectories intersect; for in this sequence, Rāmīn's conduct comes perilously close to that of Mawbad, and in consequence he risks losing everything. The moral equivalence of Rāmīn and Mawbad is made clear by the identity of their goal—exclusive possession of Vīs—and their mutual resort to violence when this goal is thwarted. Violence is the most concrete manifestation of injustice; the equation of the two is vividly conveyed in the scene in which the Nurse finds Rāmīn at the hunt, surrounded by dead game, in a landscape empty of life and drenched with blood, a scene that directly follows his marriage to Gul. Violence, whether the hunt or warfare, becomes equated with injustice, disloyalty, disorder, and the return of evil for good.[14]

In his description of the heavens on the night Vīs was delivered up to Mawbad, Gurgānī described, among the many inauspicious signs, "a Scales with all its connections severed, its two pans left but the beam broken." The image provides an appropriate emblem both for the problematic nature of justice (an issue I will take up in the following chapter) and for the love triangle itself. The beam is Vīs, who, though incapable of supporting either of the two rivals (that is, of decisively choosing between them), is nevertheless the point with reference to which the actions of both are judged; while the severed connections necessitate that the respective positions of the rivals, though related, will not be symmetrical or in balance, but out of harmony, each moving independently. Mawbad and Rāmīn

[14] This negative equivalency—reinforced by the fact that Rāmīn is acting as Mawbad's *marzbān*, i.e., in his name—bears particularly on the question of kingship, discussed in chapter 5.

embody opposing conceptions of the role of lover; while Mawbad, as king, seeks to possess Vīs by means of force and domination, Rāmīn adopts the conventional stance of courtly lover, weeping, sighing, and wasting away with love.

Throughout the bulk of the poem, the portrait drawn of Rāmīn is that of the courtly lover par excellence. Exemplary in this respect is Rāmīn's description of his state—as he confides in the Nurse—which could well serve as prototype and model for all subsequent writers of love poetry.[15]

> Rāmīn again replied to her, "None is so wretched as a lover! His heart is an enemy within the gates, seeking every day some pretext against him. Now he moans in the agony and grief his lover brings him, now weeps because of the brand of separation from his love. Although he becomes wretched at love's hand, he becomes reckless of his very life for its sake. . . . Love keeps his eyes now sleepless and now moist with tears because of his hopeless desire. He ever longs for the unattainable, and turns from what he attains. He gives his body over to love's catastrophe, and thereafter counts pain as pleasure. If a man could but enjoy sleep together with love, passion for the beloved would be even as pure wine, for its sweetness is the companion of its bitterness, as its delight matches its aftereffect. A lover is in love like a drunken man, for good appears as abominable in his eyes. He is disturbed in love like a drunken man; from sleeplessness he is like one

[15] The question arises as to what were Gurgānī's sources for such descriptions of the lover's state. They far exceed anything heretofore depicted in the Persian *qaṣīdah*. Their most conspicuous literary precedent is the portrait of the lover found in the poetry of al-ʿAbbās ibn al-Aḥnaf and his school, which focuses on the lover's self-image and portrays all the possible permutations of his state; the popularity of al-ʿAbbās's poetry in Iran makes this a likely source (see *EI*[2] s.v. "al-ʿAbbās b. al-Aḥnaf"). Another probable source lies in the Arabic prose treatises on love and anthologies dealing with famous lovers that were compiled in the ninth and tenth centuries, such as the *Kitāb al-Muwashshā* or Ibn Dāwūd's *Kitāb al-Zahrah*, works that, drawing on both the poetic tradition and *akhbār*, constitute anatomies of love. (On this type of work see Giffen, *Theory of Profane Love*; Vadet, *Esprit courtois*, pp. 267–430.)

asleep. It is reason that tells bad from good; once love comes on the scene, reason does not remain in the body. . . . One day a wind suddenly arose and showed me the face of a daughter of the Ḥūrīs. When I looked, Vīs was that moonlike beauty; she made me distant as the moon from sleep and food. From the moment my eyes fell upon that glorious paradise my heart fell a prisoner in Hell. It was as if that was no wind, but a cataclysm; it unveiled to me all of a sudden the face of my disaster.

"You nursed me in my childhood and have seen me constantly since then; but you have never seen me in such a condition as this: betwixt life and death from agony of heart. . . . My body is transformed, my color turned; the one you would suppose a hair, the other, gold. The very eyelashes on my eyes have become as nails, the hairs on my body like snakes. If any day I hold a feast with my friends it is as if I were in battle against my enemies. In times of recreation I am so mournful and wretched that you would say I was doing battle with disaster; if I wander in the garden to take my ease I am like a man lost in a reedbed.

"At night on my bed and cushion of brocade it is as if I am drowned in the depths of the ocean. In the daytime, in the midst of confidants and friends, I am like a polo ball before the polo sticks of the players. I lament as pathetically at dawn as the nightingale amid the spring blossoms. In the early morning I weep as copiously in my distress as the December cloud on the mountain crag. From those arresting eyes thousands of arrowheads have rained on my heart. From those captivating locks thousands of chains of every kind have looped around my heart. . . . Now I crave your mercy, implore the aid of your chivalry; show what chivalry you have—have mercy on this helpless child! . . . Your heart has mercy on strangers and likewise pities madmen; well may you consider me a stranger, mad and lost to sense! By any standard I am worthy of mercy, caught as I am in the jaws of a fierce dragon! You, too, if you are human, have mercy on me, increase love for me in your heart by your goodness." (*VR*, pp. 77–78; 40:51–94).

There is more, for Rāmīn's catalogue of his woes is by no means exhausted; but this passage serves to illustrate the whole, as it contains all the topoi that become commonplaces of later love poetry. Rāmīn falls in love through a *coup de foudre*; he constantly declares that he has no control over his situation. By contrast, Vīs, though she suffers similar pangs, allows herself to return his love only after due deliberation, and, once committed, never swerves from her devotion to him. Rather than being a passive victim of love—the typical stance of the courtly lover—Vīs guides her lover toward the self-realization that ensures the fruition of their love.[16]

Rāmīn's self-image as lover contrasts with that of Mawbad; for while Rāmīn typically avoids activities associated with manly prowess (warfare, the hunt), preferring song and the refined conduct of the love affair, Mawbad shows a predilection for violence, which he justifies both by his kingly status and on the grounds of the insult to his honor and repute. His attitude is clearly seen in the letter he writes to Vīrū, with whom Vīs has taken refuge after Mawbad has cast her out of Marv.

> He straightway sent a letter to Vīrū, making his pen a sword, so angry was he. He said to him, "Who has directed you, pray, to seek preeminence and perpetrate injustice at my expense? Who is your protector, who your support? for your aims are exceeding high and selfish! . . . How do you presume to take my wife, helpless and weak as you are? Although Vīseh is your sister, how can my wife sit as your spouse? Why do you hold her in your house? I shall listen to no excuse for this deed. . . .
>
> "It may be that since I saw your abode your support and refuge have become rather more substantial than before! In all the time you have been stalwart and champion

[16] Though Vīs herself is not entirely consistent in this respect, her inconsistency derives less from fluctuation in her own self-image (as in the case with Rāmīn) than from her tendency to sympathize with the various competitors for her affections in turn.

> I have never seen any renown gained by you in the world. Never on any one day have you imprisoned a king, nor defeated an enemy, nor levied tribute on a land, nor conquered a city in triumph. I have never witnessed your prowess nor heard of it from friend or enemy. . . . I see you shoot arrows in every pursuit such as hunting and archery—not, however, in battle. . . . So long as you are in the palace seraglio you finely display the accomplishments of heroes: but once you enter the battlefield and face your opponents, you run as women do before men! . . . Perhaps you have forgotten my blow which robbed your soul of reason, your body of sense, the blows, too, of the famed warriors, renowned champions of Marv, skilled horsemen. . . . That same sword and arm of mine stand ready that have wiped enemies from the face of the earth! When you read this letter, heed my words, for my sword is hungry for your blood.
>
> . . . "Dispose your army till I come; for I shall quickly undo your defenses. . . . I shall make your land a plain from the numbers of the dead; I shall cause a Tigris of blood to flow over the plain. I shall bring Vīs, barefooted and unveiled, on foot in front of the army like a dog. I shall so humiliate her that henceforth no one shall dare make an enemy of the great!" (*VR*, pp. 127–29; 51:46–84)

A greater contrast to Rāmīn's stance of courtly lover could scarcely be found. Mawbad's response to Vīs's infidelity is not that of the lover betrayed, but of the king dishonored, and he replies in kind. Both stances, however, prove to be inadequate, because both are formulated in terms of the lover's self-image, and the goal of each is possession, that is, the gratification and aggrandizement of the self.

It is this lesson that Rāmīn finally comprehends in what marks the poem's true climax, his dramatic moment of self-revelation in the storm, when he realizes that love must be pursued not for what it can gain for the self, but selflessly, and that this, paradoxically, is the only means by which the lover can attain true union. (It is no accident that the lovers' joyous reunion which follows is described in the imagery of a paradisal garden.) This is the decisive moment in Rāmīn's quest, the point at which his trajectory takes its final upward turn. For it is only following his recognition of love's demand for self-sacrifice that he is able to achieve the final and decisive dedication that will enable him to win his beloved forever.

> "My heart, how long will you deem this plight proper wherein you suffer months of grief, years of calamity! . . . My heart, if you are a lover, why so fearful? Why ask of everyone remedy and cure? Who will hearken to your cry and lamentation? So long as you do not strive for yourself, who is going to strive for you? . . . Take on your head this heavy load; reveal this hidden secret from your heart. Now either the bonds must be broken or the head laid once and for all on the line in submission. . . . I am no man if I can exercise restraint any longer; let this secret become known! What can the world bring me worst than death? . . . How shall one who courts danger shrink from enemies, how shall a pearl diver abhor the sea? . . . Happiness is not to be found through ease; nor success through avoidance of travail." (*VR*, pp. 334–35; 97:6–22)

The larger implications of the lovers' final reunion and their accession to the throne of Marv will be dealt with in the following chapter. What is clear is that they triumph not because of but despite their adultery, a moral negative they are finally able to transcend through the acquisition of self-knowledge and an understanding of the true nature of love.

If *Vīs u Rāmīn* has proven an embarrassment to commentators, the romances of Niẓāmī have received abundant attention; they are customarily viewed as depictions of ideal love which supply a corrective to Gurgānī's questionable morality. Marshall Hodgson's description of Niẓāmī's romances of love, *Khusraw u Shīrīn, Laylī u Majnūn*, and the *Haft Paykar*, reflects the mainstream of critical opinion. Discussing Niẓāmī's use of material found in Firdawsī's *Shāhnāmah*, Hodgson observes:

The story of the lovely Shîrîn and the Sâsânian emperor Khusraw Parvîz is also in Firdawsî; but . . . Niẓâmî stresses the romantic colour. Persian painters have loved to depict the scene at which Khusraw first sees Shîrîn—she is on a trip and has stopped to bathe in a stream when Khusraw, on a trip in the opposite direction, chances to ride by. Niẓâmî exploits fully the pathos in the story of her lover, Farhâd, who, to gain her hand, is set the task of hewing a way through the rock of the great mountain Bihistûn . . . and who faithfully proceeds with his labour for years, till when he is almost done Khusraw has someone send him a false report that Shîrîn has died; whereupon he kills himself. By the code of honour, no other solution to the story was possible; the lord Khusraw must triumph. But Niẓâmî also portrayed, subsequently, a love in which the lover who truly triumphs is he who has renounced his object. The story of Majnûn (the "madman") and Laylâ, his beloved, comes from ancient Arabian lore; Laylâ is given by her father to another, but Majnûn refuses to renounce her and wanders distraught in the desert, befriended only by wild beasts. When her husband dies, she comes to him, but he is too crazed to know her. Niẓâmî tells us they were finally united in Paradise. Though Niẓâmî's treatment is not primarily a Ṣûfî work . . . yet it bears a Ṣûfî stamp.

The last mas̄navî of Niẓâmî's quintet deals again with a figure from Firdawsî, the Sâsânian emperor Bahrâm Gûr, famed as a hunter and fierce as the wild ass he hunted. The greater part of the story, however, moves into a realm yet further removed from history, being made up of seven fanciful tales retold by seven princesses whom Bahrâm Gûr has wooed (on the basis of the beauty of their portraits) and won; the princesses represent the seven regions of the world . . . so expressing both the glory of Bahrâm Gûr and the romantic wonder of the exotic.[17]

This passage raises a number of important issues. The implicit assumption that love is always in the right arises from an

[17] Hodgson, *Venture*, 2:302–303.

uncritical equation of that term with a conception of romantic love that is inappropriately applied to medieval literature. The problem of Niẓāmī's relation to his sources—traditionally discussed in terms of "influence" or "borrowing," categories that are also inefficient when applied to medieval compositions—was touched on in chapter 2 and will be returned to in the present one. With respect to the individual romances, Hodgson's observations are even more problematic. The precise function of the bathing scene, and the significance of the story of Farhād, in *Khusraw u Shīrīn*, and the assumption of Majnūn's "triumph" and of the presence of Sufi overtones in *Laylī u Majnūn*, will be discussed in the present chapter, while the fantasy and exoticism of the *Haft Paykar*, and the particular significance of Bahrām's seven brides and the "fanciful" tales they tell, will be dealt with in the next.

Khusraw u Shīrīn is organized around the love of its kingly protagonist for the Armenian princess Shīrīn. Its relationship to *Vīs u Rāmīn*, already touched on in connection with the use of imagery, is even more complex with respect to the depiction of character. It is often assumed that Niẓāmī meant to criticize the "immorality" of the earlier work by presenting a picture of idealized love; but a careful consideration of the many parallels on the level of character demonstrates that this is not the case. The problems of self-knowledge and of the protagonist's interpretation of his role as lover explored in *Vīs u Rāmīn* are developed with greater complexity in *Khusraw u Shīrīn*, in which the question of identity is a key issue. The poem focuses on the problem of the personhood of its protagonist Khusraw and the manner in which this is established (or revealed) in the course of his quest for union with his beloved.

In his study of European romance Robert Hanning identifies "the complexity and precariousness of individual identity" as a "major theme" of the genre; he continues:

> The hero remains the same person throughout the story, yet may also change his identity during his adventures through a change of personality . . . disguise, or a stroke of misfortune. . . . Making our various identities (and the destinies they imply) fall together in and through time is

> one of the goals of romance. . . . The implication of the synthesis of those identities which adventure has foisted upon the hero is that man can, in and of himself, give meaning to the disparateness of experience by his own attainment of happiness, that individual experience is important, with its unifying focus located within rather than outside the individual. We are more than what someone else thinks we are, what we may temporarily pretend to be, or what fortune makes us; our many identities cannot defeat, though they may long deny, the personal destiny that is ours alone. . . .
>
> The diverse identities used by romance to explore the nature of personhood include natal (identity by parent and inherited title or situation), qualitative (identity by the intermingling of virtues and vices), circumstantial (who the world judges us to be in a given situation), assumed (strategic disguises), and desired or destined (whom we want to be or become again). In a romance world of change and adventure . . . the hero cannot always control his identity; yet the unstated principle of the genre is that *in time* his qualitative identity will enable him to regain his natal, or gain his desired, identity, passing in the course of his quest through various circumstantial (and sometimes assumed) identities. In other words, identity in romance is at once a *given*, a *process*, and a *goal*—a past, a present, and a future.[18]

The problem of identity was expressed in *Vīs u Rāmīn* through the preoccupation of Mawbad and Rāmīn with their own self-images, their sensitivity to the opinion of others, and, most graphically, through Rāmīn's nearly disastrous choice of prowess (that is, of violence) over love, a choice through which he aligned himself morally with Mawbad. In *Khusraw u Shīrīn* confusion of identity becomes a major theme. A striking feature of the poem is the frequency with which its characters either appear in disguise or are, for other reasons, unrecognized by one another. Two episodes stand out in particular in

[18] Hanning, *Individual*, pp. 201–203 (author's emphases).

this connection: the first is that in which Khusraw first encounters Shīrīn, the second his much later meeting with the courtesan Shakar in Isfahan.

The first episode contains the famous bathing scene so frequently, if sometimes inaccurately, depicted by artists. The prince Khusraw, having fallen in love with Shīrīn on hearing her description, sends his closest friend Shāpūr to bespeak her; Shīrīn, in turn, falls in love with Khusraw's portrait, drawn by Shāpūr, and leaves, secretly, to join him. Meanwhile Khusraw, accused of striking coins in his own name (false accusations provide a variation on the theme of confused identity), is forced to flee the king his father's wrath; his path crosses that of Shīrīn, whom he spies bathing in a stream, while she observes him watching. Neither recognizes the other, for Shīrīn is naked and Khusraw in disguise—a distinction that provides an emblematic statement of the difference in their characters, expressed on the verbal level by their contrasting reactions to the situation. Khusraw, despite his self-confessed passion for the princess he has never met, burns with desire for this beauty (as well as coveting her magnificent horse Shabdīz): "If this idol were my love," he says to himself, "what harm would it do? and if this horse belonged to me, what harm would it do?" (*Gar-īn but jān-i man būdī chih būdī; / v-ar īn asb ān-i man būdī chih būdī?* [*KS*, p. 80]). The parallelism of *jān* and *ān* effectively reveals Khusraw's attitude to both woman and horse: both are objects to be possessed. Shīrīn, becoming aware of the watcher, covers herself with her long hair; Khusraw chivalrously averts his gaze, allowing her to flee. Struck by Khusraw's appearance and by his (somewhat belated) gallantry in turning away, Shīrīn suspects that he is, in fact, her love—else why would her heart respond so?—but cannot be sure, since he is not wearing princely clothing.

> For she knew not that kings on journeys bent
> their garments change, for fear of bad intent.
>
> (*KS*, p. 84)

Uncertain, she avoids a confrontation, for the heart cannot have two masters (literally, one cannot pray in two directions:

Ravā nabūd namāzī dar du miḥrāb [*KS*, p. 84]). No such strictures afflict Khusraw, who, having not the slightest suspicion of, or care about, the identity of the mysterious beauty, laments his lost opportunity:

> I saw a rose, but plucked it not at dawn;
> alas! night fell, and with the wind it's gone.
>
> (*KS*, p. 86)

The question of identity—and more particularly, the confusion between what Hanning terms "circumstantial," "qualitative," and "assumed" identities—is a crucial element in this scene. Shīrīn is naked, clad only in her own flowing hair; her physical beauty, and the nobility of character it reflects, are clearly apparent. Khusraw, on the other hand, is in disguise; although his own beauty and his belated chivalrous conduct suggest his princely identity, his clothing creates an element of doubt.[19] The irony lies in the fact that Khusraw's unprincely garb is a truer emblem of his qualitative identity than the princely nature it supposedly conceals; for Khusraw's outward handsomeness and chivalry mask a self-indulgence and an opportunism that become increasingly apparent. His opportunism is concretely exemplified by his first marriage, for reasons of political expediency, to Maryam, daughter of the Byzantine emperor,[20] while self-indulgence provides the motivation for his second, to the courtesan Shakar, in a segment that consti-

[19] In medieval thought, beauty is a moral, and not merely a physical, quality: outward beauty is the reflection of the soul's inner light. Cf. Nasr, *Introduction*, p. 69; J. Lomba Fuentes, "La beauté objective chez Ibn Ḥazm," *CCM* 7 (1964), 161–78.

[20] Contrary to the opinion of Peter Chelkowski, Khusraw undergoes no soul-searching prior to his marriage to Maryam, and neither does he do so "with tortured heart" (*Mirror of the Invisible World*, p. 32); it is only after his restoration—i.e., after he has obtained his immediate goal—that he has the leisure to reflect on his lost love: "When Khusraw with both throne and crown was blest, / the thought of Shīrīn caused him great unrest. // Yet from his heart he could not drive that grief, / nor summon her in whom lay his relief; // For he, by duty bound, kept Maryam near, / by whom his sovereignty reached the Sun's sphere" (*KS*, p. 166).

Khusraw Spies Shīrīn Bathing (John Rylands Library Ms. Pers. 856)

tutes a structural and thematic analogue to the marriage of Rāmīn and Gul.

The theme of confused identities, of the discrepancy between the apparent and the real, the circumstantial and the qualitative, is further developed in this segment, often ignored by commentators who sense that it ill accords with the image of Khusraw as ideal lover.[21] The consummation of the love of Khusraw and Shīrīn is long delayed. When they finally meet (when Khusraw, in flight from Bahrām Chūbīn, takes refuge in Armenia), the conflict between their personalities suggested in the bathing scene is intensified; for while Khusraw's goal is the physical possession of his beloved, not only does she refuse to become his outside of marriage, but declares that she will never share him with another wife (an allusion to Vīs—who had three husbands but only one lover—which suggests a further confusion of identities as well as of roles). Their love affair has many ups and downs, including the episode of Farhād (to which I shall return); the story of Shakar follows closely on the deaths of both Farhād and Maryam and is precipitated by Khusraw's renunciation of Shīrīn and his determined pursuit of the pleasures of the flesh.

In contrast to Shīrīn, whose chastity and steadfast love for Khusraw have become legendary, Shakar has acquired equal

[21] In the introduction to his French translation, Henri Massé considers the affair with Shakar a strategy used by Khusraw to win Shīrīn by making her jealous (*Le roman de Chosroës et Chîrîn*, p. 10). Maḥjūb states that the episode was composed solely for the purpose of imitating *Vīs u Rāmīn*: "In the story of *Vīs u Rāmīn* there is included a subordinate story [*dāstān-i farʿī*] consisting of Rāmīn's falling in love with Gul and his marriage to her. The story of Shakar of Isfahan . . . is also a subordinate story; from the beginning to the end of it, it is clear that Niẓāmī composed it in order to make his poem resemble *Vīs u Rāmīn*. . . . In *Vīs u Rāmīn*, Rāmīn's marriage to Gul has a reasonable cause and a logical excuse. But in *Khusraw u Shīrīn*, only the outward form of the story has been constructed in imitation of *Vīs u Rāmīn*; no attention is paid to the problem of why the king does not marry Shīrīn and why, without preface, he brings Shakar (whose former employment was the encouragement of prostitution) to the royal castle and makes her queen of Iran" (*Vīs u Rāmīn*, pp. 92, 94). On the contrary, the question of why Khusraw is so long in marrying Shīrīn is central to the romance; for (like Alexander and Soredamors in *Cligès*), there is not only no obstacle to their marriage, but every reason for it.

repute as a courtesan of surpassing beauty whose one fault is a too-liberal distribution of her favors. When Khusraw seeks her out, he finds the lady—who is the poet tells us, "Like Vīsah, a seductress in her honey'd kisses; and like the nurse, a marvel of dissimulation" (*KS*, p. 280)—equal to her reputation. But when the crucial moment arrives, she excuses herself and sends in a slave girl who resembles her and is wearing her clothes. Khusraw (who has drunk freely) is completely deceived; and although he discovers the truth in the morning, Shakar produces a convincing explanation. The deceits and deliberate equivocations with regard to identity practiced by Shakar are not without their comic aspect; but the poet's intent is quite serious. Shakar, pestered by Khusraw as to why she will not surrender herself to him—since, after all, her reputation is well known—finally reveals that her pose as courtesan is all a sham, for, in fact, no man has ever possessed her. Khusraw, impressed by her wit, takes her to wife; but, like Rāmīn, he soon longs for his old love, who still remains unattainable.

The complexities of this segment arise not only from the uncertainties of identity observed at the explicit level of the plot, but, and perhaps more important, from the intertextual echoes evoked. Khusraw's marriage to Shakar parallels that of Rāmīn to Gul: Is Khusraw thus like Rāmīn? And is this likeness positive or negative? Is Shakar, like Gul, a wrong choice? She is compared explicitly to Vīs: Are they alike in their reputation for being seductresses (their apparent nature), or by virtue of the fact that each gives her body to only one man (a fact of some ambivalence in moral terms); and is that man, by implication, either in actuality or *in potentia*, an ideal lover? Shakar is also compared to the nurse: Does their likeness derive from the fawning duplicity of both, or from some other aspect of similitude?

In dicussing *Vīs u Rāmīn* I suggested that the moral trajectories of Rāmīn and Mawbad intersected at the point where Rāmīn abandoned Vīs and married Gul. Mawbad, the willful king, and Rāmīn, the self-styled courtly lover, are the base points of the love triangle whose apex is Vīs, to whom they both aspire. *Khusraw u Shīrīn* is a story of two lovers, not a triangle of rivalries; but the single figure of Khusraw subsumes the two identities, which were treated by Gurgānī as separate persons: those of king and of lover. If Khusraw, in his pursuit of Shīrīn, has adopted the stance of the courtly lover (in which he resembles Rāmīn), his conduct often seems closer to that of Mawbad (as exemplified by his treatment of Farhād). The episode of Shakar raises the question of which aspect of Khusraw reflects his true or qualitative identity; a possible answer is suggested by the line that explicitly links Vīs and the nurse as dual aspects of Shakar.

A single episode in *Vīs u Rāmīn* presents these figures as commingled and opposes them to Mawbad in an overtly sexual context, an episode in which the confusion of identities is central. Vīs, in order to be with Rāmīn, persuades the nurse to take her place in bed beside Mawbad, who, in his drunken sleep, is (like Khusraw with the slave girl) completely deceived. Like Khusraw, he becomes aware of the substitution in the morning, when he grasps the wrinkled hand of the nurse, and flies into a rage; Vīs, returning, places her hand in his and convinces him that she has never been absent from his side (*VR*, pp. 153–55; 59:182–269).[22] Both episodes make a somewhat obvious moral point about the blindness of concupiscence and the willingness to be deceived; but the deliberate confusion of identities in *Vīs u Rāmīn* is transformed by Niẓāmī into an exploration of the precariousness of his protagonist's identity

[22] The story of Shakar provides a variation on the "substitute bride" motif, which recurs once more in *Khusraw u Shīrīn* on the lovers' wedding night. Shīrīn has enjoined Khusraw not to drink wine on this night but to make of her "both wine and *sāqī*," since "two drunkennesses do not bespeak an undivided heart" (*kih natavān kard bā yikdil du mastī* [*KS*, p. 387]). (The line recalls Shīrīn's earlier observation that one cannot pray in two directions; it also takes up a motif common in bacchic poetry since Abū Nuwās: that of being twice drunk, with the wine and the beauty of the *sāqī*.) To test Khusraw's sobriety, Shīrīn dresses a withered crone in her own garments and sends her to him; Khusraw—although "in such a state of drunkenness that he could not tell one thing from another" (*dar chishm āsmānash rīsmān būd*)—is not so drunk that he cannot tell the difference: he can yet perceive "that the spring quail walks more gracefully than this" (*KS*, p. 389), and the lovers are, at long last, united.

and raises questions as to the nature of his quest and of its object as he himself perceives them. If Khusraw is simultaneously following the paths of Rāmīn and of Mawbad, which will he choose, that of self-perfection or of self-destruction? And what is the relationship between his two "circumstantial" identities, as king and as lover, with his own qualitative identity? The answers to these questions are further complicated by what the reader has learned from the story of Farhād.

Shīrīn has commissioned Farhād, a skilled engineer, to build a canal that will bring fresh milk to her castle. Farhād falls in love with her, but knowing her devotion to the king he conceals his love and serves his lady without hope of reward. Shīrīn, for her part, treats him with cordiality and compassion, but no more; there is no question of her returning his love. When his passion overwhelms him, Farhād flees to the desert, where he weeps and bemoans his unfortunate state; his erratic conduct reveals his condition, and the news soon reaches the king. Khusraw, inflamed by jealousy, consults his advisers for a remedy; he fears that if he leaves Farhād alone, this rival will supplant him, yet if he kills him he will be guilty of shedding innocent blood. The advisers suggest the impossible task of tunneling through the mountain of Bīsitūn. Summoning Farhād, Khusraw interrogates him concerning his love; the readiness of his answers, and the evident purity of his motives, further enrage the king. Perceiving the true nature of Khusraw's love—his assumption of ownership, and his lack of concern for Shīrīn's reputation, evidenced by his sealing the contract with an oath on her honor—Farhād agrees to the task on condition not that Khusraw give Shīrīn to him, but that he renounce his claim to her—an important distinction that emphasizes the moral distance between the two.

Farhād, in Khusraw's eyes, stands in relation to him as Rāmīn did to Mawbad: as rival for the affections of the woman he desires. Two crucial differences, however, escape the king. First, not only is Shīrīn not his wife, but his attempts to possess her have conspicuously failed to include an offer of marriage—hence her resistance. Second, Shīrīn does not return Farhād's love but on the contrary has made it clear that she can love no one but Khusraw; thus there is no question of Farhād ever possessing her. The king's perception of their rivalry amounts to a projection of his own motives onto Farhād and a failure to understand the lesson finally learned by Rāmīn: that true love is both single-minded and selfless. Khusraw's subsequent action—when, learning that Farhād inspired by love is near success, he sends the false report of Shīrīn's death which causes Farhād to die of grief—lacks even the technical justification that Mawbad's acts of violence against the adulterous lovers might claim; and his mocking letter of condolence to the innocent Shīrīn further emphasizes the baseness of his motives. Khusraw's triumph over his rival reflects no "code of honour" which must, willy-nilly, be observed but demonstrates his own lack of honor.

Khusraw's dual identities, as king and as lover, are shown in the Farhād episode to mirror one another: his injustice, as lover, to Shīrīn, manifested by his infidelities and his suspicions, is paralleled by his injustice as king to Farhād, for whose death he is responsible. The two identities merge to constitute his true, qualitative identity: he is neither a worthy lover nor a just king. Although the lovers are at last united in marriage (significantly, Shīrīn's final arguments, which persuade Khusraw to treat her with the honor due her, are made, not in her own person, but through the minstrel Nakīsā, just as Khusraw's replies are conveyed through Bārbad), and although, through her good counsel, he is finally persuaded to practice justice and piety and to seek wisdom,[23] their happiness is

[23] Shīrīn's warning to Khusraw constitutes an exemplary counsel to kings: " 'O king,' Shīrīn entreated, bowing low, / 'From song towards wisdom turn your efforts now. // 'Long have you striven pleasure's joys to gain; / strive now the heart's fulfillment to attain. . . . // 'How many a mirror held by kings, to black // has turned, as men cry out at justice's lack. // 'When kingly power turns its face away / from the right path, his deeds as well will stray. . . . // 'Oppression, tyranny are evils twain; / 'twere best with love your subjects' trust to gain. . . . // 'Towards your salvation in the next world strive, / remembering that *this* station you must leave. // 'He who amasses gold and silver: say, / how shall he then dispose for Judgement Day? // 'Retain it, and your wealth will prove your bane; / but it will guard your path, if it's well given. // 'The tales of Darius and Jamshīd read well: / how the Sun's game with each of them did

short-lived. Khusraw is murdered by Shīrūyah, his son by Maryam, who lusts after both the throne and Shīrīn (that is, after his father's dual identities).[24] Shīrīn, pretending to agree to wed Shīrūyah and affecting indifference to Khusraw's death, enters his tomb to pay her last respects; there, she stabs herself and dies embracing Khusraw's corpse. The final stage of Khusraw's quest, in which the possibility of becoming a new person was offered him, is doomed to failure because of his earlier inability to perfect his own nature.

Niẓāmī prefaced his romance of *Khusraw u Shīrīn* with a great hymn in praise of love, which testifies to his conception of that virtue as a cosmic force and which concludes:

> All essences towards one another move;
> this movement the philosophers call love.
> If you but contemplate with Reason's eye,
> 'tis love maintains the world's stability.
> And if the heavens of love devoid should be,
> the earth would never find prosperity.[25]
>
> (*KS*, p. 34)

By contrast, he does not term his poem a love story, but a *havasnāmah*, a tale of passion. Commissioned to write a poem about passion, he describes his undertaking in a passage in which the word *havas*, singly and in compounds, is repeated

---

deal; // And so comport yourself, 'neath these nine veils, / that you may learn the mysteries they conceal' " (*KS*, pp. 398–99). The ancient kings Darius and Jamshīd are used as exempla of the transience of worldly power.

[24] Khusraw was accused by Bahrām Chūbīn of parricide (another of the false accusations that complicate the problem of identity); the accusation is, in retrospect, ironic, since Khusraw himself becomes the victim of the very crime for which he was wrongly accused.

[25] At the beginning of this passage Niẓāmī asserts, "The world has no *miḥrāb* save that of love" (*KS*, p. 38), introducing the motif repeated later by Shīrīn. The view of love expressed resembles that of both the Ikhwān al-Ṣāfa' and the Sufis, in whose beliefs "the whole world seeks the Creator and loves Him" and who "make the power of yearning (*shawq*) the very cause of the coming into being of things and the law governing the universe" (Nasr, *Introduction*, pp. 53–54), as well as that expressed by Naṣīr al-Dīn Ṭūsī (see *Nasirean Ethics*, pp. 195–211).

no less than seven times in four lines, contrasting with the repetition of *ʿishq* in the passage praising love.[26] *Havas*—passion, desire, caprice—is the quality that characterizes Khusraw's love; his equation of love with possession amounts to a moral confusion of terms that parallels the distinction on the level of language. Mawbad's error was a similar one; it resulted in his replacement, in all capacities, by Rāmīn. Khusraw, combining in his person the identities of lover and of king, is unable to perfect either; his replacement by Shīrūyah testifies to the tragic consequences, both private and public, of such a failure.

Niẓāmī's second romance, *Laylī u Majnūn* (1188), is also concerned with the relationship of private conduct to public responsibility; in it too the question of identity becomes a crucial issue. The story of the ill-starred lovers was taken from the Arabic tradition, where it is related in poems and anecdotes concerning the poet Qays al-ʿĀmirī, known as Majnūn, the mad lover. Niẓāmī, so the story goes, was reluctant to undertake the composition of this poem for fear that the slenderness of the story would not produce a work of much significance. A passage in the prologue reflects the poet's dilemma: how to convey, through this tale whose brevity is determined by its matter, the deeper significance the poet perceives it to contain. Niẓāmī's praise of the finished product suggests that he was not entirely displeased with it; his boast of the pains he has expended on it belies the supposition that he viewed his task with repugnance. Moreover, his stated misgivings were perhaps intended to function as a modest disclaimer for any imperfections the poem might appear to have, particularly in view of the unconventional treatment the poet gives to his traditional material.[27]

Niẓāmī's retelling of the story of Laylī and Majnūn reveals the destructive aspects of love's power and poses fundamental moral questions concerning the lover's conduct of his quest and his definition of its object; for, in this romance, all who are

[26] See *KS*, p. 32; Farhād's passion is also termed *havaskārī*. The repetition of *havas* also contrasts with the description of Firdawsī's treatment of the story as a *ḥadīth-i ʿishq* (p. 33).

[27] Cf. chapter 6, n. 33.

touched by Majnūn's passion are either altered or destroyed by it. Majnūn's love for his cousin Laylī, though sincere and deeply felt, becomes an obsession almost from the start. His conduct, when he is first smitten with love, recalls that of Farhād: he wanders about distractedly, repeating Laylī's name and composing verses about his love and the suffering it causes him. But where Farhād concealed his passion and was content to serve his lady with silent devotion for the sake of preserving her good repute, Majnūn makes a public display of his emotions. His excessive, self-willed suffering, and the damage done thereby to Laylī's honor, earns him the enmity of her father, who refuses to marry his daughter to such an obvious madman and rejects all efforts to persuade him otherwise. Although his refusal is motivated largely by self-interest and a concern for what others will think—"You know what fault-finders the Arabs be," he tells Majnūn's father; "should I do this, what would they say of me?"[28] (*LM*, p. 59)—his attitude, though conservative, is scarcely unreasonable. Majnūn's reaction is to make a public spectacle of his grief—tearing his garments, heaping dust on his head, repeating Laylī's name, and uttering impassioned verses about his grief, before finally falling senseless to the ground.

Shīrīn reproached Khusraw for his divided loyalties: "To have two loves does not bespeak a single heart" (*KS*, p. 308), she reminded him, in a passage recalling her earlier words in the bathing scene: "One cannot pray in two directions." Her assertion that "loverhood can only be the affair of one for whom the beloved is everything in this world" (*KS*, p. 340) anticipates the moral dilemma subsequently explored in *Laylī u Majnūn*. If Khusraw represented a heart divided—and an identity that was, correspondingly, precarious—Majnūn embodies the opposite extreme, that of excessive devotion to a single purpose. Majnūn can pray only in one direction—a metaphorical description of this state, which is concretely exemplified in the scene where, when his father takes him on pilgrimage to

[28] All page references in the text are to *Laylī u Majnūn* (*LM*), ed. Vaḥīd Dastgirdī.

Mecca in the hope of curing his madness, he seizes the door ring of the Kaʿbah and prays to God to make his love ever increase: "A love as steadfast as this, let it increase a hundred fold" (*LM*, p. 67).[29]

The object of such a prayer is not union, but division; it is the decisive proof of Majnūn's madness, as his grieving father correctly perceives. Majnūn's prayers are directed to only one *miḥrāb*; but it is not that of the Kaʿbah, described by the poet as "the goal of the whole world's pilgrimage, the *miḥrab* of heaven and earth" (*LM*, p. 66). Moreover, though he refers to the beauty of Laylī's face as the *miḥrāb* of his prayers (*LM*, p. 192), the ultimate object of Majnūn's adoration is not Laylī herself, but his own self-image as lover.[30] Majnūn's prayer before the Kaʿbah—that he become ever more desirous of the sight of Laylī's face, that the years of his life be added to hers—is, in the light of ensuing events, ironic for he will ultimately reject the sight of that face, preferring his own visions, and she will die before he does. Majnūn's passion, like a consuming flame, feeds on itself and seeks to destroy everything in its path; for, like the raging fire to which it is repeatedly likened, it knows no bounds, no limits, and is beyond control.

Majnūn becomes increasingly alienated from his fellow men, and his flights into the desert, where he wanders naked among the wild beasts, grow more and more protracted, as he comes to prefer his isolated state. While Romantically inclined critics may see in Majnūn a rebel against the constricting values of society, Niẓāmī's judgment of his moral condition is quite otherwise; we may fruitfully recall Naṣīr al-Dīn Ṭūsī's dictum that one cannot seek perfection in isolation. The negative aspect of Majnūn's passion is revealed not only by the ac-

[29] The episode is recounted by al-Washshā', *al-Muwaššá*, p. 58.

[30] Religious metaphors abound throughout the poem: Majnūn's love for Laylī is a miracle (*āyat*, p. 63); his frequenting of her neighborhood is described as *ṭawāf*, "circumambulation" (as of the Kaʿbah) (p. 66); the scene in which they fall in love abounds with allusions to the story of Joseph (pp. 62–63); Majnūn visits Laylī *labbayk zanān u bayt gūyān* (that is, both repeating the formula of obedience to God and spouting poetry, p. 68); his torn clothes are likened to torn pilgrim's garb (*iḥrām darīdah*, p. 74). (See further note 32.)

tion but by the poem's pervasive imagery, in particular the systematic contrast between desert and sown: Majnūn is regularly associated with the sterile, inhospitable desert, a place fit only for animals and madmen but not suitable for human habitation; Laylī, on the other hand, is associated with gardens and verdant greenery, symbolic of a fertility that her constancy to Majnūn will ultimately prevent her from realizing.

The need for human society and for the ameliorating power of social institutions is graphically demonstrated when the mad, naked, and emaciated Majnūn is found in the desert by the Arab lord Nawfal and taken under his protection. In the desert, Majnūn is no better than an animal, for which he is easily mistaken; but once restored to human company, his condition improves dramatically:

> When easeful food and clothing he obtained,
> with kindly care good order he regained.
> His face, once yellow, took on ruddy hue;
> his stature bent reedlike now supple grew.
> Once more his downy beard, like precious musk,
> his moonlike face encircled with its dusk.
> When gentleness breathed easy on that flower,
> all that the wind had robbed it did restore. . . .
> The madman of the plain, his sense regained,
> unfettered dwelt at home, now unconstrained.
> Calm grew the verdure in the garden's close;
> the wine-cup graced the hand of the red rose.
>
> (*LM*, p. 107)

The conviction that man's natural state is among his fellows is clear from this fruitful blending of man and nature in the restored Majnūn. But this restoration is not to last, for Majnūn pursues his obsessive quest, manipulating the Arab chief's promise of support to his own end of obtaining Laylī at whatever cost. The wars conducted by Nawfal against Laylī's tribe result in bloodshed and destruction; ultimately he is obliged to forgo victory, and Majnūn, reviling his friend, retreats once more into the desert.

Nawfal, his honor compromised, is a victim of Majnūn's obsession; so, in time, are Majnūn's parents, who die alone and grieving, their son lost to them forever. So is Ibn Salām, Laylī's husband, whose despair at her coldness robs him of the will to live. Laylī, for her part, lives only for the thought of Majnūn; but her steadfastness, unlike that of Vīs or of Shīrīn, who combined with it an active moral stance, reflects a passivity that is at odds with the imagery of fertility and verdancy with which she is associated. She herself is the final victim of Majnūn's passion. When he rejects her, unable to abandon the image created by his mind for the real woman, she dies of grief, after enjoining her mother to adorn her as a bride before placing her in her tomb. Desert has triumphed over garden.

Moral passivity is a key issue in *Laylī u Majnūn*. At the root of Majnūn's surrender to the excesses of his passion, and of his public display of this passion, lies an inability to struggle against adversity and a willingness to become its victim—qualities that also doom Laylī to die unfulfilled. Niẓāmī announced this theme in his prologue to the romance, in the section entitled "Advice to His Son," under the rubric "One must not endure injustice" (*bīdād-kish nabāyad būd*).

> Why bow before the wishes of the base?
> fall prey to those not worthy of their place?
> Why before vile abuse your head bend down?
> why suffer that injustices be done?
> Stand firm and resolute, like the high hill;
> show sturdiness against the weak of will.
> . . . .
> Submissiveness will lead to inward flaws,
> sufferance of injustice baseness cause.
> Shoulder your weapon, like the martial thorn,
> if heaps of roses to your breast you'd strain.
> "Alas! alack!" are words that sap man's power;
> "alas!" will bring about man's death for sure.
>
> (*LM*, p. 53–54)

Majnūn's self-indulgence also involves a denial of his obligations to his fellow humans, and specifically to those to whom he is bound by ties of blood. The value of family ties is another theme announced in the prologue: into the lengthy section of advice to his son the poet inserts a tribute to deceased members of his family—father, mother, and maternal uncle—as well as to his departed friends (*LM*, pp. 48–51). The value of human companionship and friendship (*hamdamī*) is stressed, as is the necessity for moderation in grief and forgetfulness of the pain of loss—principles conspicuously ignored by Majnūn.

> For grief outstrips all bounds that one can span;
> it is a whirlpool deeper than a man.
> The cup of sorrow so much greater looms
> than in a thousand hours can be consumed.
> The remedy for boundless pain and grief?
> Only forgetfulness will bring relief.
>
> (*LM*, p. 49)

Majnūn's suffering, however, is an indispensable part of his self-image; he resists all attempts at consolation. His abandonment to grief and his habituation (*khū kardan*) to life among the beasts amounts to a denial of his own humanity—a denial that he himself admits, when his father reproaches him:

> "Even the dog admits a home; but you
> do not; and yet you *are* a man, 'tis true.
> "If then you are a man, behave like one;
> if demon, demon-like through deserts roam."[31]
>
> (*LM*, p. 154)

He responds, "In my own wildness I have gone astray; / a wild beast amongst humans cannot stay" (*LM*, p. 157).

For many critics, Majnūn's conduct can be excused because

[31] Dastgirdī's gloss is apt: "Demons, ghouls and jinni are, in popular belief, the same, and it is said of the jinn that they can take different shapes. The meaning of the lines is this: If you are a demon, then like demons and ghouls, who with great difficulty take on the shapes of men, you too take on a man's shape; but if you are a man, why then do you live in the abode of ghouls and become their like?" (*LM*, p. 154 n. 5).

his passion, however excessive, inspires him to compose beautiful verse. Gelpke's judgment is typical:

> To his Arab biographers Majnūn is suffering from an illness, a broken man, who has lost his way, to be reproached, pitied or derided. Niẓāmī understands the three elements of the traditional Majnūn, his love, his insanity and his poetical genius, as three aspects of one, indivisible unity. Only when he is driven out of the paradise of his early love does Majnūn become both insane and a poet. Insanity and poetical genius are two expressions of the same state of mind, of a soul estranged in the world of men. And the same people who reproach, pity and deride Majnūn because of his insanity, memorize and admire his poetry. Has the tragic ambiguity of the artist's position in the world, the paradox of unbounded desire in a limited body, ever been described more aptly?[32]

Unfortunately, the "tragic ambiguity of the artist's position in the world" invoked by Gelpke is a construction of the Roman-

[32] *The Story of Layla and Majnun*, trans. R. Gelpke, p. 219. Gelpke also accepts a mystical reading of the poem: "It would be wrong to consider Majnūn's and Laylā's fate as 'tragic' in the western sense of the word. That there could be no fulfillment of their love on earth is a foregone conclusion for Niẓāmī's mysticism. His Laylā states clearly, that in the religion of love close intimacy is perilous. . . . If, therefore, our lovers' sufferings are not 'tragic', they must also not be interpreted from a point of view of conventional morals. The Persian mystical poets have never been puritans! The lovers' grief breaks through the limitations of human nature, enabling them to become free of the 'Self' which is tied to the transitory world. Death is the gate to the 'real' world, to the home which our wandering soul desires" (ibid., 219–20). Much of this misunderstanding stems from too literal a reading of the "religion of love" topos: to the truly pious (or to the rational philosopher—Niẓāmī is both) such a love is sheer idolatry, and Majnūn is indeed mad. Compare Glynnis Cropp's analysis of similar topics in the poetry of the troubadours: "Madness lies in forgetting one's religious obligation, through moral transgression or through sin. It is therefore hardly surprising that, in the courtly domain, madness signifies a transgression. Its cause is, most often, love, which by its irrationality robs the lover of his ability to judge rationally, and makes him forget to conduct himself with moderation. . . . Love sweeps man away toward unreason, which allows every kind of aberration" (*Le vocabulaire courtois des troubadours*, pp. 133–34).

tics and their successors. For the medieval poet, the alienation represented by Majnūn is just that: a refusal to take one's proper place in the world. The "Paradise of love" enjoyed by Majnūn is his childhood state of loving Laylī without realizing that he does so; once this feeling is understood and named, that is, once Majnūn becomes aware both of himself as a lover and of the practical demands love makes on the adult, he is driven mad, a madness that in part reflects his inability to come to terms with adult responsibilities.

The poetry inspired by this passion is a perverted art precisely because it is limited to self-expression and knows no higher purpose; like the desert in which it is produced, it is sterile. Just as Laylī's passivity dooms her to deny her own potential for fertility and the creation of new life (a denial for which the description of the withered garden in autumn which precedes her death provides a fitting emblem), Majnūn's madness causes his poetry to provide, not guidance toward right conduct (the proper function of poetry), but misguidance—it is, in short, a negative exemplum. This is made clear by the story of Salām of Baghdad, a lovesick youth who seeks out Majnūn in the desert but finds communication with him impossible. Salām begs of Majnūn that he be allowed to be his constant companion on his desert wanderings; Majnūn replies, "I am a wild beast; you seek companionship. Go seek of he whose kind you are" (*LM*, p. 222), playing on the words *vaḥshī*, "wild beast" or "savage," and *uns/ins*, "companionship"/"humankind." "You will find not a moment's friendship [*hamdamī*] from me," he tells the youth. The ironic contrast between the self-styled "king of love" and the lovestruck youth is heightened by Salām's efforts to win Majnūn's friendship in simple human fashion, by inviting him to break bread with him; but Majnūn prefers his savage state, and when his provisions run out, Salām finally abandons Majnūn to return to Baghdad, where he recites Majnūn's poetry to the admiration of all (*LM*, pp. 219–26).[33]

[33] Majnūn's impassioned versifying is most frequently referred to as *ghazal-sarā'ī* or *bayt guftan* (occasionally his poems are called *qaṣīdah*). Some doubt

There is, indeed, a literary lesson to be learned from the story of Majnūn, but it is a negative one. Majnūn, much like Rāmīn in the early portions of *Vīs u Rāmīn*, mistakes literary convention and poetic stance for reality; his self-image is modeled on what is essentially a literary conception of the lover, of the sort reflected in courtly *ghazal*. The artificiality of this model (as well as the fact that the stance it provides cannot cope with the problems of real life) is seen clearly in Majnūn's encounter with the black-clad messenger who brings him word of Laylī's marriage (against her will, and never consummated because of her unswerving fidelity to Majnūn) to Ibn Salām. The messenger concludes his report with a most uncourtly tirade against the female sex—a tirade that (as he himself is forced to admit, when Majnūn takes it seriously) is all lies and has been calculated to encourage Majnūn to forget his lost love:

"A woman—nay, a thousand if there be—
a creature is of little constancy.

. . . .

"Oh yes, she loves—but only till such time
as none but you to love her heart can find.
"And when she's found another man's embrace,
she'll never wish to see again *your* face.

. . . .

"How many 'neath her cruelty have groaned,
and loyalty in women never found.

. . . .

"A foe, she brings disaster to the world;

---

is cast on both the quality of the poems and the integrity of their maker in an interesting passage describing Majnūn when he is encountered by a passer-by: "He saw him [Majnūn] seated beside a mirage, fallen ruined into a ruin, // Limping like the balance of his own verses, their sense abundant, their rhyme restricted; // Saying: 'From now on I have no-one; and he who has no-one is in disorder [*bī-qāfiyat*]' " (LM, p. 84). (*Bayt-i khīshtan* in the second line can also refer to the poem itself—to which Niẓāmī referred in the prologue in much the same terms [p. 27]—as well as to Majnūn's "house" or family [cf. n. 39].)

a lover, wreaks destruction on the soul.
. . . .

"Tell her to do a thing—she pays no mind;
but tell her not—she's doubly there inclined.
"In your unhappiness she finds her joy;
but if you're happy, grief will her destroy.
"These women's ways to all quite plain appear;
the magic spells of women's wiles are clear."
(*LM*, p. 144).

Majnūn's response is to fall on the ground and heap invective on Laylī; even when the messenger hastens to tell him that he has lied, his grief is not lessened.

When Majnūn knew that all that he had heard
a two-faced mirror was, all lying words,
His sorrow slackened from its former spate;
his violent grieving did somewhat abate.
He stood there, like a bird with broken wing;
his head was broken from that battering.
From tearful sighs he lustrous rubies strung,
and on those broken vows some verses sung
. . . .

And his angelic reason then became
"Majnūn"—distraught—e'en more than was his name.
. . . .

"Where now those colloquies when, side by side,
we sat? with myriad vows our pact we tied?
"Where now those hopes we placed in union meet?
that bowing low in love's submission sweet?
. . . .

"Your heart's abandoned loyalty, I see;
where now that vain pretense of love for me?
"For you my soul I've bartered; but you've naught
to sell to me but words, so cheaply bought.
"Your love I purchased with my life so dear;
another's love you've chosen to prefer.
. . . .

"My youth was spent all in your garden's care;
alas, for all the gardener's pains I bore!
"This dove did toil to make that garden grow;
its fruit, once ripe, was eaten by a crow.
"Although your dates are ripened now, and sweet,
all men but I will only sharp thorns meet.
"My sighs will set up such a scorching wind
that none will from your garden nurture find.
"O jasmine-breast, you're like the cypress tree:
fruit from the cypress men have yet to see.
. . . .
"Other than this, no recourse can I see
but to give up my own dear life for thee:
"To choose to suffer, with a loyal heart:
your cruelty, your injustice set apart:
"Make patience my companion; bear each ill
for you, and let life take me where it will."

(*LM*, pp. 146–49)

The messenger's uncourtly tirade (introduced at the outset as an explicit fabrication) is a parody of the courtly concept of love;[34] in this view love, far from being ennobling, only brings affliction. The point seems to be proven by Majnūn's immediate response: rendered totally incapacitated, he can only beat his head against the stones and cry out in anguish. His second response, when the message is belied and Laylī's fidelity reasserted, is equally illuminating: his grief abating somewhat, he begins to versify, producing a love plaint of which any courtly poet might be proud. The manner in which this "*ghazal*" is introduced leaves no doubt as to the poet's evaluation of it: Majnūn is even madder than his name.[35] His madness is patent

[34] Shihābī takes this passage as exemplifying Niẓāmī's views on women (*Niẓāmī*, pp. 205–206); similarly, Chelkowski sees it as reflecting the poet's "need to present all facets of human experience" (*Mirror*, p. 67). Even the latter view ignores the fact that the lines are spoken by a specific character for a specific purpose (a purpose that includes the poet's goal of parody).

[35] Majnūn's madness is explicitly and negatively judged in the reference to

in his reversion to the familiar self-image: literature wins out over life. The self-centeredness of the passage is remarkable, as is its destructiveness; if he cannot have Laylī (and it is clear that he will not), no one will.

W.T.H. Jackson has observed of Chrétien's romances that his protagonists talk most when their love (from the poet's viewpoint) is least sincere.

> To me it is clear that Chrétien uses the love dialogue, the characteristic of early romances, only when love is not sincere in his sense. In other words, if Alexander and Soredamurs, Cligès and Fénice are courtly lovers, then Chrétien wants no part of courtly love. His real lovers never indulge in the love monologue or love dialogue when they are truly in love.[36]

This observation strikes me as being equally relevant to the two early romances of Niẓāmī (as well as to his attitude toward *Vīs u Rāmīn*, illuminating one aspect at least of his commentary on it). Khusraw, like Rāmīn before him, talked incessantly about love; but his motives were, to say the least, questionable. His "concentration [was] entirely upon a formalized analysis of his own feelings, which proves in the end . . . to be thinly disguised urgings of the flesh." Majnūn does not merely talk about love but writes poetry about it; but again, "it is the effect of love, not of the beloved, which is being examined."[37]

By Niẓāmī's time both the courtly and the mystical *ghazal* had emerged as independent forms and were flourishing. Niẓāmī's poems reflect a growing tension between lyric and ro-

---

his "angelic reason" becoming distraught or deranged (*Gasht khirad-i firishtah-fām-ash / majnūn-tar az ānkih būd nām-ash*). It is reason that brings man closer to the angels (and hence to the divine); disruption of this faculty draws him down to the level of the beasts. Cf. *RIS*, 1:448–9; Naṣīr al-Dīn Ṭūsī, *Nasirean Ethics*, pp. 46–51, 61–3, et passim.

[36] W.T.H. Jackson, "Problems of Communication in the Romances of Chrétien de Troyes," in *Medieval Literature and Folklore Studies*, ed. J. Mandel, p. 49.

[37] Ibid., p. 42; this is, of course, even more true of Rāmīn, and *Vīs u Rāmīn* at times appears much closer to *Cligès* than does *Khusraw u Shīrīn*.

mance, which possess, as separate genres, disparate goals, much like that seen in twelfth-century European romance (for example, in the *Tristan* of Gottfried of Strassburg, as well as in Chrétien). While the lyric might present an ideal of love calculated to inspire its audience to the pursuit of virtue by playing on their identification with the role of lover, romance asserts that the courtly lover's self-involvement ill prepares him to survive in the real world where he must continually interact with others. In particular, as Niẓāmī's romances imply, the courtly lover's stance is unsuited to either kings or poets as a real attitude to the world; the implication is strengthened by the more pragmatic (but paradoxically more idealistic) view of love that informs the *Haft Paykar*. Bahrām Gūr, as we shall see in the following chapter, talks little about love; he listens, however, far more than either Khusraw or Majnūn is capable of doing. In short, Niẓāmī's true lovers, like Chrétien's, are not given to extensive divagations on the topic of love.

> For Chrétien [and for Niẓāmī as well] the communication of real love, as distinct from the formalized games of the court, apparently came through action and through indirect communication of affection. He clearly mistrusted the rhetoric and dialectic of earlier romances as a method of representing love in its higher aspects and used them principally to parody the type of love he rejected. If we are right in assuming that he regarded married love as that which best fulfilled the aspirations of both man and woman, then we must also assume that he felt that such love needed no elaborate verbal communication. True love expressed itself in mutual trust, not in the artifices of cunningly wrought words.[38]

Both of Niẓāmī's early romances suggest strongly that he, too, saw married love as the highest stage of human loving; the *Haft Paykar* will make this message even plainer.

The view that Majnūn triumphs by renouncing the object of

[38] Ibid., p. 50.

his love does not reckon with the fact that this object is not, ultimately, Laylī herself, but his own self-image, which is never renounced. His madness, at first a symptom of his lovesickness, becomes an end in itself, symbolic of his failure to accept his own humanity and to live among his fellows; his exclusion of his own kind extends even to Laylī, and when she summons him following the death of her husband, he cannot confront her, preferring his own mental image of her (an image that is, like his own self-image, a profoundly literary construction) to the woman of flesh and blood. It is indeed true that the values of the society from which Majnūn becomes alienated are questioned as much as his own actions are; the conduct of Laylī's father, and of Ibn Salām in particular, is shown to be motivated by self-interest and concupiscence and presented in a most unpraiseworthy light. This only compounds the central dilemma of the poem by calling attention to the moral complexity of the human condition; for if the actions of these individuals are ethically questionable, those of others—notably Majnūn's parents and the Arab Nawfal—demonstrate profound concern for their fellow beings. It follows that, just as the individual cannot seek his own perfection in independence, so society cannot perfect itself without justice toward its individual members.[39]

[39] One of the central themes of *Laylī u Majnūn* is the need for both family and social solidarity and in particular the duty of filial piety; introduced in the prologue, it is stressed throughout in the series of destroyed relationships that Majnūn's passion leaves in its wake: with parents, with friends (Nawfal and Salām), and ultimately with Laylī herself. In this connection it is curious that Chelkowski's notion that Majnūn's love is "ideal" is supported by a line from a scene in which Majnūn fails to recognize his father: "When Majnūn, waking, opened his eyes wide, / he saw a strange companion [*damsāz*] by his side. // He looked upon his father, but he knew / him not, and from his closeness quick withdrew. // He who's forgotten of his self all trace: / how should he then recall another's face?" (*LM*, p. 151; see Chelkowski, *Mirror*, p. 67). Such an evaluation of this line—and of the entire scene—demonstrates the unwisdom of ignoring authorial prefaces to romance, which customarily provide specific indications of how the poet intended his poem to be read, and of concentrating merely on the "story." Niẓāmī's point throughout the poem is that, however sincere it may be, the love that can thrive only by turning its back on the world

Although Majnūn's life in the desert may superficially resemble the ascetic's renunciation of the world, the ascetic's purpose—unlike Majnūn's—is self-control, his method the discipline of the senses. Neither is a Sufi interpretation any more tenable; Majnūn's goal is not self-annihilation in the beloved, but separation from her, and his love is thus not selfless but selfish in the extreme, producing not union, but multiplicity. Establishing his identity as lover, Majnūn's ultimate goal is to feed and to enhance this image; and while his quest may lead to the image's perfection, such perfection is perverse, since it is accomplished at the cost of his own humanity.[40]

---

is doomed to failure. On the hierarchical ordering of society and the necessity for love in maintaining its order and harmony, see Naṣīr al-Dīn Ṭūsī, *Nasirean Ethics*, pp. 193–96; see also al-Fārābī, *Fuṣūl al-Madanī*, pp. 53–55.

[40] Cf. Naṣīr al-Dīn Ṭūsī: "The farthest of men from virtue are those who depart from civilized life and sociability and incline to solitude and loneliness. Thus, the virtue of Love and Friendship is the greatest of virtues, and its preservation is the most important of tasks" (*Nasirean Ethics*, p. 252). In an addition to the poem, the story of Zayd and Zaynab (which many critics consider an interpolation), Zayd sees in a dream a vision of Laylī and Majnūn reunited in Paradise. If indeed Niẓāmī was the author of this section (presenting a contrasting tale of love, which thrives because it is conducted within accepted social norms, and which may well have been intended as commentary on the story of Majnūn), the vision cannot be interpreted as validating Majnūn's obsessive passion, but rather as emphasizing the distinction between the human and divine worlds, between which there can be no equivalence. The same distinction is emphasized at the close of *Vīs u Rāmīn*, when after Vīs's death Rāmīn renounces his throne to take up residence in the fire temple: "He descended from the royal throne and went to the *dakhmeh*, the throne of the next world. He took up his abode at the fire temple and dwelt there; he attached his pure heart to God. God that day granted him kingship when he chose contentment and saintliness. Although before this he had been a prince, he was ever the slave of desire. The world carried out his orders and he in turn from the craving of his heart was the obedient servant of desire. When he disabused his heart of the world's desire, he freed his body from desire and his heart from care; be sure that a heart which has escaped from the hurly-burly and desire of this world has escaped eternal punishment" (*VR*, p. 350; 104:16–22). The souls of Vīs and Rāmīn are also united in Paradise (as are ʿAyyūqī's lovers, resurrected by the Prophet); the topos is a recurrent one in romance. Compare the motif of the "entwined trees" in the Tristan romances (see Pierre Gallais, "Les arbres entrelacées dans les 'romans' de Tristan et le mythe de l'arbre androgyne primordial," in *Mélanges Pierre le Gentil*, pp. 295–312). Majnūn's

Thus far our discussion of character in romance has focused on its protagonists and the manner in which their individual traits, qualities, and attitudes are established through their words and actions, as well as through more subtle means such as imagery and the sort of intertextual echoes evoked, for example, in *Khusraw u Shīrīn*. It is self-evident that, while the words of individual characters are presented through monologue and dialogue, their actions are presented through narration; and this act of narration may function to reveal not only the qualities of the characters, but those of the voice that recounts their adventures. In the preceding chapter it was suggested that this voice, in romance, cannot always be equated with that of the poet himself, and that different modes of presentation are often present in the same work, corresponding to differing degrees of authorial "presence" as well as to different narratorial personae. Such authorial interventions, usually in the form of commentary on the action, often purport to present the author in the persona of omniscient storyteller:

> The author himself . . . interrupts the story to comment upon and to explain the sense of the situation not only in terms of the story, but also in terms of universal, moral, and psychological values. The *persona* of the author becomes one of an omnivident, omniscient sage who divulges to us not only the secrets of his hero's heart and mind, but also the great truths of human existence.[41]

Such passages abound in romance, Persian and European alike; while they have certain advantages as "excellent devices for suspending the narration and adding to it a deeper ideological significance and wider moral sense," they also have shortcomings, in particular the "clear, unavoidable danger of generalization and of *sententiae*-making which is fundamentally alien to a successful presentation of a real, identifiable human

love, like Rāmīn's, is of this world, hence imperfect; however, although the distinction between the imperfect human world and the perfect world of the divine is upheld, perfectability (within the framework of human limitations) is perceived as a goal toward which human beings should strive.

[41] Dembowski, "Monologue," p. 110.

situation."[42] We have already seen, in the case of Gurgānī, that such interventions are not necessarily ideologically consistent but deliberately seek to present the complexities of a given action or situation and to reflect the ambiguities of the human condition. Still more complexity arises when the narratorial voice is treated, not as the omniscient poet (the voice of prologue and epilogue) speaking *in propria persona*, but as a character in the poem. This strategy, which enhances the potential for irony already afforded by any authorial intervention, may not be—indeed usually is not—employed consistently throughout the poem; it more often appears sporadically (particularly at crucial moments in the action) and takes the form of a comment on that action, which reflects the fallibility of human judgment and the conflict of values or the moral dilemma that the action itself exemplifies. The most striking example of this strategy in Persian romance is provided by Niẓāmī's *Haft Paykar* (1197), where the narrator who recounts the exploits of the hero, the Sassanian emperor Bahrām Gūr, emerges as a distinct character in his own right, in the medieval sense of "character" as exemplary of conduct or belief.

This narratorial persona is seen to best advantage in one of the poem's most important episodes, the story of Bahrām and

[42] Ibid., pp. 113, 114. Discussing Chaucer's *Troilus*, Bernard Huppé identifies three types of narratorial interjection: first, "allusions to the 'auctour,' . . . investing the narrative persona with the role of 'translator,' a literal-minded instrument for transmitting his source on the level of sense"; second, "by comment and explication," which, "where these exist independently of the role of the translator, . . . tend to suggest a further role as narrative commentator"; and third, "rhetorical interpolations and apostrophe, often lengthy and elaborate and involving personal judgment and interpretation, evoking themes like that of fortune," which "provide a rhetorical frame for the narrative . . . [and] place the whole . . . in the context of a special viewpoint, that of the narrator whose sympathy for the characters of his story is as evident as is his ambiguous relationship to them, and as evident as his ineptness" ("The Unlikely Narrator: The Narrative Strategy of the *Troilus*," in *Signs and Symbols in Chaucer's Poetry*, ed. J. P. Hermann and J. J. Burke, Jr., pp. 189–90). All three types of interjection can be found in the romances of Gurgānī and Niẓāmī; a systematic study of the topic would not only be of great value, but would undoubtedly aid in laying to rest the tendency to take every line of every poem as a statement of the poet's personal beliefs.

the harp girl Fitnah (an episode that, as we shall see in chapter 5, is particularly illuminating with respect to Niẓāmī's relation to his sources). Bahrām, hunting for onager in the company of his favorite, Fitnah, is irritated when she withholds praise of his prowess, and he asks what he must do to impress her; she challenges him to transfix a wild ass through hoof and ear with a single arrow. When he obliges, instead of praising him she points out that this act is the result of practice rather than innate ability. Angered, Bahrām orders an officer to kill her; she succeeds in persuading the officer to spare her and to tell Bahrām that she is dead. Ultimately the two are reunited, after Fitnah has taught the king a much-needed lesson.[43]

The voice of the narratorial persona is established early in the episode. He appears at the outset to be slightly bewildered by the events he recounts; his bemusement is manifested by his comments on Bahrām's prowess as a hunter, and his naiveté by the repeated wordplay on the conceit of "striking fire":

> His bolts of tempered steel hurled down
> now fire, now game, upon the ground.
> With haunch of game, and purest wine,
> it wants a fire to roast the chine.
> Did then the royal spear strike fire
> for this, while slaying onager?
> His lance's heat, with grisly wound,
> cooked well the prey he brought to ground.
>
> (*HP*, 25:7–10)

The belaboring of this conceit establishes the narrator's perspective as a pragmatic one, concerned with the literal level of events. The metaphorical sense of the conceit is ignored in favor of its literal meaning; but the insistent repetition of *ātish*, "fire," three times in three lines, and the figurative associations of *pukhtan*, "to cook," and *kabāb*, "roast meat," suggest to the reader that there is a significance to the action of which the

[43] See *Heft Peiker* (*HP*), ed. H. Ritter and J. Rypka, sections 25 and 26. All line references in the text are to the numbering in this edition. For a fuller discussion of this episode, see chapter 5.

narrator is unaware. Thus his somewhat ludicrous query—did Bahrām's arrows "strike fire" in order to kindle a blaze by which to cook his prey?—must be examined for its figurative meaning: those arrows (metonymically, Bahrām's skill as a hunter) are the agents that kindle within him, first the desire for praise, then anger at the woman who withholds it, and thus set in motion a course of events that will, through suffering, lead to the king's acquisition of wisdom.[44] All of this is apparently lost on the narrator, who sees Bahrām's exploits in purely pragmatic terms.

The inadequacy of the narrator's response to the events he reports, his tendency to oversimplify and his literalness become even more obvious from his proverblike comment on Bahrām's anger at Fitnah (a fine example of "*sententiae*-making"):

When bent on vengeance, kings should wait:
slay only when in better state:
Else they 'gainst young gazelles would ride,
and make their fur coats from dogs' hide.[45]
(*HP*, 25:42–43)

This warning against hasty action on the part of kings echoes a point much stressed in mirrors for princes, and it might seem that the narrator intends to criticize Bahrām's action; but, as the ensuing line makes clear, it is not the justice of his act that is at issue, but its propriety. Bahrām's own observation that "brave heroes cannot slaughter women-folk" (25:46), coming hard on the heels of the narrator's comment, is so like it that the two are revealed to be of a kind, emanating from the same

[44] The figurative sense of *kabāb*, "roast meat," is that of suffering in love; it is a poetic commonplace to describe the lover's heart as "roasted" by love's flames, his sighs rising like smoke, and he himself becoming "well done" (*pukhtah*, "cooked"), i.e., mature, through this suffering. The verb used with "striking fire," *angīkhtan*, is also used in constructs with the sense of provoking or instigating a chain of events (specifically a revolt or sedition), as in the construct *fitnah angīkhtan*, a usage certainly not lost on the reader of Niẓāmī's poem.

[45] For line 44 I prefer the variant reading in the edition of Vaḥīd Dastgirdī (*Haft Paykar*, p. 110).

moral perspective: no more do heroes slay women than they ride to hunt young gazelles, or make *pūstīns* from dog skins. The passage establishes an identity between the values by which the king judges Fitnah and those of the narrator: both assume that Bahrām is in the right and that he has (by delegating responsibility for the actual execution) observed the proprieties of kingly conduct.

A final revealing comment occurs in the second portion of the episode, in which Fitnah performs an amazing feat of strength in order to teach Bahrām a lesson. Describing Bahrām's amazement at this feat, the narrator observes:

> He stood amazed: what might this mean?
> some gain?—yet he knew not *what* gain.
>
> (*HP*, 26:64)

The imputation of ignorance to the king suggests that the narrator knows what will turn to Bahrām's gain. There follow, in rapid succession, the king's recognition of Fitnah and their reconciliation, his apology, Fitnah's explanation (her seeming taunt was motivated by the desire to avert the evil eye), and their wedding. Fitnah is forgiven and restored to favor, and the king and his bride live happily ever after. The gain seems to lie in the happy conclusion of the affair and thus is purely pragmatic: a wrong has been righted, the basis for the confusion has been cleared up, the lives of those involved resume their normal course. Its true nature, however, proves to be more complex than the narrator, with his essentially materialistic viewpoint, can perceive; for the full meaning of Bahrām's gain from this experience does not depend on this episode alone.[46] It is, however, incomprehensible to the narrator of the episode in any but the most concrete sense.

The narratorial persona that emerges from this episode can be seen as the embodiment of the didactic stance characteristic of the authors of mirrors for princes. As we shall see in the next

[46] Dastgirdī equates the unrecognized "gain" (*sūd*) with Fitnah herself (ibid., p. 118 n. 2). The motif of gain is part of an important group of motifs that recur throughout the poem; the final gain achieved by Bahrām is his acquisition of wisdom and accession to spiritual kingship (see chapter 5).

chapter, Niẓāmī intended that the *Haft Paykar* be read, on one level, as a princely mirror; he also intended—as is clear from both his treatment of his sources and the career of his royal protagonist—that it transcend the limitations of both such works and the epic tradition from which he took much of his *matière*. The naive and unreliable narrator of the Fitnah episode, with his pragmatic orientation and his mundane morality, exemplifies the limitations of the mirror genre; his moral alignment with Bahrām also exemplifies the similar limitations of the heroic ethos of epic. This narratorial voice, distinct from that of the poet (as heard in the prologue and epilogue), acquires the status of another character, providing yet another perspective on the action in the poem.[47]

Character is thus a means not only for the presentation but

[47] Niẓāmī's fictional narrator may be compared to the notorious "unreliable narrator" of Chaucer's *Troilus* (cf. Huppé, "The Unlikely Narrator"). Robert M. Jordan's comment on the relation of narrator to story in this work is instructive: "The goal of the poem's movement is a level of perception from which the narrator—who has always represented the 'reality' from which we viewed the Trojan fiction—is ultimately to be seen not as a historian, not as a commentator, a master of recalled events, but as a dupe of time, a sham authority—in sum, a mortal" (*Chaucer*, p. 96). Niẓāmī's narrator is similarly rooted in reality (as well as limited by the generic stances he represents); a dominant theme of the *Haft Paykar* is the deceptive nature of appearances, the distinction between *visibilia* and truth. As Huppé comments on the *Troilus* narrator, "The apparent contradiction of narrative voices [along with other ambiguities and contrasts] are too interwoven, too omnipresent, not to be part of a design. Perhaps the fact of the narrator as character, however ambivalent, may provide the clue to Chaucer's strategy of design" ("The Unlikely Narrator," p. 191). As D. H. Green observes concerning the strategy of the naive narrator, "The rhetorical purpose of this naivete . . . is to prompt the audience to react against it and adopt what has been the poet's critical attitude all along" (*Irony in the Medieval Romance*, p. 221; see also pp. 213–49 for an extensive treatment of the topic and the contrast between romance and epic narratorial strategies). For a further discussion of the narratorial persona in medieval poetry, with particular reference to authorial prefaces and in the general context of artistic self-representation in literature and the other arts, see Martin Stevens, "The Performing Self in Twelfth-Century Culture," *Viator* 9 (1978), 193–212; and see also Linda Parshall, *The Art of Narration in Wolfram's Parzival and Albrecht's Jüngerer titurel*, pp. 116–220, for an illuminating comparison of the narratorial stances employed in those works.

for the interpretation of the events of the poem, a means by which the issues with which the poet is concerned are defined and through which their ambiguities are explored. The genre of romance "by its very nature favours variety rather than consistency";[48] such variety is perhaps seen to best effect in the multiplicity of perspectives and the fact that no final explicit statement is made as to which may be right or wrong.

> The [romance] poet is reporting the fact that characters perceive reality differently according to their personal situation or awareness; no evaluation is involved, but rather an observation of how difficult it is to make valuative assumptions, or determine what is really happening in the world, given the limited perceptions of individuals particularly placed at particular moments.[49]

This does not mean that the poet himself is not ideologically committed, or that his own final judgment remains obscure, but rather that he seeks, through his art, to show the problems that arise from conflicting values and codes and to demonstrate that many of these problems are perhaps insoluble. It is in this sense that the writer of romance becomes an allegorist (a mode not far removed from that of irony—and, indeed, medieval writers viewed the two as essentially akin), practicing "a mode well adapted to deal with man's epistemological dilemma" and accepting, as part of his poetic task, a "double responsibility: to re-fashion Paradise in imagination . . . and to provide a clue to the labyrinth of this world, where we are perplexed by hints, guesses, lights that go out, a language that continually betrays us."[50] It is this dimension of romance—its combined effort to illuminate life's labyrinth and to refashion Paradise—that will be explored in the following chapter.

[48] Vinaver, *Rise of Romance*, p. 32.

[49] Hanning, *Individual*, p. 174.

[50] Isabel MacCaffrey, *Spenser's Allegory*, p. 37.

· V ·

Romance as Mirror: Allegories of Kingship and Justice

MORE than any other genre of courtly poetry, the verse romance deals with the specific ethical concerns—both immediate and far-reaching—that were shared by the poet and his audience. One of the most pressing of such concerns was without doubt the question of kingship. The proliferation of mirrors for princes during the period in which Persian romance flourished (from the advent of the Saljuqs to the Mongol invasion) testifies to the widespread interest not only in establishing the practical ethics of kingly conduct, but in defining the nature of kingship and the qualifications of the ideal sovereign.[1] It is scarcely surprising to find this preoccupation shared by writers of romance and to discern in their works, as an inseparable dimension of their didactic concerns, much that bears directly on this issue.

> Who is the king? On a conscious level for medieval men, the king is the man ordained to keep peace and render justice, to further the earthly happiness of his subjects. He is also the man ordained to defend and strengthen the faith, to help his subjects gain eternal bliss. On a slightly less conscious level, the king is the man whose life subsumes the experiences of his nation, making its victories

[1] In this respect the Saljuq period resembles the early Abbasid: both are marked by a preoccupation with ethics (and particularly those of kingship and government), by the proliferation of other genres, which exist in a complementary relationship with the *qaṣīdah*, and by a general florescence of the arts. On Saljuq mirrors for princes, see F.R.C. Bagley's introduction to his translation of al-Ghazzālī's *Nasīḥat al-Mulūk* (*Book of Counsel*, pp. xiii–xvi); Lambton, "Mirrors," 424–38, and idem, *State and Government in Medieval Islam*, pp. 106–29.

and sufferings his own and enabling his people to sense these all the more keenly in his person.[2]

The concept of kingship reflected in the work that is the subject of these remarks (the twelfth-century Middle High German *Kaiserchronik*) is shared by medieval Islam. The king is expected to maintain justice and prosperity through pursuing peace, to uphold religion, and to provide a moral exemplar for his subjects; for, as al-Ghazzālī observes, "Sages have said that the character of subjects springs from the character of kings; for the common people and the royal officials and troops become good or bad through the instrumentality of their kings inasmuch as they acquire their habits from them."[3] The prin-

[2] Henry A. Myers, "The Concept of Kingship in the 'Book of Emperors' ('Kaiserchronik')," *Traditio* 27 (1971), 205. The twelfth-century *Kaiserchronik* resembles the nearly contemporary *Rāḥat al-Ṣudūr* (1202–1203) of Muḥammad ibn ʿAlī Rāvandī in constituting not a factual but an exemplary history designed "to show what true kingship is" (ibid., 206). While purporting to trace the fortunes of the Saljuq dynasty, Rāvandī in practice limits himself to selecting exemplary events characterizing each reign and adds many "digressions" on the nature of kingship and justice. He also employs poetic quotations (including many from Niẓāmī, chiefly from *Khusraw u Shīrīn* but also from *Laylī u Majnūn*) to illustrate the principles of kingship adumbrated by the work as a whole, the usage of which, as authoritative statements, demonstrates the close relationship of poetry and ethics and sheds light on the contemporary reception of romance. For a study of the exemplary nature of Islamicate historical writing in connection with Bayhaqī's *History*, see Marilyn R. Waldman, *Toward a Theory of Historical Narrative*, especially pp. 1–25, 121–42. Waldman stresses the importance of analogical reading, especially of the interpolated poetic and story material, in interpreting this work, and calls attention to the author's "direct exhortation for wise men to think analogically" in connection with "two lines of poetry on the inconstancy of lovers" which should be "understood [as] analogous to the situation between Amīr Muḥammad [of Ghaznah, r. 1030; deposed by his brother Masʿūd I] and his followers" (pp. 73–74; see *Tārīkh-i Bayhaqī*, pp. 76–77).

[3] Al-Ghazzālī, *Book of Counsel*, p. 60. The King's assumption of the experience of the people is exemplified in the *Haft Paykar* by the account of the famine that directly precedes the Fitnah episode. After several years of prosperous rule Bahrām's kingdom is visited by a four-year famine, which is relieved by his generosity in opening the royal granaries to provide the people with sustenance. So great was his liberality that only one soul died in the famine; and so intense was his grief at this single death that, by decree, his domains

ciple "that good men are good through the instrumentality of kings and that the conduct of mankind varies with their conduct"[4] extends the sense of the king as embodiment of the experience of his nation to encompass the moral character of that nation as a whole; it thus reflects the concept of man as microcosm and as mediator between upper and lower levels of creation, and the special place of the monarch in this system of correspondences, as the Perfect Man of the age.[5]

Three of the romances dealt with in this study—*Vīs u Rāmīn, Khusraw u Shīrīn*, and the *Haft Paykar*—directly address the matter of kingship. All three do so in the context of the love quest; but there is a clear progression from the first, where love is the predominant element, through the second, where love and kingship are more or less in balance, to the third, where kingship is the chief preoccupation.[6] In all three, the protagonist's conduct as lover reveals his fitness, or unfitness, for kingship; this aspect of his qualitative, or ethical, identity depends directly on his capacity to be guided by love and to understand its nature correctly as encompassing, not merely private passion, but public order. All three romances explore (as does, in a more generalized context, *Laylī u Majnūn*) the relationship between love and justice, and specif-

---

were granted a four-year reprieve from death (*HP*, 24:1–30). "It would seem that God, His saints, and His angels generally are more touched by suffering in the king's person and more moved by the king's prayers than by those of the people at large"; moreover, "there is only a thin line between the king whose prayers are answered with miraculous alacrity and the king whose person has magic power" (Myers, " 'Kaiserchronik,' " 223–24)—suggested, in Bahrām's case, by the reprieve from death.

[4] Al-Ghazzālī, *Book of Counsel*, p. 62.

[5] On the Perfect Man, see Nasr, *Introduction*, pp. 66–70; Naṣīr al-Dīn Ṭūsī, *Nasirean Ethics*, pp. 52-63; *EI*[2], s.v. "al-Insān al-kāmil", and see note 64.

[6] A progressive concern with kingship is likewise seen in the romances of Niẓāmī, as he moves from the portrait of the king as lover in *Khusraw u Shīrīn* and the depiction of Bahrām's progress to perfect kingship through love in the *Haft Paykar* to the detailed account of the two aspects of kingship—temporal and spiritual—in the portrayal of Alexander in the two books of the *Iskandarnāmah*, the *Sharafnāmah* and the *Iqbālnāmah* (cf. Rypka, "Poets and Prose Writers," p. 583).

ically the role of love as the source of that wisdom which leads both to justice and to universal harmony.

In the broadest terms, *Vīs u Rāmīn* is an account of the replacement of one sovereign by another. The true outcome of the rivalry between Mawbad and Rāmīn is not the latter's physical possession of Vīs, which occurs early in the poem, but his accession to the throne; his conquest of Vīs as woman anticipates his possession of her as queen—and his replacement of Mawbad as both husband and king—while at the same time it sets in motion a series of events that finds its resolution only when he has overcome the negative aspects of his love. These aspects are figured by the adulterous nature of the liaison but go beyond the fact of adultery to its cause: Rāmīn's absorption in a succession of delusive self-images, first as courtly lover, and then as warrior. The crucial issue is thus not the conflict between the private values of love and the public values of society—each of which makes equally valid claims on the individual, so that the conflict becomes essentially unresolvable—but the separation of these values: the faulty conception of love as merely private and of the lover's goal as exclusive possession of the beloved. The lover must learn that love must lead to a goal beyond itself, to a wisdom and a happiness that transcend the personal, transient dimension of human experience, and that the immediate object of his desire is but a figure for the ultimate object of union.

The conduct of the love quest is initially determined by the protagonist's self-image, his assessment of his circumstantial identity, as well as of his desired one; his success or failure is determined by the extent to which this self-image corresponds, or fails to correspond, to the ideal and by the protagonist's ability to correct errors in his perception of this image. In their pursuit of Vīs, Mawbad and Rāmīn embody two distinct and opposing self-images: Mawbad acts in the fashion of a king seeking dominion, while Rāmīn adopts the stance of the long-suffering courtly lover. Mawbad's progress is marked by increasing violence and injustice in both the private and the public spheres, as his rage against the lovers leads to acts that threaten not only them, but the well-being of his kingdom; he thus appears increasingly unfit for kingship.

Mawbad's capacity for irrational and unjust acts is suggested in the poem's opening episode, when, as a young ruler, he seeks the hand of the queen Shahrū. When she declines, stressing the unsuitability of such a match (she is considerably older), he extracts her promise that should she ever bear a daughter, that daughter will be his in marriage. This is the first of several similar contracts; the second is the marriage contract of Vīs and Vīrū, the third and climactic one the lovers' oath of Vīs and Rāmīn—both founded, in contrast to the first, on the eminent suitability of the partners. The peculiar nature of this contract (and of its outcome, the ill-assorted "marriage of Spring and December") establishes Mawbad's nature as hasty, willful, and self-centered, qualities that cast doubt from the beginning on his fitness for sovereignty and that jar with the description of his prosperous rule with which the story begins.[7] Shahrū's breach of this unnatural contract is morally less reprehensible than is her subsequent delivery of Vīs in response to Mawbad's flattery and bribes; while Mawbad's insistence on its fulfillment points to a concern with the letter of justice, rather than its spirit. The three contracts point to a disparity between justice conceived of as socially legislated equity and as the result of love. While society's concept of justice may demand the fulfillment of any and all contracts, the problematic nature of these three suggests that loyalty, though a cardinal virtue, must be motivated by a higher principle; for not all oaths are just. That Mawbad is motivated by no such principle, but rather by self-interest alone, is shown by his violation of the marriage contract between Vīs and Vīrū and his initiation of the war in which Vīs's father is killed and he himself is forced to flee the field.[8]

[7] See *VR*, pp. 20–21; 8:19–33. Gurgānī's description of Mawbad's New Year celebration employs the garden motif to suggest the prosperity of his reign; it parallels the account of Rāmīn's triumphal entry into Marv.

[8] All three contracts are, in the last analysis, motivated by self-interest; moreover, Rāmīn violates his oath by his marriage to Gul. Only after he renounces self-interest to dedicate himself to love does he succeed.

The relation between violence and injustice is further illustrated in the crucial segment in which Rāmīn embarks on his career of knight-errantry, when the moral trajectory of his quest intersects with that of Mawbad. This negative equivalency is suggested when Rāmīn, having determined to renounce Vīs, comes to bid her farewell. Entering her presence, he seats himself on the king's throne, from which she angrily bids him, " 'Arise from the King's place! Since you are of lesser state, avoid the place of the great! For you to presume to sit in the King's place is as much as to seek his position. It is premature for you to seek this position; perhaps your demon has tempted you along this road' " (*VR*, p. 213; 73:17–21). Before he can become worthy of Mawbad's queen (and thereby of his throne), Rāmīn must move from the stage of loss represented by this segment to that of recovery.[9]

Rāmīn's loss is not merely of Vīs herself but of his claim to loverhood in both the true and "courtly" senses of the word. His decision is the result of the counsel of a sage, ironically named Bihgū ("Well-saying"), who reminds him, "You will be king one day and take in your grasp any desire you wish. . . . Why are you downcast? Why do you not redouble your joy and pleasure? You have youth and a royal throne; when these two are to hand, what more do you want?" (*VR*, p. 204; 70:4, 7–8). Bihgū reproaches Rāmīn for his lack of manliness: "They do not know anyone as rancorous [*bad-gamān*] as you in the world; they call you nothing but unchivalrous [*nā-javān-mard*]" (p. 207; 70:74). The peroration of his lengthy speech amounts to encouraging Rāmīn to equate himself with Mawbad:

> "You have enjoyed the desire of your heart from Vīs; have plucked the fruit from the branch of love. Even if you see her for a hundred years she will be the same. . . . If you seek you shall find a thousand superior to her in beauty and purity. How can you dissipate life and youth with one

[9] In the episode of the "substitute bride," when Mawbad, made suspicious by the substitution of the nurse for Vīs, raised an angry outcry, Rāmīn suggested his murder but was dissuaded by Vīs (*VR*, p. 155; 59:235–46).

woman in this profitless manner? If you take another lover, you will hold your bond to her as naught in your heart. . . . Seek out an abode for yourself in every quarter, seek out a silvery-bosomed beauty from every city. . . . Enjoy fortune and life; ever slake your desire of this world.

"How long will you sit thus in misery? . . . The time has come for you to seek your desire of youth; to quest for fame in banquet and battlefield; to bear in mind greatness and act upon an auspicious omen. You should now seek kingship, for you are worth no less. . . . Your companions seek sovereignty; you, sport and impurity. Your days of sport and play are past: how long will you go on galloping over the field of play? What demon is this that has cast a spell on your soul and thus made you quite feeble? You are in thrall to a sinister demon, not in obedience to the lord of the world."[10] (*VR*, pp. 207–208; 70:84–108).

Equating fitness for kingship with martial prowess, Bihgū correspondingly relegates love to the level of physical gratification, in other words, to the satisfaction of concupiscent passion. His vision of Rāmīn's "demon" as the immoderate pursuit of passion is diametrically opposed to that of Vīs, who sees

[10] Bihgū serves as spokesman for the "heroic" values admired by Mawbad and his court, as his advice to Rāmīn to be patient until he is king and can take what he wishes by force, and his accusation of "unchivalry," make clear. His viewpoint (though equally "courtly") is antithetical to that of the nurse, whose advice to Vīs that only love matters suggests "new," more refined values which, like the old, have their limitations. These two advisers represent two moral poles between which the lovers must establish a balance. The recurrent references to demons responsible for human aberration in *Vīs u Rāmīn* recall the view of the Ikhwān al-Ṣafā' that "the qualities and perfections belonging to the various levels of the hierarchy of being are not in any way 'subjective' or 'anthropomorphic,' but, being a part of their ontological status, are completely independent of the whims and fancies of the 'thoughts' of men. In the three kingdoms of mineral, plant, and animal, good and evil . . . souls are mixed independently of human will. The beautiful and good qualities of these kingdoms are manifestations of the good souls, while what is ugly is due to the evil souls, which the Ikhwān call 'satanic forces' (*shayāṭīn*)" (Nasr, *Introduction*, p. 69).

it as the immoderate pursuit of sovereignty. Of the two, her assessment is the more correct: Rāmīn will not prove himself fit for kingship until he proves himself fit for loverhood.

Rāmīn's new dedication to prowess figures his injustice, as lover, to Vīs; its climax is the final infidelity of his marriage to Gul. For both Mawbad and Rāmīn, violence becomes a symbolic projection of their frustration at failing to achieve fulfillment in love, which each interprets as exclusive physical possession of Vīs. In their pursuit of this goal, both Mawbad's aggressive stance and Rāmīn's courtly lovesickness prove inadequate, as each reflects a lack of moderation in their natures—a lack of moral balance emblematically represented by the Scales with the broken crossbeam. Rāmīn is initially obsessed with both the idea of love (much as was Majnūn) and its physical pleasures; his self-absorption enables him to practice any deceit to gain Vīs and to renounce her when he believes his honor besmirched by their affair. His lack of moderation is paralleled by Mawbad's alternating rages and pathetic pleas for reconciliation. Both (like Bihgū) conceive of love and kingship as pertaining to separate spheres of existence and fail to perceive their interrelationship and the necessity that both be governed by justice.

Rāmīn alone is able to overcome this error, when, in the midst of the storm, he is moved to repent his injustice to Vīs and to beg her forgiveness. Their reunion paves the way for a dramatic shift in the poem's focus from its concentration on the internal state of the lovers to the political consequences of their renewed dedication to love. Vīs assists her lover to enter Mawbad's castle secretly by night and to make off with the royal treasure; aided by Mawbad's disaffected nobles, he sets himself up in successful opposition to the king, whose reaction to the news betrays his persistence in error.

> When they brought the news to the camp the nobles did not pass the news to the King: for he was an ill-natured monarch, and there is no worse fault in kings than this! . . . For three days the secret remained hidden from him. . . . When he learned of it the world fell about his ears;

you would have sworn a Judgment Day had arrived for him. . . . [Debating what remedy to seek, he laments:] "My army is in feud against me, they will one and all choose Rāmīn as king. . . . He has appropriated all my treasure; I am impoverished and he rich. I neither enjoyed the treasure nor gave it away; but laid it up—all for him!"[11] (*VR*, p. 341; 100:1–15)

The treasure Mawbad has lost is not merely the royal hoard, or yet Vīs herself, but the legitimacy that possession of both symbolized. Mawbad, who saw warfare as a means of preserving his good name, and whose willful wars in pursuit of personal revenge have brought death and desolation upon the land, loses the support of both nobles and populace.[12] Ironi-

[11] The equation of Vīs with the king's treasure suggests that the prosperity of the kingdom depends on her, as does her association with the garden, i.e. fertility. By contrast, Mawbad expresses his loss in material (almost commercial) terms: he is "bankrupt" (*muflis*), having neither "eaten of that blessing" (the prosperity conferred by Vīs) nor shared it (100:15: *Nah khurdam ānhamah niʿmat nah dādam*). (*Niʿmat* has the further connotation of a divine gift that must be properly administered.) It is tempting, and perhaps not too farfetched, to see in the story of Vīs and Rāmīn echoes of an ancient myth that recounted the struggle for a feminine fertility genius (Rāmīn's name is derived from Rām, an ancient Iranian pastoral divinity [see *VR*, p. 102 n. 1], while Mawbad suggests a sacral figure perhaps associated with the other world). Compare the Welsh "Tristan fragment" in which (in a Celtic reprise of the Persephone myth) the two rivals for Esyllt, March and Trystan, are commanded by King Arthur to share her: "And then Arthur adjudged her to the one when the leaves were on the trees, and to the other when there were no leaves on the trees, and that the husband should be allowed to choose. And he [March] chose the time when there would be no leaves on the trees because the night would be longest at that time" ("The Welsh Fragment of Tristan," trans. R. L. Thomson, in *The Tristan Legend*, ed. Joyce Hill, p. 4). The assumption of mythological antecedents for *Vīs u Rāmīn* seems borne out by the poem's astrological symbolism; cf. Hartner and Ettinghausen, "The Conquering Lion," 161–64. Such antecedents may account for the story's continued popularity (despite its apparent immorality) in later times, as well as for the need felt to rediscover its signification in terms of later preoccupations.

[12] On war and its causes, Naṣīr al-Dīn Ṭūsī states: "The utmost efforts should be made to win over enemies and to seek agreement with them, and matters should be so ordered . . . that the need for fighting and warfare does not arise. If such need does befall . . . either one begins (hostilities) or one is the

cally, it is neither in battle nor at the hand of Rāmīn that Mawbad meets his end; on the morn of the anticipated final combat, he is gored to death by a wild boar that suddenly rushes into the camp, against which he is unable to protect himself (*VR*, p. 343; 101:120–40).[13] His death exemplifies both his own moral impotence (in battle, against the boar; in love, with Vīs) and the rightness of Rāmīn's claim, the justice of whose accession is emblematized by the description of his triumphal entry into the city of Marv, which recapitulates the motif of the garden-state.

> When King Rāmīn entered choice Marv he saw a Paradise with decorations massed in it; in beauty like the blossom of Nourūz on the trees; in fairness like the fortune of the lucky, the nightingale of a thousand strains playing the lute with its melodies; the blossoms the garments of the fair. Above hung a cloud of smoke from musk and ambergris, silver, gold, and gems raining from it. The decorations that had been put up remained for three months; people scattered down jewels from them day and night. Not only did choice Marv take part in these rejoicings; the whole of Khurāsān was even thus. For years people had suffered tribulation at the hand of Moubad; after his death they gained ease. Once they had escaped from his injustice they rejoiced in the justice of King Rāmīn. You would have sworn they had escaped quite from Hell and now sat in the shade of the Tuba tree. Ill fortune is the end

---

defender. In the former case, the first requirement is that one's purpose shall be only Pure Good and the quest of the Faith, and that one is on guard against any seeking after superiority or domination" (*Nasirean Ethics*, p. 235). Compare Christine de Pisan's distinction between lawful and willful war in the *Book of Fayttes of Arms and of Chyualrye*, and the parallels in the *Morte Arthure*: Arthur's reverse progress from lawful to willful kingship is expressed through the nature of his wars—the first a lawful one against oppression, the last a war of aggression—in much the same way as is Mawbad's declining fortune (see John Finlayson, "The Concept of the Hero in 'Morte Arthure,' " in *Chaucer und seine Zeit*, ed. A. Esch, pp. 249–74).

[13] As Morrison points out, there is a striking parallel between this event and Marjodoc's dream in the *Tristan* of Gottfried, in which a boar enters Mark's bedchamber and fouls his bed (*VR*, p. 345 n. 1).

> of the bad; their name remains eternally accursed. Neither perform nor meditate evil in the world; for if you do evil, evil shall be requited. How truly spoke Khosrou to the treasurers: "God created the evil out of Hell. In the end he will return them to the selfsame matter from which he created them in the beginning." (*VR*, pp. 345–46; 102:42–54)

The lovers' triumph, despite the moral negative of their adultery, involves a translation of the principles by which they learn to govern their private relationship to the public sphere. It also reflects a perceived discrepancy between appearance and reality: Mawbad, in appearance a prosperous sovereign, is morally unfit to rule; the apparently immoral adulterers are found to possess true virtue. While this is demonstrated in the context of love, the principle of justice provides a link between love and kingship, as is made clear through the shift in the action from personal to political. The poet's exhortation, "Neither perform nor meditate evil in the world," together with the *sententia* that follows the death of Rāmīn—"Happy is he whose end is good, happy he who leaves behind a good name!" (*VR*, p. 351; 104:409)—recalls his announcement of the poem as "sage advice" and suggests that the specific addressee of this advice is the patron, for whom this piece of exemplary fiction may serve as a reminder that injustice will not thrive and that a good name depends on more than power, wealth or prowess.[14]

[14] The entire passage is instructive as to Gurgānī's purpose: "Happy is the man who takes [the Lord] as a friend and reckons all things on the basis of carrying out his behest! Happy he whose end is good, happy he who leaves behind a good name! Even as we glean tidings of those who have passed away, tomorrow perforce they [i.e., others] shall glean tidings of us. We who have sought reports shall ourselves become a mere report; we who have spoken idle words shall become mere idle words. They shall tell of us in the world as we have told the tale of Vīs and Rāmīn" (*VR*, pp. 351–52; 104: 48–53). Morrison's translation alters the sense of these lines: the "they" of 51b (*zi mā fardā khabar gīrand nāchār*) clearly means "those who will come after us"; no "mere" precedes "report" in 52a (*Khabar gardīm u mā būdah khabar-jūy*); and *samar* in 52b (*samar gardīm u khvad būd samar-gūy*) is not used here in the sense of "idle talk" but to mean an exemplary fiction (as in ʿAyyūqī's pro-

Gurgānī's romance illustrates the principle voiced by his contemporary al-Fārābī, at the other end of the Islamic world, that "justice follows upon love."[15] Naṣīr al-Dīn Ṭūsī, who defined love as "the quest for nobility and virtue and perfection," asserts the natural superiority of love over justice on the grounds that

> Justice requires artificial union, whereas Love requires natural union; at the same time, the artificial in relation to the natural is like an outer skin, the artificial imitating the natural. . . . It is obvious that the need for Justice . . . in preserving the order of the species, arises from the loss of Love; for if Love were to accrue between individuals, there would be no necessity for equity and impartiality.

Equity, Naṣīr al-Dīn reminds us, is an equal division of a disputed object, and thus a cause of multiplicity; whereas love is a cause of union, thus ethically preferable.[16]

Vīs u Rāmīn illustrates the error of equating justice with mere equity, and hence with multiplicity. As the figure of the

---

logue to *Varqah u Gulshāh*; see chapter 3, n. 19). The effect of the translation is to make Gurgānī condemn his own effort, whereas he sees its purpose as inspiring his patron to virtue and thus ensuring his lasting fame as an exemplar of good rule.

[15] Al-Fārābī, *Fuṣūl al-Madanī*, p. 53. Al-Fārābī's remarks on "voluntary love," though addressed to the relations between inhabitants of a city, apply by analogy to private relationships as well: love, which unites the city's members, may be natural, or willed, "its beginning being in voluntary things followed by love. Voluntary love comes in three ways: (*a*) by sharing in virtue; (*b*) on account of advantage; and (*c*) on account of pleasure." Sharing in virtue "is connected with thoughts and actions" concerning "the beginning" (the accepted doctrinal beliefs and moral principles of the community), "the end," which is happiness, and "what lies between," i.e., "the actions by which happiness is attained. . . . When the opinions of the inhabitants of the city are agreed on these things, and that [agreement] has been completed by the actions by which happiness is mutually attained, there follows mutual love, of necessity." True love between Vīs and Rāmīn follows their agreement on the nature and demands of love and is not to be equated with their earlier concupiscent passion, which is merely its accidental cause (a "voluntary love" engaged in "on account of pleasure").

[16] Naṣīr al-Dīn Ṭūsī, *Nasirean Ethics*, p. 196. Al-Fārābī considers equity "a species of the more general justice" (*Fuṣūl al-Madanī*, p. 55).

Scales suggests, there can be no justice in an equitable division of the disputed object, Vīs; such equity would be a mockery of both justice and love. Love demands a choice; as Shīrīn reminded Khusraw, it does not admit divided loyalties; yet it must, paradoxically, transcend the limitations of private passion to encompass the individual's public life as well. Vīs and Rāmīn become at last able to distinguish love from the mere concupiscence with which it is equated by both Mawbad and Bihgū. By contrast, Khusraw's attempt to achieve equity—to divide his heart between his various attachments—results in calamity for both himself and his beloved and leads to his failure not merely as lover, but as king.

As was the case in *Vīs u Rāmīn*, an early and crucial episode in *Khusraw u Shīrīn* establishes the protagonist's character. This is the bathing scene, in which Shīrīn's naked beauty and the inner purity that it reflects contrast with Khusraw's external disguise and interior duplicity. Niẓāmī's relative neglect of Khusraw's kingly activities is not merely due to his wish to emphasize the love story; the depiction of Khusraw as a seeker of pleasure, a pursuer of the delights of the flesh who would not willingly let pass an opportunity for self-indulgence, underscores his unsuitability for the role of king.[17] The just war against the usurper Bahrām Chūbīn is of less interest to him than are his attempts to seduce Shīrīn (whom he characteristically blames for "distracting" him from his duty, after she recalls him to it); his other pastimes during his sojourn in Armenia—notably the polo game at which he is unable to best Shīrīn and her ladies (we may recall a parallel episode in *Vīs u Rāmīn*)—further reveal his pleasure-seeking nature and his somewhat cavalier attitude to both love and kingship.[18]

[17] Massé observes that Khusraw "shows himself to be frivolous, pleasure-seeking, and a liberal drinker, thus fairly mediocre . . . but he redeems himself by the tones of sincere passion which Niẓāmī assigns to him, and he finally moves the reader by his noble acceptance of his tragic fate" (*Chosroës et Chîrîn*, pp. 11–12). Khusraw's pleasure-seeking nature is neither "fairly mediocre" nor morally reprehensible, but it is excessive and uncontrolled (compare the example of another pleasure-loving king, Bahrām Gūr in the *Haft Paykar*); his inability to master his appetites is figured by his habitual drunkenness.

[18] *KS*, pp. 121–25; the polo game in *Vīs u Rāmīn* is discussed in chapter 3.

In both spheres, Khusraw's conduct is governed by will rather than by law—a distinction emphasized more explicitly in the later romance of the *Haft Paykar*.[19] His willful nature and unthinking capacity for injustice are demonstrated in an early episode in which, as a young prince, his drunken feasting in a village causes loss and deprivation to the unfortunate villagers.[20] His lack of concern for the welfare of others—a quality not outgrown as he matures—characterizes both his kingship (as his treatment of Farhād demonstrates) and his conduct of love.

The potential duplicity of language is a major theme of the poem, reflected in its reliance on discourse, and specifically on dialogue, rather than on action. Khusraw's original infatuation with Shīrīn (with whom he falls in love on hearing her description) testifies to his willingness to use and interpret words

[19] On the distinction between kingship by will and kingship by law, see n. 34. Niẓāmī's portrayal of Khusraw departs from those of the historical sources and of the *Shāhnāmah*; in the latter, he appears as a victorious ruler who, after making his realm secure from aggression, inexplicably and without apparent motive turns from just to unjust role and thus precipitates his downfall. Compare the treatment in the *Kaiserchronik* of the Byzantine emperor Justinian, historically famous as a lawgiver, but there portrayed as the prototype of the unjust ruler. The parallel with Khusraw is marked: "The typical bad ruler ignores the law and either rules by capricious whim or is so wrapped up in the temptations of palace life that he scarcely rules at all. . . . Justinian, the great Lawgiver, is incompatible with the author's Justinian, the near tyrant, and so Justinian is not the great Lawgiver at all; what worldly success he does have is the result of the perceptiveness and resourcefulness of his queen" (Myers, " 'Kaiserchronik,' " 213.)

[20] Khusraw, tired from the hunt, stops in a village to rest and make merry; his horses devour the crops, his music disturbs the villagers, and his servant steals the harvest of green grapes (*ghūrah*). When his father, King Hurmūz, is informed, he makes compensation by disbanding Khusraw's stable, bestowing his servant on the villager he robbed, restoring the ravaged fields, giving Khusraw's richly carpeted seat to the owner of the house wherein he held his feast, and dismantling his elegant lute, the sound of which had troubled the ears of those not the prince's familiars (*nā-maḥram*). Khusraw humbles himself before the king and begs forgiveness on the grounds of his youth and inexperience; irony is brought to the episode when the same courtiers who advised the king to punish his son severely (blood should not stand in the way of justice) also plead with him to forgive Khusraw (blood demands compassion), thus anticipating the conflict between Khusraw and Buzurg-Ummīd over the fate of Shīrūyah (*KS*, pp. 43–45; cf. n. 24).

(as well as natural events) to his own advantage.[21] The focus of such interpretations is always himself; thus, for example, when he questions Farhād as to the nature of his feelings for Shīrīn, he cannot understand Farhād's answers in the sense in which they are intended but projects his own interpretation on them, equating Farhād's pure love with his own concupiscent passion. The poem's many passages of dialogue stress the inadequacy of verbal expression, as the parties involved most often speak at cross-purposes and fail to communicate at all. This failure of communication encompasses Khusraw's willingness (as king) to accept bad counsel rather than good, preferring what serves his interests rather than what is just.[22]

Thus, though Khusraw's passion for Shīrīn may be "sincere," in the sense that it is intensely felt, he woos her in accordance with his own misinterpretation of its goal, mistaking *havas* for *ʿishq*. Khusraw seeks, not lawful union in marriage,

[21] Shāpūr's description of Shīrīn is a rhetorical *descriptio* delivered as part of a tale of marvels, told during a gathering devoted to the recounting of exemplary narratives which follows Khusraw's dream of his ancestor, Khusraw Anūshīrvān (see n. 23). This dream so preoccupies him that he is unable to rest ("Both day and night his tongue was stilled; his ear / the words of that ancestral shade did hear. // Nightly he wakeful gathered with wise men / to ask, and tell, instructive tales with them" [*KS*, p. 48]). Khusraw takes this account to heart, dwelling day and night on Shāpūr's tale (designated as *ḥikāyat, afsānah, dāstān* [*KS*, p. 54]). As an exemplary account, it should inspire him to pursue virtue; that he will fall short of this expectation is anticipated when he expresses his decision to win Shīrīn in typical fashion. Sending Shāpūr to find her, he tells him: "If she, like wax, impressionable prove, / go then, and set my seal upon her love. // But if her heart's of iron, stay not; return, / and say; let me not beat upon cold iron" (*KS*, p. 55). Khusraw's sending a substitute upon this errand (observing a protocol more proper to kingship than to the love quest) is the first in the series of equivocations regarding identity which mark the poem, while his disinclination to waste his time "beating upon cold iron" should Shīrīn prove intractable suggests the self-centered nature of his pursuit of her.

[22] The motif of bad counsel figures importantly in all the romances that deal with kingship. Both Mawbad and Khusraw exhibit a willingness to listen to bad counsel in preference to good, which arises from their preoccupation with their own interests. The motif is less in evidence in the narrative portion of the *Haft Paykar* but crucial in the tales, where, along with its corollary (failure to heed good advice), it supports one of the poem's central themes, the necessity for right guidance.

but immediate (even if illicit) gratification; he is motivated not by love, but by concupiscence. Like Rāmīn, Khusraw fancies himself as a courtly lover; but like Mawbad, he views Shīrīn's resistance as demeaning to his status not only as lover, but as king. He himself is less than loyal to his love; the infidelity in thought alone witnessed in the bathing scene anticipates the infidelity in deed represented by his wedding, first Maryam (both for reasons of political expediency and out of spite), and then Shakar (whom he pursues because of anger at Shīrīn's rebuff and out of his own unwillingness to deny himself any immediate gain). This capacity for easy and unthinking injustice, undesirable in a lover, is all the more so in a king.

Khusraw's final achievement of his heart's desire is marred by his recollection, at the peak of happiness, of mortality and mutability.

> When Tāqdīs, Bārbad, Shīrīn and Shabdīz
> all four adorned the royal king Parvīz,
> That long-gone dream of old he did recall,
> which caused his happy heart in ruin to fall.
> He knew that all from earth and water made,
> though prospering, at last in ruin is laid.
> The new moon, while it waxes, grows in light;
> when past the full, then wanes its lustre bright.
> The fruit tree, while the fruit is raw, grows tall;
> but when that's ripe, its leaves begin to fall.[23]
>
> (*KS*, p. 397)

[23] On Shīrīn's advice to Khusraw, see chapter 4, n. 23. The account of Khusraw's pursuit of knowledge parallels the scene in which he hears Shāpūr's description of Shīrīn—a scene that closely followed his dream of Khusraw Anūshīrvān, in which he was promised that the possessions of which he was deprived by Hurmūz's punishment—servant, banquet couch, horses, and lute—would be replaced by four far greater possessions: a beloved "sweeter" (*shīrīn-tar*) than any ever seen (to compensate for the "bitterness" of the loss of his grape-stealing servant); Tāqdīs, the throne of the kings of Iran (on which he is seated when he hears the account of Shakar; see *KS*, pp. 274–79); the marvelous horse Shabdīz (originally belonging to Shīrīn); and the minstrel Bārbad (his spokesman in his final arguments with Shīrīn [*KS*, pp. 47–48]). As is evident from the circumstances surrounding Khusraw's attainment or use of all four, their possession is fraught with moral ambiguities. Incited by this promise, and by the description of Shīrīn which seems to presage

It is this thought that moves him, on Shīrīn's advice, to the belated pursuit of wisdom rather than pleasure. His resulting decision to pass his declining years in pious observance in the fire temple (a final parallel with *Vīs u Rāmīn*) ironically leads to the doom his earlier unwisdom has made inevitable: his murder by Shīrūyah, who takes advantage of Khusraw's occupation in prayer to seize the kingdom and imprison the king, followed by the suicide of Shīrīn, who, like Farhād, becomes a martyr to love. Khusraw's brief span of just rule is thus brought to an end; the irony of this end is compounded by the fact that he was counseled by his minister Buzurg-Ummīd to be forbearing with Shīrūyah (whose nature showed itself early) in the hope that maturity would bring him wisdom.[24] In his last moments, Khusraw performs his first selfless and spontaneous act of concern for another, when, stabbed by a murderer who creeps in by night when king and queen are asleep, he wakes to find his life's blood draining away but refrains from waking Shīrīn for fear that she will be distressed beyond measure at his state.

> Thus he let slip his life, that loyal king,
> in bitterness, when he woke not Shīrīn.
>
> (*KS*, p. 418)

---

its early fulfillment, he begins his quest for what Shīrīn properly defines as the gratification of his own desires (*kāmrānī* [p. 398], an ironic use of a conventional epithet of panegyric denoting a fortunate ruler). Now that the four are his, he is reminded of their transient nature and his own mortality. His pursuit of wisdom includes a series of dialogues on philosophical questions and the recital of forty tales from the *Kalīlah wa-Dimnah* (parallelling the parables told by the ladies-in-waiting), each one summarized in a one-line moral (*nuktah*; see *KS*, pp. 406–10).

[24] The irony of Buzurg-Ummīd's advice concerning Shīrūyah is clear: though maturity may (as in Khusraw's own case) bring wisdom, if the quest for wisdom is delayed, events may be set in motion which cannot be altered. The fact that this is one instance in which Khusraw heeds what is supposedly good advice, rather than following his own judgment, adds further complexity to the situation. There is a marked parallel between Shīrūyah and Arthur's son Mordred in the Arthurian cycle, and particularly in the *Morte Arthure* (see Finlayson, "Concept of the Hero," p. 274 et passim): both represent the consequences of "sowing bad seed" and provide tangible evidence of moral error.

Between the account of Khusraw's death and that of Shīrīn's awakening, the poet has inserted a brief passage announced as a *tamsīl*, or parable.

> Regard the blooming rosebush, sunny-faced;
> its hope in the green world's constancy it's placed.
> A swift and drunken cloud arose instead,
> with sword in hand, the basil's blood to shed.
> The hail with such aggression did descend
> that from the rose nor branch nor leaf remained.
> The sleeping gardener, once awake, will see
> that neither rose nor rosegarden there be.
> Then say: why not, in mourning for the rose,
> weep sore; when roses fall, rosewater flows.
>
> (*KS*, p. 418)

In this analogical image, the king becomes the rose, the central figure in the garden of the state,[25] while Shīrīn is likened to the gardener who nourishes and cares for it. More than a pretty conceit, the rose emblematizes both kingship and the prosperity destined to elude both Khusraw and his kingdom, as well as the fertility that brings him only grief. The angry cloud blots out the sun, the royal basil's blood is spilled; there remains only to mourn for the lost promise of the garden.

In *Khusraw u Shīrīn*, as in *Vīs u Rāmīn* and the *Haft Paykar*, the process of *becoming* king in truth rather than merely *being* so in fact is of central importance. All three poems focus on the protagonist's success or failure in achieving the qualities that will make him king *de natura* rather than merely *de jure*. This is the larger implication of the love quest, its final goal (in terms, at least, of this world). Khusraw's failure as a lover figures his failure as a king; the qualities that mar his courtship of Shīrīn—willfulness, self-interest, and a mistaken and delusive self-image—ensure that he will sow the seeds of his own downfall. With the exception of the final brief period of his reign, Khusraw's kingship exemplifies kingship by will, and his gov-

[25] This analogy is central to the *ghazal* of Ḥāfiẓ (QG 81) discussed in chapter 6.

ernance is determined by caprice or expediency rather than by principle; his is the rule of might, rather than of law. Khusraw's qualitative identity thus proves to be other than either his natal or circumstantial identities would indicate and fatally delays the realization of his desired identity of successful lover and exemplary ruler. For Niẓāmī, as for Gurgānī before him, marriage provides the ultimate symbol of the success or failure of the lover's quest. Khusraw's delay in wedding Shīrīn, and his two "false marriages" to Maryam and Shakar, stress the importance of marriage as the only true union and suggest a criticism of courtly attitudes toward love as incapable of leading to true wisdom.[26]

If *Khusraw u Shīrīn* illustrates the failure of kingship when directed by will, the *Haft Paykar* affirms the possibility of transcending this state to that of kingship by law. The story of the

[26] Alfred Adler has defined the central topic of *Yvain* as "*love in marriage, and as the result of knowledge of oneself*" ("Sovereignty in Chrétien's *Yvain*," *PMLA* 62 [1947], 301; author's emphasis). Adler's analysis of Yvain's ethical progress shows illuminating parallels with both *Khusraw u Shīrīn* and the *Haft Paykar*. Yvain's first quest is motivated by *curiositas* ("the beginning of evil ways"); it amounts to "the seeking of a *mervoille*," as does Khusraw's initial suit for Shīrīn. "*Curiositas* breeds *superbia*," seen in Yvain's treatment of Esclados, which, like Khusraw's of Farhād, "is the picture of selfish pride. . . . To this bad attitude, corresponds love in its objectionable form, *cupiditas*, so much manifested by Yvain . . . that his undisciplined love for [Laudine] has long been thought to constitute the kernel of the romance. *Curiositas, superbia* and *cupiditas* cause dispair. The spiritual road upward starts with the recognition of the frailty of one's self, and of human nature in general, that is, by the recognition of man's state of *necessitas*. . . . [That is] the beginning of self-knowledge. . . . For the man who through self-knowledge has conquered his selfishness, the reward is *Amor Dei*. This love has its fulfillment equivalent to love in marriage" (ibid., 302–303). Rāmīn, Khusraw, and Bahrām Gūr in the *Haft Paykar* all dedicate their declining years to pious observance. On the relation of the virtues and vices, see Naṣīr al-Dīn Ṭūsī: "Corresponding to every virtue are two classes of vice, the virtue standing at the middle-point and the two vices at two extremes. . . . The classes of virtues are four; hence the classes of vices are eight. Two correspond to Wisdom, namely Ingenuity and Foolishness; two correspond to Courage, namely Foolhardiness and Cowardice; two to Continence, namely Greed and Sluggishness of Appetite; and two correspond to Justice, namely Injustice and the Suffering of Wrong." Ingenuity (analogous to *curiositas*) "is the use of the reflective faculty on what is not obligatory or beyond the obligatory extent" (*Nasirean Ethics*, pp. 86–87). It is this vice that initiates the quests of both Khusraw and Yvain.

Sassanian king Bahrām V, the depiction of his progress to become, in all senses, the perfect sovereign, provides a commentary on courtly values—in particular those of mirror literature and of epic—and presents a vision of kingship that transcends the limitations of both.

The romance constitutes, on one level of interpretation, an allegorical mirror for princes in verse. In his prologue Niẓāmī recounts the circumstances leading to its composition. He was commissioned by the Ahmadili ruler of Maraghah, ʿAlā' al-Dīn Körp-Arslān, to write a poem that would be a masterpiece of eloquence, beyond the understanding of ordinary people.[27] Whether the poet himself selected the subject of his poem, or whether it was suggested by his patron, is unstated; but its specific topic is kingship. Niẓāmī's intent to provide instruction in the principles of just rule is expressed in a passage in which, praising his royal patron, he states:

Four kings four royal jewels have owned;
and you the fifth—your life be long!
Much wisdom Alexander bore
from Aristotle's precious store.
Nūshīrvān's feast with heaven vied,
since Buzurjmihr his earth did stride.
Parvīz a Bārbad had, whose airs
a hundred—nay, a thousand were.
That great king, Malikshāh by name,
had his Niẓām, of pious fame.
But you, whose crown far greater be,
have such a poet as Niẓāmī.

(*HP*, 6:35–40)

Niẓāmī presents himself as fifth in a series of illustrious advisers to princes and authors of courtly mirrors: Aristotle, whose letters to Alexander the Great on matters of kingly con-

[27] See *HP*, 4:1–16. The wished-for poem, like the crescent moon that appears on the eve of the new lunar month (here *shab-i ʿīd*, i.e., ʿĪd al-Fiṭr, marking the end of the Ramaḍān fast) should be "So slim a moon, that not an eye / shall it through darkness' veil descry" (4:4). *Bārīk*, "slender," has the metaphorical sense of abstruse or difficult meaning. On Niẓāmī's patron, see *CHI*, 5:171, and *EI*², s.v. "Aḥmadīl."

duct were well known in their Arabic version of the *Sirr al-Asrār* long before the medieval Latin translations; Buzurgmihr, minister of the Sassanian emperor Khusraw I Anūshīrvān "the Just" (r. 531–579), to whom was attributed a work preserved in Arabic known as the *Ethics of Buzurgmihr* (*Ādāb Buzurjmihr*); Bārbad, the famed poet-minstrel of Khusraw Parvīz; and Niẓām al-Mulk, minister to the Saljuq king Malikshāh, Niẓāmī's predecessor by some hundred years, and author of the famous *Siyāsatnāmah* or *Book of Government*.[28] Niẓāmī clearly considered himself not only the heir to the tradition represented by his predecessors, but its continuator and culmination, uniting in himself their several attributes of poet, philosopher, and adviser to princes. But the *Haft Paykar* is more than a versified mirror for princes (just as it is more than the "light and charming" romantic poem it is often taken to be);[29] a deeply serious work, elegantly and painstakingly composed, it exemplifies allegorical romance at its peak, where every element contributes its multileveled meaning.

The full scope of Niẓāmī's intent is also revealed in the prologue, in the section entitled "In Praise of Discourse." After describing discourse as being like "a flawless spirit which guards the treasure-house of the unknown," and which "knows stories yet unheard, and reads books yet unwritten," the poet continues:

> Look round: of all that God has made,
> what else, save discourse, does not fade?

[28] On the letters attributed to Aristotle, the *Secretum Secretorum*, and their versions and reception East and West, see M. Manzalaoui, "The Pseudo-Aristotelian *Kitāb Sirr al-Asrār*: Facts and Problems," *Oriens* 23–24 (1974), 147–257; W. F. Ryan and C. B. Schmitt, eds., *Pseudo-Aristotle, The Secret of Secrets: Sources and Influences*; on the *Ādāb Buzurjmihr* (preserved in Miskawayh's *al-Ḥikmah al-khālidah [Jāvīdān khirad]*) see D. Gimaret, *Le livre de Bilawhar et Būḏāsf*, pp. 38–41; on Bārbad, see chapter 1, and especially the references cited in n. 7; on Niẓām al-Mulk, see Browne, *LHP*, 2:212–17, and *The Book of Government or Rules for Kings*, trans. H. Darke.

[29] Gabrieli's statement that the *Haft Paykar* "recounts the romantic adventures of the Sassanian ruler Bahrām Gūr" ("Versioni da Niẓāmī," *AION* 10 [1937–38], 33) is taken over almost verbatim by R. Levy (*The Persian Language*, p. 81); see also Marshall Hodgson's remarks quoted in chapter 4.

Strive, from the worlds of mineral,
plant, animal, and rational,
To learn what in creation lives
that to eternity survives?
He who his own self truly knows
triumphant over this life goes.
Who knows not his design must die;
but who can read it, lives for aye.

(*HP*, 3:5–10)

Self-knowledge is announced as the explicit goal of the quest that will be undertaken by the protagonist of this exemplary fiction, while discourse is the medium by means of which he, like the audience to whom the poem is addressed, may learn the nature of his own design.

The prologue to the *Haft Paykar* also contains Niẓāmī's most explicit statement on his relation to his sources, and specifically to Firdawsī. In *Khusraw u Shīrīn* he announced that he would tell the part of Khusraw's life that was as yet untreated—the love story; in the *Haft Paykar* he expands on this topic and declares that he will tell that which his predecessor left unsaid concerning the matter of kingship. Describing his search for material, he states:

I searched through books both fine and rare
for what would free the heart from care.
Whatever chronicles might say
of kings, that in books chosen lay,
An earlier poet, of keenest mind,
had ordered all in verse refined.
From it, some ruby chips remained,
shards from which others something feigned.
I, from those fragments, jeweller-wise,
this precious treasure cut to size,
So that the experts who assay
all efforts, *this* most worthy weigh.
That which was left by him half-said
I say; the half-pierced pearl *I* thread;
While that which I found right and true

just as before I've left to view.
I strove that this fair jointure, too,
should be adorned in foreign hue.
Again I sought, from books concealed
and scattered through the world's broad field;
From Persia's speech, and Araby's—
Bukhārī's pen, and Ṭabarī's—
From other texts, all scattered wide:
each pearl, in hiding, cast aside.
The pages which came to my hand
I wrapped in leather, tied with band.
When all was chosen, ordered well,
when 'neath my pen's black ink all fell,
A poem I wrote that would win praise,
and not the scholars' laughter raise.[30]

(*HP*, 4:18–32)

Besides providing a description of the poet's method (a topic to which I shall return in chapter 7), this passage—particularly the metaphorical assertion that he will "thread the half-pierced pearl"—suggests that Niẓāmī's approach to the matter of kingship will be not merely different from but more "true" than that of Firdawsī, boasting a spiritual dimension absent from the epic.

[30] The "shards" from which other poets had made something refers to the minor epics produced after the *Shāhnāmah* (see Molé, "L'épopée," 377–93). The poet refers to his work (or to the process of composing it) as a *tarkīb*, which I have rendered "jointure," as it is clearly analogous to Chrétien's *conjointure*. Cf. chapter 3, n. 20; and see further Douglas Kelly, "Theory of Composition in Medieval Narrative and Geoffrey of Vinsauf's *Poetria Nova*," *Medieval Studies* 31 (1969), especiall y 126–28, 140–43; idem, *Sens and Coinjointure in the Chevalier de la Charrette*, especially pp. 86–97; and Allen, *Ethical Poetic*, p. 184 et passim. On the association of *conjointure* with descriptions of well-wrought objects (analogous to descriptions of the poet's craft), see Freeman, *Poetics*, pp. 140–67; on metaphors of craft as descriptions of poetic art, see Jerome Clinton, "Esthetics By Implication," *Edebiyat* 4 (1979), 73–96; R. Hanning, "Poetic Emblems in Medieval Narrative Texts," in *Vernacular Poetics in the Middle Ages*, ed. Lois Ebin, pp. 1–32; and see also chapter 7. On Bahrām Gūr in historical and literary sources, see Mechthild Pantke, *Der Arabische Bahrām-Roman*.

Such authorial directives to the readers of Niẓāmī's poem are reinforced by its style and structure. Since questions of structure have received little attention here, I will focus on this aspect of the *Haft Paykar* as the key to its meaning. Framed by the prologue and epilogue, the body of the poem consists of two structurally distinct but interrelated parts: First, the narrative account of Bahrām's life, and second, a central interlude comprising the seven tales told by his brides, which divides the narrative into two unequal portions. The first and longest portion recounts the story of Bahrām's birth, his upbringing and education at the court of the Arab king Nuʿmān ibn Munẕir, his early prowess as a hunter (which achieves for him the epithet of Bahrām Gūr, "Bahrām of the Wild Ass," the onager being his favorite prey), his accession to the throne of Iran after establishing the legitimacy of his claim, and his marriage, after his victory in a war with China, to the Princesses of the Seven Climes, followed by a feast that takes place in winter in an indoor pleasure palace. Then follows the central interlude, in which Bahrām visits each princess in the dome he has had built for her, feasts, drinks, enjoys her favors, and listens to a tale. The narrative is resumed when Bahrām, emerging from the domes in spring to hold court in his royal pleasance, learns that his evil minister, in his absence, has abused his power and ravaged the kingdom, which is again threatened by war with China. Bahrām brings his minister to justice, reestablishes order, and successfully concludes the war. After a long and prosperous reign, he disappears into a mysterious cave from which his body is never recovered.[31]

[31] The poem's tripartite division evokes a variety of tripartite classifications in medieval ethical thought. The Ikhwān al-Ṣafā' categorized the three stages of knowledge of the self as being, first, observation of the body and its characteristics; second, observation of the soul and its qualities and faculties; and third, observation of the two in concert (see *RIS*, 2:379); in the *Haft Paykar*, the first stage is represented by action, the second by reflection, the third the two in combination; see also the remarks of Naṣīr al-Dīn Ṭūsī on the role of the speculative faculty, quoted in n. 34 to this chapter. The Ikhwān's "philosophic liturgy" (as described by Nasr) "took place three evenings each month, at the beginning, middle, and some time between the 25th and the end of the month. The liturgy of the first night consisted of personal oratory; that of the

Niẓāmī's retelling of the story of Bahrām Gūr focuses less on the king's emotional or erotic life than on his achievement of kingship; the poem thus partakes of the heroic mode, in that there is more emphasis on action than in Niẓāmī's previous works, yet his hero is still a hero of romance, whose subjective state is of greater importance than are his deeds of prowess. Bahrām (like the Arthur of the *Morte Arthure*) is that "combination of romantic hero, epic warrior and actual king" in whom "elements of all sorts are handled in such a way as to give complexity to the character [while] the material is arranged and proportioned so as to present the picture of a man of many traits, some individual, some typical, none of which is inconsistent with the guiding conception."[32]

Bahrām's progress involves his assertion, in successive segments, of his natal, circumstantial, and desired identities, which ultimately merge into the single identity of king.[33] The

---

second of a *cosmic text* read under the starry heavens facing the polar star; and that of the third night of a philosophical hymn (implying a metaphysical or metacosmic theme) which was a 'prayer of Plato,' 'supplication of Idris,' or 'the secret psalm of Aristotle.' There were also three great philosophical feasts during the year, at the time of entry of the sun into the signs of the Ram, Cancer, and Balance. The Ikhwān correlated these feasts with the Islamic feasts of *ʿīd al-fiṭr* at the end of Ramaḍān, *ʿīd al-aḍḥā*, the 10th of *Dhū'l-ḥijjah*, and the *ʿīd al-ghadīr* on the 18th of the same month, the date of the investiture of ʿAlī ibn Abī Ṭālib by the Prophet as his successor . . . which they made correspond to the fall feast. For the winter season, however, there was a long day of fasting instead, for the time when 'the seven sleepers are sleeping in the cave' " (*Introduction*, p. 35; author's emphasis). There is a further analogy with the structure of the universe (an analogy already applied to poetic structure by Sanāʾī in the *Sayr al-ʿibād*): "The three main divisions of [the universe]—viz. the material world, the astral world and the world of the universals—symbolize the three levels on which the human soul may be. The lowest level is that of the human soul which has not yet been able to free itself from the domination by the animal soul. As long as one has not moved upwards beyond this stage by gaining control of the lower passions, one has not really reached the level of human existence" (de Bruijn, *OPP*, p. 205). Each of these levels, moreover, has its own internal divisions.

32 Finlayson, "Concept of the Hero," p. 255.

33 The question of Bahrām's accession—when, his natal claim being deemed insufficient, he must prove his right to the throne in other ways—both foreshadows a central theme (the nature of true kingship) and contrasts with the

two portions of the narrative depict his attainment, successively, of kingship by will and kingship by law. The first is symbolized by the wedding to the seven princesses; here, at the pinnacle of success, Bahrām is, to all appearances, the perfect ruler. This judgment is rendered problematical, however, by the intervention of the tales, which constitute nearly half the poem; at their conclusion, and in view of the events that follow, we become aware that the true nature of kingship has yet to be defined.

Three distinct but interrelated structural patterns provide complementary ways of organizing events in the poem, in both narrative and tales, and of unifying its tripartite form (the account of Bahrām's life, divided into two unequal portions by the tales). Constituting different dispositions of space and time, these interacting patterns represent contrasting but mutually interdependent ways of perceiving the meaning of events. The first of these is the linear pattern of Bahrām's biographical movement through time, paralleled by his spiritual progress from ignorance to wisdom, and from the stage of kingship by will (temporal kingship) to that of kingship by law (spiritual kingship); it is mirrored by the progress from spiritual darkness to illumination, represented in the sequence of the seven tales.[34]

treatment of the topic in *Khusraw u Shīrīn*, where the insistence on hereditary succession culminated in the combined regicide-parricide committed by Shīrūyah.

[34] Bahrām's temporal wedding to the seven princesses, symbolizing his achievement of kingship by will, is paralleled by his spiritual wedding to the single principle of Justice in the second portion of the narrative. Islamic political thought recognized three kinds of kingship; as defined by Ibn al-Muqaffaʿ, "The first was that founded on religion; the second was based on the will to power and the third on personal desire." The first was considered best, the second acceptable but likely to meet with opposition, the third ephemeral (Lambton, *State and Government*, p. 55; cf. Finlayson, "Concept of the Hero," pp. 257–66, and the distinction between lawful and willful war discussed in n. 12). The distinction between willful and lawful kingship is considered in much mirror literature; cf. Lambton, "Mirrors," 424 and especially 426–36, discussing the *Baḥr al-Favāʾid*, in which work "kingship exercised in accordance with the *sharīʿa* is contrasted with kingship exercised in accordance with desire. The former was true happiness (*saʿādat*), while the latter was

The second pattern is that of alternance, which, in the narrative, takes the form of a loose but systematic alternation between two types of segment (which may contain one or more episodes), the first of which may be characterized by the rubric "adventure," the second by "kingship." Kingship episodes characteristically take place at court and involve public issues relating to the establishment and maintenance of social order: matters of statecraft, the adminstration of justice, and the conduct of war. Adventure episodes, by contrast, occur in natural settings, depict an action or encounter of a private nature, and typically lead to the discovery of something hitherto unknown. Adventure episodes are introduced by Bahrām's departure for the hunt, a pursuit that bears him far from the court and its restraints and protocols, transporting him into an area of uncharted, magical space in which anything can happen.[35] In the tales, the alternation is between the contrasting yet complementary moral faculties of concupiscence and irascibility as dominant motivating impulses for the action.[36]

---

tantamount to endless misery, and, moreover, very dangerous" (426–27). The dangers inherent in "kingship by desire" are well illustrated in the *Haft Paykar* by the successive Chinese invasions and by the abuses perpetrated by Bahrām's evil minister.

[35] The hunt functions both structurally, as a framing device separating adventure segments from the main narrative, and thematically, signaling the extraordinary nature of the events about to take place. On the importance of the hunt in medieval European literature, see M. Thiébaux, *The Stag of Love*, especially pp. 47 ff.; see also D. H. Green, "The Pathway to Adventure," *Viator* 8 (1977), 155–56, 185–87; W. L. Hanaway, Jr., "The Concept of the Hunt in Persian Literature," *Boston Museum Bulletin* 68 (1976), 21–34.

[36] Tales I, III, V, and VII depict actions motivated by concupiscence, II, IV and VI by irascibility. In Islamic ethics these faculties can motivate for either good or evil; the important point is that equilibrium be established between them. As to how this may be accomplished, Naṣīr al-Dīn Ṭūsī writes: "The student of virtue must first examine the state of the faculty of appetite, and then that of the faculty of irascibility, ascertaining whether either is naturally disposed in accord with the law of equilibrium or divergent therefrom. If it is in accord with the law of equilibrium, he must strive to preserve that equilibrium and to make habitual the procession therefrom of that which is fair relative to the faculty; if it be divergent from equilibrium, he must take steps first to restore it to equilibrium, and then to acquire the habit in question. When he is acquitted of the correction of these two faculties, he must occupy himself

The third ordering arrangement is the spatial pattern of the circle, which links a series of four analogical adventure episodes—two preceding and two following the central segment of the tales—identified by the repetition of a cluster of specific motifs whose constituent elements, while remaining functionally identical, undergo significant contextual variations. These four episodes represent increasingly more advanced stages in Bahrām's progress toward perfect kingship. In the first episode, Bahrām kills a dragon; the second is the story of Fitnah; the third recounts Bahrām's encounter with the shepherd; and the fourth, his final disappearance into the cave.

The following diagram illustrates the relationship between these patterns (K indicates "kingship" segments, A "adventure" segments).[37]

---

with perfecting the speculative faculty, observing (due) classification therein" (*Nasirean Ethics*, pp. 111–12). The tales, which exemplify divergences from equilibrium, assist Bahrām in perfecting his speculative faculty so that he may achieve it in himself.

[37] Further analogies with both spatial and numerical arrangements suggest themselves. The three patterns according to which events are disposed recall the classification of types of motion by the Ikhwān al-Ṣafā'. The sixth type, defined as "translation, or local movement (*naqlah*)—passage in space and time from one point to another" (which may be physical, *jismānī*, or spiritual, *rūḥānī*)—is itself divided into three types: straight (*mustaqīmah*), circular (*mustadīrah*), or a combination of the two (*murakkabah minhumā*) (see Nasr, *Introduction*, p. 66; *RIS*, 2:13–16). The biographical pattern of the narrative (the kingship episodes) provides linear movement; the chiastic arrangement of the four adventure episodes is, with respect to thematic motifs, circular (its intersection with the linear pattern provides a spiral movement; see n. 52); while the pattern of alternance between kingship and adventure episodes is a "combined" arrangement, reflecting as well a thematic alternation between appetite (adventure) and irascibility (kingship), as does the ordering of the tales. The organization of the four linked episodes recalls the fourfold classification of men into "ranks of perfection or deficiency . . . determined according to will and reason" described by Naṣīr al-Dīn Ṭūsī: according to their degree of perfection of these faculties, men are able to rise to "the highest of the ascending degrees of the human species," that is, the third stage, of persons who "by revelation and inspiration, receive knowledge of truths and laws from those brought close to divine majesty," and can proceed to the fourth: "And so to the limit, where is the abode of Unity, and there the circle of existence meets, like a curved line beginning from a point and returning to the same point" (*Nasirean Ethics*, p. 46). The Ikhwān al-Ṣafā' associated the four degrees of

Prologue (sections 1–8)

K(1) Bahrām's birth and childhood (9); building of Khavarnaq and disappearance of Nuʿmān (10–11); Bahrām's education and hunting (12–13)

A(1) Bahrām kills the dragon and finds the treasure in the cave (14); Bahrām sees the portraits of the Seven Princesses (15)

K(2) Death of Yazdigird (16); Bahrām's accession and reign (17–23); famine averted (24)

A(2) Bahrām and Fitnah (25–26)

K(3) First war with China and Bahrām's victory (27–28); Bahrām weds the Seven Princesses (29); Bahrām feasts in winter, building of the Seven Domes (30–31)

Bahrām sits in the Seven Domes and hears the tales told by the Princesses

I. Saturday/Saturn/Black (32)
II. Sunday/Sun/Yellow (33)
III. Monday/Moon/Green (34)
IV. Tuesday/Mars/Red (35)
V. Wednesday/Mercury/Blue (36)
VI. Thursday/Jupiter/Sandal (37)
VII. Friday/Venus/White (38)

K(3′) Spring: Bahrām celebrates the New Year and learns of the second war with China (39–40)

A(2′) Bahrām and the shepherd (41)

K(2′) Trial and punishment of the minister (42–50); apology of the Chinese ruler; Bahrām's wedding to Justice (51)

A(1′) Bahrām's disappearance into the cave (52)

K(1′) Homily on the transience of the world (52)

Epilogue (53)

---

perfection with the classes of craftsmen, religious and learned men and political chiefs, kings and sultans, and prophets and sages, and categorized their own membership accordingly (Nasr, *Introduction*, pp. 31–32; see *RIS*, 4:119–23). Four is also the essential number by which the categories of creation are subdivided (ibid., 1:229–32 et passim). In Pythagorean number symbolism, three and four are numbers of the cosmos (cf. Heninger, *TSH*, pp. 152–78 et passim). Numerical symmetries and symbolisms are seen in the division of the *Haft Paykar* into sections: the poem's culmination, Bahrām's marriage to Justice and his apotheosis, occurs in sections 51 and 52, making

That the two portions of the narrative exemplify the two types of kingship suggested is further established by other sets of analogous kingship episodes: for example, the two wars with China, resolved in markedly contrasting manners. In the first, Bahrām achieves military victory through a combination of ruse, strategy, and prowess and is able to defeat the Chinese in battle despite their vastly superior numbers; the second war is concluded when Bahrām receives an apology from the Chinese king, who withdraws his forces and sues for peace, having been drawn into the war through the scheming of Bahrām's evil minister who plotted to divide the kingdom between them. The implication is that the perfect ruler, guided by the light of justice, will have no need of force to preserve his claim, because his moral right will be universally acknowledged.

Such paired episodes, based on the repetition and variation of specific motifs (another instance is the building of Khavarnaq and of the seven domes), provide varied perspectives on the problems dealt with in the poem. With the presentation of similar actions, modified by developments and changes in space and time, "the appearance and meaning of external reality changes, and our understanding and apprehension develop and change progressively as well. This type of multiple perspective is a mimesis of the individual's learning process as it results from his interaction with earthly experience."[38] In the *Haft Paykar*, perhaps the most important in this array of shifting perspectives is the series of four adventure episodes the chiastic arrangement of which establishes the poem's circular pattern. Each episode represents a crucial moment in Bahrām's progress and redefines the journey on which he is engaged.

---

midpoint; section 7 contains the "praise of discourse," and section 14 Bahrām's encounter with the dragon. On the importance of spatial, temporal, and numerological patterns in literature generally see R. G. Peterson, "Critical Calculations: Measure and Symmetry in Literature," *PMLA* 91 (1976), 367–75; W.J.T. Mitchell, "Spatial Form in Literature," in *The Language of Images*, ed. W.J.T. Mitchell, pp. 271–99; in romance specifically, see Lacy, "Spatial Form"; K. M. Boklund, "On the Spatial and Cultural Characteristics of Courtly Romance," in *Semiotics and Dialectics: Ideology and the Text*, ed. P. V. Zima, 387–443.

Bahrām Gūr and the Dragon (John Rylands Library Ms. Pers. 36)

The first, which initiates the journey and in which the basic elements of the identifying motif cluster are introduced, recounts how the young prince, already renowned as a hunter, goes in pursuit of his favorite prey, the onager (*gūr*). Several lines repeat the pun on the word *gūr* in its double meaning of "onager" and "grave." In addition to serving as a reminder of the onager's emblematic significance (its appearance both signals the beginning of an adventure and points to Bahrām's skill), the pun involves a basic irony: the paradox of the king who hunts the wild ass while the grave is hunting him, a reminder of human mortality and the transience of worldly glory.[39]

After Bahrām has killed a number of beasts, there suddenly appears a female onager of extraordinary beauty:

> So many felled he, by his power,
> the plain with bones was covered o'er.
> A female onager appeared
> at last, whose sight the whole world stirred.
> A vision of the soul she seemed;
> bright was her face, her forehead beamed.
> . . . .
> Her rosy mane, in housing's place,
> a silken veil cast o'er her face.
>
> (*HP*, 14:4–6,9)

This marvelous beast, a veritable queen of onagers, leads Bahrām to a remote cave at the mouth of which lies a terrible

[39] The pun recurs in the final adventure episode, where the capping irony is provided by Bahrām's disappearance into the cave from which he is apotheosized: although in appearance the cave becomes his grave, in reality his grave is never found. The pun on *gūr* was a poetic commonplace both before and after Niẓāmī; a famous example is ʿUmar Khayyām's (d. 1122) line: *Bahrām kih gūr mī-giriftī hamah ʿumr / imrūz bi-ngar kih gūr Bahrām girift* ("Bahrām, who took the wild ass all his life: / see how, today, the grave has taken him"). It is echoed by Ḥāfiẓ (who had the benefit of Niẓāmī as a precursor): *Kamand-i ṣayd-i Bahrāmī biyafkan jām-i Jam bar dār / kih man paymūdam īn ṣaḥrā: nah Bahrām-ast u nah gūrash* (QG 278: "Cast down the lasso of Bahrām, and take up Jamshīd's cup instead; / for I've traversed that desert: neither Bahrām nor his *gūr* is there").

dragon. The prince surmises that the onager has led him there so that he may render her some service:

> He knew well, from the beast's alarm,
> she'd suffered from the dragon harm,
> And sought the prince—whom just she knew—
> to do her justice on the foe.
>
> (*HP*, 14:31–32)

In fact, the dragon has devoured the onager's foal, as Bahrām finds when, having slain the beast, he splits open its stomach, from which the foal emerges unharmed. The onager leads him into the cave, where he discovers a fabulous treasure, which he subsequently distributes with great liberality.

This episode introduces a sequence of actions and a cluster of thematically related motifs whose recurrence marks the four major adventure episodes. The sequence of actions consists of: (1) hunt, (2) encounter, (3) conflict, (4) resolution, and (5) discovery (result); the major participants are Bahrām himself and a second figure who functions as guide (here, the onager). The paradigmatic scheme with respect to this episode may be rendered thus: (1) Bahrām *hunts*, (2) he *encounters* the onager who leads him to the cave, (3) he *fights* with the dragon, and (4) *slays* it, thereby (5) *revealing* the onager's foal, and (as a secondary result) *discovers* the treasure in the cave.

From this sequence of actions derive the motifs linking the four episodes. The introductory structural motif of the hunt establishes the thematic "space" of the episode as that of adventure. The second motif is that of guidance, associated with the encounter: the onager guides Bahrām to the cave where he slays the dragon and leads him inside to discover the treasure.[40] The third important motif, one that is central to the

[40] For the association of the pursued animal with guidance, cf. Thiébaux: the animal (which often had uncanny qualities) "would entice the intent pursuer into an alien setting, an actual or psychic wilderness where he must wrestle with the beast. A function of the quarry was . . . to achieve the separation of the protagonist from his familiar notions of reality and order and procure for him his isolation." Further, "the original contest between man and quarry might become transferred to some other power or adversary" (*Stag of Love*,

poem (and to romance as a genre), is the disparity between appearance and reality and the assumption that the one serves to conceal the other. The onager is no ordinary beast but possesses extraordinary powers; the existence of the dragon in its remote cave was hitherto unknown; the foal, apparently dead, is miraculously alive; the cave conceals a treasure. This motif, constantly escalating, extends beyond things that are literally hidden to encompass the disparity between Bahrām's (and the narrator's) evaluation of his nature, and specifically the assumption of his inherent justice, which will be questioned in the Fitnah episode that follows. The foal concealed in the dragon's belly and the treasure in the cave are analogues of the true nature of the individual, concealed within the soul and revealed by actions. The resolution of the conflict involves the disclosure of the reality behind the appearance and is usually expressed through the motif of rebirth—here, the foal delivered from the dragon's belly. This motif also incorporates a figurative as well as a literal sense: just as the foal's restoration to life anticipates that of Fitnah, so Bahrām's emergence from the treasure cave prefigures his spiritual rebirth after his passage through the domes, as it does his final apotheosis. The final motif is that of gain: the gain resulting from the successful resolution of the conflict and the accompanying revelation—here, the foal restored to its mother and the treasure that enriches Bahrām. All of these motifs are introduced in concrete terms on the literal level of the action. Striking enough in this episode, their full significance is revealed only as they are encountered again in subsequent ones.

The second of these linked episodes, that of Fitnah, causes us to look back on that of the dragon with deepened understanding, as we recognize the analogies, while at the same time it prepares us for further recurrences and transformations. In this adventure, both the basic sequence of actions and the motifs associated with it are modified in the direction of complexity, a complexity that arises in the first instance from the seg-

p. 56). In Persian literature the onager often figures as such a magical quarry; cf. Hanaway, "Concept of the Hunt," 27-28.

ment's bipartite structure, consisting of a first portion calqued on the episode of Bahrām and Āzādah in Firdawsī's *Shāhnāmah*, and a continuation. Consequently, the conflict itself partakes of two phases, in which the roles of the participants are reversed, and the nature of the conflict between them becomes problematical.

The first portion of the Fitnah episode was described briefly in the previous chapter; its crucial importance to the poem makes it worthy of a more detailed discussion here, in the context of its significance for Bahrām's progress. The parallel episode in the *Shāhnāmah* told how Bahrām, still prince, went hunting with his favorite, the harp girl Āzādah, who challenged him to transform the female of a pair of gazelles into a male, the male into a female, and to transfix the latter through head, ear, and hoof. When Bahrām accomplished this feat (the details of which are described at length), Āzādah burst into tears and accused him of "unmanliness" (*nā-mardānagī*): only a demon would so abuse dumb beasts. Bahrām, enraged, forthwith set his riding camel to trample her and never took women hunting again.

Niẓāmī's treatment of the story differs markedly, both in the attention given to Fitnah herself—whose charms are catalogued in detail, whereas Firdawsī, for whom Bahrām's skill as a hunter is central (both structurally and thematically), describes Āzādah only briefly—and in the alteration of many details. The episode takes place when Bahrām is king, the hunt is for onagers, the challenge itself is simplified, and its circumstances changed; while Fitnah's "death" at the end of this first portion, though believed real by Bahrām, is in fact only apparent, as is revealed in the continuation.

Taking refuge in the castle of the officer who has saved her, Fitnah prepares herself for confrontation with Bahrām. After some years have elapsed, she urges her protector to invite the king to take refreshment at the castle when he is on one of his hunting expeditions. After entertaining Bahrām, the officer tells him of a marvelous woman who can carry a full-grown ox up the sixty steps that lead to the tower room where they are seated. Bahrām demands to see this feat; Fitnah, heavily veiled, performs it for him, and, when questioned as to how she has accomplished it, replies that it is through her own strength. To the king's objection that she can only have mastered this feat through constant practice, she retorts:

. . . "The king a great debt owes:
'practice' the ox—not the wild ass?
"Am I, who to the roof have borne
an ox, for 'practice' to be known?
"Why, when *you* shoot a wild ass small,
dare no one *your* deed 'practice' call?"
(*HP*, 26:72–74)

Bahrām is delighted to find Fitnah alive; she explains that her apparent taunt was inspired by love and the desire to avert the evil eye from him, and, struck by her ability and wit, he marries her.

The hunt motif establishes the episode as one of adventure; but the emblematic wild ass encountered therein serves only as the immediate stimulus for the action, not as its effective cause. The function of guidance is displaced to Fitnah—a displacement anticipated by the parallelism in both position and content of the passages describing each. The two share, not only their common sex, but the attributes of beauty, cleverness, and luminosity, attributes directly associated with guidance.[41] The rebirth motif that accompanies the act of discovery is also displaced to Fitnah, whom Bahrām believed dead; the disclosure

[41] The onager was described as being of bright face and broad forehead (*tāzah-rū'ī gushādah-pīshānī*); Fitnah is "bright-faced as spring in Paradise" (*tāzah-rū'ī chun naw-bahār-i bihisht*), an allusion to the rebirth motif as well. (*Tāzah-rū* is also used in the prologue of the Prophet Muḥammad: summoned by the angel Gabriel to undertake his heavenly journey [*miʿrāj*], he is told, "Be like a brilliant lamp to guide the stars; be bright-faced like a garden's blooming flowers" [*HP*, 3:14].) The onager's rosy mane, which falls over its forehead and shoulders and is compared to a veil (*burqaʿ*) worn in place of horse's housing, anticipates the veil with which Fitnah conceals her own luminous, moonlike visage; however, the colors are reversed, as Fitnah's veil is camphor colored, while her face is rosy (*HP*, 26:58). Camphor is used in preparing the dead, who are wrapped in white shrouds, for burial; the description emphasizes Fitnah's figurative death.

is expressed both literally and symbolically when Bahrām removes the veil beneath which Fitnah concealed her identity, and which was prefigured by the onager's "veil-like" mane—both suggesting that there is more to their owners than meets the eye. The restoration of Bahrām's love causes Fitnah, in her own words, to be restored to life; and—as the foal was liberated from the dragon's belly, and the treasure from the cave—she is freed from the tower in which she had been virtually imprisoned while in hiding.

The significance of this episode is indicated at the outset by Niẓāmī's change of the harp girl's name from Āzādah (suggesting willfulness) to Fitnah, which, while not inappropriate as a feminine appellation, seldom occurs as a name and carries a wide range of associations: besides its connotation of physical charm and seductiveness (hence, of sexual temptation), it refers to incitement to morally reprehensible acts (*rusvā'ī*), and more specifically to civil war and revolt against the true faith and rightly designated authority. It is also associated with the supernatural, with magic, and with possession. All of these connotations are derived from the root meaning of the verb: to put to the test, to tempt.[42]

The importance of the harp girl's name is emphasized by the poet's delay in revealing it, and his restriction of its use to three occasions, on each of which it is repeated in contexts that stress the wordplay on its various senses. She is first named in a line that repeats the word *fitnah* four times:

Fitnah-nāmī hazār fitnah dar ū;
fitnah-i shāh u shāh fitnah bar ū.
Fitnah her name, of thousand *lures*;
the king's *temptress*, he *charmed* by her.

(*HP*, 25:13)

[42] On the meanings associated with *fitnah*, see J.-C. Vadet, "Quelques remarques sur la racine *ftn* dans le Coran et la plus ancienne littérature musulmane," *REI* 37 (1969), 81-102; see also *EI*² s.v. "Fitna." On Fitnah as a name, and on the name of Bahrām's favorite in historical sources, see Pantke, *Bahrām-Roman*, pp. 133-36. The episode of Fitnah, and its relation to the poem as a whole, is discussed in greater detail in J. S. Meisami, "Fitnah or Āzādah? Niẓāmī's Ethical Poetic" (forthcoming).

Fitnah's designation as the "king's temptress" (or temptation) will prove accurate in a far more meaningful sense than the initial suggestion that he is infatuated with her allurements. These are subsequently catalogued in detail and stress her grace, her pleasing voice, and her skill at music.[43]

The next mention of Fitnah by name is when Bahrām orders her execution, labeling her a "disturber" whose death is therefore licit:

Fitnah-i bārgāh-i dawlat-i māst;
fitnah kushtan zi rū-yi ʿaql ravāst.
She has *disturbed* our stately court:
death to *disturbers* reason supports.
(*HP*, 25:49)

The third and final mention follows her disclosure of her identity to Bahrām and their reconciliation:

Chun zi fitnah-garān tuhī shud jāy,
pīsh-i khvad Fitnah-rā nishānd zi pāy.
Fitnah bi-nishast u bar gushād zabān;
guft k-ay shahriyār-i fitnah-nishān:
Ay marā kushtah dar jidāʾī-yi khīsh;
zindah kardah bah āshnāʾī-yi khīsh. . . .
When from *disturbers* the place was free,
he made "*Disturbance*" seated be.

[43] Fitnah's association with music, and hence with harmony and order, contrasts with her apparent role as a disturber. Music is included in the mathematical branch of the philosophical sciences (*riyāḍīyāt*); based on number and proportion, it is closely associated with poetry, whose metered cadence also reflects such principles (see *RIS*, 1:196–97, 206–34). On the power of music and poetry to incite various types of action, see ibid., 1:184 ff. On the association of the world-soul with music and the notion that both music and poetry, being based on number, bear witness to divine order, see also Heninger, *TSH*, especially pp. 101–105; L. Spitzer, *Classical and Christian Ideas of World Harmony*, pp. 29-34 et passim. Niẓāmī designates Fitnah's instrument (*sāz*) as the harp (or lute, *chang*), and Bahrām's as the arrow (*HP*, 25:19), an association that finds a parallel in Heraclitus: "The lute and the arrow are alike in form; this fact, and the fact that both are attributes of Apollo, are for Heraclitus symptomatic of the ease with which strife . . . can turn into harmony" (ibid., p. 9).

Fitnah sat down, her speech began:
"O king, who sets *disturbance* down,
Whose absence made me die of grief;
whose love has brought me back to life."

(*HP*, 26:81–83)

The very banality of employing *fitnah nishāndan* in the literal sense of "to make Fitnah sit down" stresses its more usual (if figurative) meaning, to suppress insurrection or sedition, and thus raises the question of the nature and locus of the "disturbance" that Fitnah represents. (It also recalls the limitations of the narrator, which include a tin ear for the subtleties of language.) Rather than being a disturber of order, she mirrors a moral conflict within Bahrām himself; her role is to restore, not upset, order, as is made clear by the transferral to her of the function of guidance. The moral dimension of this guidance is suggested by the qualities she possesses (and which she shares with the onager of the dragon episode): beauty, wit, grace, and, most important, luminosity.

Fitnah's luminosity is suggested not only by her physical description ("bright-faced"), but more specifically by the recurrent likening of her to the moon—again, like her name, in contexts that suggest its special significance. To compare a beautiful woman to a moon is to employ a time-worn convention of Persian poetry; but in the case of Fitnah a conventional interpretation is mediated against by the symbolic dimension of the likeness: the comparison is not metaphorical but analogical. This dimension is first suggested when the officer brings Bahrām the false report of Fitnah's death, telling him that he has "given the Moon to the Dragon" (*HP*, 25:71)—an allusion to the belief that the moon, in eclipse, is swallowed by the "tail of the Dragon" (*al-dhanab*), i.e., the moon's descending node. (We may recall the fate of the onager's foal.)[44] The maleficent

[44] In the commentary to his English translation of the *Haft Paykar*, C. E. Wilson equates this "Dragon" with the constellation Draco (*The Haft Paikar*, 2:102, n. 905). Kunitzsch, correctly identifying *al-dhanab* (in Gurgānī's description of the night) as the moon's descending node, notes: "The two nodes of the moon's orbit . . . are often counted, in Islamic astrology (following In-

influence of this Dragon is invoked again when Fitnah, explaining to Bahrām why she withheld her praise, attributes to it the distortion of the true meaning of her words.[45]

Two further references to Fitnah as moon in an astrological context occur in connection with her feat of strength: first, when the bemused narrator hits on the clever conceit of likening the moon of beauty carrying the ox-calf on her shoulders to the sun entering the house of Taurus in spring (*HP*, 25:80: "The Sun does bear the Calf in spring; / who's seen a moon do such a thing?"); and second, when she begins her feat:

> This fortnight's moon, when by love led,
> her seven adornments had arrayed,
> Like a full moon drew near the ox:
> the moon finds strength in Taurus' house.
> (*HP*, 26:59–60)

This particular conjunction has been anticipated from the beginning of the narrative: when Bahrām's natal horoscope was cast, the moon was in exaltation in Taurus; Saturn was in strength, with the Dragon's tail turned toward it. Fitnah acts out this combination of signs, to become the human analogue of the ascendant moon, escaping the malevolent influence of the Dragon and of Saturn, and rising to her fullest exaltation as she bears the ox to the top of the tower. Her action thus interprets the significance of the horoscope, as both moon (Fitnah) and sun (Bahrām) are released from the sky's influence—an influence that does not determine their fate but provides an analogue for their moral status.[46]

---

dian models), among the planets, and are assigned similar virtues in the calculation of a horoscope. Thus, the Descending Node is of a maleficent influence" (" 'Description,' " 108; on the powers of the moon's nodes, see *RIS* 4:285). On Niẓāmī's use of astrological elements, see n. 63.

[45] *Ghabnam āmad k-azhdihā-yi sipihr / tuhmat-i kīnah bar nihād bar mihr* ("The sky Dragon made me appear / at fault; my love as hate seemed clear" [*HP*, 26:90]). The line highlights the ambiguous nature of language, with the pun on *mihr* (which can mean "love" or "sun"), suggesting that it was the king (the sun) who committed an injustice against Fitnah (the moon), by believing a false accusation (*tuhmat*).

[46] Bahrām's horoscope is glossed by Wilson with the aid of Alan Leo (again

The eclipsed moon reappears to resume her function of guidance, which she performs by virtue of her luminosity. The association of the moon with guidance as well as with beauty in medieval Islamic thought is a complex one. Just as the moon reflects and mirrors both the sun's light and the divine luminescence, so the beauty of the individual mirrors the inner light of the soul; thus the conceptual link between beautiful form and moon transcends metaphor to encompass the analogy of physical with spiritual beauty.[47] By virtue of this relationship, Fitnah is transformed from a willful and impudent slave girl to a spiritual guide who embodies that beauty the love of which has as its analogue the desire for moral perfection; at the same

---

confusing the "Dragon's tail" with Draco; see *Haft Paikar*, 2:63–65, n. 533). The horoscope is typical of that of a great man, with all the planets at their exaltations; cf. David Pingree, "Mashā'allāh: Some Sassanian and Syriac Sources," in *Essays on Islamic Philosophy and Science*, ed. George F. Hourani, pp. 5–14, and especially p. 6. On the ancient association of the moon and Taurus, see M. Mokri, "La lumière en Iran ancien et l'Islam," in *Le thème de la lumière dans le Judaïsme, le Christianisme et l'Islam*, pp. 359–61.

[47] Cf. Mokri, "Lumière," pp. 381 ff. Ibn Ḥazm articulates the relationship between beauty and moral action: "Two sources of perfection in the human soul are its moral actions . . . and the erotic life, which produces the impression of beauty in the lover" (Lomba Fuentes, "La beauté objective," 164; see also 162–63). Corbin comments on the idea of beauty in the thought of Ibn ʿArabī: "A veritable *spiritual potency* invests the human Image whose beauty manifests in sensible form the Beauty that is the divine attribute par excellence, and because its power is a spiritual power, this potency is *creative*. This is the potency which creates love in man, which arouses the nostalgia that carries him beyond his own sensible appearance, and it is this potency which, by provoking his Active Imagination to produce for it what our troubadours called 'celestial love' (Ibn ʿArabī's spiritual love), leads him to self-knowledge, that is, to the knowledge of his divine Lord. That is why feminine being is the Creator of the most perfect thing that can be, for through it is completed the design of Creation, namely, to invest the respondent, the *fedele d'amore*, with a divine Name in a human being who becomes its vehicle" (*Creative Imagination*, p. 164). The moon is the mediatory power between the celestial and material worlds (see *RIS*, 2:147); it is also associated with the Universal Intellect (*ʿAql-i Kull*) which informs and animates the universe (Nasr, *Introduction*, p. 77). Its powers are analogous to the powers of speech: "As the Moon receives its light from the Sun and casts it over the twenty-eight mansions, so does the power of speech receive its power from the intellectual faculty and transmit it through the twenty-eight letters of the (Arabic) alphabet" (ibid., p. 101).

time, she is a mirror in which Bahrām sees reflected the qualities of his own soul and learns that the temptation against which he must strive has its source in his own nature.[48] The wedding of Bahrām and Fitnah, the conjunction of Sun and Moon, is the symbolic climax of the action generated by this complex of analogies.

These two episodes, each involving a question of justice, precede Bahrām's achievement of temporal sovereignty, marked by his victory over the Chinese and his wedding to the seven princesses. The two corollary episodes follow the interlude of the tales and complete the pattern. The first, Bahrām's encounter with the shepherd, follows his celebration of the New Year, when he learns that his kingdom is in disorder and that the Chinese ruler has again invaded his domains. The cause (which no one dare reveal) is the abuse of power, in his absence, by his minister Rāst-Rawshan.[49] Seeking to alleviate his cares, he goes hunting alone—not, this time, for onager,

[48] "Woman is the mirror, the *maẓhar*, in which man contemplates his own Image, the Image that was his hidden being, the Self which he had to gain knowledge of in order to know his own Lord" (Corbin, *Creative Imagination*, p. 161; see also pp. 157–75). A Prophetic tradition states, "The believer is the mirror of the believer," Discussing the Koranic uses of the root *f-t-n*, Vadet cites another (perhaps spurious) tradition to the effect that "Temptation dwells within our souls and . . . man is continually at war with himself" ("Remarques," 93). Bahram must struggle to achieve equilibrium between the concupiscent and irascible faculties of his own soul; the first motivates his unseemly desire for praise, the second his anger at Fitnah. On the desire for fame Ibn Ḥazm observes, "One of the evils implicit in the love of fame is that it renders good works barren and fruitless, because he who performs them does so only so that people may speak well of him" (Lomba Fuentes, "La beauté objective," 167).

[49] The invasion is termed a *fitnah*, a sedition encouraged by the evil minister, whose name, Rāst-Rawshan (like Fitnah), provides an example of Niẓāmī's technique of allegorical naming. Its literal meaning ("upright and bright") suggests the disparity between appearance (name) and reality (nature, revealed by action): what we choose to call something is not necessarily what it really is. Rāst-Rawshan is called by the epithet *ʿālam-sūz*, "world-burner" (Shīrīn referred to Khusraw's exploits as *jahān-sūzī*, with a strong negative implication); over and above the conventionality of the epithet, we may perhaps discern a topical reference to the Ghurid leader ʿAlā' al-Din Ḥusayn "Jahān-Sūz," who took and sacked Ghaznah in 1150–51 (cf. *CHI*, 5:160–62).

but for leopard, lion, and boar. On his return homeward, suffering from a burning thirst, he searches for water but finds none; he sees only a trail of black smoke which, rising dragonlike into the sky, guides him to a shepherd's tent. Outside this tent Bahrām observes a mound of dead sheep and a sheep dog hung on a gibbet. The old man who receives him gives him water and explains that the dog, for years a faithful guardian of the flock, had finally betrayed his trust; infatuated with a she-wolf, he enjoyed her favors in return for a gift of fat sheep. For this breach of trust, the shepherd punished the dog by hanging him from the gibbet.

> My dog a wolf in ambush deep
> became—nay, butcher of my sheep.
> He trust with treason did repay:
> to traitor sold his charge away.
> . . . .
> Whoso with wrongdoers in like ways
> deals not, let no one give him praise.
>
> (*HP*, 41:64–66)

Bahrām at once understands the object lesson (*ʿibrat*) conveyed by the old man's speech: that he, as king, is the shepherd of his people and responsible for their well-being. Hastening back to court, he loses no time in bringing the culprit to trial and hangs him for his misdeeds.

The episode of the shepherd—like its direct analogue, that of Fitnah—is also modeled on a well-known and easily recognized source: a story whose fullest account occurs in the *Siyāsatnāmah* of Niẓām al-Mulk.[50] The distinction between these models—the *Book of Kings* and the *Book of Government*—places them in opposition and emphasizes the contrast between kingship by will and kingship by law. But their relationship is more complex than that: the structural positioning of this opposition indicates its ethical nature. Both sources rep-

[50] See Niẓām al-Mulk, *Book of Government*, pp. 24–31. Niẓāmī's rendition of this story is markedly more faithful than his treatment of the story of Āzādah; his major change is to increase the number of witnesses against the minister to seven, in keeping with the number symbolism of the *Haft Paykar*.

resent incomplete visions of kingship; for the series of linked episodes is not yet complete, and the fourth and final one will show that Niẓāmī's ideal of kingship transcends Niẓām al-Mulk's emphasis on kingship as statecraft as it does Firdawsī's concept of temporal kingship as based on lineage and prowess.

After a long and prosperous reign, one day Bahrām, setting aside crown and throne, goes hunting with a group of his nobles. While they seek literal beasts, his quarry, we are told, is himself:

> *They* sought the wild ass of the plain,
> but *he*, the lonely tomb to gain.
> He sought a grave in which to dwell:
> gazelles, but of himself, did fell.
> From this salt plain gazelle, wild ass,
> seek not: one tomb, the other vice.
> At last, from desert side appeared
> a wild ass, towards the ass-king veered.
> That angel beast, the king knew then,
> would set him on the path to heaven.[51]
>
> (*HP*, 52:16–20)

The onager leads Bahrām to a remote cave in which lies a deep, water-filled chasm. The king plunges into the chasm on horseback, "consigning the kingly treasure to the cave" and embracing therein the Companion of the Cave (*yār-i ghār*). The circle is complete; Bahrām, having passed through the grada-

[51] The poet plays on the dual meanings of *āhū* ("gazelle," "vice") and *gūr* ("onager," "grave"). This emblematic use of gazelle and onager provides further commentary on the Āzādah episode, where Bahrām's quarry was a gazelle (interpreted retrospectively as an allegory of his own vice). Animals of various sorts are often used as emblems of the *nafs-i ammārah*, man's animal soul; the "leopard, lion and boar" sought by Bahrām in section 41, as well as the wolf and the dog, should be read in this sense. A restive horse is another such emblem; at the beginning of the Fitnah episode, Bahrām's charger is described as "dancing beneath him," inviting him to the sin of pride (*HP*, 25:5). Gūr-Khān, "Ass-King," was, according to Dastgirdī, Bahrām's title (*Haft Paykar*, p. 350, n. 2). Historically, the title was borne by the non-Muslim rulers of Qarakhitay, whose first king defeated the Saljuq monarch Sanjar in 1147 (see *EI*², s.v. "Gūrkhān").

tions of love, consigns the treasure of his soul to the first and final beloved, its source and the goal to which it returns.[52]

The completion of this circle would not be possible without the intervening tales, which prepare Bahrām for the transition from kingship by will to kingship by law. The tales come at a climactic point in Bahrām's career, when his position as ruler of the world is made secure; his wedding to the daughters of the Kings of the Seven Climes sets the final seal on this success. Much has been made of Bahrām's "love" for these princesses, said to have obsessed him following his discovery of their portraits in a mysterious room in the palace of Khavarnaq where he has spent his youth.[53] Entering this room (the existence of

[52] For the relevant traditions concerning Bahrām's disappearance, see Pantke, *Bahrām-Roman*, pp. 194–97. Dastgirdī glosses *yār-i ghār* as the solitude (*tanhā'ī*) sought by Bahrām (*Haft Paykar*, p. 351, n. 1), Wilson as the divine beloved (*Haft Paikar*, 2:200, n. 2005). The epithet is commonly applied to Abū Bakr, the Prophet's uncle, to whom Muhammad is said to have taught the "silent *dhikr*" (personal, private prayer) while they were in hiding in a cave during the emigration from Mecca to Medina (A. Schimmel, *Mystical Dimensions of Islam*, p. 169; see Koran 9:40); by association, it may be applied to the Prophet, or to God (a Ḥadīth Qudsī states, "I am the companion of he who remembers Me" [*anā jalīsu man dhakaranī*]). Sanā'ī in the *Ḥadīqat al-ḥaqīqah* compares "the relationship between reason and the soul to the relationship between the Prophet and his faithful servant Ṣiddīq (i.e. . . . Abū Bakr), [and] shows how the soul takes advantage of this companionship to perfect itself" (de Bruijn, *OPP*, p. 240). The Prophet's *mi'rāj*, described in the poem's prologue, is the prototype for Bahrām's spiritual journey, the movement of which might better be termed spiral than circular; the completion of the circle (the meeting of beginning and end, *mabda'* and *ma'ād*, the soul's rejoining of its source) is complemented by the upward motion associated with Bahrām's acquisition of self-knowledge (see n. 61). On the importance of the spiral as a compositional principle in Islamic art (especially in painting), see A. Papadopoulo, *Islam and Muslim Art*, tr. R. E. Wolff, pp. 96-102. Papadopoulo comments that the spiral "symbolized the 'helicoidal movement,' which . . . descends from God to the soul of man and then returns heavenward to its Maker . . . adopted by the Muslim mystics in their explanations that this movement initiates with God, passes through the 'circle of prophecy' and then through the 'circle of initiation' to reach its end in the soul of the mystic" (ibid., p. 102). See also Pierre Gallais, "Hexagonal and Spiral Structure in Medieval Narrative," in *Approaches to Medieval Romance*, ed. Peter Haidu, pp. 115–32.

[53] Cf. Pantke's assertion that despite Bahrām's success in establishing his claim to the throne "his happiness is not yet complete, for the love of the prin-

which was hitherto unknown) one day upon returning from the hunt, he sees these seven portraits—the *haft paykar* of the poem's title—ranged in a circle round his own, and beneath them, writ in gold, the legend that he is destined by divine decree to possess them. The princesses are not mentioned again until Bahrām's temporal sovereignty is complete; his desire for them must thus be read as a metaphor for his determination to rule the world, rather than an erotic obsession. Moreover, he in no way "woos" them but sends to their fathers, peremptorily demanding them as his due (even to the threat of war); his subsequent erotic relations with them are relegated to a few formulaic phrases preceding and following each tale. On the level of the poem's symbolic imagery, the princesses represent Bahrām's worldly achievement; on the level of its plot, they exist for the purpose of telling the tales.

Bahrām hears these tales as he visits each princess in the dome or pavilion he has had built for her. Each dome is dedicated to a specific day of the week, governed by that day's planet, and characterized by an emblematic color. The sequence of the tales is governed by the order of the days of the week, beginning with the black dome of Saturn on Saturday and finishing with the white dome of Venus on Friday; the entire interlude covers the passage from winter to spring. The tales, which exploit a wide range of storytelling techniques, all deal with love: physical love and its frustration or fulfillment. Their outcomes range from loss and despair in the first tale, through renunciation of the world in the fifth, to marriage and prosperity in the remaining tales, but most conspicuously in the seventh. Although the tales are frequently treated as though they were separable from, and incidental to, the main

---

cesses leaves him no rest" (*Bahrām-Roman*, p. 133; see also pp. 91–98). The parallel between the building of Khavarnaq and of the seven domes, and the contrasting fate of the kings who build them (Nuʿmān, overtaken by worldly pride, kills the architect Simnār lest he duplicate this wonder for another; subsequently, in remorse, he abandons his throne and disappears into the desert), points to the distinction between building for this world and for the next. The two edifices are explicitly linked by Shīdah, the apprentice of Simnār and the architect of the seven domes.

narrative, they are organically related to it with respect to their central themes as well as by their symbolic imagery. Tales and narrative alike emphasize the disparity between appearance and reality, and more important, the problem of self-knowledge.

The tales make possible Bahrām's transformation from a perfect ruler in appearance to one in reality; their structural and thematic organization (reinforced by symbolic imagery) both parallel and predict the course of his spiritual progress. The king's journey toward self-knowledge is mirrored by the movement in the tales from the darkness of moral ignorance (symbolized by the black of the first dome) to the light of illumination (symbolized by the white of the seventh and final dome, the color of purity and worship and of the garments donned by the protagonist of the tale as he prepares to wed his radiant bride)—a progression that is also from mourning to marriage, from the sterility of frustrated concupiscence to the fertility of desire governed by law, passing through the stage of renunciation in the fifth tale, itself another form of mourning for lost desires. The tales thus constitute, in the guise of a series of entertaining love stories, an anatomy of ethical man, in which love is the means by which man's inner nature becomes externalized and can be explored.

The tales are a further means by which the poet establishes his purpose, for they stand in relation to Bahrām as Niẓāmī intends his poem to stand in relation to its audience: as a source of instruction and as an incitement to the acquisition of virtue and self-knowledge. Further complexity is added by the alternation between tales in which the protagonist is motivated chiefly by the concupiscent faculty (represented as temptation or desire for gain, in tales I, III, V, and VII) and those in which the dominant faculty is the irascible (represented by anger or by steadfastness in pursuit of a worthy goal, in tales II, IV, and VI). This pattern brings home the necessity of mastering these complementary faculties (either of which, if allowed to dominate, leads to vice) and establishing equilibrium between them.[54] It also recalls Niẓāmī ʿArūẓī's assertion that the poet, "by acting on the imagination[,] . . . excites the faculties of anger and concupiscence in such a way that by his suggestion men's temperaments become affected with exultation or depression; whereby he conduces to the accomplishment of great things in the order of the world."

A final link, both structural and symbolic, between narrative and tales is the motif of the garden. At the heart of Bahrām's progress from temporal to sacred kingship lies an inward journey symbolized by a movement from garden to garden. Three of the most important tales (I, V, and VII) are set in gardens, while the interlude as a whole is framed by the two gardens of the narrative: the garden in winter, cold and bare, from which Bahrām takes refuge to feast in the comfort of indoor chambers and to order the construction of the seven domes, and the royal pleasance in spring, described in imagery of Paradise, rebirth, and resurrection, where the action leading to the restoration of order is set in motion. The progress from ignorance to enlightenment is thus closely bound up with the opposition of barrenness to fertility (symbolized by the contrasting outcomes of tales I and VII) as well as with the themes of right guidance and the disparity between appearance and reality.

The garden of the first tale, to which its kingly protagonist is magically transported, is ultimately lost by him when, embracing the beautiful maiden Turktāz with whom he has fallen in love and failing to heed her enjoinders to be content for a while with what he has (that is, with any other maiden in the garden), both she and garden vanish. The black robes of mourning that he dons are the outward emblem of the spiritual ignorance in which his failure to master his desires dooms him to remain, while the lady Turktāz, consistently described in terms of brightness and illumination, is another of the poem's figures of guidance. The garden itself, described as filled with flowers

[54] See Naṣīr al-Dīn Ṭūsī, *Nasirean Ethics*, pp. 79–81. Another example of the symbolic alternation between concupiscence and irascibility is found in Chrétien's *Perceval*; cf. Pierre Gallais, *Perceval et l'initiation*, pp. 122–27.

of all sorts, figures the assault of worldly beauty on the senses also suggested by the lady's name; its disappearance points to the transient nature of such beauty and to the necessity for contentment and continence.[55]

The garden of the fifth tale is also lost by its protagonist, the beautiful youth Māhān, who finds it after wandering several days in the desert where he has been enticed by a demon in the guise of a friend, and where he is tormented by other demons and by a seven-headed dragon.[56] Like the king of black, Māhān too finds a beautiful lady in his garden; but when he embraces her, she turns into a dreadful *ʿifrīt*, "created of God's wrath" (*HP*, 36:363). Falling in a swoon, Māhān wakes to

[55] The name Turktāz, "Turkish Raid," signifies the assault of beauty on the senses, which awakens the concupiscent faculty. (Some manuscripts give the variant Turknāz, which is accepted by Ritter and Rypka but not by Dastgirdī [see *Haft Paykar*, p. 166, n. 7]. On the Turk as an emblem of beauty, see further chapters 2 and 6.) Turktāz enjoins her would-be lover, "He who with contentment's pleased / will ever find a life of ease; // But he who makes desire his friend // will be a beggar in the end" (*HP*, 32:345–46). Contentment, *qināʿat*, is subsumed under the general category of *ʿiffat*, continence, one of the four cardinal virtues: " 'Continence' signifies that the faculty of appetite is obedient to the rational soul, its controls being in accordance with the exigency of the latter's opinion; moreover, the operation of freedom should be apparent in it, and it should be quit of bondage to the soul's passion and of servitude to pleasures" (Naṣīr al-Dīn Ṭūsī, *Nasirean Ethics*, p. 81; see also p. 252). The King of Black's fault is akin to the sin of *curiositas* (see n. 28): his adventure is motivated by his unrepressed desire to learn the secret of the "City of Black," of which he has heard from travelers, at whatever cost to himself or others, while his loss is precipitated by his impatience to possess his beloved. His perpetual mourning is as excessive as was the immoderate desire that caused it.

[56] The dragon represents the "sky," that is, the material world; its four feet are the four elements, its seven heads the seven planets (Wilson, *Haft Paikar*, 2:1645, n. 1616; Dastgirdī, *Haft Paykar*, p. 244, n. 1). Cf. the narrator's interjection, when Māhān wakes to find the garden vanished: "And he knew not that all we prize / is but a Dragon, in Moon's guise. // See—if the curtain he'd but raise— / for what the fool his love displays" (*HP*, 36:407–408). This emblematic reading is further supported by the fact that the tale is told in the "turquoise dome"—a common metaphor for sky and world. Māhān's wanderings in the desert recall the Manichean conception of hell as a waterless waste inhabited by fiends; cf. Mary Boyce, *The Manichaean Hymn-Cycles in Parthian*, pp. 87–91.

find the garden transformed into a wasteland, "a Hell in place of Paradise" (36:390). Despairing, he throws himself on God's mercy and is miraculously transported to his own garden by the prophet Khiẕr; there, he dons blue robes, which recall the ascetic's cloak of abstinence and which are emblematic of his renunciation of the world of the senses. With the exception of Khiẕr, the guides encountered in this story are false; the garden itself is illusory and represents the deceptive evidence of the senses, the source of error when not mediated by reason or right guidance.[57]

[57] Māhān's loss is the result of his desire for gain, which motivates his actions from his first acceptance of false guidance to his final embrace of the lady-ʿ*ifrīt*. The garden he finds is a false Paradise (though it might have proved a true one: the signs that identify it are ambiguous); Māhān's inexperience and naiveté prevent him from interpreting these signs correctly: "reading" the garden in material, not spiritual, terms, he succumbs to temptation. (Compare Spenser's method, in the *Faerie Queene*, of juxtaposing visual illusion and transcendent reality, discussed by Heninger, *TSH*, pp. 352–57.) For Niẓāmī (as for Chrétien) "the garden is a symbolic place, representing marriage, or rather the love relationship, as seen from both personal and social points of view. . . . Even a highly metaphorical place will not mean the same thing to all who see or enter it, and the dominance of one or another viewpoint in the garden . . . will endow it with its social meaning, as well. . . . [Chrétien's] method depends . . . on the basic assumption that external reality is endowed with significance by individual, not universal or absolute, perspectives" (Hanning, *Individual*, p. 170). Unable to rely either on his senses or on reason, Māhān takes refuge in *tavakkul*, reliance on divine guidance, personified by Khiẕr, the "Green Man" of Islamic tradition (see *EI*², s.v. "Khaḍir"). (Right guidance is another of the virtues subsumed under ʿ*iffat*; see Naṣīr al-Dīn Ṭūsī, *Nasirean Ethics*, p. 83.) The transformation of the lady into an ʿ*ifrīt* recalls the Zoroastrian conception of the *daēna*, which greets the soul of the deceased after death: if he has been righteous, his *daēna* takes the form of a beautiful maiden, but if he has done evil, it is embodied in an ugly hag (see Molé, "Jugement," 143–75, and chapter 1, n. 49). Comparison of the world to an ugly crone with many bridegrooms is a commonplace in Islamic literature and suggests the continued influence of this tradition. Ritter's comment on Niẓāmī's comparison of Māhān, when he encounters Khiẕr, to a thirsting man finding the Fountain of Life (*HP*, 36:429)—"surely plain water would have been enough"—and the implication that a forced correspondence is established "to fit the mood" of the scene (*Bildersprache*, p. 28), misses the point; as the legend of Khiẕr itself exemplifies, right guidance leads precisely to this fountain. Māhān's donning of blue robes is glossed by Dastgirdī as *hamrangī-yi rūzigār*, the

Only the garden of the seventh tale remains in the possession of its protagonist, the young master who, like his precursors, also becomes enamored of a beautiful lady who mysteriously appears therein. The repeated frustration of his attempts to win her finally lead him to the realization that the fault is due to his failure to guide his desire into lawful channels, whereupon he resolves to marry the lady, whose name is Bakht, "Fortune." The tale ends with a hymn to the color white, symbol of worship and purity; the protagonist's ability to master his desires and govern them by law enables him to achieve the prosperity symbolized by his radiant bride.

> See how his luck clear water showed,
> and he did drink as was allowed:
> A source as pure as sun is bright,
> like jasmine clean, like silver white.
> In whiteness is the day's pure light;
> the world-illuming moon is white.
> All colors show duplicity
> save white, which cannot tinted be.
> In worship, at the time of prayer,
> the custom 'tis pure white to wear.
>
> (*HP*, 38:318–22)

The three gardens of the tales are arranged in ascending order with respect to their proximity to reality: the first is in a magical country beyond time and space, the second proves to be a dream and an illusion, the third is explicitly located in the real world. This sequence is expressed through a controlling metaphor likening each to the legendary Garden of Iram, the earthly Paradise of Islamic tradition: the first is explicitly identified with that garden, the second described as better than it,

---

acquisition of immunity to the world's afflictions by taking on its color (*Haft Paykar*, p. 267, n. 1). "Color," however, is indicative of dissimulation (*takalluf*; cf. *HP*, 38:321); its stain can be removed only by inner purity. For parallels in medieval Christian literature, see Peter Dronke, "Tradition and Innovation in Medieval Western Colour-Imagery," *Eranos-Jahrbuch* 41 (1972), 60–71.

the third is merely like it.[58] This progression from illusion to reality, which accompanies that from ignorance to enlightenment, illuminates the nature of the gardens by which the tales are framed. Bahrām's indoor winter garden, while a marvel of art that dispels the winter cold, does but mimic a real garden;[59] like the gardens found and lost by the King of Black and by Māhān, it testifies to the unreliability of the uninterpreted evidence of the senses. The garden of the seventh tale leads directly to the royal pleasance in spring; this is the true garden, and Bahrām's emergence into it signifies his spiritual rebirth and his readiness to attain the state of kingship by law.[60]

This is accomplished when Bahrām correctly interprets the shepherd's tale of his errant sheep dog both as an allegory of the evil minister who has betrayed his charge and as pointing

[58] On Iram's Garden, see *EI*[2] s.v. "Iram"; and see chapter 6, n. 71. The means by which the three protagonists find and enter their respective gardens are of interest: The King of Black, carried into the sky by a magical bird that has lifted him from the top of a tower where he sits waiting in a basket, alights in a grassy plain, sleeps, and awakens to find himself in a garden. Māhān, trying to escape his tormentors, at last finds a stream and descends, for safety, into a pit, a breach in which leads to the garden. The young master, hearing strange sounds in his own garden, penetrates it through a hole he makes in the wall, the gate being locked. The symbolic suggestiveness of these various means of entry into the garden is self-evident. The garden tales are told in the domes governed by Saturn, Mercury, and Venus; on the association of these planets with love, see al-Masʿūdī, *Les prairies d'or*, 6:382–84. The gardens of the *Haft Paykar* are discussed in J. S. Meisami, "Allegorical Gardens in the Persian Poetic Tradition: Neẓāmī, Rūmī, Ḥāfeẓ," *IJMES* 17 (1985), 229–60.

[59] Bahrām feasts in a heated chamber (*tābkhānah*), taking respite from the winter cold that envelops the real garden (now bleak and bare). The *tābkhānah* maintains the aspect of the four seasons; its perfumed airs, abundant fruits, and incense-laden fire soften the bite of winter. It mingles qualities of Hell (Dūzakh) and Paradise (i.e., warmth and light), and mimics the aspect of a real garden (see *HP*, 30:1–50).

[60] In Persian poetry the association of spring imagery with the topics of accession and restoration is of course associated with the New Year; Niẓāmī exploits the cosmic significance of this event to figure Bahrām's spiritual rebirth. On the symbolism of New Year rituals in Iranian tradition, see M. Molé, *Culte, mythe et cosmologie dans l'Iran ancien*, pp. 90–91, 120–25, et passim; in European literature, see Hanning, *Individual*, p. 197, and Garrison, *Dryden*, pp. 70–72. See also A. J. Wensinck, "The Semitic New Year and the Origin of Eschatology," *Acta Orientalia* 1 (1922), 158–99.

to his own "human exemplar" (*nimūdār-i ādamīyat*), his divinely ordained role in the cosmic hierarchy (*HP*, 41:70).[61] His ability to make this interpretation is the result of his acquisition of wisdom by means of the tales, as the several quests of their protagonists figure forth the potential for success or failure of Bahrām's own quest and guide him toward wisdom. Bahrām's passage through the seven domes constitutes a truancy in which his apparent neglect of duty in reality prepares him for a new and perfected understanding of his true identity;[62] he thus succeeds, where Niẓāmī's earlier heroes failed, in achieving self-knowledge, the prerequisite to justice.

In his translation to ideal kingship, Bahrām's natal, circumstantial, and desired identities merge and are subsumed by the true, qualitative identity he ultimately attains. This fusion is symbolically enacted (as are the other crucial stages in Bahrām's progress) by a wedding, as, following the trial of the evil minister, he puts aside his seven brides, who represent both his

[61] In addition to being termed an object lesson (*ʿibrat*), the shepherd's speech is also called *ramz* (allegory or parable) and *tadbīr* (counsel) (*HP*, 41:67–69). The concept of the king as shepherd, found in ancient Iran, permeates Islamic ethical and political writings, as well as poetry; cf. Morony, *Iraq*, pp. 35–36, and Lambton, *State and Government*, pp. 283–84.

[62] The truancy is a favorite device of romance which takes on added complexity in connection with kingship, as a central issue of kingly ethics is the ruler's accessibility to his subjects, and his obligation to devote full attention to affairs of state (see al-Ghazzālī, *Book of Counsel*, pp. 95–96; Lambton, "Mirrors," passim). Khusraw's truancy at the Armenian court has graver implications than do Rāmīn's love idylls with Vīs; Bahrām's dalliance in the domes enables the forces of disorder, in the person of the evil minister, to ravage his kingdom. Bahrām's truancy somewhat resembles Calidore's sojourn among the maidens of Mt. Acidale in book 6 of Spenser's *Faerie Queene*, an idealized pastoral similarly located in magical space with only the most tenuous relationship to reality, which recalls both the voluptuous isolation of the seven domes and the gardens of the tales themselves. Calidore's prowess and courtly manners, like Bahrām's valor and statecraft, are insufficient to avert the inroads of unjust elements, because they are not informed by the inner illumination necessary to transcend the world of appearance. For both, this illumination is provided by the power of love incarnated in poetry; it is tempting to find a parallel between Niẓāmī's princesses and the Muses invoked by Spenser. (On Calidore's truancy, see Javitch, *Poetry and Courtliness*, pp. 145–59.)

own desire for worldly glory and the multiplicity that results when justice is conceived of, in human terms, as merely equity. Bahrām's final bride, in the succession that includes Fitnah and the seven princesses (and that is anticipated by the triumphant wedding of the young master to his "Fortune"), is the single principle of justice: a justice whose source is love and whose guiding light is law. To this beloved he dedicates himself totally, renouncing his seven brides and converting their domes to temples.[63]

Bahrām's kingship thus incorporates the dual functions of priest and king, echoing both an ancient Iranian ideal of kingship and the Islamic concept of the king as Perfect Man.[64]

[63] Ritter reads this episode as indicating that the influence of astrology on Bahrām's life has been "overcome" and that he has replaced the false guidance of the stars with the right guidance of religion (*Bildersprache*, p. 50). The function of astrological elements in Niẓāmī is analogical rather than predicative: the planets and stars forming part of the cosmic order created by God, and the existence of a parallel, independent order being unthinkable, the heavens mirror the divine decrees rather than exerting their own influence. As the Ikhwān al-Ṣafā' make clear, "Astrology does not pretend and has not the right to pretend to an anticipated knowledge of events. Many people believe that astrology proposes to study the science of the unseen (*ghaib*), but they are definitely wrong. What they call the science of the unseen is really the science of indetermination, the gratuitous pretention of anticipating the future without recourse to any symptom or reasoning, be it causal or deductive. In this sense the unknown is accessible neither to the astrologers, nor diviners, nor prophets, nor sages. It is the work of God only" (*RIS*, 1:153; translated by Nasr, *Introduction*, p. 82 [translator's emphasis deleted]). The Ikhwān stress that the study of the stars is not for all men, but for the wise it is a means to progress to higher things (*RIS*, 1:155–56). Allen writes, "Mere fortune-telling is a cheap distortion of what intends, essentially, to assert that heavenly and human realities operate according to the same rules and forces and definitions and therefore operate in parallel to one another" (*Ethical Poetic*, p. 208). Niẓāmī denies the predicative role of astrology in his prologue to the *Haft Paykar* (1:17–41). Compare Chaucer's use of astrological symbolism discussed by Charlotte Thompson, "Cosmic Allegory and Cosmic Error in the Frame of the *Canterbury Tales*," *Pacific Coast Philology* 18:1–2 (November 1983), 77–83.

[64] "In the perfect man, who has realized his Divine Origin, the process [of ascent toward the Creator] has come to an end. Man's 'evolution' is therefore inward . . . because man, by virtue of being able to return to his origin, fulfills the purpose of the whole of creation" (Nasr, *Introduction*, p. 73). De Bruijn comments on the mystical and secular aspects of the concept of the Perfect

Aided by the power of love—no longer wrongly interpreted as either possession or self-immolation, but correctly, as the true source of justice and a cosmic force for harmony and order—Bahrām awaits his final union, the ultimate stage of love, which is possible only in the next world: the oneness with the divine beloved, which follows his apotheosis from the cave, an event that lifts Niẓāmī's romance from the status of a versified mirror for princes to that of an eschatological vision of kingship.[65]

Man as reflected in Islamic writings (as well as on the pre-Islamic origins of the concept), but, like most other writers on the topic, does not clarify its association with kingship (see *OPP*, pp. 216–18; see also *EI*², s.v. "Al-insān al-kāmil"). The idea of the king as Perfect Man is, however, a logical extension both of the connection of kingship and the imamate (that is, the ruler as the regent of God) and of the concept of man as microcosm (the king embodying the highest level of mankind); it is reflected perhaps most fully in al-Fārābī's ideal of the philosopher-king (see Lambton, *State and Government*, pp. 69–82, 288–306, 316–25, et passim; see also *EI*² s.v. "Imāma"). Cf. Naṣīr al-Dīn Ṭūsī: "When Man reaches this degree, so that he becomes aware of the ranks of generables universally, then are realized in him, in one way or another, the infinite particulars subsumed under the universals; and when practice becomes his familiar, so that his operations and acts are realized in accordance with acceptable faculties and habits, he becomes a world unto himself, comparable to this macrocosm, and merits to be called a 'microcosm'. Thus he becomes Almighty God's vice-gerent among His creatures, entering among His particular Saints, and standing as a Complete and Absolute Man. . . . At length, between him and his Master no veil intervenes, but he receives the ennoblement of proximity to the Divine Presence" (*Nasirean Ethics*, p. 52).

[65] In the course of his progress Bahrām passes (either personally or vicariously, by means of positive or negative examples) through the varied gradations of human love to reach this ultimate stage. On the types of love, see *RIS*, 3:178–84; Naṣīr al-Dīn Ṭūsī, *Nasirean Ethics*, pp. 198–99. On the Beatific Vision, see also Lomba Fuentes, 169–72. By his disappearance into the cave, Bahrām becomes associated with such Messianic figures as the Sunnite *imām mahdī*, the Shiʿite *imām ghā'ib*, and their precursor the Zoroastrian Saoshyant, the savior who will incorporate in his person the functions of king and priest and bring about the renovation of the world. (The ancient Iranian god Varhrān [= Bahrām], whose name was taken by a number of kings, was considered a forerunner of this final savior. See J. Duchesne-Guillemin, *La religion de l'Iran ancien*, pp. 261–64, 353–54; H. Corbin, *Avicenne et le récit visionnaire*, 1:282–96; and compare Gallais, *Genèse*, pp. 73–74.) Rather than reflecting any covert Imamite or Batinite beliefs on the part of Niẓāmī, I take this conflation of Bahrām, Saoshyant, and *imām* as an effort to reconcile these conflicting beliefs in one figure and thereby to deny any essential opposition be-

Bahrām's status as Perfect Man suggests that, for the poet, the sense in which the ruler embodies the experience of his people is not merely political but ethical: the king is Everyman, and the moral conflicts that exist within his soul exemplify those of mankind as a whole. By mastering his nature, he achieves a state of harmony with the cosmic order and thus is able to fulfill his mediatory role between macrocosm and microcosm: to become "the monarch as the many in the one,"[66] uniting nature and mankind. Niẓāmī demonstrates that neither heroic valor nor clever statecraft is sufficient to make the perfect ruler, who, as the embodiment of all virtue, cannot display valor or dispense justice without the informing power of love; his poem thus stands as a commentary on, and corrective to, both the heroic ethos of epic and the pragmatic values of mirror literature.[67] Fulfilling the promise of the prologue, it teaches man the nature of his own design, and, in so doing, reveals to him his place in that "cosmic cathedral" which is the ordered hierarchy of the universe, and which the poet, through his artistry, has recreated in verse.[68]

---

tween them. (The "three levels" of knowledge alluded in n. 31 also have an Ismaili significance, and it is possible that in the figure of Bahrām Niẓāmī intends an allusion—political rather than doctrinal—to the Caliph al-Nāṣir [1180–1225], who attempted to restore the power of the caliphate and who was successful in achieving an alliance with the Nizari Ismailis [cf. *CHI*, 5:168–70, 458 ff.; Hodgson, *Venture*, 2:280–81].) Ritter's comment on the "dreadful senselessness" of Bahrām's end (*Bildersprache*, p. 68) is, under the circumstances, inappropriate, as is Rypka's interpretation of his disappearance as a sign of "the vanity of all things" ("Les Sept Princesses de Nizhami," pp. 108–109); although in worldly terms the event may occasion grief (as the mourning of Bahrām's mother—introduced for the first and only time in the poem for precisely this purpose—suggests), in terms of eternal truth it is an occasion for joy. Bahrām's progress has also been interpreted as an allegory of the mystical path (see, for example, Wilson, *Haft Paikar*, 1:xvii–xix); but while the work contains obvious mystical allusions (for example, the tales depict a progress through the spiritual stations of Contentment [I] through Right Guidance [IV] to Law [VII]), mysticism is only one of the facets of human experience that the poet sets himself to explore.

[66] Myers, " 'Kaiserchronik,' " 222–23.

[67] The spiral structure of the *Haft Paykar* contrasts with the overall linear movement of the *Shāhnāmah*; in so doing, it presents a contrasting view of time and of human history. Bausani observes that in the *Shāhnāmah* "the ancient instrument of Iranian symbol, Cyclical Time, uniting the primordial be-

ginnings with the eschatological end, is . . . broken, and Time becomes linear Time" ("Muhammad or Darius?" p. 48); Niẓāmī's reinstatement of the ancient view of time functions as further commentary on the epic. This conception of time as circular—reflecting the absorption of neo-Platonic ideas into Islamic thought—recalls the cosmological system of al-Bīrūnī, concerning which Nasr comments: "The traditional idea of cycles implies a qualitative notion of time in such a way that an analogy exists between two points in the unfolding of time. This conception can be symbolized by a helix whose turns have analogies with each other without ever repeating one another" (*Introduction*, p. 119, n. 6; cf. n. 52). On the contrast between cyclical and linear time and their complementary relationship, see Heninger, *TSH*, pp. 220–27. Niẓāmī's treatment of the female element in the *Haft Paykar* is noteworthy as departing from both the male-oriented ethos of epic and the typical misogyny of mirror literature and resembles the attitude of such mystical thinkers as Ibn ʿArabī and Jalāl al-Dīn Rūmī, who gave special importance to the feminine principle, as did the Ikhwān al-Ṣafāʾ in their philosophical writings. The episode of Fitnah specifically functions as a criticism of the code of male honor and vengeance for insults that prevailed during the period, on which see Hodgson, *Venture*, 2:140–46.

[68] I have borrowed the phrase *cosmic cathedral* from S. H. Nasr, who observes (concerning the beliefs of the Ikhwān al-Ṣafāʾ), "In this Universe of purpose where 'God, Most High, has created nothing in vain,' there are correspondences and analogies, descents and ascents of souls, differentiation and integration, all knit into a harmonious pattern which is very far from a 'rationalistic castle.' It is rather the 'cosmic cathedral' in which the unicity of Nature, the interrelatedness of all things with each other, and the ontological dependence of the whole of creation upon the Creator, is brought into focus" (*Introduction*, p. 55; see chapter 7 of this book for the particular relevance of this figure).

· VI ·

Ghazal: The Ideals of Love

IN THE *qaṣīdah*, the topic of love serves as a preliminary to panegyric; however essential it may be in establishing the poem's ethical and/or topical context, as formal subject matter its role is subsidiary to that of the primary topic of encomium. In romance, while love is the central topic around which the plot (typically, the protagonist's love quest) revolves, it also provides a means of exploring analogous or related issues. At first glance, it appears that in the *ghazal* the topic of love at last comes into its own. The *ghazal*, which emerged as an independent poetic genre with distinctive structural characteristics in the twelfth century, ultimately eclipsed the *qaṣīdah* as the most prominent lyric genre; and though it soon expanded thematically to incorporate other types of material—gnomic, encomiastic, and satiric—it remained (and still remains) primarily identified as a vehicle for expressing the varied aspects and perspectives of the experience of love.

Like romance, the *ghazal* is a distinctively Persian genre that has no exact counterpart in Arabic. Its relatively sudden emergence as a formal genre distinguished from the *qiṭʿah* by specific structural characteristics, notably the obligatory rhymed hemistichs of the *maṭlaʿ* and the mention of the poet's name in the *maqṭaʿ*, has led to wide speculation concerning its origins.[1]

[1] The main theories concerning the origins of the Persian *ghazal* are summarized by A. Bausani as follows: (1) that it originated in a separation of the *nasīb* from the *qaṣīdah* and its subsequent development in isolation; (2) that it originated as an offshoot of earlier Iranian folk poetry, about which admittedly almost nothing is known; and (3) a compromise thesis, advanced primarily by A. Mirzoyev, to the effect that both Arabic and indigenous elements played a part in its development, and that a distinction must be made between the "technical" *ghazal*, as manifested in the formally distinct Persian form ap-

Evaluation of the various theories in this regard does not concern us here; it seems clear that many factors contributed to the formation of the *ghazal*, not least its close association, almost from its inception, with mysticism and the effect of this association on its structure and, more particularly, its language.[2] This chapter focuses on the development and function

---

pearing in the twelfth century, and the "generic" *ghazal*, a more generalized love lyric which (in Bausani's words) "owes its origins to folk poetry, later refined at the courts under Arabic influence" (*EI*[2] s.v. "Ghazal"). All these theories ignore contemporary rhetorical usage, which treats *ghazal* as a content-defined genre encompassing love poetry in general (including the *nasīb*), and which does not recognize a distinct formal genre (formal genres are usually defined prosodically, e.g., *rubāʿī, masnavī*, etc., with no distinction as to content). See also Rypka, *History*, pp. 248–53, and the references cited on pp. 274–75, nn. 8–30. Bausani has elsewhere suggested a Chinese origin for the *ghazal*; see "Considerazione sull'origine del ghazal," *Quaderno dell'Accademia Nazionale dei Lincei* 160 (1971), 195–208.

[2] The association should be broadened to include the effect of the growth of religious poetry in general during the period in question (eleventh–twelfth centuries); as de Bruijn observes, "On the level of meaning, the emergence of religiously inspired poetry, expressed in almost any form available in the tradition, was undoubtedly the most decisive process with regard to the future. It left a permanent mark on Persian poetry, noticeable in works of a predominantly profane nature as well as in those which are genuine religious poems" (*OPP*, p. xii). Bausani views this interpretation more negatively: "The passage from [the lyric] style [of such poets as Rūdakī and ʿUnṣurī] to that of the golden classic age [e.g., Ḥāfiẓ] is characterised above all by the penetration of gnostic-mystical features . . . into the heart of the lyrical composition, a penetration which shatters the harmony of the composition and gives rise to that typical feature of the classic *ghazal*, the conceptual independence of the several verses" ("The Development of Form in Persian Lyrics: A Way to a Better Understanding of the Structure of Western Poetry," *East and West*, n.s., 9 [1958], 149). (On the problem of the *ghazal*'s unity, see also n. 69.) Marshall Hodgson's discussion of the functional role of Sufism in Islamic society is illuminating in this connection. Pointing to the fact that from the eleventh century onward all devotional life is influenced by Sufism, he analyzes its interrelationship with the Sharīʿah: "The usual justification of Ṣûfism with regard to the Sharîʿah did not depend on dialectical subtleties or even on rigoristic rules, but on a frank division of labour. It was explained . . . that the Ṣûfis dealt with the inward side (bâṭin) of the same faith and truth of which the Sharʿî ʿulamâʾ scholars were concerned with the outward side (ẓâhir); and that both were completely valid and necessary. In all respects, the inward paralleled the outward, complementing it, not contradicting it" (*Venture*, 2:219;

of the *ghazal* in the courtly milieu—a task that will require, if not the total abandonment, at least a considerable modification of many assumptions that have traditionally characterized discussions of the genre.

For the *ghazal* is, perhaps, the most opaque and elusive of Persian poetic genres. The initial impression of spontaneity, or of "sincerity," produced by its ostensible status as a love lyric that expresses personal emotion gives way, on reading many such poems, to a conviction of its repetitiveness and extreme conventionality. Notwithstanding (or perhaps due to) its great popularity and attractiveness for poets and critics alike, it has suffered conspicuously from both misinterpretation and neglect. Having had, initially, the most immediate appeal to those scholars who sought throughout Persian literature for the expression of the poet's "personal voice"—rarely (and often mistakenly) perceived in the panegyric *qaṣīdah*, and equated with the narrator's didactic or pseudoautobiographical musings in epic and romance—the "authentic" *ghazal* was subsequently identified with the mystical subgenre, while the courtly *ghazal* (insofar as its existence was admitted) was rejected as the empty repetition of stereotyped formulas.

The views of G. M. Wickens cited in the Preface reflect the tendency of many critics—who assume a priori the detrimental effects of courtly patronage—to regard "the use of a mystical setting and mystical imagery" as "one of the most ingenious devices to escape from the boundaries of social convention and taste."[3] However, the tendency of modern scholars to view literature through a socioeconomic filter, and thus to see the use of mystical themes as a means of combating an oppressive regime or of achieving self-affirmation (personal, class, or national),[4] has, like the assumption of earlier generations that mystical poetry alone embodied the genuine expression of a

see also 2:201–30). This complementary relationship makes it difficult (as well as virtually unnecessary) to distinguish between an authentic Sufi and a non-Sufi in the absence of other (historical or biographical) evidence.

[3] Wickens, "Persian Literature," p. 72.

[4] Cf. the views of I. S. Braginsky on Ḥāfiẓ, quoted by Rypka, *History*, p. 269; and see also the discussion of Ḥāfiẓ in this chapter.

deeply moving personal experience,[5] proved inadequate to deal with a large body of *ghazal* poetry, in particular that composed for courtly audiences. Moreover, the persistent allegorization of *ghazal* poetry—interpreted in terms of a code that posited, concealed behind the apparent celebration of secular love, physical beauty, and the pleasures of real wine, an esoteric mystical meaning that endowed the poem with spiritual value—has further obscured understanding of the genre, chiefly by assuming a uniformity for it that is not, in fact, the case.[6]

For the *ghazal* is neither uniformly mystical nor a mere succession of sterile imitations of prescribed, inherited stereotypes in which content is subordinated to form. While it is true that during the centuries when it was at its peak, from Sanā'ī (d. 1150?) to Ḥāfiẓ (d. 1390?), its language, imagery, and thematic content show little apparent development—so that, presented with a random sample of unfamiliar *ghazal*s (lacking, of course, the *takhallus̱*), one would be hard put to identify their

[5] Examples of this response to Persian mystical poetry (particularly strong in Nicholson) are too numerous to cite; cf. (as one instance) A. J. Arberry's "Autobiographical Sketch" in the preface to his translation of *Mystical Poems of Rumi: Second Selection* (pp. ix–xiv).

[6] The popularity of this method reflects the attachment of some early translators of Ḥāfiẓ (notably Wilberforce Clarke) to indigenous efforts to allegorize the works of this and other poets (beginning primarily with Jāmī), and their reliance on such commentaries as those of Muḥammad Davānī and Muḥsin Fayẕ Kāshānī, and on the *Gulshan-i Rāz* of Shabistarī (d. 1320) and its commentaries—works belonging rather to the exegetical than to the critical (i.e., rhetorical) tradition. It is likely that the immediate causes of such indigenous trends were political (or politico-religious) rather than literary (a topic that requires systematic investigation). The Victorian quest for Eastern spirituality, coupled with the tendency of nineteenth-century scholarship to equate "courtly" love with a Platonic or "pure" love in which the sexual element was, if not absent, rigidly suppressed or sublimated, further encouraged the mystical allegorization of much *ghazal* poetry, while insistence on viewing the lyric as autobiographical, as reflecting a factual relationship between the poet and his beloved (whether human or divine), contributed further to the trend. For a discussion of the various interpretations of Ḥāfiẓ see especially A. Schimmel, "Ḥāfiẓ and His Critics," *Studies in Islam* 16 (1979), 1–33. On comparable problems in medieval European literature, see Dronke, *Medieval Latin*, 1:56–97.

authors, or even the periods in which they were composed—it is also clear that (to quote Robert Rehder) "men for hundreds of years wrote ghazals not out of mere habit, but because the *ghazal* expressed what they wanted to say in a way which pleased them."[7]

As Peter Dembowski points out, court poetry is, by its very nature, marked by a stability and longevity that transcend the fluctuations of historical realia; its internal equilibrium of vocabulary and structure ensures that its evolution will be so gradual as to be almost imperceptible, yet this very stability renders it capable of addressing a wide variety of changing issues.[8] Similarly (Rehder notes),

> There is no question that Persian poetry is very conventional, and that a limited number of conventions are used over and over. This, however, does not make all ghazals interchangeable. What is interesting is that *within these narrow limits* some poems seem artificial, trivial and insipid while others generate great power and beauty, and that whatever their quality there is a great variety of poems. It is very important to discriminate between the different ways in which a given poet made use of the tradition.[9]

Perhaps more than any other genre of Persian poetry, the *ghazal* is, paradoxically, both highly conventional and highly flexible.

If this flexibility, this potential for variety, does not reside in the *ghazal*'s language or thematic content per se, it must derive (as Dembowski and Rehder both emphasize) from the "third dimension" of the poem, that is, from the uses to which its essentially conventional elements are put—in other words, from what the poem "means": a meaning not to be equated with some hidden allegorical (i.e., mystical) sense, but that must be understood in terms of the poem's function. The functions of

[7] Rehder, "Unity," 65.

[8] Peter Dembowski, "Vocabulary of Old French Courtly Lyrics—Difficulties and Hidden Difficulties," *Critical Inquiry* 2 (1976), 775–6.

[9] Rehder, "Unity," 72; author's emphasis.

the *ghazal* are manifold: It is an entertainment, a diversion (particularly as it is frequently accompanied by music), a "background" for courtly gatherings; it figures in a poetic competition or is presented on a specific occasion. It may be composed in response to an issue of immediate topical importance or may bear a more general message. The varied and ephemeral occasions for which it is composed do not account for its longevity as a genre; this must be attributed to its ability, in all periods of its popularity, to remain both sufficiently stable to ensure continued appeal and sufficiently flexible to meet changing needs. Both these conditions are met by the continued and universal appeal of it primary generic topic—love—and by the wider implications of this topic, implications that have already been explored in connection with the *qaṣīdah* and romance and that are even more significant in preserving the *ghazal* as a perennially viable genre.

In the light of these observations, it is clear that interpretation of the *ghazal* is not aided by considering its language and imagery as fixed conventions but depends on an analysis both of the ways in which these are put to use by individual poets, and of how they may have been received by the audience. The problems that present themselves in connection with the *ghazal* in many ways parallel those described by Judson Allen with repect to the *grand chant courtois*:

> The problems presented to modern understanding by the lyrics of the *grand chant courtois* are not problems of literal meaning, nor of social context, historically understood. We know well enough what these poems say, and we know the social class and the typical biographies of the people who liked, commissioned, wrote, heard, and supported them. What we have not decided for sure is their rhetorical character—we do not know what they are as a part of a complex involving audience, doctrine, and ideal or real behavior.[10]

[10] J. B. Allen, "The *Grand Chant Courtois* and the Wholeness of the Poem: The Medieval *Assimilatio* of Text, Audience, and Commentary," *L'Esprit Créateur* 18:3 (1978), 11.

Allen proposes that, in terms of this larger complex, the love celebrated by this poetry is a means by which the poet communicates a more general ideal of human conduct: "Correct love, when submitted to, permits one to achieve that posture of selfhood which is true, and in which therefore one is a true self." The "textuality" of such poems, in Allen's view, exists at the level of tropology—the level of ethical meaning—where, by making analogical demands on its audience, the poem points ultimately to anagogy,

> the perfect, iconic life, in which persons find themselves transformed into personifications. Here, I suggest, is the proper place to locate the real audience. In other words, this scheme . . . suggests that the only fit use of the *grand chant courtois*, as a piece of language with rhetorical effectiveness, is to teach mortal aristocratic people how to exist as the achieved personifications of their roles.[11]

We may recall Niẓāmī's statement in the *Haft Paykar* that the purpose of discourse is to teach man the nature of his own design—a precept supported by the example of Bahrām, who learned from various types of discourse how to become such an "achieved personification" of his own *nimūdār-i ādamīyat*, his "human exemplar." Although the fourfold scheme to which Allen alludes is specific to Christian exegesis, the underlying belief "in language as an analogizing system which includes, rather than excludes, the world," is common to medi-

[11] Allen, "*Grand Chant Courtois*," 15, 16; cf. idem, "Grammar, Poetic Form, and the Lyric Ego: A Medieval *A Priori*," in *Vernacular Poetics in the Middle Ages*, ed. Lois Ebin, especially pp. 205–209; the medieval lyric is defined as "a definite and informing ego position within which any given human hearer is invited to become true" (p. 208). Michel Zink observes, "In order for the poem to make an impression on its reader, the latter must make it his own . . . and place upon himself the affective burden which the poet has put into it. The poem succeeds if the reader finds himself therein, that is, if the *I* of the poem is also he. The entire effect of the poem is in this tension between distance and familiarity: this *I* both is not, and could be, myself" ("Remarques sur les conditions de l'anonymité dans la poésie lyrique française du Moyen Age," in *Mélanges Michel Foulon*, p. 423).

eval thought both East and West.[12] While it is evident that mystical poetry, through its depiction (or rather, its evocation) of personal experience, aims at just such an encouragement toward the anagogic, it has generally gone unrecognized that the courtly *ghazal* similarly depicts an idealized relationship on which its audience is encouraged to model its own behavior.

In generic terms, the *ghazal* exists in a complementary relationship with the *qaṣīdah*; while in the latter the love situation is subordinated to the encomiastic, and the virtues held up for emulation are public rather than private, the *ghazal* focuses on

[12] Allen, "*Grand Chant Courtois*," 6. Clarifying his heuristic model, Allen observes: "What the fourfold schema of exegesis defines for literature is not a range of possible meanings of a text . . . but rather a range of possible kinds of reality a text may assimilate. . . . Thus the literal level normally includes . . . remembered facts and stories. . . . The consuetudines and credulitates which are really what poetry is about . . . correspond to the allegorical level. The tropological level is the reader or hearer . . . who may occur dramatically within texts . . . as well as in the more conventional place of audience. . . . The anagogical level . . . normally . . . is not the text, but something extra-textual which may be assimilated. . . . Generalizing, anagogy is significance in some ideal sense" (*Ethical Poetic*, p. 214). Allen relates this scheme to the medieval notion of *assimilatio*, under which "the principle of parallel, and of parallel systems, was the basis on which language in general and poetry in particular should be understood" ("*Grand Chant Courtois*," 7). "In that version of Aristotle's *Poetics* which was accepted and read in the Middle Ages [Hermann Alemanus' translation of Averroes' "Middle Commentary"], *assimilatio* displaces *mimesis*. It means, broadly, 'likening' . . . [and] refers, without distinction, to a variety of different linguistic acts which we habitually distinguish—simple reference, the relation between a description and the thing described, the relation between the two halves of a simile or metaphor, the relation between the two parts of a simile or comparison, and the relation among the parts of a proportionate analogy" (ibid., 6). The Latin rendering of Averroes' *tashbīh* by *assimilatio* supports the view that the meaning of this term is broader than that of *simile*, by which it is customarily translated. The anagogic end of discourse is reflected in Rūmī's response to the question, "What is the use of expressions and words?" "The Master answered: The use of words is that they set you searching and excite you, not that the object of the quest should be attained through words. . . . Words are as when you see afar off something moving; you run in the wake of it in order to see it, it is not the case that you see it through its movement. Human speech too is inwardly the same; it excites you to seek the meaning, even though you do not see it in reality" (*Discourses*, p. 202; *Fīhi mā fīhi*, pp. 193–94).

private relations between individuals and is thus more subjectively oriented. The *ghazal*'s private dimension—its generic subjectivity—reflects the less formal nature of the occasions on which it was composed; the type of love that it depicts is one that was cultivated in refined aristocratic circles. The frequent crudities and barbarities witnessed on the political scene should not blind us to the fact that to be a devoted servant of love was one of the cardinal virtues of *murūvat* and a defining quality of any man who claimed to possess *adab* (which might, in this context, best be rendered as *savoir-faire*).[13] Moreover, although the refined and idealistic nature of love was certainly stressed, its physical aspect was by no means ignored; even in mystical *ghazal*s, the sensual and spiritual sides of love typically coexist as analogues, rather than alternatives.[14] Reluctance to admit that poets extol (in veiled or open terms) the joys of sex, and not merely love in the abstract, and that their love service is not merely a conventional metaphor but is envisioned as leading to concrete rewards, has placed unnecessary obstacles in the path of interpretation of much *ghazal* poetry.

A distinctive component of the Persian *ghazal*, and one that has often proved disconcerting, is its overt homoerotic content. The gender ambiguity characteristic of Persian lyric poetry has traditionally been exploited to permit the critic to construe the beloved as feminine. While this is possible to some extent in the *qaṣīdah*, where explicit descriptions tend to be relatively infrequent and where the analogy between beloved and patron is conventionally predicated on the contrast between the sexes implicit in the complementary relationship between *nasīb* and *madīḥ*, it is less justifiable for the *ghazal*,

[13] See, for example, the ideals adumbrated in the *Kitāb al-Muwashshā* and similar works. Poirion notes: "This seething violence, this cruelty ever ready to display itself, require discipline rather than stimulation. Action must become subject to the word in order to regain the humanity which will founder if not tamed. Words are reborn as precepts. It is through words that one becomes nobly involved in life. Language makes possible the passage from instinct to will" (*Le poète et le prince*, p. 68).

[14] Cf. Schimmel, *Mystical Dimensions*, pp. 289–93.

where the male gender of the beloved, often explicitly indicated, becomes a standard convention of the genre.[15] Critics uneasy with this situation have attempted to rationalize it in various ways, either by allegorizing the male beloved as a neo-Platonic human reflection of divine love, or by invoking such sociohistorical factors as the prohibition on the open reference to women in love poems.[16] But while such factors lend a certain verisimilitude to the fictive world of the *ghazal*, reliance on them to explain away the presence of a male beloved ignores the fact that such love—which might or might not include a carnal dimension—was not only not condemned, but widely tolerated and frequently highly esteemed.[17]

[15] Many *qaṣīdah*s, of course, feature homoerotic motifs in the *nasīb*; a case in point is the second *qaṣīdah* by Manūchihrī discussed in chapter 2. This is most frequent when (as in that instance) an explicit parallel is intended between the "beloved" of the *nasīb* and the *mamdūḥ* (often linked by the topos of the "cruel Turk"); see, for example, Farrukhī's *qaṣīdah* in which the *nasīb* is addressed to a Turk who is requested to doff his warlike garb and take up the harp instead (with appropriate wordplay on *jang* and *chang*), while the *madīḥ* extolls Maḥmūd of Ghaznah's victory at Hazār-Asb and, implicitly, stresses the desire for peace (*Dīvān*, pp. 206–208).

[16] Cf. Hodgson, *Venture*, 2:303. Compare the parallel situation with respect to Urdu *ghazal* (heavily influenced by Persian) discussed by C. M. Naim ("The Theme of Homosexual [Pederastic] Love in Pre-Modern Urdu Poetry," in *Studies in the Urdu Ġazal and Prose Fiction*, ed. M. U. Memon, pp. 122–23).

[17] See Hodgson, *Venture*, 2:145–6, for a brief discussion of this topic. Naim contrasts the attitude of medieval Islam with the intolerance of homosexuality in medieval Christendom: "If the European response to homosexual love has been totally antagonistic, the Islamic East has neither celebrated it in an unequivocal fashion nor looked at it with total impassivity"; while condemned by the orthodox (who found in Koran 4:16 a censure of the practice), a number of alleged Prophetic traditions were adduced in support of it (Naim, "Homosexual Love," pp. 120, 134, n. 8). Traditional sources attribute the introduction of pederasty into Abbasid society to Persian influence (and specifically to the practices of the Khurasanian army); the attribution presumably formed part of the anti-Shuʿubid arsenal and as such can be given little validity. On homosexuality and related practices in Abbasid society, see Mez, *Renaissance of Islam*, pp. 352–61. It is related concerning al-Amīn that, "to cure her son of his passion for eunuchs the mother of the Caliph Amin smuggled among them several slender, handsome maids with short hair, dressed up as boys in tight jackets and girdles. Court circles and common-folk all alike followed this

The idealizing tone of Persian homoerotic poetry contrasts markedly with that which is generally typical of Arabic, where the *ghazal bi-al-mudhakkar*—poetry on the love of boys—is often salacious, if not downright obscene, and frequently (as in the poems of Abū Nuwās) constitutes a parody on the ideal of courtly love expressed by poets like al-ʿAbbās ibn al-Aḥnaf. Al-Washshā''s condemnation both of the love of boys and, more specifically, of their praise in poetry, is representative of an attitude not uncommon among writers on love:

> Among the praiseworthy practices [*madhāhib*] of the *ẓurafā'* is their inclination to the love of women and flirtation with singing-girls. . . . The love of boys [*ghilmān*] does not find praise among them, nor is it found in their customary behavior; they have ever preferred the love of women to that of boys, and have praised them with fullest eloquence. . . . Love of [women] is more suitable, and they are fitter for men [than are boys]. . . . Never have I seen any of the Arabs of old, or their most excellent [*mufaḍḍal*] poets, resort, in their poems, to mentioning any but women, or beginning their *qaṣīdahs* with anything but erotic verses [*tashbīb*] describing women.[18]

While examples abound, in both verse and prose, of the passionate attachments of older men for beautiful youths, such re-

---

fashion and similarly dressed-up their slave-girls and called them *Ghulamiyyah*" (ibid., p. 357). Such *ghulāmiyāt* figure prominently in the poetry of Abū Nuwās.

[18] Al-Washshā', *al-Muwaššá*, pp. 104–105. Al-Washshā' draws support from the example of the Prophet, who approved of poets who introduced their qaṣīdahs with the traditional *nasīb*; he concludes (in a passage which has a distinctly apologetic tone): "Were the mention of women in poetry something prohibited [*munkar*], the Prophet—peace be upon him!—would have been the first to prohibit it; and were the mention of other than women more worthy of presentation in poetry than their mention, the Prophet—peace be upon him!—would have been the first to command the former, and condemn the latter. And if the mention of women in poetry were an obscenity, an indecency or an abomination, those poems uttered in praise of the Prophet should have avoided all mention of what is reprehensible, just as they avoided all mention of males, and love of them" (pp. 105–106).

lationships are generally denied the ennobling status of heterosexual love. There are no male counterparts to the idealized Salmās, Laylīs, and Hinds who populate the mainstream of Arabic love poetry.[19]

The more tolerant Persian view of homosexual love perhaps reflects antecedents in ancient Iranian culture, where the courtly view of love may have extended to homosexual relations.[20] The tendency found reinforcement in Islamic times, particularly at the courts of Turkish princes, first that of Ghaznah and, later, those of the Saljuqs; the attachment of Maḥmūd of Ghaznah to the slave Ayāz is legendary and has become a literary commonplace for devoted love.[21] The prevalence of youths as objects of love is closely linked to the manners and protocols of courtly drinking gatherings (*majālis-i sharāb*), which themselves provided both an occasion for the composition of *ghazal*s and a conventional fictive setting for them.

> There is no genre of Persian poetry which has been more impregnated by the atmosphere of these drinking-bouts than the poetry of love. All the elements which constitute the thematic complex of *taġazzul* are in one way or another related to this real background, whether they are meant in a profane [or] in a religious sense.[22]

The practices associated with drinking gatherings reflect the continuity of ancient Iranian tradition in Islamic courtly soci-

[19] Compare the discussions by Norman Roth, " 'Deal gently with the young man': Love of Boys in Medieval Hebrew Poetry of Spain," *Speculum* 57 (1982), 20–51, and J. Schirmann, "The Ephebe in Medieval Hebrew Poetry," *Sefarad* 16 (1955), 55–68.

[20] According to Burton, Herodotus claimed that the Persians learned pederasty from the Hellenes, whereas Plutarch asserted that the practice antedated Persian contacts with Greece; see *Love, War and Fancy: The Customs and Manners of the East*, ed. Kenneth Walker, p. 179.

[21] Clint, *Manūchihrī*, p. 122. On Maḥmūd and Ayāz, see C. E. Bosworth, *The Ghaznavids*, pp. 103, 128, and "Maḥmūd of Ghazna in Contemporary Eyes and in Later Persian Literature," *Iran* 4 (1966), 85–92. A *qaṣīdah* of Farrukhī praises Ayāz (*Dīvān*, pp. 163–65).

[22] De Bruijn, *OPP*, pp. 158; see Mez, *Renaissance of Islam*, on drinking gatherings in Abbasid society.

ety.[23] A central figure therein was the *sāqī*, or cupbearer, who served the wine—not (as so often in Arabic poetry) a lissome slave girl, not even exclusively a youth with downless cheeks, but frequently a young male slave noted equally for beauty and bravery, as was Maḥmūd's Ayāz. (Such individuals often rose to high positions, as was the case with Albtegīn, founder of the Ghaznavid dynasty, and his son, Maḥmūd's father Sabuktegīn.)

> At their best, such slaves were excellent soldiers and fine horsemen, played a musical instrument, were refined in their manners and proved delightful companions, as amply attested by the poetry of the period. Some could even engage in discussions on highly specialized literary techniques.[24]

Such persons were frequently the objects of amorous attachments; moreover, unlike heterosexual affairs, such relationships could be referred to openly, without impropriety. Thus their reflection in poetry—the mirror of ideal love—is to be expected.

> It is the social position, training and characteristics of these youths, within a socially accepted pattern of love relationship, that determines some of the main traits of Persian love poetry. . . . Unless one is mindful of the fact that the beloved, as a type, is very often a young soldier cupbearer, who combines the warlike qualities of a warrior with the refinements of a sociable wine server, many aspects of Persian love poetry, and for that matter, much of Ottoman, Urdu, and Islamic Arabic poetry remain puzzling.[25]

[23] Ehsan Yar-Shater, "The Theme of Wine and Wine-Drinking and the Concept of the Beloved in Early Persian Poetry," *Studia Islamica* 13 (1960), 45, and see the references cited in nn. 1 and 2; see also de Bruijn, *OPP*, pp. 157–60.

[24] Yar-Shater, "Wine and Wine-Drinking," 49; the description recalls Anvarī's frequent portrayal of the beloved in his *nasīb*s (cf. chapter 2).

[25] Ibid., 52; cf. Naim, "Homosexual Love," pp. 121–22.

Such a beloved is depicted in this *ghazal* by Sanā'ī:

> Once again you have saddled up your horse, and preferred the road to home.
> To me you have brought the path of wakefulness, and made my heart lost and sorrowful.
> You have put on the coat of mail instead of fox-skin robes, and have taken up the spear instead of the wine-cup.
> You have stretched your hand towards bows and arrows, and turned your face towards battle and ambush.
> You think not of Time's afflictions, nor do you have mercy on the earth's creatures.
> For so long as I do not see your moon-like face, I will rain dew from my eyes upon the Pleiades.
> When I lie down to sleep, because of your absence, my bed will be sorrow, and my pillow, confusion.[26]
>
> (*ghazal* no. 324)

In the *ghazal*, the love of man for man that such an example suggests, however, perhaps is less frequently depicted than is the more familiar model of the love of man for boy. Sanā'ī's *ghazal*s abound with poems addressed to the youthful ephebe, the "sweet boy" (*shīrīn pisar*) of Persian love poetry.

> The curling locks above your ear, my lad,
> has set the world about *its* ears, my lad.
> Who in the world is there could gaze on you
> while heart and head remain unmoved, my lad?
> You are a moon who bears a cup, O slave;
> you are a cypress in a gown, my lad.
> A cypress next my heart, a moon embraced,
> I hold when you are in my arms, my lad.
> Why do you strive so to be cruel, O slave?
> Strive rather towards fidelity, my lad.
> Tonight you've caught me in a snare, my love,

[26] Sanā'ī, *Dīvān*, ed. M. Mudarris Raẓavī; all references are to the numbering in this edition.

since from my arms you flew last night, my lad.
Oh, may you from your rubies grant a kiss
so sweet, and ever drink sweet wine, my lad.
Cease this oppression; seek not to do ill:
the Lord of Justice's near; be still, my lad.

(*ghazal* no. 161)

Such evocations of the youthful cupbearer making the round of the courtly drinking-party, attended by the prince or patron, the "lord of justice" (*mīr-i dād*) to whom the distraught lover may appeal, and before whom the poet sings his song of love, recur time after time in the *ghazal* (as in the *nasīb*; we have already seen an example in the poetry of Manūchihrī). Other commonplace topics of pedophilic verse also abound, such as the description of the down that appears on the beloved's cheek, signaling the end of youth.[27]

The convention of homoerotic poetry, however, must be placed in its proper perspective. The lovely youths addressed and extolled in the Persian *ghazal*, like the ladies to whom such Arab poets as Bashshār and al-ʿAbbās ibn al-Aḥnaf dedicated their verses, should not be construed as literal participants in a factual love affair (or the poems as revelatory of the poet's sexual proclivities). Like Salmā and Hind, they provide the occasion for the poet's song and the pretext for his presentation of the various states of love. In *ghazal*, as in courtly love lyrics in general, it is the portrayal of this experience that is central; any similarity, so to speak, between the poet, the beloved, and the audience to whom the poem is addressed, to any real persons, is purely coincidental, while the experience itself is both an ideal and a fiction.

This concept of the central experience of the love poem as a fiction provides a useful tool for analysis. Frederick Goldin notes in connection with the poetry of the troubadours:

> The basic fiction which provides the subject matter of these lyrics is everywhere the same, and it is every bit as

[27] Cf. *ghazal* no. 137, notable for its use of Koranic allusions and its wordplay, which suggests that the beloved is, in fact, a person of noble status.

> stereotyped as all the other elements of courtly love poetry, both lyric and romance. In the lyric, this fiction is fragmented, analyzed into a fixed register of episodes, moods, and postures, from which the poet draws in order to arrange a certain nonnarrative pattern. . . .
>
> The courtly audience knew this fiction thoroughly, and once it heard the opening lines it would place each lyric at a specific point in the round of courtly love. At the beginning of every song there is a clear indication as to where the lover is, in the pattern of his amorous career. . . . The opening lines, like the opening moves of a game, determine the possibilities that can follow. Every lyric finds its place in the fixed and universal fiction of courtly love.[28]

It is the sharing in this "fiction" that enables the lyric—in our case, the *ghazal*—to perform its function of guiding the audience toward an understanding of the ideals of love and their transcendence of the *realia* of love's actuality. Pending the opportunity for a more detailed study of the formal and thematic elements of the fiction the *ghazal* unfolds, it is this aspect—what Allen terms the lyric's "tropological textuality"—that will be the focus of the present chapter.

The *ghazal*s of Sanā'ī provide a useful introduction to the genre. In them we find its major conventions already well established; they illustrate, moreover, both the inherent stability and the potential flexibility of the form. A widely popular but critically neglected poet, Sanā'ī is usually classified as a mystic, despite the fact that much of his poetry was written in and for courtly circles. His impact on later poetry, both courtly and mystical, was profound; his *ghazal*s perhaps best exemplify the blend of courtly elements and spirituality so characteristic of the genre and the chief cause of difficulties in interpretation.[29]

[28] Goldin, "Array of Perspectives," pp. 52–53.

[29] As de Bruijn comments, "Sanā'ī was a prolific writer of *ġazals*. . . . Although perhaps more of these poems were composed for the purpose of his homiletic poetry than appears at first sight, there can be no doubt that he also produced poems of this genre for entertainment only" (*OPP*, p. 161). The con-

Sanā'ī's *ghazal*s constitute a veritable anatomy of love, in which all its varied phases and gradations are depicted. In their presentation of all the seemingly conflicting aspects of the fiction of love, they provide exemplary illustration of the manner in which the courtly lyric encourages its audience, through identification with the ideal lover, to become (in Allen's phrase) the "achieved personification" of that role, and in so doing to transcend love's human limitations.

> The unattainability of the lady and the suffering of the lover are ethical necessities in the fiction of courtly love. Courtly love . . . is the love of courtliness, of the refinement that distinguishes a class, of an ideal fulfilled in a person whom everyone recognizes. This love-relation enables the courtly man to declare his commitment to the ideals of his class, and to exemplify the behavior in which those ideals are realized: steadfastness, optimism, devoted service, formality, personal grace, self-esteem, self-sacrifice. The singer describes for his audience how, in his devotion to this mirror of courtliness, he has known such suffering and joy as only a man of inherent nobility can experience. He suffers loneliness because he must remain distant from his beloved; uncertainty, because she is capricious as grace itself; despair, because gazing on her beauty and her moral perfection he understands he must renounce every claim to requital. But the surprising thing

---

flicting aspects of Sanā'ī's poetry are discussed in de Bruijn's study of Sanā'ī, which became available to me in the concluding stages of this work. De Bruijn correctly observes that *mystical* is too limiting a term to describe Sanā'ī's religious poetry (which he prefers to call homiletic); he also raises the important question of the influence of patronage on the type of poetry composed on any given occasion (see especially pp. 246–48). In an earlier article de Bruijn stressed the necessity of recognizing the essential nature of the blend of sacred and profane in Sanā'ī's poetry; see "Sanā'ī and the Rise of Persian Mystical Poetry," in *La signification du bas moyen âge dans l'histoire et la culture du monde musulman*, pp. 35–43. The problem of defining mystical poetry is discussed by Lowry Nelson, Jr., "The Rhetorical of Ineffability: Toward a Definition of Mystical Poetry," *Comparative Literature* 8 (1956), 323–36. On Sanā'ī's influence on later court poets, see de Bruijn, *OPP*, p. 12, and p. 253 nn. 51–60.

> is that this despair brings him great joy, for it proves beyond all doubt the steadfastness of his devotion. In renouncing his vassal's "right" to requital, he proves that the lady's virtues are more precious to him than any common pleasure: for these are the virtues that define the courtly class, and his devotion proves his courtliness. Somehow, miraculously, through love, he has been brought to a level of refinement where a greater joy awaits him than any he ever knew or hoped for. The signal of that joy is the lady's smile of pleasure, but its source is his awareness of his own worth and nobility.[30]

Although requiring some modification, Goldin's analysis of the central fiction of the courtly lyric provides a useful preamble to a discussion of Sanā'ī's *ghazal*s as exemplary of the genre. Central to this fiction is the beloved's superiority (in both physical and moral terms, physical beauty being but the outward mirror of the soul's virtue), a superiority emphasized in poem after poem, in both temporal and spiritual terms. The epithets applied to the beloved reflect the status accorded her (or him: I use the feminine pronoun only for convenience): she/he is a king who has dominion over heart and soul, a "king of idols" (*shāh-i butān*) whose lovers are numerous as an army, while the lover is a servant (*bandah, chākar*) who wears the earring of slavery (*ḥalqah-i farmān*) in his ear (a conceit referring to the beloved's ringlike curls). Hyperbolic description abounds: the beloved is a moon lighting the path of those who have gone astray, the dust beneath her feet is collyrium for the spiritual, her appearance is an epiphany. Her exaltation is intensified until she becomes equated with the essential elements of creation, while the lover's existence is defined solely in relation to her. This exaltation can lead to the point of adoration: the beloved's face becomes the direction (*qiblah, miḥrāb*) toward which the lover prays, her house a shrine (Kaʿbah). Such expressions invoking the "religion of love" should not be taken as proof that the love described is spiritual rather than physical; they exemplify the analogical habit of thought which sees the beloved's place in the lover's world as parallel to that

[30] Goldin, "Array of Perspectives," pp. 54–55.

of God for the believer, setting the beloved at the highest point of the lover's universe.[31]

In the courtly *ghazal*, it is not the sex or even the "real" status (human or transcendent) of the beloved that is of primary importance, but the qualities she embodies. The beloved (whether youth, man, or woman, slave or free, or God Himself) is accorded absolute supremacy in the love relationship because she is, by definition, the noblest of creation; her word is law unto the lover, over whom she holds the power of life and death. Cruel and kind by turn according to her whim, she is adored as idol, as liege lord, as divinity; and while she may have many lovers without the taint of infidelity (for, after all, who could resist her?), the long-suffering lover is permitted only one beloved.

Separation is the lover's natural state; and the vast majority of *ghazal*s are love plaints addressed to the absent (or indifferent) beloved. For, as Goldin points out, it is the unattainability of the beloved, and his own consequent service without expectation of requital, that permits the lover to demonstrate his own value and his membership in the company of those ennobled by love. For, while the Persian poet typically is of lesser social degree than the members of his audience, as the *ghazal* makes clear, nobility is not conferred by birth, but by the state of loving.[32]

[31] On similar analogical parallels in troubadour poetry (specifically in connection with the poet's suit), Cropp observes: "There is more than one parallel to the courtier's suit: a Christian praises God and gives thanks to Him, prays God to forgive him and to aid him; similarly, if the occasion arises, a vassal asks his lord for certain privileges. In short, every individual who is dependant upon a superior must ask some favor in this way. He may, perhaps, be granted it more quickly if he is clever enough to praise his patron and to be patient. For these reasons, praise, expectant waiting, suits, and service constitute the poet-lover's experience" (*Vocabulaire courtois*, p. 183).

[32] In courtly circles East and West, love is regarded as an aristocratic pursuit not proper to base people. Al-Washshā', for example, declares that love is "suited only to four (types of person): to those with evident *murūwah*, those who are pure, those who have abundant wealth, or those of outstanding *adab*; it is unbecoming in all others" (*al-Muwaššá*, p. 117). Elsewhere he cites a verse of Maḥmūd al-Warrāq to the effect that love is "among the qualities of the noble [*min shiyam al-kirāmi*]" (ibid., p. 47). Cf. Steadman, "Courtly Love," especially pp. 11, 18–20, 28–30.

The *ghazal* poet identifies himself, first and foremost, not as an individual, but as a member of a class. He is, as Sanāʾī observes, one of the *khāṣṣagān-i ʿishq*, the elite (or aristocracy) of love; he is also, paradoxically, love's slave, wearing the ring of servitude in his ear and abasing himself before the beloved. While the beloved is frequently addressed as a ruler, love itself is often personified as a *shāh* or *sulṭān* who holds sway over this aristocracy and who has numberless servants and vast armies under his command. Service to this king requires true manliness (*mardānagī*): "If you have not a man's courage, do not serve the ruler" (*ghazal* no. 311: *Zahrah-i mardān nadārī, khidmat-i sulṭān makun*); and it is love—now defined as an inward quality embodying the ideal virtues—that distinguishes *mard* from *nā-mard*, the "manly" from the "unmanly":

> In the field of name and shame, what save love and
> choice have distinguished the true man from the
> false?
>
> (*ghazal* no. 143)

Love is a prerequisite of *mardānagī* in its dual sense of aristocratic manly virtue and humanity: "A man is not a man until he has tasted the pain of loverhood" (*ghazal* no. 61).

Mardānagī is distinguished from *khājagī*, "lordship," to which it is clearly opposed: "O Sanāʾī, lordship is not a condition for love of the beloved. . . . In pursuit of the love of idols, manliness is required" (*ghazal* no. 63). *Khājagī* designates mere wordly status, while manliness does not depend on birth or wealth, but on loverhood. Similarly, *javānmardī*, "courtesy" or "chivalry," is contrasted with mere wordly wisdom (*khirad*), which is unable to fathom love's secrets:

> The hands of the chivalrous have loosed the secrets of
> your ruby;
> but the chains of your curls have bound the feet of the
> wise.
>
> (*ghazal* no. 42)

Javānmardī, which encompasses the cardinal virtue of loyalty, should inform the bond between lover and beloved:

The loyal services I performed had cruelty as their
 reward;
O idol, enough of lack of courtesy [*nā-javānmardagī*];
 may God judge you on my behalf.

(*ghazal* no. 76)

Compared to the *khājagān*—the noble in name only—the lover also boasts that he is a *darvīsh*, one who has renounced worldly pursuits in order to devote his entire existence to the beloved. Often he is an outcast as well, an *āvārah*, a homeless wanderer, an exile, whose single-minded dedication to love is viewed by society as excessive or improper, since it often reaches the ultimate degree of love madness exemplified by Majnūn (whose function in lyric is quite different from the treatment given him by Niẓāmī in his romance).[33]

All these designations constitute sets of binary oppositions derived from the various systems that provide, not merely metaphors for love, but analogues of it—oppositions that distinguish the initiate from the pretender, the true aristocrat from the parvenu, the wise from the ignorant, or, as the commonplace has it, the raw (*khām*) from the cooked (*pukhtah*).[34] In the courtly hierarchy, the *khāṣṣagān*, the aristocracy of love, are distinguished from the *khīshtan-bīnān*, the self-seeking, whose pursuit of love is motivated by selfish ends, and who boast of their love for purposes of self-aggrandizement. Similarly, the *darvīsh* is defined by contrast with those whom Sanā'ī terms the *tavāngar-pīshagān*, who make the pursuit of worldly power their way of life:

Naught has been added to your worth by the works of
 the power-hungry,

[33] In lyric, Majnūn is typically (though not always) treated as the ultimate embodiment of the ecstatic poet-lover and martyr of love, a view presumably dating from ninth- and tenth-century Arabic writings. Al-Washshā' cites the verses of a contemporary, ʿAmr ibn Qanān, concerning such martyrs of love: "Those of old who died in the religion of love found death a honeyed spring: / / Qays [Majnūn], ʿAmr, and al-Muraqqish before them were explications [*ta'wīl*] of love's revelation [*tanzīl*]" (*al-Muwaššá*, p. 56).

[34] This opposition is common in Persian poetry: *khām* signifies the inexperienced lover who naively hopes for union, *pukhtah* the lover matured through suffering (cf. chapter 4, n. 44).

who out of passion have raised buildings to the skies;
Your worth the *darvīsh* knows, who sees hovering,
like a vulture on the airs, the seventy times seventy
(warring nations).

(*ghazal* no. 4)

Similarly, in the analogous system of religion, which has its own hierarchy and its own signs of initiation, the *khāṣṣagān-i ʿishq*, love's elite, correspond to the *rahruvān*, the travelers on love's path, likened to pilgrims journeying toward a sacred shrine. To the outsider (the uninitiate) the religion of love appears as idolatry and unbelief; to the lover it is the one true faith. The beloved—the object of worship in this religion—is described conventionally as a beautiful idol; but she is contrasted with the idols of ordinary men, identified by Sanāʾī as the things of this world, material objects that distract from love.

Things are idols; since we have donned pilgrims' robes,
it is not a condition that we worship idols.

(*ghazal* no. 19)

Such examples, focusing as they do on the nobility of the lover, express the ideal aspect of the love portrayed in the *ghazal*; but there is another, more "realistic" one, which draws on the same complex of metaphors in order to evaluate, not the lover, but the beloved. Although the vassal of love may elect to serve without requital, secure in the knowledge that his love service provides proof of his innate virtue and nobility, such a renunciation of his rights does not absolve the beloved of obligation toward him. It is here, I think, that the depiction of idealized love by the Persian poets departs most significantly from that of their European counterparts: in the assumption that the beloved, however exalted, is still a partner in a relationship that confers both rights and obligations on each member. Love is a contract (*ʿahd, paymān*) that binds both parties, and the contractual nature of the love relationship is stressed by the metaphors drawn from its analogues to describe it. Just as the object of worship has an obligation toward the adoring

The Suppliant Lover (British Library Ms. J.56.8)

believer, as the master has to the slave and the feudal lord to his subject, so the beloved has the obligation to conduct herself according to the protocols that govern such relationships; more specifically, it is the beloved who, precisely because of her exalted status, must observe in her conduct the principles of justice.

Thus it is possible for the same poet who in one *ghazal* absolves his beloved of guilt—

> Whatever comes from that sun-faced one is all justice
> and equity;
> our oppression comes from this windowless turquoise
> dome.
>
> (*ghazal* no. 45)

—to accuse her in another of infidelity and warn her of the consequences:

> Should you think there is no punishment for you from
> God on Judgement Day for the blood of lovers such
> as I—there is!
> And should you believe that you do not, despite your
> beauty and grace, possess likewise a disloyal nature
> and an unfaithful habit—you do!
>
> (*ghazal* no. 51)

Such an apparent contradiction represents, not an inconsistency in the poet's "philosophy of love" or in the "courtly code" that his poetry is presumed to reflect, but rather the generic status of the *ghazal* as a vehicle for "representing every viewpoint on love conceivable in courtly society."[35] Although the basis of this representation, and the source of the varied perspectives on love that the *ghazal* presents, is the presumed response of various sectors of the poet's audience, in contrast to romance, all these perspectives are filtered through the perception of one subject and heard in the words uttered by one voice: that of the poet in his persona of courtly lover.

For the primary focus of the *ghazal* is on the lover, equated

[35] Goldin, "Array of Perspectives," p. 71.

implicitly—when not explicitly—with the poet; the kaleidoscopic panorama of love is reflected in the persona of the poet-lover as in a mirror. Even in poems where the ostensible subject is the beloved, the governing sensibility is that of the lover, who is the poem's real subject. Yet for all the emphasis on this subject, whose fictional experience provides a unifying feature of the *ghazal*, it exhibits little real subjectivity. When one attempts to define or describe this ever-present "I," its transparency becomes evident, as the poet-lover disappears behind (or rather into) the words of his song, which define him while defining the particular occasion of that song.

Thus, despite its emphasis on personal experience, the "I" to whom both love and song relate proves elusive; the song is not personal, the "I" not flesh and blood. Some critics go so far as to see in the "I" of medieval lyric a mere grammatical convention:

> In all its types, discourse either begins with a first person or ends with one. It is noteworthy that these *I*'s and *me*'s do not go back to any referent included in the text but, purely and simply, designate the speaker of the song (who may be assumed to vary).[36]

This "absence of referentiality" in the courtly lyric is seen variously as reflecting the "closed" nature of the poetic text (i.e., as self-referentiality) or as evidence (as in Allen's view) that the poem's real "textuality" is external to it.[37] That both views are extreme may be seen from the example of the *ghazal*, whose closely structured texture betrays a preoccupation not merely

[36] Paul Zumthor, "Le *je* du chanson et le moi du poete," in *Langue, texte, énigme*, p. 185.

[37] Compare, for example, Zumthor's view that the absence of referentiality in the *grand chant courtois* reflects the status of the poetic text as closed, its own subject turning in upon itself like Narcissus losing himself in the mirror of the pool ("De la circularité du chant," *Poétique* 2 [1970], 139), with Allen's, who finds in such impersonality evidence that "medieval poems are larger than their textuality" ("*Grand Chant Courtois*," 17). Cf. also Zink, "Anonymité," on the varying degrees of impersonality in different genres of medieval lyric.

with its "message" but with the letter of the text, while its impersonality points to a wider dimension beyond the text proper, to which it refers and of which it is typical.

The convention of the *takhalluṣ* points to the fact that the "I" of the *ghazal* functions neither as a grammatical convenience nor as a depersonalized type or universal exemplar, but as a deliberately constituted persona—that of the poet-lover, who is simultaneously identified with and distanced from his poem through the agency of the *takhalluṣ*. The presence of this convention, which functions as an explicit declaration of an assumed identity, also decrees that the speaker in the poem cannot be equated with a specific, nameable individual caught in the toils of a factual, literal love affair, that is, that the poem is not to be interpreted autobiographically. The "I" of the *ghazal* is presented as an idealized (and often fallible) participant in the kind of love affair to which his audience may be presumed to aspire: one that establishes their virtue by reason of the quality of this participation and of the object with which they desire to be united. This bestows on the poet a dual, generic identity: he is (*qua* lover) on the same level as the audience of his poem, while his function as its singer sets him apart from them—not only as a member of a different class, but as one who is more deeply initiated into the mysteries of love.

The poet thus stands at the point of intersection between poem and audience, while the poem itself points simultaneously outward toward its audience (to whom it presents a model of conduct) and inward toward its maker. The *ghazal* poet stands in relation to his lyric song much as Niẓāmī did to his romance: as sage and craftsman, as one who perceives the signification of his material and, through his art, recreates that truth, in words, for his audience, while embodying, in his persona, the ideal to which his audience aspires. The ultimate function of the *takhalluṣ* (as might be guessed from its derivation) may be seen as analogous to its role in the *qaṣīdah*: it places the poet (rather than the patron) at the pinnacle of praise.[38]

[38] The problem of the *takhalluṣ* demands more extensive investigation than

I will return to this question of language in a moment; first, however, I wish further to explore the relation of the poet, or of his persona, to his audience, and specifically the way in which his poem fulfills its function of guidance toward a higher ethical ideal. As suggested above, the poet's words are not directed solely to those members of his audience who stand parallel to him in the role of dedicated servant of love, but also to those who occupy the position of beloved, as he points not only to the obligations enjoined by the state of loving, but to those concomitant with the state of being loved. If the beloved's face is equated with the brilliance of justice, it is because she has escaped the temptation of injustice, which is also part of her nature and a potential trap:

> That is no curl which he has let fall over his shining
> cheek;
> it is the tyranny of Ẕaḥḥāk, which he has placed over
> the justice of Anūshīrvān.
>
> (*ghazal* no. 81)

This is no mere "decorative" metaphor for dark locks falling over a luminous visage, but one that points to the moral values implied by the light-dark contrast, as well as to the poem's courtly context. The choice between good and evil, loyalty and infidelity, kindness or oppression is perhaps the most significant act of the beloved and certainly the most important in terms of the formation of the ideal self. For if the lover has no choice but to love and to serve, the beloved, by contrast, does have the choice between justice and injustice. And while the

---

it has hitherto received. The emergence of the *ghazal* as a distinct formal genre is marked by the increasing and self-conscious employment of the poet's pen name in the *maqṭaʿ*; this, in turn, has been linked to an increased concern with problems of authorship (and of individual creativity) seen also in the poet's self-naming in romance (compare Gurgānī and Niẓāmī) and in the *qaṣīdah* (Sanāʾī, for example, regularly addressed himself in this genre as well as in the *ghazal*), as well as in the growing use of signatures by artisans in other crafts; see Rypka, "Poets and Prose Writers," p. 552; Hodgson, *Venture*, 2:328; O. Grabar, "The Visual Arts, 1050–1350," *CHI*, 5:552; for parallels in the medieval West see Stevens, "The Performing Self"; and see chapter 4, n. 2, and chapter 7.

lover, in his self-sacrificing mode, may attribute his suffering to the turning sphere rather than to the beloved—who is, by definition, "all justice and equity"—her shortcomings are nevertheless noted.

> Heart-ravisher, when I read the writ of dismissal
> from union with you,
> how much blood—O heart!—flowed from my eyes
> upon my face.
> I never reached the target of your merciless heart,
> though I loosed every arrow which was in my quiver.
> Think not, my soul, that I have renounced loverhood,
> or that I have freed my heart from grieving for you.
> If I make less outcry and wailing in love, it is because
> the fire of my heart has been extinguished by the
> water of my eyes.
> Do not set at naught the rights for my many services;
> for I was once summoned, if now I am dismissed.
> Hear my cry for succour, for the sake of old respect;
> have pity on me, my idol, for I am quite distraught.
>
> (*ghazal* no. 210)

Injustice is still *nā-javānmardī*, particularly when committed by the person who should, as the repository of all virtues, be the human embodiment of justice.

> Love has renounced those faithless sweethearts,
> beats his head in despair at this bunch of base
> dominion-seekers.
>
> (*ghazal* no. 73)

The poet's words are also addressed to those elements in the audience that are hostile to him, and whose very existence is defined in relation to his love and to his poem. We have already considered the opposition between initiate and uninitiate in the secrets of love; the latter include a whole range of dramatis personae who people the *ghazal* and who appear to encompass a great variety of types, but who in actuality are all aspects of two shared qualities: they are proponents, and practitioners, both of false love and of false poetry.

> Every courtly love poet must, for the sake of his exalted theme, accommodate the hostile elements in his audience. The song is a pattern of the moves he makes to outmaneuver them, in order to save his song and to be a credible witness for the vision of his friends. These enemies, therefore, precisely because of their incomprehension and destructive intent, are an essential element in the lyric; the vindication of the friends takes the form of a triumph over the enemies.[39]

Such enemies include "the vulgar people" (for Sanā'ī, the *'āmmah*, those who are not numbered among love's elite [*khāṣṣah*]), who "know that no man with a living body can swear this consuming fealty to another human being . . . forever beyond his reach," and consider the singer either "a fool, or a liar," or one "who is putting on airs, as sometimes one has to do in court." They include the "false lovers," who

> listen to the singer, hear his song as a strictly technical achievement, the mastery of a certain manner which, for them, is all that courtliness is. They hear the song as an advertisement of prowess addressed to a woman, or intended to impress the other false lovers, who are, in either case, too full of lust to bother about the question of security. And so, when they behold the singer, they behold a man who is just like them, a hypocrite, and his resemblance to them is never more pronounced than when he claims to be different from them on the grounds that he really means what he says.[40]

About these—the *mudda'īyūn*, "pretenders," encountered earlier in Manūchihrī's complaint about his rivals—I will have more to say in a moment, as they play a role central to the poem and to its ethical message. Other enemies, "or other aspects of these same enemies," include "the talebearers and spies" (*raqībān*, *ghammāzān*, *vushāt*), who "are blinded by their carnality, for they understand nothing of this love affair

[39] Goldin, "Array of Perspectives," p. 87.
[40] Ibid., pp. 87–88.

except that it is illicit, and they would like to expose it."[41] The poet plays to all these negative voices, invoking their criticisms and castigating their shortsightedness; but without them, his poem, and the message it conveys, would lose its completeness. He needs them in order to display the superiority of the ideal over the limitations of the real, and he needs them "because the sweet chant of the nightingale will not sound genuine unless it is heard over the croaking of the frogs."[42]

This brings us to another topic addressed by the *ghazal*: that of poetry itself, and more specifically of the relation of language to experience, and of the efficacy of poetic language in conveying the poet's message to friends and enemies alike. As for the troubadours and trouvères, for the *ghazal* poet to love is to sing (as exemplified by the archetypal figure of this relationship, the nightingale).[43]

> When the ruby rose showed its face, in its joy the
> nightingale knew no rest.
> Long has the nightingale—like myself—been in love
> with the garden and the rose.
> If, day or night, he does not sleep, it is no wonder; for all
> are sleepless in the beloved's presence.
> I am slave to the tongue of that nightingale who, last
> night, sang the praises of the ruby rose:
> whoever has heard his song will have deaf ears for (all
> other) music.
> . . . .
> Sāqī, give (me) rosy wine in the season of the rose; for
> no one has commanded repentence in that season.
>
> (*ghazal* no. 29)

The state of loving is inseparable from the words used to describe it. Sanā'ī repeatedly underscores this equation: the whole world is the *ghazalkhān* of the beloved (*ghazal* no. 32).

[41] Ibid., p. 88. Ferrante views such figures as representing the baser aspects of the lover's own nature (see *Woman as Image*, pp. 72–73).

[42] Goldin, "Array of Perspectives," p. 88.

[43] Cf. Zumthor, "Circularité," 136–37.

O moon-faced one, throughout the world your
song is echoed;
the affairs of unachieved lovers are in tune to your
music.
Wherever there is sweet verse, it is the tales of love
of you;
wherever there is beautiful prose, it is the stories
of your elegance.

(*ghazal* no. 28)

By virtue of his command over language, the poet is able to occupy the place of both lover and beloved—to speak, that is, for both of them.

If I am, in quality, a soul-less image, I resemble both
idolhood and loverhood.
Sometimes, like lovers, I join a hundred corteges;
sometimes, like the beloved, I join with a hundred
souls.
I am bi-colored, like the face and hair of the idol;
because of this, I am both unbelief and faith.
If you look at my form, I am this; if you look at
my lines [*khaṭṭ*], I am that.
Sometimes I am bent, like the stature of lovers;
sometimes I smile, like the lips of the beloved.
Sometimes I am curved like the posture of lovers;
sometimes I am broken like the curls of beloveds.
I have the quality of the beloved's cheeks and curls;
because of this, I am the crown for lovers' heads.[44]

(*ghazal* no. 237)

The system of language stands in parallel to the system of love, which it depicts through an ordered and frequently predictable disposition of words, figures, and propositions. Participation in this system, in this ordering of things, is shared by poet and audience; true understanding of it, however, is lim-

[44] The poem suggests itself as a riddle (*lughz*, *muʿammā*), particularly since in one manuscript it appears among the *muqaṭṭaʿāt*, where the placing of such poems is more appropriate; however, it also provides a telling image of the poet's ability to identify with, hence express, all aspects of the love experience.

ited to those who share with the poet true understanding of the system of love itself. Moreover, though words may sometimes prove inadequate to express love, this does not invalidate the centrality of poetry to the state of loving; the true poet—like the true lover—is one who knows when to speak and when to be silent.

In terms of this interrelationship of poetry and love, the *muddaʿī*, the false lover, becomes identified with the false poet, whose verses are inspired by self-seeking and not by love. The ultimate proof of this is that he is never speechless before the majesty and awesomeness of love: he never knows when to stop talking.

> Bring on the silence of the spiritual, and do a great work;
> burn the garments of the pretenders and throw them
> away.
> What is the silence of the spiritual? inability, and
> stillness.
> What is the garment of the pretenders? long-winded talk.
>
> (*ghazal* no. 172)

As Ḥāfiẓ will say later, "The words of love are not those which come to the tongue" (QG 81). The true lover must ultimately stand speechless before the ineffable marvel of love:

> Every pretender, from one end of the world to the other,
> boasts in vain of your love.
> No angel can aspire to your face: no-one ever makes a
> profit from the money-changer.
> The light of your cheeks burns the soul; the mine
> of your perfection splits the heart.
> . . . .
> How can Sanāʾī describe you, when your beauty has
> gone beyond all description!
>
> (*ghazal* no. 197)

The *muddaʿī*'s verses are mere words, false boasting; his poems are worldly vanities, composed for self-advancement rather than being the fruit of love's inspiration. The true poem acquires its worth by being the genuine product of the lover's suffering:

> From my eyes I brought forth pearls and cast them in
> my lap;
> when I looked at my skirt, lo! there was a bride's dowry
> therein.
>
> (*ghazal* no. 113)

Love is not a "toy or a vain tale" (*ghazal* no. 58), neither is it mere "pleasure and passion" (*ghazal* no. 30), as the ordinary mistakenly believe. It is, like poetry, an art, to the learning and mastery of which one must dedicate one's entire being; and its mastery comes from the heart rather than the head:

> The path of love is not by way of reason; thus it is very
> difficult;
> for it is not the path of form and foot, but the way of
> the heart.
>
> (*ghazal* no. 40)

The equation of love with art will be developed more fully, and more explicitly, by Ḥāfiẓ; but it is already clear, in the *ghazal*s of Sanā'ī, that love and song are inseparable.

Sanā'ī's *ghazal*s present the lover's inner world as an ethical microcosm in which virtue and art alike are equated with, and find their source in, good love. Placed between the idealized (though sometimes imperfect) object of this love and its detractors, the poet-lover's goal is to demonstrate that the perfection of his own love enables him to transcend the limitations of reality and move toward the level of anagogy, becoming the embodiment of the ideal he seeks to inspire in his audience. This transcendent quality of love, and of loverhood, is a major theme in Sanā'ī's *ghazal*s; and the ideal love they depict ultimately unites lover and beloved as participants in a single, indivisible entity.

> The cause of loving is not loveliness; the lovers'
> affliction is not the moon-faced beauty.

Love has no share in qualities; idol-worship stems only
from shame [*siyāh-rū'ī*].
Love is both lover and beloved; love has not two faces,
but one.
Know that the essence of love is lack; he who says
otherwise tells a vain tale.
I have cut short my speech, before it was completed:
for lovers, ease lies in little speech.

(*ghazal* no. 54)

Sanā'ī's ethical message to his courtly audience, implicit in this picture of ideal love, carries more general implications as well, as befits his broader homiletic purpose.[45] While specific issues of courtly ethics are strongly suggested, for example by the opposition of the *khāṣṣagān-i ʿishq* and the *darvīsh* lover, who are content with love service, to the *tavāngar-pīshagān* and the *riyāsat-jūyān* ("seekers of dominion"), whose worldly preoccupations make them ignorant of true love, as well as by the courtly settings and terminology of many of the *ghazal*s, Sanā'ī rarely addresses such issues directly.[46] This feature of his poetry presumably reflects the fact that he did not consistently compose for courtly audiences but wrote his poems for a variety of patrons; thus their applicability would need to be broader. As the *ghazal* grew in popularity, other poets, with closer ties to court, availed themselves of its potentials and put its generalized ideal of love to the service of the related and analogous ideal of courtly conduct. The most notable poet in this respect is Ḥāfiẓ, who, some two centuries after Sanā'ī,

[45] On Sanā'ī's homiletic poetry, and the uses to which it may have been put, see de Bruijn, *OPP*, especially pp. 169–70; see also Rūmī, *Discourses*, pp. 215–16 (*Fīhi mā fīhi*, p. 207) for a revealing anecdote concerning the practice of illustrating sermons with poetic quotations.

[46] Having said this, it is still difficult to avoid reading many of Sanā'ī's *ghazal*s as deliberately intended for a courtly audience, and more specifically for the moral edification (if not the practical reminder of obligations) of an aristocratic patron. Of the poems referred to in this study, *ghazal* no. 4 seems critical of courtly society; no. 73 equates that society with irreligion and hypocrisy; and it is difficult to read no. 210 as anything but a reference to the poet's falling out of favor with an aristocratic patron.

brought the courtly *ghazal* to its peak in terms of both artistic achievement and ethical signification; and it is to this aspect of Ḥāfiẓ's *ghazal* that the remainder of this chapter is devoted.

Discussions of Ḥāfiẓ as a court poet have been limited primarily to two aspects of his *ghazals*, which are neither original with him nor particularly characteristic of his style: the use of erotic verse for encomiastic purposes and the insertion of topical references. Roger Lescot attributes to Ḥāfiẓ the "innovation" of preferring the *ghazal* to the *qaṣīdah* as a vehicle for encomium.

> One of his original innovations was to use the *ghazal*, in preference to the *qaṣīdah*, to praise the virtues of his patrons. In this manner he revitalized Persian lyricism, opening up to new themes a type of poem till then reserved for the expression of love, whether profane or mystical. He also freed himself thereby from the constraints imposed by a bombastic genre, artificially introduced into Iran and falsified, from its beginnings, by its foreign origins.[47]

While it is true that Ḥāfiẓ devoted his talents to the *ghazal*, in preference to the *qaṣīdah*, to an extent perhaps greater than did any of his contemporaries (even in an age when the *ghazal* enjoyed unprecedented popularity), and that, in adapting it to many of the purposes ordinarily associated with the longer form, he greatly deepened and enriched its thematic scope as well as its ethical relevance, it is not true that prior to him the genre was used for love alone, or that he was the first to use it for panegyric. Neither should the reasons for his specialization in *ghazal* necessarily be sought in dissatisfaction with the longer, "foreign" genre of the *qaṣīdah*, which, as we have seen, had been thoroughly acclimated to Iranian conditions and which served the needs of poets for many centuries without, presumably, their feeling that it was unduly encumbered (let alone "falsified") by its foreign origins. Despite the fact that Ḥāfiẓ's age was, so to speak, the "age of *ghazal*," which had

[47] Roger Lescot, "Essai d'une chronologie de l'oeuvre de Ḥāfiẓ," *BEO* 19 (1944), 59.

come to rival, if not surpass, the *qaṣīdah* in popularity since Saʿdī's time over a century earlier, the *dīvāns* of Ḥāfiẓ's contemporaries (Khājū-yi Kirmānī, Salmān Sāvajī, Ibn-i Yamīn, and others, including the great satirist ʿUbayd-i Zākānī), as well as of Saʿdī himself, testify to the fact that the *qaṣīdah* was by no means neglected. Thus the reason for Ḥāfiẓ's preference must be sought in a combination of personal inclination and temperament (the boast that he is the unchallenged master of the genre resounds throughout his *ghazal*s) and of changing patterns of patronage and literary taste that affected Persian culture after the Mongol invasion.

Such changes involved a variety of factors, to no single one of which can the *ghazal*'s increased popularity be exclusively ascribed. It is assumed, by Rypka in particular, that since the display of the poet's erudition formed a standard component (not to say requirement) of the *qaṣīdah*, the form could appeal (or be addressed) only to patrons sufficiently rooted in the tradition to appreciate such erudition, and that since the Mongols, like many princes of the local dynasties that succeeded them, lacked such roots, the *qaṣīdah* met with little favor on their part. This assumption is highly debatable in view of other cultural achievements of the period, particularly in the visual arts, and has been challenged; moreover, the *ghazal* itself did not lack for such displays, not only in Ḥāfiẓ's time but earlier, as demonstrated, for example, by Sanāʾī's frequent use of Koranic references, or the extreme allusiveness of a poet like Khājū. The increased popularity of mystical poetry (which should not be interpreted solely as a response to the disturbed times and to the wish to escape from reality, but which also reflects an increased demand for such poetry by the Sufi orders, which formed a growing center of power and influence—and hence of patronage—in Mongol times) may have contributed to a greater flexibility in the *ghazal*'s style, while it certainly enriched its associative resonances. Increasing urbanization and the growth of the middle class have been seen as encouraging the production of brief lyrics and of entertaining and didactic *maṣnavī* poetry, on the grounds that these appealed to the sensibilities of this class in ways that the panegyric *qaṣīdah*, with its aristocratic overtones, could not; yet we must not forget that the *qaṣīdah* itself, as a formal structure, underwent considerable thematic modification and was used for a variety of ends, including religious and didactic.[48]

All of these factors created conditions that encouraged diversity in poetic production. A poet was not bound to seek his fortune at court if not inclined to do so, since there were other centers and other patrons to support him; neither was he obliged to function solely, or even primarily, as a writer of panegyric *qaṣīdah*s but could specialize in other, "minor" genres such as *ghazal* or satire. He was, however, still bound to earn his living from patronage, which thus continued to be an influential factor on the types of poetry produced. If the *ghazal* appears to have held pride of place in the eyes of poets and patrons alike, it is perhaps because its brevity, its inherent ambiguity of diction and style (and hence its potential for polysemy), and its universally appealing subject (which lent itself to a wide variety of interpretations) gave it a flexibility and an appearance of spontaneity that made of it, so to speak, a genre for all seasons.

Ḥāfiẓ was not, however, the first poet to employ the *ghazal*

[48] For a discussion of the various factors to which are attributed the increased popularity of the *ghazal* at the expense of the *qaṣīdah*, see Rypka, *History*, pp. 248–49, 252, 282, and idem, "Poets and Prose Writers," pp. 550–56 et passim. The assumption that the Mongols and their successors fell short of the literary and artistic standards of appreciation of earlier periods is challenged by Hodgson in particular, who regards this "middle period" as one of the most brilliant, and diversified, of Islamic (and especially Persian) culture; see *Venture* 2:437–500, and especially 484–93. On Ḥāfiẓ in particular Hodgson observes, "It is perhaps the very richness of what he could presuppose in sophisticated traditional expectations that made possible Ḥâfiẓ's excellence" (488). Hodgson takes issue with the view that correlates the rise of mysticism (and, by extension, the increased popularity of mystical writings) with political instability, seeing in it rather a reflection of "a growing complexity and sophistication generally" (2:202; see also 201–14); he also notes (in contrast to Rypka) the "decreasing prominence" of the mercantile classes, during the post-Mongol period, "in the high culture, which moved away from the market place and perhaps even from the mosque, to focus more frankly on the court (with its love of preciousness) and, complementarily, on the khâniqâh" (2:409–10).

for encomiastic purposes; neither is Lescot's evaluation of the pre-Ḥāfiẓian *ghazal* an accurate one. Before discussing the tradition of which Ḥāfiẓ represents the culmination, rather than the unique member, we may refer to Lescot's description of his technique:

> It is well known that every *qaṣīdah* is introduced by a few amorous verses which, separated from the rest of the poem, might often pass for an independent *ghazal*. . . . The procedure adopted by Ḥāfiẓl consists, if you like, of having retained, of the original framework, only this prologue, reducing the panegyric proper to a minimum: a few verses, sometimes only one, appended to the *ghazal* in the fashion of an envoi. . . . Frequently, as well, the name of the *mamdūḥ* and the poet's *takhalluṣ* appear together in the *maqṭaʿ* . . . (but) most often—and this is the logical conclusion of this reform—the poem's addressee is mentioned in the body of the poem. . . . It also happens that the poet dispenses with naming the patron to whom he addresses his poem explicitly, designating him only by his title . . . or by some epithet clear enough to contemporary audiences, but less easy for us to decipher.[49]

The procedures Lescot considers typical of Ḥāfiẓ (and, it is implied, his invention) are already evident in the *ghazal*s of Sanāʾī, several of which conclude with an encomiastic cap in which the *mamdūḥ* is named, while others, ostensibly addressed to the beloved, employ titles or are couched in language that suggests they are in fact addressed to a person of rank, who may or may not be equated with a patron.[50] A

[49] Lescot, "Essai," 59–60; the epithets he cites include such locutions as *khājah-i jahān*, *Āṣif*, *māh-i ṣāḥib-qarān*, etc., the presence of which suggests that the *ghazal* is addressed to a specific patron.

[50] Cf. Sanāʾī, *ghazal* no. 80, addressed to Aṣīl al-Mulk Khājah Asʿad, i.e., Khajah Aṣīl al-Mulk Ḥasan Asʿadī Haravī (*Dīvān*, pp. *q-qā*); and no. 272, addressed to "Ghiyāṣ al-Dīn." De Bruijn states that Sanāʾī wrote panegyric *ghazal*s for Bahrāmshāh Ghaznavī but does not specify the numbers in the *Dīvān* (*OPP*, pp. 80, 264, n. 3). Expressions such as *shāh-i butān*, "king of idols" (no. 49), *mīr-i khūbān*, "prince of the noble" (no. 137), etc., are sufficiently

younger contemporary of Sanāʾī, Ḥasan-i Ghaznavī (d. 1160), known as Ashraf, employed the *ghazal* for panegyric purposes with some regularity.[51] A number of his *ghazal*s are encomiastic from start to finish; they are distinguished from "brief" *qaṣīdah*s by the use of the erotic language typical of the *ghazal*, and by the fact that the name of the *mamduḥ* (who is most frequently the Ghaznavid ruler Bahrāmshāh) characteristically appears in the *maqṭaʿ*, or concluding line (a feature that may have contributed to this line's association with the *takhalluṣ*, or *gurīzgāh*, of the *qaṣīdah*, and to the eventual identification of the term *takhalluṣ* with the poet's pen name). More frequent, however, is the model described by Lescot, in which a love poem concludes with an encomiastic cap. It is not always possible (as Lescot suggests) to consider this cap as "tacked on" and unrelated to the body of the poem, since the inherently ambiguous language of the *ghazal* and the conventional analogy between poet and lover make it feasible to read the poem as a courtier's suit rather than (or as well as) a lover's.

> My heart and soul are devoted to the beloved; to be
> again united with him: that is life.
> I will practice contentment humbly, for my hand is
> bound by the tyranny of separation.
> My suffering at his absence is more than the Sphere
> itself could endure.
> The state of separation of two intimate friends:
> how can I tell of it? for it cannot be known.
> Be joyful, Ḥasan, in your grief for him, for he is
> both the affliction and the remedy.
> I fear that the king will not hear that grief for him is
> king over my heart:
> The king Bahrāmshāh, (son of) Masʿūd, he who is
> the form of sovereignty and the image of life.[52]

---

ambiguous that they may designate either a patron or the beloved, hyperbolically addressed.

[51] On Ḥasan-i Ghaznavī, see Rypka, *History*, p. 197; de Bruijn comments on the influence on him of Sanāʾī (*OPP*, p. 12).

[52] Ḥasan-i Ghaznavī, *Dīvān*, ed. T. Mudarris Raẓavī, p. 266, *ghazal* no. 7.

Such a love plaint, in which separation from the beloved may be read as loss of favor with the patron, points to the ease with which the *ghazal* lends itself to the poet's suit for redress or forgiveness. At the same time, it shows how the *ghazal* incorporates a basic motif of the *qaṣīdah*: the patron's favor compensates for the cruelty of the beloved. This example also illustrates a typical formal characteristic of Ḥasan's encomiastic *ghazal*s: the occurrence of the poet's name a few lines before that of the *mamdūḥ* (which generally occurs in the *maqṭaʿ*), bearing out the assumption that this is the focal point of praise in the *ghazal*, serving—like the *gurīzgāh* in the *qaṣīdah*—as a transition to the encomium that links the topics of love and praise and emphasizes the poet's dual status as lover and courtier.

The appearance of Bahrāmshāh Ghaznavī as *mamdūḥ* in the majority of Ḥasan's panegyric *ghazal*s, as well as in others by his contemporaries, suggests that the court of the later Ghaznavids favored this kind of poetic game in which the lover's suit figured the poet's.[53] The stylistic features that (as Clinton observes in connection with the *qaṣīdah*) reinforce the inherent ambiguity of the love poem—notably the "harmony of images" that exists between *nasīb* and *madīḥ*, the analogy between poet and nightingale as singers of love, and the identification of the beloved with the beautiful, often warlike "Turk"[54]—at the hands of the poets of this period become

[53] Sanāʾī's contemporary, Masʿūd-i Saʿd-i Salmān, also wrote panegyric *ghazal*s addressed to Bahrāmshāh (de Bruijn, *OPP*, p. 152). Anvarī also turned the *ghazal* to encomiastic purposes on occasion, perhaps most notably for his patron Majd al-Dīn Abū al-Ḥasan ʿImrānī, *raʾīs* of the town of Sarakhs in Khurasan and a familiar of Sultan Sanjar until he lost that ruler's favor, was imprisoned and subsequently killed (see *Dīvān*, introduction, pp. xliv–xlv, text pp. 468, 490). There is also a *ghazal* addressed to an unnamed *sulṭān* which resembles remarkably the style of Ḥasan-i Ghaznavī (ibid., p. 508). Anvarī's encomiastic *ghazal*s are also notable for the fact that they contain few of the customary conventions: there is no Turk, *rind*, or nightingale, and there are few of the allusions typically used by other practitioners of the genre.

[54] Clinton, *Manūchihrī*, pp. 94–122; see also Schimmel, "Ḥāfiẓ," 30. On the Turk as an emblem of beauty see especially A. S. Melikian-Chirvani, "Bouddhisme," and A. Schimmel, "Turk and Hindu: A Literary Symbol," *Acta Iranica* 3 (1974), 243–48.

commonplaces of the *ghazal* as well. Doubtless the strong homoerotic convention of love poetry, which is also seen in the *qaṣīdah*s of the Ghaznavid poets, further facilitated the use of *ghazal* for encomiastic purposes, making the transference from beloved to lord even easier because of the absence of what I may be excused for calling a gender gap.

Thus the potential for addressing the patron directly using the erotic language of the *ghazal*, which Lescot views as a sign of Ḥāfiẓ's originality, is in fact exploited far earlier. It is clearly visible in the *ghazal*s of Saʿdī (d. 1292), who is generally considered the foremost practitioner of the form prior to Ḥāfiẓ, and in whose poems the growing tendency toward abstraction and ambiguity in the treatment of love topics is strikingly clear.[55] Though Saʿdī's *ghazal*s appear less explicitly encomiastic than do those of Ḥasan, the very generality of the language and conventions used—and the greater possibility for multiple interpretations that results—increases their potential for conveying messages that are more specific than they appear on the surface. Is the following *ghazal*, for example, merely a simple love plaint, or does it suggest as well a suit for favor?

> Happy that spot wherein my love abides:
> there soul's ease and the sick heart's cure resides.
> Here, I am but a lifeless form, no more;
> my soul is there, where that rash love abides.
> Here is my body, sick; there dwells my soul;
> here is the sky; its planets there reside.
> O Zephyr, should'st thou chance to bring a breeze,
> pass by Shiraz, where my beloved resides.
> Whom may I tell my woes? in whom confide?
> let me go there, where secrets' lord resides.
> My heart longs not to gaze on meadows fair:
> my gaze is there, where my beloved resides.
> What worth this ruin, Saʿdī? 'tis not thy place;
> pack up! the lovers' dwelling there abides.[56]

Such examples show that the way was already prepared for

[55] On Saʿdī and his achievements in *ghazal*, see Rypka, *History*, pp. 252–53.

[56] Saʿdī, *Kulliyāt*, ed. M. ʿA. Furūghī, *ghazal* no. 49.

Ḥāfiẓ's "audacious innovations," for what Lescot terms "this manner, peculiar at first sight, of flattering princes and ministers," exemplified by the *ghazal* like the following:

O blessed time, when my beloved shall return:
when that one dear to those who grieve for love return.
My eyes, two piebald steeds, await his phantom troop's
approach, in hope that royal rider will return.
I dwell inside the road that he will take, like dust,
and wish that he may pass along it, in return.
If my head rolls not within his mallet's curve,
of head what shall I say, which way will my head turn?
That heart which had a pact with his two curling locks:
think not that to that heart sweet peace will e'er return.
What cruelty the nightingales have felt at winter's hand,
in hopes that, once again, the springtime will return.
There is, Ḥāfiẓ, this hope, from Fate's great Artist, that
that beauty, cypress-like, will to my hand return.[57]

(QG 235)

Lescot dates this poem to the period of Shāh Maḥmūd (1363–66), who for a brief time forced his brother Shāh Shujāʿ (Ḥāfiẓ's patron) to flee Shiraz; thus the "absent lover" is equated with the ruler in flight.[58] The poet invites his audience to identify with him in his longing for the absent ruler's return, while the allusion to the suffering of the nightingales at the hand of winter specifically refers to the status of poets under Maḥmūd. The fusion of erotic elements with specifically courtly topics is quite complete, but to equate the poet's strategy in such a

[57] I follow the order in Pīzhmān's edition (P 199; see bibliography). Sūdī adds two lines (between 2 and 3, and between 5 and 6), which are essentially amplification, adding nothing to the poem's sense, and which may well be later interpolations (*Sharḥ-i Sūdī bar Ḥāfiẓ*, trans. ʿIṣmat Sattārzādah, 2:1333–37). Sūdī also gives *shāh-i khiyālash* (for P and QG *khayl-i khiyālash*) in line 2, which is perhaps equally acceptable.

[58] Lescot, "Essai," 66, 73, where the association of the epithet *shahsuvār* with Shāh Shujāʿ is noted; Schimmel also comments on the connection with Shāh Shujāʿ's surname, Abū al-Fawāris, and considers the period of Shāh Maḥmūd's reign to be one in which Ḥāfiẓ was "estranged" from his royal patron ("Ḥāfiẓ," 7–8). Sūdī makes no mention of the possible political implications of the *ghazal*, glossing it as a straightforward love plaint.

poem with the mere adaption of the erotic conventions of *ghazal* to panegyric, and to consider such poems as essentially comprising no more and no less than "occasional poems" of which the "true import of their content" is merely prince-pleasing flattery,[59] is to ignore their more general implications and to make as grave a mistake in interpretation as does the critic who sees a mystic in every lover and divine love in every cup of wine.

Ḥāfiẓ's *ghazals* illustrate perhaps more than those of any other Persian poet both the potential for polysemy and the importance of the ethical dimension that are characteristic of the genre. Both features can be illustrated by a careful examination of the second aspect of his *ghazal* that has been considered to reflect its courtly (and, more generally, social) milieu: the use of literary allusions and of historical and legendary exempla. On the basis of such allusions (and largely as a corrective to excessive mystical allegorization) Rypka proposes a "literalistic" reading of many poems, viewed as the mirror of contemporary political realities.

> If it used to appear as though Ḥāfiẓ's lyrics reflected nothing of contemporary events and as if only the peace of God and an infinite heavenly bliss hung permanently over Shiraz, the reason for this was twofold: insufficient acquaintance with the metaphors applied to public life and, on the other hand, sublimation on principle of all erotic and bacchantic elements into mystic allegory.[60]

Citing Ritter's warning against such allegorization, Rypka supports the view that many *ghazals* "require a literal and cer-

[59] Lescot, "Essay," 60. Cf. A. J. Arberry's discussion of QG 148, of which he observes: "The flattering description of the wine-bearer [in this poem] is . . . to be understood as directed at the prince who is giving the party; the party is the prince's audience; the wine which Ḥāfiẓ craves is the gold with which he hopes the appreciative prince will fill his mouth; to earn it, the poet is ready to protest the most servile adoration" ("Three Persian Poems," *Iran* 2 [1964], 4). Arberry treats this level of the poem's meaning as distinct from the Sufi sense he also discerns in it; the two are united only by the "commonplace" identification of the prince with the Perfect Man of his age (ibid., 5).

[60] Rypka, *History*, pp. 266–67.

tainly not a mystical interpretation," and that even when Ḥāfiẓ utilized mystical imagery or concepts,

> he did so mainly in order to give a mystical flavour to the whole and, by means of an explanation projected into mysticism, to gain an opportunity of escaping blame for his antinomies and blasphemies. . . . If his protector cherishes a disposition for mysticism, it is in this direction that Ḥāfiẓ tries to curry favour with him. . . . Yet it cannot be denied that some of the *ghazals* are composed entirely in the spirit of mysticism—concessions to the prevailing fashion, experiments knowing only a "today" and no "tomorrow," because they did not come naturally to Ḥāfiẓ.[61]

Thus, for Rypka, Ḥāfiẓ's *ghazal*s must be read as a mirror of the political and social realities of the time, and the array of characters in them—*rind* and *muḥtasib*, *ʿārif* and *zāhid*, the *muddaʿī* and even the beloved—as historic individuals, players in a real-life drama of revolt and oppression conditioned by political injustice and religious conservatism.[62]

[61] Ibid., pp. 267–68.

[62] Schimmel observes that "the discovery that Ḥāfiẓ was probably more of a court poet than we had realized and that his verse was neither erotic nor mystical but rather panegyric, even 'political', led some Persian and Russian scholars to the assumption that wine, beloved, and *muḥtasib* should all be interpreted afresh, thus turning Ḥāfiẓ into a political poet" ("Ḥāfiẓ," 25). Between the two poles of mystical and political allegorization the characteristics of Ḥāfiẓ's style have become obscured. Ḥāfiẓ, however, is not an obscure poet, as is assumed by P. N. Khanlari (for example), who equates symbolism with obscurity: "The difficulty in grasping the deeper meaning of Hafiz's poetry stems in the first instance from his symbolism. For him, all is metaphor, allegory, and symbol." However, "In his symbolism [Hafiz] was only following the poetic tradition of his homeland and the inclinations of his age. He expresses himself in terms veiled by metaphors, so that most of the time one does not know whether he is addressing a beloved or a prince" ("Hafiz de Chiraz," in *L'âme de l'Iran*, pp. 163, 164–65). On the problems of distinguishing between "difficult" and "clear" lyrics, Judson Allen notes, "There is an important difference, easily obscured by the passage of time, between a text whose difficult code its ideally expected reader experiences by decoding, and a text whose complex use of convention intends for its ideally expected reader a refined and even mannerist but immediately intelligible experience" ("Grammar, Poetic Form, and the Lyric Ego," p. 202). Ḥāfiẓ's lyric is of the latter sort.

This assumption arises from an essentially modern separation of the relevant categories: the worldly, courtly, political, erotic, mystical aspects of experience are each viewed as excluding the others. Such a separation, as Ḥāfiẓ's *ghazal*s demonstrate fully, is hardly possible for a medieval poet, who sees each as an analogue of the other, and who invites his audience to participate in his poem according to their various stations in life. If we are to take even half-seriously Ḥāfiẓ's constant reiteration of the topic of worldly transience, if we are to regard it as more than a merely conventional commonplace, we must realize that the ultimate level of reality cannot be located at the level of day-to-day events but must reside rather in the exemplary or transcendental significance of these events.

Yet Ḥāfiẓ must be distinguished from a poet like Sanā'ī, who was never fully committed (or fully accepted) as a court poet; for Ḥāfiẓ aspired to a connection with the court from the very beginning of his career and continued in the association (to the best of his ability) to the very end of it.[63] This fact of his biography makes it necessary to distinguish, among the various members of his audience to whom his poems may be addressed and whom he encourages to identify with the stance portrayed within them, one very specific addressee of a large proportion of the *ghazal*s: the patron, who in many poems is the intended recipient of their ethical message. The assumption of the patron as addressee in a significant number of Ḥāfiẓ's *ghazal*s is supported by analysis of the function of the topical allusions and historical references that occur in such poems.

The frequency of such allusions and exempla has been noted by Lescot and others, although Ḥāfiẓ is less obtrusively allusive than, say, his contemporary Khājū, or even Sanā'ī; his allusions are, so to speak, more assimilated into the text of the poem as a whole. What has been less often observed is that they function, not only on the level of political (or mystical) allegory, but as signs pointing to other areas of meaning. The

[63] Cf. Schimmel, "Ḥāfiẓ," 4–9; on Ḥāfiẓ's biography, and particularly on his association with the court, see especially Qāsim Ghanī, *Bahs̱ dar āṣār u afkār u aḥvāl-i Ḥāfiẓ*, 1:*Tārīkh-i ʿaṣr-i Ḥāfiẓ*; and ʿAbd al-Ḥusayn Zarrīnkūb, *Az kūchah-i rindān: dar bārah-i zindagī u andīshah-i Ḥāfiẓ*.

rhetorical device of *talmīḥ* not only subsumed references to well-known stories, proverbs, legendary figures, and the like, but extended to the use of technical terminology belonging to specific disciplines (science, law, philosophy, etc.) and characteristically functioned to represent particular concepts or to provide types figuring moral or spiritual qualities, as well as metaphors for topical or personal references.[64] Although the material from which such allusions are drawn is, as has been noted, extremely limited, their application in practice is much more flexible than is usually granted, as the examination of the use of any specific figure would undoubtedly show. Thus, though the range of associations of a particular figure is relatively fixed, their interpretation may vary considerably from poet to poet and, at the hands of any individual poet from poem to poem as well. Allusions, whether ostensibly topical or exemplary, are integrated into the context of the poem as a whole, and the relationship between the two is a mutually supportive one.

As an example we may take the famous reference to the deposition of Ḥāfiẓ's early patron Shaykh Abū Isḥāq Īnjū, whose reign in Shiraz (1343–53) was a period of relative prosperity, although accompanied by political insecurity.

Indeed, the turquoise ring of Abū Isḥāq flashed brightly;
but it was a transient fortune.

(QG 207)

The reference occurs in a *ghazal* composed much later, which is glossed by commentators (largely on the strength of the al-

[64] Shams-i Qays defines *talmīḥ* as "when a few words point to a great meaning" and associates it with brevity of discourse (*ījāz*) (*al-Muʿjam*, pp. 245–46). See also Browne, *LHP*, 2:77–80; J. S. Meisami, "Allegorical Techniques in the *Ghazals* of Hāfez," *Edebiyat* 4 (1979), 23–31; G. M. Wickens, "The Frozen Periphery of Allusion in Classical Persian Literature," *Literature East and West* 18:2–4 (1974), 171–90. Wickens's strictures on the limitations, with respect both to material and associative content, of allusions in Persian poetry fail to take into account the ahistorical attitude of medieval writers in general, who value allusions not for whatever historical or factual veracity they may have, but because they provide the particular example that illustrates a general principle.

lusion) as a lament for that ruler.[65] The *ghazal*'s general topic is that of the absent friend; a look at the whole poem will aid in pinpointing the precise function of the allusion within its more general context.

Remembered be the time when I dwelt in your street,
and my eyes took light from the dust of your door.
Indeed, like lily and rose, because of that pure friendship,
whatever was in your heart was on my tongue.
When Heart repeated the lessons learned from the Elder
of Reason, Love explained whatever he found
difficult.
In my heart I thought never to be without a friend. What
can be done? mine and my heart's efforts were in
vain.
Last night, in memory of my companions, I went to the
tavern; I saw (only) the vat, blood in its heart, its
feet in the mud.
Much did I wander seeking the cause of separation's
pain; but the *muftī* Reason was ignorant in this
matter.
Indeed, the turquoise ring of Abū Isḥāq flashed brightly;
but it was a transient fortune.
Alas for the cruelty and injustice of this snare; and alas
for the elegant pleasures of that feast.
Saw you the laughter of that strutting partridge, Ḥāfiẓ,
who was heedless of the claws of the royal falcon of
Fate?[66]

[65] Lescot, "Essai," 207. On Shaykh Abū Isḥāq, see also Browne, *LHP* 3:274–76; and cf. Zarrīnkūb, *Az kūchah-i rindān*, pp. 13–30.

[66] I follow the version in Sūdī (*Sharḥ-i Sūdī*, 2:1205–1209). In line 6 Sūdī has *pas* "then," for *bas*, "often, much," which appears to be a typographical error since he glosses it as *khaylī*, "much." Sūdī interprets the image of the wine vat in line 5 as an allegory (*tashbīh*) of man's soul, "since until the vat is emptied (i.e., the soul is emptied of worldly attachments) its feet must be in the dust" (1207). The general relevance of the example of Abū Isḥāq is reinforced by the fact that *būsḥāqī* (= "of Abū Isḥāq") is a term used of a particularly fine type of turquoise. Ḥāfiẓ also uses the figure of the partridge in QG 133: "O gracefully strutting partridge, where are you going? stop! be not deceived

This *ghazal*, like the preceding one, takes the form of a lament for the absent beloved. It may be divided into three segments: lines 1–4, where the poet recalls the old attachment, and his vain assumption that he "would never be without the beloved"; lines 5–6, in central position, which depict his search for the cause of separation and, more specifically, of mutability, questions that no authority (neither of inebriation nor of wisdom) can answer satisfactorily; and lines 7–9, the conclusion: the transitory nature of the world is a given and incontrovertable rule to which all are subject. In this context, the reference to Shaykh Abū Isḥāq serves as the particular example that demonstrates the truth of the general precept. More specifically, with respect to the poem's implicit addressee—the present ruler—it serves as a reminder that worldly power will not last and that the fate that carried off Abū Isḥāq will one day do likewise with his successor. Over and above the immediate practical aspect of this principle—which might be phrased "as ye sow, so shall ye reap," a motif frequently met with in Ḥāfiẓ's *ghazal*s—is its more general implication: that since this world is mutable, one must live not only for it, but for the next as well. We can do no better than to recall al-Ghazzālī's advice to the ruler, that the treasure of this world is good repute, while that of the next is salvation.

Ḥāfiẓ's achievement (the secret of his artistry, if one will) does not lie either in his adaptation of the *ghazal* to encomiastic ends, or in the extent to which his poems mirror historical actuality or biographical fact, but in the manner in which all these elements are placed at the service of a concept of poetry which views the poem—and the totality of the poet's work—as an ethical artifact. Ḥāfiẓ's *ghazal*s do indeed function as a

because the ascetic cat has said its prayers." Although often interpreted as a topical allusion (cf. Browne, *LHP*, 3:280), in both instances the partridge stands as the type of preoccupation with worldly attractions and heedlessness of the hereafter. (In ʿAṭṭār's *Manṭiq al-Ṭayr* the partridge is treated in similar fashion and is characterized as constantly searching for jewels; see *The Conference of the Birds*, tr. A. Darbandi and Dick Davis, pp. 41–42.) Sūdī glosses the figure in QG 133 as "a *talmīḥ* employed as a *tamṣīl* [allegory]" (*Sharḥ-i Sūdī*, 2:825).

mirror, but a mirror of transcendental truth, rather than of historical *realia*. If Sanā'ī, in his general depiction of love, incorporated material that had specific relevance to courtly conduct, requiring therefore a reading of his *ghazal*s (or at least some of them) that moves from general to specific, Ḥāfiẓ demands a reading in the reverse direction: his advice to his patron (the implied addressee of such poems) moves from this specific, courtly context to a more general one. However, in order to understand the nature and meaning of this progression, it is essential that Ḥāfiẓ's *ghazal*s not be divorced from their courtly context; for the concept of poetry they reflect relates directly to the poet's vision of his function in the courtly milieu. His *ghazal* subsumes the ends of all the genres of courtly poetry and presents itself, therefore, as the ultimate wisdom.

A careful reading of Ḥāfiẓ's *dīvān* reveals that, perhaps more explicitly than is the case with any of his contemporaries, the ultimate end of his *ghazal*s is a moralizing one.[67] It is this ethical purpose that constitutes the major unifying element of his *ghazal*s, ordering their apparently unrelated topics into a coherent whole. Ḥāfiẓ has frequently been accused of lack of "unity" in his *ghazal*s, beginning with the famous criticism of his patron Shāh Shujā' to the effect that the poet shifted from topic to topic within a single poem, "contrary to the practice of the eloquent."[68] What is generally overlooked in such criti-

[67] An evident exception, among court poets, is Ḥāfiẓ's older contemporary 'Ubayd-i Zākānī, chiefly known as a master of satire (often highly obscene), who exerted a profound influence on Ḥāfiẓ's style. Unfortunately the limited scope of this study precludes a consideration of courtly satire, a topic to which I hope to be able to address myself in the future; a perusal of 'Ubayd's *Kulliyāt* is most revealing with respect to the conditions of the age in which he, and Ḥāfiẓ, lived.

[68] Quoted by van Gelder, *Beyond the Line*, p. 207. Van Gelder uses this anecdote to support his conclusion that Arabo-Persian poems lack overall coherence and that the poets were not concerned with this problem, stating: "Ḥāfiẓ, in his reputed reply, did not contest this by trying to show the hidden unity in his poems. While admitting the truth of the king's words (he may merely have been polite) he pointed out that his poems were more popular than those of his rivals [including, one may note, those of Shāh Shujā' himself]. *Ḥāfiẓ is utterly*

cisms is that the ethical dimension of the poem, conceived of in the broadest terms, provides the essential element with respect to which the apparently disparate topics are related by the principle of analogy. The operation of this principle—which affects all aspects of the poem's structure, language, and imagery—is especially evident in a particular type of *ghazal* which figures importantly in Ḥāfiẓ's *dīvān*, and of which the following poem provides an example.[69]

At dawn the bird of the meadow said to the new-risen
    rose:
"Less coquetry! for many like you have flowered in this
    garden."
The rose laughed: "Indeed, the truth does not disturb us;
but no lover ever spoke a harsh word to his beloved.
"If you desire to drink the ruby wine from that
    bejewelled cup,
many a pearl must you string with the tips of your
    eyelashes.
"The scent of love will never come to the nostrils of one

---

unconcerned with the accusation of incoherence" (p. 207; my emphasis). That Ḥāfiẓ was indeed unconcerned with such an accusation I accept; he knew better, as, I submit, did Shāh Shujāʿ. For discussions of the problem, see Rehder, "Unity"; Michael C. Hillmann, *Unity in the Ghazals of Hafez*; Rypka, *History*, pp. 269–71. Judson Allen comments on the propensity of medieval critics to discuss poems in terms of single lines: "The most important principle one must see in this habit of analysis by division is that there must have existed, in the medieval awareness of the material of their poetry, a firm conviction that the material involved had a unity, an integrity, an essence, a stability, so strong that analysis by mere division would reveal and not obscure its essence" (*Ethical Poetic*, pp. 141–42; see also p. 124).

[69] Most critics of the *ghazal* in general, and of Ḥāfiẓ in particular, appear to assume that all *ghazal*s are alike. The analysis that follows is part of an attempt to establish a typology of Ḥāfiẓ's *ghazal*s, and of a larger effort to identify the *ghazal*'s various subgenres. A detailed analysis of this particular *ghazal* was presented in a conference paper entitled "The Analogical Structure of a Persian Courtly Lyric: Ḥāfiẓ's 81st Ghazal," delivered at the Nineteenth International Congress on Medieval Studies, Kalamazoo, Michigan, May 1984. The *ghazal* is also discussed in the context of Ḥāfiẓ's use of garden imagery in J. S. Meisami, "The World's Pleasance: Ḥāfiẓ's Allegorical Gardens," *Comparative Criticism* 5 (1983), 163–64.

who does not sweep the sill of the wineshop with his
forehead."
Last night in Iram's Garden, when, with the gentle air,
the hyacinth's curls were stirred by the dawn breeze,
I said, "O Throne of Jamshīd, where is your world-
seeing Cup?"
It answered, "Alas, that waking fortune slept."
The words of love are not those which come to the
tongue:
Sāqī, bring wine, and cut short all this talk.
Ḥāfiẓ's tears have cast wisdom and patience into the sea:
what can he do? the burning of love's grief cannot be
hidden.

(QG 81)

The poem's eight lines can be divided into three segments with no apparent transition between them, which I shall call segments A, B, and C. Segment A (lines 1–4) consists of a dialogue between nightingale and rose, those quintessential lovers of Persian lyric. The nightingale's admonition to his beloved is rebuffed by the rose, who reminds him that it is not seemly for the lover to complain; his role is to suffer, shed many tears (expressed by the metaphor of "stringing pearls"), serve his lady devotedly, and humble himself before her, in order to prove himself worthy of her favor (the "ruby wine" of her kisses, dispensed from the "bejewelled cup" of her mouth, with its pearl-like teeth). (I refer to the beloved as female only, again, for convenience.)

Segment B (lines 5–6) presents another dialogue: that of the poet (or more precisely, of a poetic persona) with the personified royal throne of Jamshīd. The garden of love in which the colloquy of rose and nightingale was set gives way to the legendary garden of Iram, built by the ancient Arabian king Shaddād and destroyed by a great tempest as a warning against worldly pride. In the Persian tradition this garden is identified with the seat of the ancient king Jamshīd, who disappeared suddenly after a long and prosperous reign, and whose magical world-seeing cup was unable to warn him of his impending doom.[70] This conjunction of garden of love with royal seat gives new significance to the nightingale's warning that roses fade; we are reminded that, just as in the garden the rose is king of flowers, best of its kind, the prince also is the best of mankind, at the head of the hierarchy of humanity.

The allusions to Iram's Garden (also the best of its kind), to Jamshīd's Cup, and to the royal throne that responds to the poet's query of *ubi sunt*, establish a courtly context for this segment in which a second relationship emerges as parallel to that of nightingale and rose in the first: that of the poet and his prince, whose presence as audience for the poem may be assumed. Segment C (lines 7–8) introduces a third such relationship: that of the lover and his beloved (absent from the scene, but certainly present in the lover's thoughts, and parallel to the prince as implied audience). Suffering from the pangs of a love that cannot be described (and that, according to convention, should not even be spoken of), the lover seeks solace in the wine cup, having been forced by the intensity of his passion to reveal his secret.

These three segments exhibit a number of similarities that reveal themselves gradually in the course of reading the poem. Each contains a passage of recorded discourse: the dialogues of nightingale and rose and of poet and royal throne, and the lover's apostrophe to the Sāqī. Each features a distinctive speaking voice: the nightingale in A, the poet in B, and the

[70] For the Koranic story of the Garden of Iram, see Suras 89:6–8, 34:16. Sūdī glosses the reference in this *ghazal* as an allusion to the pleasance of Ḥāfiẓ's patron Shāh Shujāʿ and states that in the Koran it refers to "one of the gardens of Paradise," which is the true sense of Ḥāfiẓ's allusion (*īhām*) (*Sharḥ-i Sūdī*, 1:510). Persian tradition identifies Iram with Persepolis (Takht-i Jamshīd), seat of the ancient Iranian kings. On Iram, see Melikian-Chirvani, "Bouddhisme," 57–58 (who identifies it with the Sanskrit *Arama*); A. J. Arberry, *Fifty Poems of Ḥāfiẓ*, pp. 149–50, n. 7. Jamshīd's Cup is consistently read by Western commentators as an emblem of mystical gnosis and divine love (cf. Arberry, *Fifty Poems*, p. 150, n. 7); Sūdī glosses it as the faded flower, signifying the fading of fortune (*Sharḥ-i Sūdī*, 1:511). Ḥāfiẓ frequently uses this allusion in a courtly context, both generally, for royal favor (as in QG 272), and more specifically (as here and in QG 486) to signify the transience of kingly power and glory (cf. Meisami, "Allegorical Techniques," 29–31).

lover in C,—all associated, by convention, with the singers of lyric. There is a progression in the distance between speaker and audience from the impersonal account of segment A through the poet's self-referential report in B to the direct address to the Sāqī in C; this progression is accompanied by an increasing specificity in the time frame of each segment, from the indefinite "at dawn" of A to the more specific "last night" of B to the present moment at which the cupbearer is asked to pour the wine in C. Each segment has its own setting—garden of love, royal pleasance, and wine shop; settings that are in fact analogous, as will be shown presently. The topics of the discourses are also parallel and contain a series of related paradoxes: the nightingale comments on the transient nature of roses, the poet muses on the similar nature of royal power, the lover laments the simultaneous compulsion to speak and the inadequacy of language. This parallelism suggests that each apparently independent segment in fact presents a variation on a common central theme.

The settings of each segment establish the parameters of this central theme by providing specific contexts for the juxtaposition in the poem of two parallel and analogous codes of conduct: that of love, expressed explicitly, and that of courtly protocol, which is implied, as well as a more general context in terms of which these codes become the subject of moral commentary. In the garden of love, the commonplace that beauty, like the rose, will fade, suggests the parallel that the prince may not always be powerful and in a position to bestow favor. "Look not to the rose's kingship and glory," says Ḥāfiẓ in another poem, "for the sweeper of the wind will scatter all its petals underfoot" (QG 429). The rose's objection that it is not seemly for the lover to complain has its courtly corollary as well: not only is it improper, but it can be unwise in the extreme, for the courtier to complain of his own situation, to criticize his prince's conduct, or to voice sentiments that may be unwelcome or offensive. The rose's rebuff emphasizes the lover's obligation to prove himself worthy of favor—proof that, for a court poet, would include composing many poems (another sense of the expression "stringing pearls") and of adopting, like the lover, the stance of a suppliant who must humble himself before the object of his devotion, if he desires to drink the ruby wine of favor from the bejeweled cup of preferment.[71] The exemplum of Iram's Garden, where the breeze ruffles the hyacinth's curls, anticipating the ruder buffets of the autumn wind, reinforces the motif of transience stated in the opening line, and the lesson that princes, like roses, fade is strengthened by the allusion to Jamshīd, who was carried away by a whirlwind. This message is left to sink in by the abrupt transition to the wine shop and the invocation of the convention of silence, with its corollary that the courtier must be circumspect; but, like the lover driven to complaint, the poet's need to remind the prince of the moral obligations that accompany his position impels him to speak out. To the convention of silence is thus opposed the topos that the possession of knowledge makes it a duty to impart it.

This final paradox points to the presence throughout the poem of an implicit opposition between the surface protocol of courtly conduct and the ethical values that should inform such conduct.[72] The tension generated by this conflict is embodied in a series of binary oppositions: between silence and speech, between power and powerlessness, and perhaps most important, between material and spiritual riches. As Ḥāfiẓ observes elsewhere, the independence and contentment that arise from the possession of spiritual wealth are not enjoyed by royal courts; he supports this notion, again, with the exemplum of Jamshīd's Cup:

> Jamshīd bore naught but the tale of the Cup from
> this world;

[71] Compare the poet's exhortation to his patron in QG 246, where the same complex of images is employed: "Drink wine to my poems, for with this princely pearl your bejewelled cup provides the adornment of the age."

[72] The parallels between the code of love and the courtly code are discussed in more detail (together with reference to mirror literature and specifically to the *Nasirean Ethics*) in J. S. Meisami, "Medieval Persian Courtly Poetry: Allegories of Love and Justice," to be published in *Love Lyrics in the Mediterranean Tradition: Studies in Memoriam Samuel M. Stern*, ed. James T. Monroe.

beware! do not fasten your heart on worldly things.[73]
(QG 486)

The opposition between apparent and true riches involves also an implied contrast between king and poet, in which the latter, content with the spiritual rewards brought by the pursuit of wisdom and the practice of the poetic art, is the possessor of real and lasting power, while that of the prince is transitory. (Not the least considerable aspect of the poet's power, of course, is his ability to preserve his patron's name and repute for posterity.)

The motif of riches (both real and apparent) is concretely embodied in the image of the cup, which appears in each segment and which constitutes both a central metaphor and an emblematic focal point around which is clustered a series of associative references; the image encompasses the jeweled cup filled with wine (by which are designated the beloved's favors), the magical cup of Jamshīd, and the wine cup in which the lover seeks comfort. In this poem virtually devoid of images, that of the gem-encrusted cup containing sparkling ruby wine stands out as startlingly concrete. It is, moreover, pregnant with multiple associations: with flowers (not only the crimson rose, but the tulip, emblem of lovers' martyrdom);[74] with jewels (specifically the ruby, also an emblem of suffering, since, according to traditional belief, the ruby is formed by the sun's rays penetrating stone);[75] with princely favor, as the jeweled cup is a typical kingly gift, while the wine suggests a position of familiarity at court; with the magical possession of Jamshīd, emblem of his worldly power and of the intoxication power brings. (We may recall the commonplace *mast-i ghurūr*, "drunk with pride.") In addition to the obvious connotations

[73] The structure of QG 486 (and particularly the juxtaposition of three parallel and analogous segments set in garden, royal pleasance, and wine shop) is almost identical with that of QG 81, reinforcing the assumption that a formal typology may be established for Ḥāfiẓ's *ghazal*s.

[74] Cf. I. Mélikoff, "La fleur de la souffrance: recherche sur le sens symbolique de *lâle* dans la poésie mystique turco-iranienne," *JA* 255 (1967), 341–60.

[75] Cf. de Bruijn, *OPP*, p. 181, and the references cited on p. 273 n. 32.

of value, in all these contexts the cup becomes a symbol of worldly transience: the beauty of rose and beloved and the gift of princely favor, as well as the power and magnificence of the prince himself, are all doomed to fade into oblivion. Opposed to these transient riches is the wine cup in which the lover seeks, not merely the consolation provided by drink, but the freedom from worldly cares symbolized by the state of drunkenness—a freedom acquired through dedication to wisdom and to poetry, riches that outlast the material things of this world and that are frequently likened, by Ḥāfiẓ, to both wine and pearls.

Thus far the system of links between the *ghazal*'s three segments has been established chiefly through a process of disjunctive and retrogressive reading by means of which the parallels between them are revealed through constant reference backward, each segment becoming progressively illuminated by, and shedding new light on, that which precedes it. Two spatial patterns of organization also serve to unify the poem. The first is a linear pattern by means of which the poem may be read as a logically constructed argument aimed at demonstrating the transitory nature of this world. Segment A presents the statement of the thesis along with its rebuttal by the rose (who admits to its truth but questions the propriety of stating it so brusquely); segment B, citing example and authority, provides evidence to support the thesis; while segment C, though it appears to abandon the argument in despair at the inadequacy of language, in fact asserts the necessary cause for stating it: love requires a commitment to a positive moral stance. The second overall pattern is that of ring composition. A slightly asymmetrical circular pattern is established by the repetition, in reverse order, of the motifs of speech, silence, and favor; the poem's center is occupied by the exempla of Iram's Garden and Jamshīd's Cup. This centrality of the symbols of princely power, by exploiting an important convention of panegyric poetry (placing the object of praise at the center), designates the true addressee of the poem as the prince. More important, it serves to illustrate the function of analogy in determining the organization of this *ghazal*, by invoking the mediatory position of the prince in the cosmic hierarchy.[76]

Ḥāfiẓ's juxtaposition of the paired and parallel relationships of king and poet, beloved and lover, and the metaphorical pair of lovers, rose and nightingale, who may signify either or both, in the analogous settings of garden, royal pleasance, and wine shop, appeals directly to the perception of identity between them arising from the belief in an ordered cosmos and in the existence of a system of correspondences between macrocosm (the created world, and specifically the world of nature), microcosm (the world of the individual), and the body politic (mediator between macrocosm and microcosm).[77] In the carefully constructed figure that informs this *ghazal*, as well as others structured on the same model, the garden represents the macrocosm, the wine shop the microcosm, and the royal pleasance (here, Iram's Garden) the body politic (with all the ironic connotations that it implies). As the rose is the focal point of the garden, and the beloved of the lover's world, the king is central to the world of human society, implementing on the microcosmic level the principles according to which the macrocosm is ordered. The royal pleasance, a metonymic symbol of royal power that encompasses both its achievements and its limitations, literally and figuratively mediates between macrocosm and microcosm. Thus the sequence of the segments, far from being haphazard, in fact observes an inalterable order, one based on no less an ordering principle than that which governs the cosmos.

Through thematic juxtapositions carried out according to a structural pattern based ultimately on a higher, cosmic order, Ḥāfiẓ's *ghazal* presents an object lesson for the ruler, as well as an ethical commentary on courtly values as perceived from a more general standpoint. In effect, he invites the specific ad-

[76] Gernot Windfuhr has pointed out another analogical pattern in this *ghazal*: the sets "unhide / untalk // untalk / unhide" (1–2, 7–8) framing the central sequence cup / scent // scent / cup (3–4, 5–6) (personal communication).

[77] See chapter 1; and see also Manzalaoui, "*Sirr al-Asrār*," 160 et passim; Nasr, *Introduction*, pp. 66–74. See also Heninger, *TSH*, pp. 10, 189–93 et passim on the Renaissance notion of man as the nexus of the "chain of being."

dressee of his poem—the prince—to consider the lesson of mutability provided by his analogue, the rose, and to conduct himself accordingly: to lay up riches, not for this world, but for the next. At the same time, he invites the more general audience for his poem—which may include not only the specific courtly gathering for which it was composed, but others who may hear or read the poem in other circumstances—to contemplate the more general lesson provided by the example of the prince himself: that all that is beautiful or desirable in this world will fade. The thorn beneath the rose provides a symbol of the unpleasant fact of mortality as well as calling attention to man's destiny of suffering; at the same time, one must not despair in the face of this fact, but rather devote one's brief sojourn in this world to the pursuit of true riches, stored in the heart and incorruptible. True happiness is achieved only by dedication to the ideals of love and virtue, devotion to which will lead to that spiritual contentment which "is not enjoyed by royal courts" (QG 486).[78]

In this context, the exhortation to silence with which the poem concludes is of particular significance. Like Sanā'ī, Ḥāfiẓ is well aware of the limitations of language (and, like his predecessor, exploits its potentials to the fullest), and of the fact that there is a moment when even the poet must fall silent before the greater mystery of love. This point, however, is typically (and perhaps conventionally) made at the conclusion of a poem, when the "secret" to which the poet alludes has been, if not revealed in its totality, at least strongly suggested. The "secret revealed," in this poem, is clearly more than the unrequited love of either nightingale or poet; it is nothing less than the power of the poet to transcend the limits of human language, a power he owns by virtue of the equation of poetry—and love—with wisdom. Sanā'ī suggested that love, like poetry, is an art that must be learned; the parallel is even more strongly emphasized by Ḥāfiẓ.

[78] These topics are discussed in Meisami, "The World's Pleasance," 166–73.

Only the bird of dawn can interpret the book of the rose;
for not all who read a page can understand its subtle
sense.

(QG 48)

Only the nightingale knows the true meaning of the rose; only the poet can, by his power of working on the imagination, convey through the example of his poetry the higher truth of which love is the earthly embodiment. "Hear the tale of love from Ḥāfiẓ, not from the preacher, even though he has put much artifice in his expression" (QG 131), Ḥāfiẓ exhorts, indulging in a pun on his own *takhalluṣ* and opposing the *ḥāfiẓ*—who holds the truth (Scripture) in his breast—to the *vāʿiẓ*, the preacher who knows only the empty forms and artifices of discourse.[79]

This opposition, here evoked on the specific level of discourse, makes it clear that the dramatics personae who figure in Ḥāfiẓ's *ghazal*s must not be read as "real" individuals (as is the view of Braginsky and others), but as types, representative of two opposing systems that might be said to embody, both in general terms and on the level of discourse, falsehood and truth. Thus to the ascetic (*zāhid*) and the orthodox, or "official," mystic (*ṣūfī*), the guardian of public morals (*muḥtasib*), and the preacher (*vāʿiẓ*) are opposed the gnostic (*ʿārif*), the libertine (*rind*), and the *ḥāfiẓ*—all three of whom are, in this system which represents the microcosmic world of human kind, equated with the poet and become the speaking voices or personae that utter the *ghazal*s themselves. In the macrocosmic

[79] The opposition between *ḥāfiẓ* and *vāʿiẓ* implies another between the latter's *ʿibārat*, "plain speech" (however adorned with rhetorical artifice, *ṣanʿat*), and *ishārat*, the allusive, elliptical language of the poet. The concept of *ishārat* is evoked by Ḥāfiẓ in QG 268: *Bi-nishīn bar lab-i jūy u guẕar-i ʿumr bi-bīn / k-īn ishārat zi jahān-i guẕarān mārā bas* ("Sit by the edge of the stream and watch life pass, / for this sign of the passing [transient] world is enough for us"). The opposition is a classical one in exegesis, where *ishārat* is associated with *taʾwīl* or allegorical interpretation; see Nwyia, *Exégèse coranique*, pp. 174–45, 313–16; Schimmel, *Mystical Dimensions*, pp. 25–30; Meisami, "Allegorical Techniques," 14, 37, n. 22, and idem, "The World's Pleasance," 154.

hierarchy, moreover, they correspond to that supreme singer (and lover) of nature, the nightingale, while in the world of the body politic, their place is held by the court poet. In the context of this system, the *muddaʿī* is distinguished by his ignorance not only of true love, and of true poetry, but of true courtiership as well, ignoring the proper role of the courtier, which is to advise the ruler to good actions rather than to bad.[80] The *muddaʿī* thus becomes the type of false love in the broadest sense, since his words are incitements to evil.

Through the use of such types and figures, Ḥāfiẓ's *ghazal* itself becomes a microcosm, a world in miniature,[81] as the analogies between poet and lover, poet and courtier, poet and moral philosopher become explicit, and all are united under the rubric of art (*hunar*). This may explain why Ḥāfiẓ so frequently, in his *maqṭaʿ*, stands aside from his poem to contemplate it as an independent object, an artifact whose existence confers glory on its creator just as the created world testifies to the glory of its Maker.

"In the garden of Eternity, from Adam's time, Ḥāfiẓ's verse adorned the pages of the book of rose and eglantine" (QG

[80] Cf. QG 105: *Shāh-i Turkān sukhan-i muddaʿīyān mīshnavad / sharmī az maẓlamah-i khūn-i Siyāvushash bād* ("The King of the Turks heeds the words of the pretenders; on him be the shame of the crime of shedding Siyāvush's blood"). The verse is glossed by Sūdī as a *tamsil* (allegory) alluding to the Il-khanid prince Sulṭān Manṣūr, who had his son Asad (considered to have been one of the poet's close friends) killed at the instigation of his ministers and nobles. Thus, "by 'King of the Turks' is meant Shāh Manṣūr, who was a descendent of Hūlāgū; and by the murder of Siyāvush is meant [that of] his son Asad, killed by his father, who heeded the words of enemies and enviers, and slew his son. May he bear the shame for the innocent blood he has shed" (*Sharh-i Sūdī*, 2:682–83). The central position of the line in the *ghazal* in question (to which it appears on the surface to be unrelated) emphasizes its importance. Lescot considers this *ghazal* to have been composed during that period of Shāh Shujāʿ's reign when Ḥāfiẓ was in disgrace and to number among those that "allude to malicious talk circulating against the poet" ("Essai," 67–68); but it is clear that the "malicious talk" was that addressed to the prince which resulted in the shedding of innocent blood.

[81] Or, to use Heninger's term, a "*mini*-cosm . . . a miniature which embodies completeness . . . a unity which imitates the *e pluribus unum* of the cosmos" (*TSH*, pp. 377–78; author's emphasis).

206), the poet boasts, in a conceit that places his poetry, by means of the linking metaphor of the Book of Nature, on a level with Scripture; in the world-garden, "you will find no better fruit than this" (QG 404). As only the nightingale knows the true meaning of the "book of the rose," only the poet can read the Book of Nature and, more important, re-create it in a parallel book: the collection of his verses. "I have seen no verses sweeter than yours, Ḥāfiẓ, (I swear) by that Koran which you hold in your breast" (QG 447), affirms the conclusion of one *ghazal*, reminding us that the poet's verses, held in memory like the sacred Scripture itself, serve like that divine text to provide guidance toward attaining the treasures of this world and the next.

Ḥāfiẓ's *Dīvān* thus provides a summa of all that the prince—or any man, or Everyman—must know to ensure his good repute in his life and his salvation in the next. It is no exaggeration to state that Ḥāfiẓ is preoccupied with the ethics of kingship and of courtly conduct; the theme runs close to the surface (when not explicitly stated) in a majority of his *ghazal*s. Yet it would be a mistake to consider his poems as somehow limited by the specific framework within which they operate. If the king is, ideally, the Perfect Man of his age, he is also, in a particular sense, Everyman, embodying the highest ideal of humanity. Combining temporal and spiritual rule, he incarnates the dual ideal of justice and love expressed by Naṣīr al-Dīn Ṭūsī and bears the responsibility for upholding and maintaining the social order of which love is the guiding force. Thus the king is in a position analogous to that of the prophets in the macrocosm and to that of the beloved in the microcosmic world of human love, and it is scarcely surprising to find him addressed in the language customarily reserved for these objects of love and devoted service.[82]

[82] Poirion's comment is apt in this connection: "The evolution of lyricism is linked . . . to that of society. There exists no natural separation between the mysteries of poetry and the secrets of politics: in the shadowy worlds of action and of language, it is the same enigmas of the human condition which are involved. But poetry—even poetry which is hermetic—tends to disclose, or to suggest, those secrets which politics seeks to conceal; for poetry responds to

Ḥāfiẓ was exceptional among the poets of his age for his success in exploiting the *ghazal*'s conventionality and flexibility to the fullest extent. It is always difficult to account for genius; though its presence is strikingly evident, its particulars are elusive and escape analysis, and it is characteristically only after the fact that we are able to point to antecedents and find signs indicating the direction of the ultimate development of a genre at the hand of a gifted poet. Thus it is at once accurate and misleading to speak of Ḥāfiẓ's *ghazal*—or Niẓāmī's romances, or Shakespeare's plays—as exemplary of the potentials of their respective genres; they are both typical and unique, as it is only the gifted poet who, perceiving the potentials of the typical, can raise it to the universal.

---

the need for expression and communication felt by all men, all societies, all civilizations. [The aspirations of medieval society] are summed up in the figure of the prince, the symbol not only of power, but of all human potentials as well" (*Le poète et le prince*, p. 11). Ḥāfiẓ's position in relation to his historical circumstances resembles Spenser's, on whom Edwards notes: "It was of course Love that theoretically validated the old metaphor of the state as ordered hierarchy, held together by reciprocal affections (and consequent duties) between degrees. Calvin and Hobbes were to preside over the formulation of new metaphors, ones that assumed not Love but Power as the basis of political order, and Spenser represents a tradition that, although it remained a pious ideal much longer, was effectively dead as a practical possibility even as he wrote. But for him it still seemed natural to locate 'public' experience in a continuum of feeling that included divine worship and amatory passion as well" (*Imagination and Power*, p. 62).

· VII ·

Conclusion: The Art of the Court Poet

IN THE prologue to the *Haft Paykar*, following the account of his search for source material and the comparison of his craft in constructing the poem to that of a jeweler working with precious stones, Niẓāmī invokes two other likenesses for poet and poem: that of the architect and the edifice he builds, and that of the painter and his paintings. The two are closely interwoven.

> This poem's design I have adorned
> with seven brides, like Magian Zand:
> So that, should the sky's brides decide
> to turn their gaze upon *my* brides,
> Through like affairs and ornaments,
> each of them aid to mine might lend.
> For when the seven lines converge,
> one point at center shall emerge.
> The painter, ten designs in hand,
> of one main thread yet grasps the end.
> If that thread from the line should stray,
> the others would be set awry.
> Though one trace not this thread aright,
> rightness remains, nor quits our sight.
> I follow this thread, painter-wise;
> on that main thread I've fixed my gaze.[1]
>
> (*HP*, 4:33–40)

[1] This passage presents a network of complex allusions. In line 33 the poet compares the design (*naqsh*) of his work to the "Magian Zand," that is, to the Zoroastrian scripture (more properly, to the commentary on the Avesta, understood by Muslim writers as an example of *ta'wīl*, allegorical exegesis [cf. al-Masʿūdī, *Les prairies d'or*, 2:167–68]); he thus announces his poem as an exegetical work. The Zand was presumably adorned with paintings of the planets (see Wilson, *Haft Paikar*, 2:18, n. 163; a conflation of the Zand with

A better emblem of Niẓāmī's analogical poetics can scarcely be found. More than a mere metaphor of craft, the likeness places the poet's construction (his *tarkīb*, or *conjointure*) in parallel with the cosmos itself and proclaims their kinship. In so doing, it correspondingly places the poet in a position par-

---

the Arzhang of Mani is also possible). A variant reading has *dayr* for *naqsh*, which would make of Niẓāmī's poem a "written temple" and is perhaps to be preferred as making explicit the link between poetry, painting, and building. (Although, as Melikian-Chirvani points out, Magian temples were not adorned with figural representations, earlier Buddhist temples were; the image of a temple adorned with figures is not uncommon in Persian poetry [*Varqe et Golšâh*, 47].) The sky's brides are the seven planets, linked with the seven princesses by the designation that associates both with the power of creation (cf. the commonplace *ʿarāyis-i fikrat*) and places the princesses, products of the poet's thought, in parallel with the planets, products of the Creator's. The sympathetic links between these "brides" (specifically, the elaborate pattern of astrological and color symbolism associated with both) ensures the success of Bahrām's brides in their task of guiding the king toward wisdom. The image suggested, of an edifice ("dome," subsuming the heavenly spheres as well) adorned with paintings, is materially embodied in the two buildings constructed within the poem, the palace of Khavarnaq and the seven domes, both adorned with the *haft paykar* (first in painted form and then in the flesh), and in the fire temples to which Bahrām consigns the princesses following his wedding to Justice. These buildings symbolize the contrast between temporal and spiritual kingship: the material achievement of Khavarnaq is transcended via the passage through the domes to the final, spiritual edifice of the fire temple. Lines 36–40 present an explication of the principles of design according to which Niẓāmī's "written temple" is constructed. Line 36 is glossed by Dastgirdī as an allusion to *raml*, geomancy, in which an arrangement of lines produces the *nuqṭah-i saʿādat*, or "point of prosperity" (not the traditional method of divination using lines and points drawn in sand, but the astrological version; cf. E. Savage-Smith and M. B. Smith, *Islamic Geomancy*, pp. 1–10; and see also Heninger, *TSH*, pp. 240–43, on geomancy and number symbolism). The passage as a whole, however, would seem rather (or in addition) to describe procedures for generating compositional patterns in architecture and painting. In lines 36 and 38, the poet refers to himself as both a *naqshband* and a *rassām*, terms that can designate either a painter or an architect. (In *Khusraw u Shīrīn*, Khusraw's rival, the architect Farhād, and his friend the painter Shāpūr divide these skills between them; they are combined in the two architects of the *Haft Paykar*, Simnār, the builder of Khavarnaq, and his apprentice Shīdah, builder of the seven domes.) Little is known about such techniques in Islamic art, which appear to have been closely guarded secrets transmitted only within the guilds of artisans (cf. Papadopoulo, *Muslim Art*, pp. 100–

Bahrām Gūr in the Red Pavilion (John Rylands Library Ms. Pers. 856)

allel to that of the Creator. Perhaps a daring analogue; but, "for an age that equated the macrocosm and the microcosm, it takes only a slight leap of the imagination to see the artist as analogous to Creator building his own universe."[2]

The contrasting images in this passage and in that which immediately precedes it—the comparison of the poem, first to a finely sculptured jewel, then to a building (a temple of words) adorned with paintings—epitomizes the evolution in the poet's conception of his art, which is reflected stylistically in the development of analogical modes of expression. Although Niẓāmī stands, historically, at the midpoint of this evolution, the *Haft Paykar* is the most ambitious expression of its full implications. Poetry is, indeed, a craft, and a demanding one; but it is more than that: it is a form of wisdom, divinely inspired. Where Manūchihrī boasted of his erudition, Niẓāmī places his poetry (as does Ḥāfiẓ still later) not merely on the level of scholarship, but on that of Scripture. The increasing pride of authorship that accompanies this evolution, evidenced by the self-naming of the poet in romance and the *takhalluṣ* in *ghazal*, as well as by increased self-address in the *qaṣīdah*, insists on the identification of the poem's creator, while the references to

---

101); Niẓāmī's association with such guilds makes it more than likely that he was initiated into their secrets (cf. Rypka, *History*, p. 210; idem, "Poets and Prose Writers," *CHI* 5:579). The most prominent structural pattern of the *Haft Paykar* is that of the spiral, a pattern known to have been of primary importance in the visual arts (especially painting), and conceived of as the design of cosmic order (see Papadopoulo, *Muslim Art*, pp. 101–102; and see also chapter 5, notes 37, 52). Niẓāmī's linkage of his poem to other, allied arts reveals a conscious preoccupation with its structure and relates its ordering design to that of the created universe, which, even if one fails to read it right, still exists and "quits us not." The passage provides the most conclusive evidence yet seen for the poet's view of his craft as analogous to that of the Creator, and of his work as recreating, through analogy, the pattern of the cosmos. For descriptions of buildings as poetic emblems, cf. Clinton, "Esthetics," 84–86; and see Heninger, *TSH*, pp. 352–57; Freeman, *Poetics*, 156–67; and Hanning, "Poetic Emblems," 10–24. As Hanning notes, and as Niẓāmī's use of such devices illustrates, "poetic emblems are valuable indices not only of the medieval artist's understanding of his task, but also of the changing functions of art in society" (p. 1).

[2] Stevens, "Performing Self," 210.

other (and specifically visual) arts establish his creation as a microcosmic mirror of the macrocosmic design.[3]

If (as Ibn Ḥazm observed) the created universe itself is a work of art,[4] what then of the poem which, like the *Haft Paykar* or a *ghazal* of Ḥāfiẓ, is designed to recreate not only the outward forms of its *visibilia*, but the divine order that underlies them?[5] The structural patterns chosen by these poets, their preference (at least in specific contexts) for circular and spiral patterns, implies their knowledge of the geometric skills necessary for perception of the divine order outlined in the writings of the Ikhwān al-Ṣafā' and evoked by Niẓāmī's contemporary Sanā'ī, who likened "the ability to behold the divine manifestation . . . to the intellectual way of perception of a geometrician":

> You only see with your imagination and your
> senses,

[3] Cf. ibid., 198. Compare Ettinghausen's comments on the art of the Saljuq period, in particular the increased "pride of the artisan in his creation" manifested in the use of signatures ("Seljuq Art," 120 et passim).

[4] "[Ibn Ḥazm] argues thus: the work of nature is marvellous in its complexity, its perfection and its variety; it must be created by an artist, who can be none other than God. The writer enumerates in full detail the perfections of all created things, from the stars to earthworms; following each description, he concludes with thoughts like these: 'All this is a work of art, certain and manifest as is the genius of the artist who created it and who has the ability to govern it'; 'all these works of art must have an artist, who fabricates it all without constraint, just as he wishes, and who devises it with total certitude and decision, so that nothing ever comes of it which is contrary to, or different from, his intent'; 'this is the work of an artist who has freely and without constraint resolved to bring it into being' " (Lomba Fuentes, "La beauté objective," 172).

[5] That the poet, like the prophet, enjoys the utmost degree of perfection of the imaginative power, is strongly implied by passages in Niẓāmī's poems describing visitations by voices from the unseen, as well as by the association (especially in the *Haft Paykar*) between poetry, music, and the active intellect, the link with the universal soul. The relation between imagination and prophecy is discussed by Richard Walzer, "Al-Fārābī's Theory of Prophecy and Divination," *Greek into Arabic*, pp. 206–19. Sanā'ī's contemporary ʿUs̱mān Mukhtārī in his *Hunarnāmah* treats the poet as the embodiment of the Perfect Man: "The perfect man is the consummate artist whose professional skill gives him a right to the benevolent attention of the patrons of literature" (de Bruijn, *OPP*, p. 197).

When you have not learned about lines, planes and
points.[6]

Such spatial organization reflects the ideal, eternal order, in contrast to linear patterns evocative of the finite limitations of human time and space.[7] Niẓāmī's cosmic circle repeats the grand design of the ultimate Artist as well as his manifestation in creation; the existence of that design, as a model for human experience, establishes the end of that experience, "the goal to be reached by man during his lifetime,"[8] as perfection. Similarly, in Ḥāfiẓ's *ghazal* the off-balance circle calls attention to the tension between the ideal pattern and the imperfect reality. In this way, structure is used both to convey a specific ethical message and to comment on the nature of poetry itself.

We are perhaps now able to form a more accurate image of the medieval Persian court poet's conception of the nature and purpose of his art, as well as to trace its conceptual and stylistic

[6] De Bruijn, *OPP*, p. 216 (the verse is from the *Ḥadīqat al-ḥaqīqah*; the translation is de Bruijn's). For the Pythagoreans, "geometry was meant to lead the soul above the mundane. . . . Study of the geometrical figures supposedly raises the soul to perusal of the eternal forms, so that, for instance, it can understand the work of God as geometer" (Heninger, *TSH*, p. 114). The Ikhwān al-Ṣafā' discuss "intellectual geometry" (*al-hindasah al-ʿaqlīyah*) as the means of passing from material to spiritual understanding (see *RIS*, 1:101–13). On the spiritual importance of geometric patterns in Islamic art, see David Wade, *Pattern in Islamic Art*, pp. 7–13.

[7] Cf. Bausani, "Muhammad or Darius?" 46–48.

[8] De Bruijn, *OPP*, p. 197. Sanā'ī and Niẓāmī are both concerned with depicting man's progress toward perfection; interestingly enough, it is Niẓāmī whose vision proves finally to contain far-reaching eschatological implications. In the *Ḥadīqah*, "Sanā'ī . . . is not really writing about eschatology. It should be remembered that his poem is, first of all, a panegyric. One could say that he deals with the introductory part of the philosophical theme of maʿād—that is, the part which is concerned with the specifically human virtues—but winds up the treatment of this general subject with a strictly individual application. The depiction of the process of moral purification does not end in looking towards an eschatological fulfilment; it stops at the top of the scale of human perfections in the contemplation of a specimen of the fullest development among the living contemporaries of the poet" (ibid., p. 213). By contrast, Niẓāmī, while implicitly reminding his patron of the possibility of his own perfection, goes beyond this pragmatic end toward an eschatological one in his depiction of Bahrām's disappearance and apotheosis.

evolution. Three major aspects of the poet's self-image may be discerned. The first element in this image is the oft-repeated definition of the poet as he who preserves the patron's name for posterity while spreading the repute of his accomplishments and virtues in his own age. As we now see, this universally acknowledged function of the court poet is only the tip of the iceberg. Devolving from it and concomitant with it are other aspects of the poet's role, aspects that reveal a conception of poetry far exceeding its technical definition as "rhymed, metred discourse indicating a meaning" so beloved of the rhetoricians.[9] The most important of these aspects is the identification of poetry with ethics. From Gurgānī's description of his romance of *Vīs u Rāmīn* as "a piece of sage advice" to Niẓāmī's definition of the *Haft Paykar* as "no fable, but a treasure" (*HP* 363), from Manūchihrī's praise of the poetry of his master ʿUnṣurī as resembling the blessings of Paradise[10] to Ḥāfiẓ's equation of his own verses with Scripture, the association of poetry with moral guidance and eternal wisdom is an informing principle that underlies much of the court poet's production and determines both his approach to his task and his manner of expression. Panegyrists, romance writers, and lyric poets shared the conviction that poetry served moral ends, although the specific manner in which these ends were to be achieved varied according to the dictates of their respective genres.

When we look back at the three major genres studied—panegyric, romance, and lyric *ghazal*—we find that they are complementary as regards their goals and style. Panegyric is, for obvious reasons, the genre that evolves least; bound to its depiction of a permanent ideal held up for emulation by a less than perfect human patron—an ideal that must by definition be viewed as unchanging and eternal—and despite its reminders of mortality and its frequent topical references, the

[9] The definition of poetry as "rhymed, metred discourse" reflects the rhetoricians' association of poetry with grammar; the philosophers, on the other hand, associated it with logic. Cf. Hardison, "Averroes' Commentary," p. 65; Ikhwān al-Ṣafāʾ, *al-Risālah al-Jāmiʿah*, p. 113; Averroes, *Talkhīṣ*, p. 203.

[10] See the passage quoted by Clinton, *Manūchihrī*, pp. 38–39.

qaṣīdah remains stylistically the least flexible of these three genres. It is consequently the least affected by the development of analogical style, even though its very basis, its raison d'être and the element that makes indirection possible, is the analogy between poet and lover, patron and beloved. Analogical modes of composition are most clearly perceived in romance and in *ghazal*; that these genres emerged at roughly the same period in time—a period of vigorous intellectual dialogue—and that they lent themselves so readily to the literary expression of that dialogue, may have contributed to the *qaṣīdah*'s decline in popularity, at least among poets. Moreover, the generic subordination of poet to patron clearly limits his ability to place himself, as creator of a poem in praise of another, in a position analogous to God.

The *ghazal* poet, even when employing the genre for encomiastic purposes, is able to free himself from this position of subordination by virtue of the *ghazal*'s generic subject, love. As an authority on love, the poet is brought closer to the divine order (the source and manifestation of love); he becomes a link between the real (as represented by his audience) and the ideal, revealing to the one the transcendental order of the other. This is the position taken by Ḥāfiẓ in those *ghazal*s that, by virtue of their analogical imagery and structure, become themselves microcosms in which both the macrocosmic order and the imperfections of the human world (and specifically of the body politic) are mirrored. The romance writer—and particularly a poet like Niẓāmī, who wrote for the court but was not of it—was perhaps most free to manipulate the conventions of his genre. Through the technique of multiple perspectives (encompassing both character and imagery) he could convey both the ambiguities of the human condition and the order underlying it, as well as express his belief in the human potential for perfectability.[11]

Because of the complementary nature of these genres, we

[11] The complementary nature of these genres is further reflected in the grammatical persons typical of each: the *qaṣīdah* is addressed to a "you" (the patron); the *ghazal* focuses on an "I" (the poet-lover); while the romance recounts the actions of a "he" (the protagonist).

should not look for consistency between the viewpoints presented in each (for example, on matters of love). This is especially true of the contrast between *ghazal* and romance; for while the lyric presents a courtly view of love intended to inspire its audience to self-perfection through identification with the lover's refined sentiments and self-sacrificing stance, romance criticizes both those sentiments and that stance, demonstrating the impossibility of applying them to relations of a more public nature without the intervening mediation of higher and more general principles.[12] Such attitudes are generic rather than philosophical; each genre conveys its message via its own conventions, and the exemplary status of each was understood by its audience in accordance with those conventions.[13]

An understanding of the ethical significance of poetry enables us to consider other aspects of the poet's craft—particularly those that have traditionally elicited negative criticism—in a new light. Among these is the status of the poet as imitator of his predecessors, often equated with servile copying, unprincipled or meaningless borrowing, and lack of sincerity and originality. The example of Niẓāmī enables us to define more accurately the precise nature of this relationship as one of intertextuality in its particular medieval sense:

> For a literary discourse that conceived of itself (1) as born of a process of textual imitation, and (2) as perpetuating

[12] D. H. Green notes that "the transposition of the theme of love from the lyric to the narrative genre means a transfer from an introspective, self-contained poetic realm (where attention and energy are largely restricted to the problem of love, artificially isolated) to a different type of fictional universe where the lover is also a man of action concerned with the world around him and where the literary theme is knightly action as well as lover's sentiment. By this change of genre the theme of love is no longer regarded hermetically, but has to justify itself against competing claims" (*Irony*, p. 104).

[13] As Poirion observes, "The role of courtly poetry is precisely to reestablish social harmony. Didactic, it teaches ideal human conduct; lyric, it sings of human aspirations and ideals" (*Le poète et le prince*, p. 131). Allen similarly notes that "late medieval [literary] theory . . . took the particulars of story, and of mental posture as defined by lyric, as immediately exemplary" (*Ethical Poetic*, p. 32).

this process while (3) renewing an ever-widening canon of . . . texts in recombination, intertextuality was an integral part of its poetics. The . . . romance text was itself a *reading*, or *re-writing*, of previous texts, and, in turn it invited both reading and re-writing. . . . Each romance, instead of being merely a reperformance of a model or paradigm, constitutes a *link* in a chain of texts—a textuality—that absorbs and rearticulates its predecessors together with articulating a reading or an interpretation of them.[14]

The assumption posited for romance may be similarly applied—with allowances for generic differences—to the other genres of court poetry, where, although such intertextual echoes customarily involve individual lines, it is not unheard of for them to encompass whole poems.[15] If the poet adds nothing new, that is, if he perceives no new meaning in his material, but merely produces a rhetorical elaboration of it, then he is, indeed, nothing but a slavish imitator. He not only must im-

[14] Freeman, "Intertextuality," 149; author's emphases.

[15] Thus, for example, A. J. Arberry's discussion of Ḥāfiẓ's indebtedness to Saʿdī misses this important point. Asserting that "in treating each theme [of his poem] . . . Ḥāfiẓ was well informed of how previous poets had worked it out, and would be striving to improve on all prior performances," Arberry's analysis consists of juxtaposing lines thematically resembling those of Ḥāfiẓ's "Shīrāzī Turk" *ghazal* with others from the *ghazal*s of his predecessor ("The Art of Ḥāfiẓ," pp. 350, 352–54). Rehder takes issue with this approach both on the ground that (quite apart from the vagueness of Arberry's conception of a "theme") Ḥāfiẓ "was probably not aware of 'all prior treatments of the themes' which he took up" (a minor quibble of language) and on the more serious ground that "to consider Ḥāfiẓ's ghazals primarily in terms of their themes stereotypes them unnecessarily, and fragments them so that there is a tendency to look more at the affiliations of parts of a poem with parts of other poems *by other poets*, and less at the relationships and functions of the parts within the poem, and at the poem as a whole" ("Unity," 59; author's emphasis). Both, however, ignore the fact that the intertextual nature of medieval composition makes it impossible for a given poem to be considered (except for purposes of limited analysis) as a self-contained artifact: the poet's audience, no less than he himself, would have been aware of other treatments of a given topic (if not of "all prior performances") and would have expected the poet to better them, not only through rhetorical elaboration, but by "making them new" within the context of his own poem.

prove on his model rhetorically, but (to quote another poet from a far different time and place) "make it new," and make it distinctively his own.[16]

It is here that the purpose of rhetorical ornament becomes elucidated. Rhetoric functions, not for its own sake (at least not among poets of the first rank), but for a double purpose: to reveal the "hidden truth" of the matter and to increase the effectiveness of its presentation. The exceptional erudition required of the poet establishes his qualifications for rereading the works of his predecessors; his rhetorical skill enables him to rewrite them effectively and in a meaningful fashion.[17] Niẓāmī's comparison of himself to a jeweler working with precious stones assumes both the inherent value of the material being worked with and the skill and effort required to make best use of it. The poet speaks of selecting, weighing, shaping, and arranging (metaphors readily extendible to composition), of recognizing value in what had hitherto been neglected as well as appraising earlier treatments fairly, of adding "ornaments" from other provenances and styles, combining all into

[16] An important function of the branch of rhetoric dealing with the study of plagiarism, *saraqāt*, is precisely the distinguishing of "good" borrowing from bad. The abundant literature on the subject makes clear that an improvement on the meaning of the topic involved (its *maʿnā*) is valued more than is mere elaboration of its verbal expression (*lafẓ*). For a survey of this type of criticism, see G. E. von Grunebaum, "The Concept of Plagiarism in Arabic Theory," *JNES* 3 (1944), 234–53. A thorough investigation of the development of theories of *saraqāt* and the complex terminology employed would add greatly to our understanding of medieval intertextuality.

[17] Such procedures also involve modification of the conceptual base of certain figures (cf. Bürgel, "Remarques," and Heinrichs, *Hand of the North Wind*, for examples of such modifications). Grabar comments on the relationship of decorative and structural elements in the visual arts of the Saljuq period, especially in architecture: decorative elements (arabesques, plant motifs, etc.) function, not independent of the overall design, but as a means of strengthening structural lines ("Visual Arts," 639–40). A similar principle may be adduced for the poetry of the period (and especially romance), where such devices as amplification, description, and the like reinforce the meaning of the action by calling attention to certain salient points (e.g., in the *Haft Paykar*, the amplification of the description of Fitnah as compared to the model in Firdawsī) or support thematic and/or structural parallels (the parallel descriptions of the onager and Fitnah).

a "treasure" so skillfully worked as to guarantee that it will, when appraised by experts, be recognized as of the highest worth. The ensuing comparison—of the poem as a temple adorned by images and of the poet as its architect and painter (i.e., as responsible for both its design and its embellishment)—proclaims the achievement of this goal.

That the nature and the scope of the court poet's accomplishment surpasses that for which he is traditionally given credit should be clear. This study, however, has been able to furnish only a glimpse of the whole picture, which remains to be reconstructed in all its detail. It is therefore appropriate to conclude by suggesting desiderata for a more thorough understanding of court poetry in the larger context of medieval Persian culture, and of possible directions to be taken by future investigations.

No complete study of any aspect of medieval Persian literature can consider it in isolation from the pre-Islamic Iranian tradition, from the Arabic tradition of which it is in large measure a continuation, and from medieval literature as a whole. Though many students of Persian literature emphasize its apartness from both Arab and Islamic elements, and though it would be a mistake to forget the very real transformations wrought by Islam on older Iranian (as well as more recent Arabic) elements in the tradition, nevertheless the literature in question must be viewed as part of a continuum, and not separated from its historical and literary past.[18] Similarly (as has been suggested throughout this study), important parallels exist between Persian medieval literature and that of the West, parallels that cannot be considered the result of "influence" but must be viewed as common responses to similar cultural circumstances. It is the task of comparative studies to investigate such problems of continuity and parallelism from a more

[18] Wickens (for example) emphasizes Iranian "apartness" ("Persian Literature," p. 71), as do those who see Persian literature as representing a "national resurgence." As Bausani warns, " 'Iran' and 'Islam' are . . . not to be thought of as two antithetical elements. One could even say that Islam assumed its familiar aspect only after the integration brought about by the great conquests of the seventh century" ("Muhammad or Darius?" p. 47; cf. chapter 1, n. 60).

objective viewpoint than has hitherto been typical, in order to elucidate the true aspects of similarity and of difference existing between these closely related traditions; it is also the task of such studies to restore the sense of Persian literature as *literature* lost by a discipline that has become increasingly the province of philologists and specialists in "area studies," who have lost contact with their own literary past.[19]

In the specific area of court poetry, more precise documentation is needed on the relations between court and poet, and particularly on the more mundane aspects of this relationship: the types of positions (other than, or in addition to, that of poet) court poets were likely to hold, the stipends or other rewards they might be expected to receive, the amount of influence they actually exerted, and so on. In addition, there is the question of education: not only that of the poet himself, but that of his audience, the members of the court in which he functioned. It is undoubtedly true that shared educational backgrounds played an important role in creating the shared expectations of poet and audience. The question of the types of literature preferred by individual patrons—which might be ascertained by the status of personal libraries, for example, a survey of works commissioned, requests for books to be cop-

[19] J. Stetkevych discusses the growing "alienation of the literary scholar as Orientalist-philologist from the standards and values of his own culture" ("Arabic Poetry and Assorted Poetics," in *Islamic Studies*, ed. Malcolm Kerr, p. 113). In Stetkevych's opinion this process (in Arabic studies) began essentially with Ahlwardt's emphasis on the philological aspect of literature and the search for the "perfect text": "From now on [he continues] it will be acceptable for the Orientalist scholar-critic to avoid taking a personal position and to evade, whenever he so desires, the burden of a value judgment concerning the subject of his study. His vehicle of evasion will be his claim to historicism." The burden of historicism, in turn, leads to the evaluation of past literatures by modern political and ideological standards and their condemnation on those grounds: which means, *mutatis mutandis*, that they must be inferior "aesthetically" (i.e., ideologically), and thus not worth the effort required to come to grips with them on their own terms. Needless to say, nineteenth-century nationalism and racism, and twentieth-century ideological disputes, played a significant part in such extraliterary value judgments. Cf. also Roger Allen, "Literature," in *The Study of the Middle East*, ed. Leonard Binder, p. 402 et passim.

ied, and so on—is also of considerable importance for ascertaining the tastes and expectations of the courtly audience; although a difficult matter to reconstruct, careful reading of documentary sources can undoubtedly carry us a long way toward clarifying such questions.[20] Further, the whole problem of reception—the extent to which romance, for example, was received as historical exemplar, or lyric poetry was put to homiletic uses—needs to be carefully investigated in order to shed further light on the uses of poetry and on audience expectations.[21]

Connected with this question is the broader one of patronage. As the example of Sanā'ī shows, changes in patronage can produce dramatic changes in style and can remove a poet from the category of court poet into another. Over and above the question of the influence of a specific patron's tastes on the type of poetry written by any given poet (Ḥāfiẓ's poems for Mubāriz al-Dīn are clearly quite different from those for Shāh Shujāʿ), the influence of an individual patron on a group of poets (did the patronage of Bahrāmshāh Ghaznavī contribute significantly to the development of panegyric *ghazal* at the hands of those poets who wrote for him?), the question of shifting patterns of patronage at different historical periods—for example, the rise of religious institutions as centers of patronage, and of religious scholars as the subjects of panegyric (again, Sanā'ī provides an instance)—requires systematic

[20] In this connection R. F. Green's book, *Poets and Princepleasers*, is exemplary in outlining the specific problems of documentation and areas which need to be considered.

[21] This question has already been touched on in connection with the use of poetry in the *Tārīkh-i Bayhaqī* and the *Rāḥat al-Ṣudūr* (see chapter 5, n. 2) and the use of *ghazal* verses in homiletic sermons (chapter 6, n. 45). The extent to which romance (as well as epic) was in fact received as history has received no consideration, most critics emphasizing the fictional, fantastic aspects of the genre; for a parallel problem in medieval English literature, see R. F. Green, *Poets and Princepleasers*, pp. 136–40. In general, the utilization of poetic excerpts in nonpoetic works (such as history, but also in such prose collections as the *Arabian Nights*) has been viewed as "embellishment" and has not been taken seriously; that it had a serious purpose is strongly suggested by the examples cited above, but the problem requires far more extensive investigation.

study and documentation, as does that of supposed "levels of appreciation" and their variation under different patrons or dynasties (the Ghaznavids or the Mongols, for example, as opposed to the Saljuqs). Associated with this problem is the interrelationship of court poetry with other types: mystical, homiletic, religious, or proselytizing (as, for example, the Isma'ili verse of Nāṣir-i Khusraw, the pro-Alid verse of other poets, and so on). Obviously many thematic features of these various types of poetry overlap, demonstrating that the motifs employed are rarely specific to one sort of poetry (although they may first appear in one or another), but lend themselves to a variety of interpretations and uses. A thorough study of such interrelationships would go far toward establishing a typology for the various genres in question, which would include both courtly and noncourtly subgenres.

Among important questions that have as yet received little attention is that of the conditions of composition and performance and their effect on the different genres of court poetry. We know that panegyric *qaṣīdah*s were presented orally on celebratory occasions; we can speculate, on the basis of stylistic features, as well as from the evidence of internal authorial comments, that romance (in contrast to epic) was composed to be read privately as well as publicly, in oral presentation; and although many *ghazal*s show evidence of having been composed to be sung or recited aloud, references in them to writing are so numerous that we must assume that they were meant to be read in private as well. No attempt has been made, however, to assemble information from either the poems themselves or from other sources with a view to arriving at a clearer picture of performance conditions. We may assume that the customary audience for panegyric was the patron and the assembled court; but were there other types of *qaṣīdah* (as implied by such examples as Manūchihrī's "Idol of Ḥiṣār" *qaṣīdah* and by some of the poems of Anvarī), composed for smaller, more exclusive gatherings—a circumstance that would have affected their style (and that may have encouraged the growth of the panegyric *ghazal*)? What was the composition of the audience of romance? Would it (as was the case in the medieval West) have included a large proportion of female members, or would it have been read at family—as opposed to public—gatherings (hence the frequent stress on filial piety)? As for *ghazal*, although it is self-evident that it was composed for more intimate settings, it is not entirely clear who would have been present at these gatherings; neither is it wise to stress too much their informality, since certainly courtly protocol would still have been observed. More important, the interrelationship of the *ghazal*—often composed to be sung—with music, and the effect of this on its style (can one distinguish, on stylistic grounds, between a *ghazal* composed specifically to be sung and one meant to be performed without music, or read privately?) requires extensive study.[22]

The question of the relation of poetry to music raises the more general one of its relation to the other arts. Most comparisons in this area have been made along quite superficial lines; the poem is said to resemble a mosaic, a miniature, an arabesque, a Persian carpet, and so on, with no clear or accurate definition of the compositional principles of either the arts in question or poetry. Most such comparisons, moreover, are heavily influenced by the "molecular" theory of composition with respect to both poetry and the other arts.[23] A. J. Arberry's

[22] Strong rhythmical features, the use of shorter meters, the presence of internal rhyme, etc., would seem to indicate *ghazal*s that were composed to be sung, as would a more conventional and less subtly expressed content; while by contrast, poems that exhibit more subtle use of allusion or wordplay—more complex features of meaning—may have been meant either for recitation or private reading. A similar problem is presented by the contrast between the Renaissance air and madrigal, the former oriented toward content, while the relatively simple verbal style of the other is determined largely by the exigencies of its musical context (cf. Maurice Evans, *English Poetry in the Sixteenth Century*, 2d ed., p. 116). It should be noted that such distinctions represent differences in emphasis rather than mutually exclusive categories: as Allen observes, "the *grand chant courtois* in particular and medieval lyric in general, is more sung than read and can, therefore, never be properly considered without major emphasis on its existence as public behavior" ("Grammar, Poetic Form, and the Lyric Ego," p. 215).

[23] The *locus classicus* of this theory is L. Massignon's 1921 lecture "Les methodes de réalisation artistique des peuples de l'Islam," published in *Opera*

attempt to reconstruct Ḥāfiẓ's "theory of the lyric" is exemplary, if only because of the generality of its assertions and the confusion of its terminology:

> Ḥāfiẓ's technique is fundamentally thematic; by which is meant, that he constructs each lyric upon the basis of a limited number of themes selected from a repertory which is itself definitely restricted, and to a great extent conventional. Having chosen his themes—as a rule not more than two or three whole themes, with fragments of others so familiar as to be immediately recognizable—he then proceeds to work out his pattern. It is supremely important to understand how vital and inevitable pattern is to the Persian poet: a people which produced craftsmen of unsurpassed skill in the arts of line and colour might indeed have been expected to throw up men of equal parts in the marshalling of verbal images and sounds; and it was natural that they should work their materials into forms essentially similar to those invented by their fellow-craftsmen, the creators of mosaics and miniature paintings. So it is a mosaic of sounds and symbols that the Ḥāfiẓian lyric is to be appreciated; and its artistry, including its unity, is to be understood as being of the order of artistic unity that is found in the finest mosaic pattern.[24]

Minora, 3:9–24; it was applied to literature by T. Kowalski, von Grunebaum, and others (see Rypka, *History*, 102; van Gelder, *Beyond the Line*, 14–19).

[24] Arberry, "Art of Ḥāfiẓ," p. 350. R. Rehder criticizes Arberry's analysis on the grounds that "analogies between the arts are sometimes very interesting, and they are necessary if one is to form any good idea of a culture as a whole, but extreme care must be taken in making them, and it cannot be forgotten that they are only analogies, suggestions of partial, putative, and commonly unessential, similarity. Painting and poetry, for example, are so different in their ways and means, in the modes of the mind which they engage, that the more one is concerned with the essential aspects of one of them, the less the help which is provided by analogies with the other. . . . The most interesting problems: meaning, style, form, unity, development, are radically different in the different arts. . . . Literary problems must be solved in literary terms" ("Unity," 60–61). Despite the obvious differences between various types of artistic production, the objection, while perhaps valid for the Romantic artists (Wordsworth and Turner) Rehder finds it impossible to compare in a mean-

Although Arberry's emphasis on pattern appears promising, he conceives of it, whether in mosaic, miniature, or poem (as his analysis of Ḥāfiẓ's "Shirazi Turk" *ghazal* shows), as being the product of a random juxtaposition of interchangeable units arranged without reference to any overall principle of composition. The shortcomings of such an assumption with respect to the visual arts have been demonstrated by art historians;[25] it is no less erroneous for the verbal ones. As the poets' own statements show (the prologue to the *Haft Paykar* is exemplary, but others might be cited), their likening of themselves to artisans in other crafts transcends metaphor to encompass shared processes of artistic conceptualization and realization. In an age when the arts were predominantly symbolic rather than representational, correspondences in principles of design and execution should be expected.[26] Investigation of such parallels between the arts will undoubtedly shed light on important general principles of composition in all of

ingful manner, appears invalidated for the medieval period by the insistence of the poets themselves on making such comparisons, and because of their obvious concern with clarifying not only the status of a finished product but the nature of the process that produced it. *Ut pictura poesis*—when not interpreted in post-Romantic "representational" terms (a basic problem in Rehder's objection)—is a useful tool in unraveling principles of composition. Studies in the medieval literature of the West have revealed significant parallels between principles of composition in literature and in other arts; see especially Jordan, *Chaucer and the Shape of Creation*, and Sandra Ihle, *Malory's Grail Quest*, especially pp. 3–30; cf. Kelly, "Theory of Composition," 118–19, 126–27.

[25] See especially Grabar, "Visual Arts," and Papadopoulo, *Muslim Art*. See also Heninger, *TSH*, pp. 385–88 on common assumptions of poetry and architecture in the Renaissance.

[26] Cf. Marshall Hodgson's observations on symbolizing art, *Venture*, 2:501–503. Hodgson's evaluation of Islamicate art as being, "compared with other arts of the Agrarian Age, . . . to a much greater degree independent of emblematically symbolic functions, either religious or political, apart from the intention of immediate visual appeal" (ibid., p. 507), is thrown into question by studies such as that of Hartner and Ettinghausen, which demonstrate a continuity of symbolic traditions at least in the early centuries of Islam, and which take issue with Hodgson's position as expressed elsewhere (see "The Conquering Lion," 161).

them, as well as on specific differences relating to generically determined styles, goals, and media employed.[27]

The existence of such parallels itself points to a final element which, while it has received some mention in this study, requires extensive further investigation. If poems such as the *Haft Paykar*, or Ḥāfiẓ's *ghazal*s, constitute "literary microcosms," or even "analogous universes" (using terms employed by S. K. Heninger), then a deeper understanding of the relationship between the way in which the world is perceived and the manner in which that perception is conveyed, as well as of the ways in which poetry was believed to function—affectively rather than mimetically—is crucial to an understanding of such poems.[28] These are far-reaching topics relating not only to court poetry but to the entire poetic tradition; the present study must therefore be seen as a prolegomenon to further investigation, at once more extensive and more specialized, of the philosophical and cosmological premises underlying that tradition.

[27] Such an opportunity is missed by Priscilla Soucek in her essay on Niẓāmī's references to painting in the romances ("Niẓāmī on Painters and Painting," in *Islamic Art in the Metropolitan Museum of Art*, ed. R. Ettinghausen, pp. 9–21). Viewing these references (among which the passage quoted from the *Haft Paykar* is not included) largely as an attempt by the poet "to present a definition of representational art that would allay the suspicions of the theologically minded" (p. 19), she often overlooks both the symbolic and the technical aspects of many of the passages in question.

[28] See Heninger, *TSH*, pp. 293–98, 339–44, and especially 364–93. Heninger comments on the important relation between faculty psychology and Renaissance poetics and on the concept of the poet as active maker (ibid., pp. 297–98); on this topic, see especially Robert L. Montgomery, *The Reader's Eye: Studies in Didactic Literary Theory from Dante to Tasso*. As Earl Miner has cogently observed, "No account of the nature of literature can be other than parochial if it fails to observe that mimesis is one of the least frequent systematic ideas about literature" ("On the Genesis and Development of Literary Systems," I, *Critical Inquiry* 5 [1978/1979], 349), a point that must be borne in mind especially when considering the Arabo-Persian tradition. (See also idem, "The Grounds of Mimetic and Non-Mimetic Art," in *Articulate Images: The Sister Arts from Hogarth to Tennyson*, ed. Richard Wendorf, pp. 70–97, and especially pp. 78–95.)

Bibliography

List of Abbreviations

Books

Aghānī	Abū al-Faraj al-Iṣbahānī. *Kitāb al-Aghānī*
CHI	*The Cambridge History of Iran*
EI^2	*The Encyclopedia of Islam*, 2d edition
HP	Niẓāmī Ganjavī. *Heft Peiker*, ed. H. Ritter and J. Rypka
KS	Niẓāmī Ganjavī. *Khusraw u Shīrīn*, ed. V. Dastgirdī
LHP	E. J. Browne. *Literary History of Persia*
LM	Niẓāmī Ganjavī. *Laylī u Majnūn*, ed. V. Dastgirdī
OPP	J.T.P. de Bruijn. *Of Piety and Poetry*
QG	Ḥāfiẓ. *Dīvān*, ed. M. Qazvīnī and Q. Ghanī
P	Ḥāfiẓ. *Dīvān*, ed. Ḥ. Pizhmān
RIS	Ikhwān al-Ṣafā'. *Rasā'il*
TSH	S. K. Heninger, Jr. *Touches of Sweet Harmony*
VR	Fakhr al-Dīn Gurgānī. *Vis and Ramin*, trans. George Morrison

Periodicals

AION	*Annali di l'Istituto Orientale*, Naples
AJSSL	*American Journal of Semitic Languages and Literatures*
BEO	*Bulletin d'Etudes Orientales* (Damascus)
BSOAS	*Bulletin of the School of Oriental (and African) Studies*, University of London
CCM	*Cahiers de Civilisation Medievale*
IJMES	*International Journal of Middle East Studies*
JA	*Journal Asiatique*
JAL	*Journal of Arabic Literature*
JAOS	*Journal of the American Oriental Society*
JNES	*Journal of Near Eastern Studies*
JRAS	*Journal of the Royal Asiatic Society*
PQ	*Philological Quarterly*
REI	*Revue des Etudes Islamiques*

Primary Sources: Poetic Texts and Translations

Al-ʿAbbās ibn al-Aḥnaf. *Dīwān*. Beirut: Dār Ṣādir, 1965.

Anvarī, Awḥad al-Dīn. *Dīvān*. Edited by Saʿīd Nafīsī. Tehran: Pīrūz, 1959.

ʿAyyūqī. *Le roman de Varqe et Golšâh*. Translated by A. S. Melikian-Chirvani. *Arts Asiatiques* 22 (1970) (special number).

———. *Varqah u Gulshāh*. Edited by Ẕabīḥ Allāh Ṣafā. Tehran: Dānishgāh-i Ṭihrān, 1343/1964.

Bashshār ibn Burd. *Dīwān*. Edited by Muḥammad al-Ṭāhir ibn ʿĀshūr. 4 vols. Cairo: Lajnat al-Ta'līf wa-al-Tarjumah wa-al-Nashr, 1950.

Fakhr al-Dīn Gurgānī. *Le roman de Wîs et Râmîn*. Translated by Henri Massé. Paris: Les Belles Lettres, 1959.

———. *Vis and Ramin*. Translated by George Morrison (*VR*). New York: Columbia University Press, 1972.

———. *Vīs u Rāmīn*. Edited by Muḥammad Jaʿfar Maḥjūb. Tehran: Ibn Sīnā, 1337/1959.

———. *Vīs u Rāmīn*. Edited by M. Mīnūvī. Tehran: Beroukhim, 1338/1959.

———. *Vīs u Rāmīn*. Edited by M. A. Todua and A. K. Gwakharia. Zabān va-adabiyāt-i Fārsī, 18. Tehran: Bunyād-i Farhang-i Īrān, 1349/1970.

Farrukhī Sīstānī. *Dīvān*. Edited by ʿAlī ʿAbd al-Rasūlī. Tehran: 1311/1922.

Firdawsī. *Shāhnāmah*. Edited by M. Dabīr-Siyāqī. 6 vols. Tehran: Ibn Sīnā, 1335/1956.

Ḥāfiẓ. *Dīvān*. Edited by M. Qazvīnī and Q. Ghanī (QG). Tehran: Zavvār, 1941.

———. Dīvān. Edited by Ḥusayn Pizhmān (P). Tehran: Beroukhim, 1318/1939.

Ḥasan-i Ghaznavī, called Ashraf. *Dīvān*. Edited by M. T. Mudarris Raẓavī. Tehran: Dānishgāh-i Ṭihrān, 1328/1949.

Manūchihrī Dāmghānī. *Dīvān*. Edited by M. Dabīr-Siyāqī. 2d ed. Tehran: Zavvār, 1338/1959.

———. *Ménoutchehri, poète persan du IIème siècle*. Edited and translated by A. de Biberstein Kazimirski. Paris: Klincksieck, 1886.

Niẓāmī Ganjavī. *The Haft Paikar (The Seven Beauties)*. Translated by C. E. Wilson. 2 vols. London: Arthur Probsthain, 1924.

———. *Haft Paykar*. Edited by Vaḥīd Dastgirdī. 2d ed. Tehran: Ibn Sīnā, 1334/1955–6.

———. *Heft Peyker, ein romantisches Epos*. Edited by H. Ritter and J. Rypka (*HP*). Monografie Archivu Orientálního, 3. Prague: Orientální Ústav, 1934.

———. *Khusraw u Shīrīn*. Edited by Vaḥīd Dastgirdī (*KS*). 2d ed. Tehran: Ibn Sīnā, 1333/1954.

———. *Laylī u Majnūn*. Edited by Vahīd Dastgirdī (*LM*). Tehran: Armaghān, 1313/1934.

———. *Le roman de Chosroës et Chîrîn*. Translated by Henri Massé. Paris: G. P. Maisonneuve-Larose, 1970.

———. *The Story of Layla and Majnun*. Translated by R. Gelpke. Oxford: Cassirer, 1966.

Saʿdī. *Kullīyāt*. Edited by Muḥammad ʿAlī Furūghī. Tehran: Iqbāl, 1340/1962.

Sanā'ī Ghaznavī. *Dīvān*. Edited by M. T. Mudarris Raẕavī. Tehran: Ibn Sīnā, 1341/1962.

ʿUnṣurī. *Vāmiq u ʿAẕrā'*. Edited by Maulavi Mohammed Shafi. Lahore: Panjab University Press, 1967.

Secondary Sources: Books and Articles

Abū al-Faraj al-Iṣbahānī. *Kitāb al-Aghānī*. Edited by Ibrāhīm al-Ibyārī (*Aghānī*). 22 vols. Cairo, 1969.

Abū Hiffān al-Mihzamī. *Akhbār Abī Nuwās*. Edited by ʿAbd al-Sattār Aḥmad Farrāj. Cairo: Maktabat Miṣr, 1953.

Adler, Alfred. "Sovereignty in Chretien's *Yvain*." *PMLA* 62 (1947), 281–305.

Ahsan, Muhammad Manazir. *Social Life under the Abbasids*. London: Longman, 1979.

Allen, Judson Boyce. *The Ethical Poetic of the Later Middle Ages: A Decorum of Convenient Distinction*. Toronto: University of Toronto Press, 1982.

———. "Grammar, Poetic Form, and the Lyric Ego: A Medieval *A Priori*." In *Vernacular Poetics in the Middle Ages*, edited by Lois Ebin, pp. 199–226. Studies in Medieval Culture, 16. Kalamazoo, Michigan: Western Michigan University, Institute for Medieval Studies, 1984.

———. "The *Grand Chant Courtois* and the Wholeness of the Poem: The Medieval *Assimilatio* of Text, Audience, and Commentary." *L'Esprit Createur* 18:3 (1978), 5–17.

———. "Hermann the German's Averroistic Aristotle and Medieval Poetic Theory." *Mosaic* 9:3 (1976), 67–81.

———, and Theresa Anne Moritz. *A Distinction of Stories: The Medieval Unity of Chaucer's Fair Chain of Narratives for Canterbury*. Columbus: Ohio State University Press, 1981.

Allen, Roger, et al. "Literature." In *The Study of the Middle East*, edited by Leonard Binder, pp. 399–509. New York: John Wiley & Sons, 1976.

Altheim, Franz. "The Most Ancient Romance of Chivalry." *East and West* 9 (1958), 129–44.

Arberry, A. J. "The Art of Ḥāfiẓ." In *Aspects of Islamic Civilisation as Depicted in the Original Texts*, pp. 344–58. London: George Allen & Unwin, 1964.

———. *Fifty Poems of Ḥāfiẓ*. Cambridge: Cambridge University Press, 1962.

———. "Three Persian Poems." *Iran* 2 (1964), 1–12.

Aristotle. *Fann al-shiʿr, maʿa al-tarjumah al-ʿArabīyah al-qadīmah wa-shurūḥ al-Fārābī wa-Ibn Sīnā wa-Ibn Rushd*. Edited and translated by ʿAbd al-Raḥmān Badawī. Cairo: Maktabat al-Nahḍah al-Miṣrīyah, 1953.

ʿAṭṭār, Farīd al-Dīn. *The Conference of the Birds*. Translated by Afkham Darbandi and Dick Davis. Harmondsworth: Penguin Books, 1984.

Badawi, M. M. "From Primary to Secondary Qaṣīdas: Thoughts on the Development of Classical Arabic Poetry." *JAL* 9 (1980), 1–31.

Baḥr al-Favāʾid. Edited by M. T. Dānish-Pazhūh. Majmūʿah-i mutūn-i Fārsī, 28. Tehran: Bungāh-i Tarjumah va-Nashr-i Kitāb, 1966.

Bausani, Alessandro. "Considerazione sull'origine del ghazal." *Quaderno dell'Accademia Nazionale dei Lincei* 160 (1971), 195–208.

———. "The Development of Form in Persian Lyrics: A Way to a Better Understanding of the Structure of Western Poetry." *East and West*, n.s., 9 (1958), 145–53.

———. "Muhammad or Darius? The Elements and Basis of Iranian Culture." In *Islam and Cultural Change in the Middle Ages*, edited by Speros Vryonis, Jr., pp. 43–57. Wiesbaden: Otto Harrassowitz, 1975.

Bayhaqī, Abū al-Fazl. *Tārīkh-i Bayhaqī*. Edited by Q. Ghanī and ʿA. Akbar Fayyāẓ. Tehran: 1945.

Bencheikh, J.-E. "Le cénacle poètique du calife al-Mutawakkil (m. 247): Contribution à l'analyse des instances de légitimation sociolittéraires." *BEO* 29 (1977), 33–52.

———. *Poétique arabe; essai sur les voies d'une création*. Paris: Anthropos, 1975.

———. "Les secrétaires poètes et animateurs de cénacles aux IIe et

IIIe siècles de l'Hégire: contribution à l'analyse d'une production poétique." *JA* 263 (1975), 265–315.

Benveniste, E. "Le *Mémorial de Zarēr*, poéme pehlevi mazdéen." *JA* 220 (1932), 245–93.

Bīghāmī. *Love and War: Adventures from the Fīrūz Shāh Nāma.* Translated by William L. Hanaway, Jr. Delmar, N.Y.: Scholars' Facsimiles and Reprints, 1974.

Blachère, R. *Histoire de la littérature arabe.* 3 vols. Paris: Adrien-Maisonneuve, 1956–66.

———. *Un poète arabe du IVe siècle de l'Hégire . . . Abou ṭ-Ṭayyib al-Motanabbî: essai d'histoire littéraire.* Paris: Adrien-Maisonneuve, 1935.

Bloomfield, Morton W. "Episodic Motivation and Marvels in Epic and Romance." In *Essays and Explorations: Studies in Ideas, Language and Literature*, pp. 97–128. Cambridge, Mass.: Harvard University Press, 1970.

———. "Understanding Old English Poetry." In *Essays and Explorations*, pp. 59–95.

Boklund, Karin M. "On the Spatial and Cultural Characteristics of Courtly Romance." In *Semiotics and Dialectics: Ideology and the Text*, edited by Peter V. Zima, pp. 387–443. Linguistic and Literary Studies in Eastern Europe, 5. Amsterdam: John Benjamins, 1981.

Bonebakker, S. A. "Poets and Critics in the Third Century A.H." In *Logic in Classical Islamic Culture*, edited by G. E. von Grunebaum, pp. 85–111. Wiesbaden: Otto Harrassowitz, 1970.

———. "Prejudice against Poetry in Early Islam." *Medievalia et Humanistica* 7 (1976), 77–99.

———. "Reflections on the *Kitāb al-Badīʿ* of Ibn al-Muʿtazz." *Atti del 3. Congresso di Studi Arabi e Islamici* (Ravello 1966), pp. 191–209. Naples: 1967.

Bosworth, C. E. "The Development of Persian Culture under the Early Ghaznavids." *Iran* 6 (1968), 33–44.

———. "An Early Arabic Mirror for Princes: Ṭāhir Dhū l-Yamīnain's Epistle to his Son ʿAbdallāh (206/821)." *JNES* 29 (1970), 25–41.

———. *The Ghaznavids, Their Empire in Afghanistan and Eastern Iran 994:1040.* Edinburgh: Edinburgh University Press, 1963.

———. "The Heritage of Rulership in Early Islamic Iran and the Search for Dynastic Connections with the Past." *Iran* 9 (1973), 51–62.

Bosworth, C. E. "Maḥmūd of Ghazna in Contemporary Eyes and in Later Persian Literature." *Iran* 4 (1966), 85–92.

———. "The Ṭāhirids and Persian Literature." *Iran* 7 (1969), 103–106.

Boyce, Mary. *The Manichaean Hymn-Cycles in Parthian*. London: Oxford University Press, 1954.

———. "The Parthian *Gōsān* and Iranian Minstrel Tradition." *JRAS* (1947), 10–45.

———. "Zariadres and Zarēr." *BSOAS* 17 (1955), 463–77.

Browne, E. G. *A Literary History of Persia (LHP)*. 4 vols. Cambridge: Cambridge University Press, 1928.

———. "The Sources of Dawlatshāh; with . . . an Excursus on Bārbad and Rūdakī." *JRAS* (1899), 37–69.

Bürgel, J. C. "Remarques sur une relation entre la logique aristotélienne et la poésie arabo-persane." *Correspondence d'Orient* 11 (1970), 131–43.

Burnley, J. D. "*Fine amor*: Its Meaning and Context." *Review of English Studies*, n.s., 31 (1980), 130–48.

Burton, Sir Richard. *Love, War and Fancy: The Customs and Manners of the East, from Writings on the Arabian Nights*. Edited by Kenneth Walker. London: William Kimber, 1964.

Cahen, Claude. "Tribes, Cities and Social Organization." In *CHI*, 4:305–28.

The Cambridge History of Iran (CHI). Vol. 4, *From the Arab Invasion to the Saljuqs*. Edited by R. N. Frye. London: Cambridge University Press, 1975.

———. Vol. 5, *The Saljuq and Mongol Periods*. Edited by A. J. Boyle. Cambridge: Cambridge University Press, 1968.

Cantarino, Vicente. *Arabic Poetics in the Golden Age: Selection of Texts Accompanied by a Preliminary Study*. Studies in Arabic Literature, 4. Leiden: E. J. Brill, 1975.

———. "Averroes on Poetry." In *Islam and Its Cultural Divergence: Studies in Honor of Gustave E. von Grunebaum*, edited by Girdhari L. Tikku, pp. 10–26. Urbana: University of Illinois Press, 1971.

Chejne, A. G. "The Boon-Companion in Early ʿAbbasid Times." *JAOS* 85 (1965), 327–35.

Chelkowski, Peter J. *Mirror of the Invisible World: Tales from the Khamseh of Nizami*. New York: Metropolitan Museum of Art, 1975.

Chenu, M.-D. *Nature, Man, and Society in the Twelfth Century; Es-*

says on New Theological Perspectives in the Latin West.* Edited and translated by Jerome Taylor and Lester K. Little. Chicago: University of Chicago Press, 1968.

Christensen, Arthur. *L'Iran sous les Sassanides.* Copenhagen: Munksgaard, 1936.

———. *Recherches sur les Rubāʿīyāt de ʿUmar Ḫayyām.* Materialen zu einer Geschichte der Sprachen und Litteraturen des vorderen Orients, 3. Heidelberg: 1905.

Clinton, Jerome W. *The Dīvān of Manūchihrī Dāmghānī: A Critical Study.* Studies in Middle Eastern Literatures, 1. Minneapolis: Bibliotheca Islamica, 1972.

———. "Esthetics by Implication: What Metaphors of Craft Tell Us about the 'Unity' of the Persian Qaṣīda." *Edebiyat* 4 (1979), 73–96.

———. "Myth and History." Paper presented at the Fifteenth Annual Meeting of the Middle East Studies Association, Seattle, Washington, November 1981.

Conger, George Perrigo. *Theories of Macrocosms and Microcosms in the History of Philosophy.* New York: Columbia University Press, 1922.

Corbin, Henry. *Avicenne et le récit visionnaire.* Vol. 1. Bibliothèque Iranienne, 4. Paris: Adrien-Maisonneuve; Tehran: Départment d'Iranologie de l'Institut Franco-Iranien, 1964.

———. *Creative Imagination in the Ṣūfism of Ibn ʿArabī.* Bollingen Series, 91. Princeton, N.J.: Princeton University Press, 1969.

Cropp, Glynnis M. *Le vocabulaire courtois des troubadours de l'époque classique.* Publications romanes et françaises, 135. Geneva: Droz, 1975.

Curtius, Ernst Robert. *European Literature and the Latin Middle Ages.* Translated by Willard Trask. Bollingen Series, 36. Princeton, N.J.: Princeton University Press, 1973.

Dahiyat, Ismail M. *Avicenna's Commentary on the Poetics of Aristotle: A Critical Study with an Annotated Translation of the Text.* Leiden: E. J. Brill, 1974.

Danner, Victor. "Arabic Literature in Iran." In *CHI*, 4:566–94.

Dawlatshāh. *The Tadhkiratu 'sh-Shuʿará' ("Memoirs of the Poets").* Edited by E. G. Browne. London: Luzac, 1901.

De Bruijn, J.T.P. *Of Piety and Poetry: The Interaction of Religion and Literature in the Life and Works of Ḥakīm Sanāʾī of Ghazna (OPP).* Publication of the de Goeje Fund, 25. Leiden: E. J. Brill, 1983.

De Bruijn, J.T.P. "Sanā'ī and the Rise of Persian Mystical Poetry." In *La signification du bas moyen âge dans l'histoire et la culture du monde musulman: Actes du Huitième Congrès de l'Union Européenne des Arabisants et Islamisants* (1976), pp. 35–43. Aix-en-Provence: Edisud, 1978.

Dembowski, Peter F. "Monologue, Author's Monologue and Related Problems in the Romances of Chrétien de Troyes." In *Approaches to Medieval Romance*, edited by Peter Haidu, pp. 102-14. Yale French Studies, 51. New Haven, Conn.: Yale University Press, 1974.

———. "Vocabulary of Old French Courtly Lyrics: Difficulties and Hidden Difficulties." *Critical Inquiry* 2 (1976), 763–79.

Denomy, A. J. "Courtly Love and Courtliness." *Speculum* 28 (1953), 44–63.

———. *The Heresey of Courtly Love*. New York: The Declan X. McMullen Co., 1947.

———. "An Inquiry into the Origins of Courtly Love." *Medieval Studies* 6 (1944), 175–260.

———. "*Jovens*: The Notion of Youth Among the Troubadours, Its Meaning and Source." *Medieval Studies* 11 (1949), 1–22.

Dragonetti, Roger. *La technique poétique des trouvères dans la chanson courtoise; contribution à l'étude de la rhétorique médiévale*. Rijksuniversiteit te Gent, Werken uitgegeven door de Faculteit van de Letteren en Wijsbegeerte, Afl. 127. Bruges: De Tempel, 1960.

Dronke, Peter. *Medieval Latin and the Rise of European Love-Lyric*. 2d ed. 2 vols. Oxford: Clarendon Press, 1968.

———. *Poetic Individuality in the Middle Ages: New Departures in Poetry, 1000–1150*. Oxford: Clarendon Press, 1970.

———. "Tradition and Innovation in Medieval Western Colour-Imagery." *Eranos-Jahrbuch* 41 (1972), 51–107.

Duchesne-Guillemin, Jacques. *La religion de l'Iran ancien*. Mana, Introduction à l'histoire des religions, 1. Les anciens religions orientales, 3. Paris: Presses Universitaires de la France, 1962.

Edwards, Thomas R. *Imagination and Power: A Study of Poetry on Public Themes*. New York: Oxford University Press, 1971.

Ettinghausen, Richard. "The Flowering of Seljuq Art." *Metropolitan Museum Journal* 3 (1970), 113–31.

Evans, Maurice. *English Poetry in the Sixteenth Century*. 2d ed., revised. London: Hutchinson University Library, 1967.

al-Fārābī. *Fuṣūl al-Madanī, Aphorisms of the Statesman*. Edited and translated by D. M. Dunlop. University of Cambridge Oriental Publications, 3. Cambridge: Cambridge University Press, 1961.

Farès, Bichr. *L'honneur chez les Arabes avant l'Islam; étude de sociologie*. Paris: Adrien-Maisonneuve, 1932.

Ferrante, Joan M. *Woman as Image in Medieval Literature, from the Twelfth Century to Dante*. New York: Columbia University Press, 1975.

———, and George D. Economou, eds. *In Pursuit of Perfection: Courtly Love in Medieval Literature*. Port Washington, N.Y.: Kennikat Press, 1975.

Finlayson, John. "The Concept of the Hero in 'Morte Arthure.' " In *Chaucer und seine Zeit*, edited by A. Esch, pp. 249–74. Tübingen: Max Niemayer, 1968.

Frappier, Jean. "Chrétien de Troyes." In *Arthurian Literature in the Middle Ages*, edited by R. S. Loomis, pp. 157–92. Oxford, 1959.

———. "Sur un procès fait à l'amour courtois." In *Amour courtois et Table Ronde*, pp. 61–96. Publications romanes et françaises, 76. Geneva: Droz, 1973.

———. "Vues sur les conceptions courtoises dans les littératures d'oc et d'oïl au XIIe siècle." *CCM* 2 (1959), 135–56.

Freeman, Michelle A. *The Poetics of Translatio Studii and Conjointure: Chrétien de Troyes's Cligès*. French Forum Monographs, 12. Lexington, KY: French Forum Publishers, 1979.

———. "Structural Transpositions and Intertextuality: Chrétien's *Cligès*." *Medievalia et Humanistica* 11 (1982), 149–63.

Fück, Johann. *ʿArabīya: Recherches sur l'histoire de la langue et du style arabe*. Translated by Claude Denizeau. Institut des Hautes Etudes Marocaines, Notes et Documents, 16. Paris: Marcel Didier, 1955.

Gabrieli, Francesco. "Note sul *Vīs u Rāmīn* di Faẖr ad-Dīn Gurgānī." *Rendiconti della R. Accademia Nazionale dei Lincei, Classe di scienzi morali, storichi e filologiche*, ser. 6, 15 (1939), 168–88.

———. "Versioni da Niẓāmī." *AION* 10:1–2 (1937–1938), 31–72.

Gallais, Pierre. "Les arbres entrelacés dans les 'romans' de Tristan et le mythe de l'arbre androgyne primordial." In *Mélanges de langue et de littérature médiévales offerts à Pierre le Gentil*, pp. 295–310. Paris: S.E.D.E.S. et C.D.U., 1973.

———. *Genèse du roman occidental; essais sur Tristan et Iseut et son modèle persan*. Paris: Tête de Feuilles/Sirac, 1974.

———. "Hexagonal and Spiral Structure in Medieval Narrative." In *Approaches to Medieval Romance*, edited by Peter Haidu, pp.

115–32. Yale French Studies, 51. New Haven, Conn.: Yale University Press, 1974.

———. *Perceval et l'initiation: essais sur le dernier roman de Chrétien de Troyes, ses correspondances "orientales" et sa signification anthropologique*. Paris: Sirac, 1972.

Garrison, James D. *Dryden and the Tradition of Panegyric*. Berkeley: University of California Press, 1975.

Ghanī, Qāsim. *Bahṣ dar āṣār u afkār u aḥvāl-i Ḥāfiẓ*. Vol. 1: *Tārīkh-i ʿaṣr-i Ḥāfiẓ*. Tehran: Zavvār, 1961.

Ghazoul, Ferial Jabouri. *The Arabian Nights: A Structural Analysis*. Cairo: Cairo Associated Institution for the Study and Presentation of Arab Cultural Values, 1980.

al-Ghazzālī. *Ghazālī's Book of Counsel for Kings (Nasīḥat al-Mulūk)*. Translated by F.R.C. Bagley. London: Oxford University Press, 1964.

Ghirshmann, R. *Iran: From the Earliest Times to the Islamic Conquest*. Baltimore: Penguin, 1954.

Giffen, Lois A. *Theory of Profane Love among the Arabs*. Studies in Eastern Civilization, 3. New York: New York University Press, 1971.

Gimaret, Daniel. *Le livre de Bilawhar et Būḏāsf*. Hautes études islamiques et orientales d'histoire comparée, 4. Geneva: 1971.

Ginsberg, Warren. *The Cast of Character: The Representation of Personality in Ancient and Medieval Literature*. Toronto: University of Toronto Press, 1983.

Goitein, S. D. *Studies in Islamic History and Institutions*. Leiden: E. J. Brill, 1968.

Goldin, Frederick. "The Array of Perspectives in the Early Courtly Love Lyric." In *In Pursuit of Perfection*, edited by J. Ferrante and G. Economou, pp. 51–100. Port Washington, N.Y.: Kennikat Press, 1975.

Grabar, Oleg. "The Visual Arts, 1050–1350." In *CHI*, 5:626–658.

Green. D. H. *Irony in the Medieval Romance*. Cambridge: Cambridge University Press, 1979.

———. "The Pathway to Adventure." *Viator* 8 (1977), 145–88.

Green, Richard Firth. *Poets and Princepleasers: Literature and the English Court in the Late Middle Ages*. Toronto: University of Toronto Press, 1980.

Hamori, Andras. "Form and Logic in Some Medieval Arabic Poems." *Edebiyat* 2 (1977), 163–72.

———. *On the Art of Medieval Arabic Literature.* Princeton, N.J: Princeton University Press, 1974.

Hanaway, William L., Jr. "The Concept of the Hunt in Persian Literature." *Boston Museum Bulletin* 68 (1976), 21–34.

Hanning, Robert W. *The Individual in Twelfth-Century Romance.* New Haven, Conn.: Yale University Press, 1977.

———. "Poetic Emblems in Medieval Narrative Texts." In *Vernacular Poetics in the Middle Ages*, edited by Lois W. Ebin, pp. 1–32. Studies in Medieval Culture, 16. Kalamazoo, Mich.: Western Michigan University Medieval Institute Publications, 1984.

Hardison, O. B., Jr. *The Enduring Monument; A Study of the Idea of Praise in Renaissance Literary Theory and Practice.* Chapel Hill: University of North Carolina Press, 1962.

———. "The Place of Averroes' Commentary on the *Poetics* in the History of Medieval Criticism." In *Medieval and Renaissance Studies*, edited by John L. Lievsay, pp. 57–81. Durham, N.C., 1970.

Hartner, Willy, and Richard Ettinghausen. "The Conquering Lion, the Life-Cycle of a Symbol." *Oriens* 17 (1964), 161–71.

Heinrichs, Wolfhart. *Arabische Dichtung und Grieschische Poetik: Ḥāzim al-Qarṭāǧannīs Grundlegung der Poetik mit Hilfe Aristotelischer Begriffe.* Beiruter Texte und Studien, 8. Wiesbaden: In Kommission Franz Steiner, 1969.

———. *The Hand of the Northwind: Opinions on Metaphor and the Early Meaning of Istiʿāra in Arabic Poetics.* Deutsche Mörgenlandische Gesellschaft, Abhandlungen fur die Kunde des Mörgenlandes, 44:2. Wiesbaden: Franz Steiner, 1977.

———. "Literary Theory: The Problem of Its Efficiency." In *Arabic Poetry: Theory and Development*, edited by G. E. von Grunebaum, pp. 19–69. Wiesbaden: Otto Harrassowitz, 1973.

Heninger, S. K., Jr. *Touches of Sweet Harmony: Pythagorean Cosmology and Renaissance Poetics.* San Marino, Calif.: The Huntington Library, 1974.

Hill, Joyce, ed. *The Tristan Legend: Texts From Northern and Eastern Europe in Modern English Translation.* Leeds Medieval Studies, 2. Leeds: University of Leeds, Graduate Centre for Medieval Studies, 1977.

Hillmann, Michael C. *Unity in the Ghazals of Hafez.* Studies in Middle Eastern Literatures, 6. Minneapolis: Bibliotheca Islamica, 1976.

Hodgson, M.G.S. *The Venture of Islam.* 3 vols. Chicago: University of Chicago Press, 1974.

Huart, C. *Ancient Persia and Iranian Civilization.* New York: Knopf, 1927.

Huppé, Bernard F. "The Unlikely Narrator: The Narrative Strategy of the *Troilus.*" In *Signs and Symbols in Chaucer's Poetry*, edited by J. P. Hermann and J. J. Burke, pp. 179–94. University, Ala.: The University of Alabama Press, 1981.

Ibn Qutaybah, ʿAbd Allāh ibn Muslim. *Introduction au Livre de la poésie et des poètes.* Edited and translated by Gaudefroy-Demombynes. Paris: Les Belles Lettres, 1947.

Ihle, Sandra Ness. *Malory's Grail Quest: Invention and Adaptation in Medieval Prose Romance.* Madison: University of Wisconsin Press, 1983.

Ikhwān al-Ṣafāʾ. *Rasāʾil Ikhwān al-Ṣafāʾ wa-Khullān al-Wafāʾ (RIS).* 4 vols. Beirut: Dār Bayrūt/Dār Ṣādir, 1957.

———. *Al-Risālah al-Jāmiʿah.* Edited by Muṣṭafā Ghālib. Beirut: Dār Ṣādir, 1974.

Intertextualités médiévales. Littérature 41 (Fevrier 1981) (special number).

Jackson, W.T.H. "Problems of Communication in the Romances of Chrétien de Troyes." In *Medieval Literature and Folklore Studies: Essays in Honor of Francis Lee Utley*, edited by Jerome Mandel and Bruce A. Rosenberg, pp. 39–50. New Brunswick, N.J.: Rutgers University Press, 1970.

Jacobi, Renate. "The Camel-Section of the Panegyric Ode." *JAL* 13 (1982), 1–22.

Jalāl al-Dīn Rūmī. *Discourses of Rūmī.* Translated by A. J. Arberry. London: John Murray, 1961.

———. *Kitāb-i Fīhi mā fīhi.* Edited by Badīʿ al-Zamān Furūzānfar. Tehran: Dānishgāh-i Tihrān, 1330/1951.

———. *Mystical Poems of Rumi: Second Selection.* Translated by A. J. Arberry. Boulder, Colo.: Westview Press, 1979.

Javitch, Daniel. *Poetry and Courtliness in Renaissance England.* Princeton, N.J.: Princeton University Press, 1978.

Jordan, Robert M. *Chaucer and the Shape of Creation: The Aesthetic Possibilities of Inorganic Structure.* Cambridge, Mass.: Harvard University Press, 1967.

Kaykāvūs ibn Iskandar. *A Mirror for Princes: The Qābūs Nāma.* Translated by Reuben Levy. New York: E. P. Dutton, 1951.

Kelly, Douglas. "*Matière* and *genera dicendi* in Medieval Romance."

In *Approaches to Medieval Romance*, edited by Peter Haidu, pp. 147–59. Yale French Studies, 51. New Haven, Conn.: Yale University Press, 1974.

———. *Sens and Conjointure in the Chevalier de la Charette*. Studies in French Literature, 2. The Hague: Mouton, 1966.

———. "Theory of Composition in Medieval Narrative and Geoffrey of Vinsauf's *Poetria Nova*." *Medieval Studies* 31 (1969), 117–48.

———. "*Translatio Studii*: Translation, Adaptation, and Allegory in Medieval French Literature." *PQ* 37 (1978), 287–310.

Khanlari, Parviz Natel. "Hafiz de Chiraz." In *L'âme de l'Iran*, pp. 153–77. Paris: Albin Michel, 1951.

al-Kīk, Viktūr. *Ta'ṣīr-i farhang-i ʿArab dar ashʿār-i Manūchihrī Dāmghānī*. Beirut: Dār al-Mashriq, 1971.

Kitāb al-Tāj fi akhlāq al-mulūk. Edited by Aḥmad Zakī Bāshā. Cairo: 1914.

Köhler, Erich. "Sens et fonction du terme 'jeunesse' dans la poésie des troubadours." In *Mélanges René Crozet*, edited by Pierre Gallais and Yves-Jean Riou, 1:569–71. Poitiers: Société d'Etudes Médiévales, 1966.

Kunitszch, Paul. "The 'Description of the Night' in Gurgānī's *Vīs u Rāmīn*." *Der Islam* 59 (1982), 93–110.

Lacy, Norris G. "Spatial Form in Medieval Romance." In *Approaches to Medieval Romance*, edited by Peter Haidu, pp. 160–9. Yale French Studies, 51. New Haven, Conn.: Yale University Press, 1974.

Lambton, A.K.S. "Islamic Mirrors for Princes." *Quaderno dell'Accademia Nazionale dei Lincei* 160 (1971), 419–42.

———. *State and Government in Medieval Islam, An Introduction to the Study of Islamic Political Theory: The Jurists*. London Oriental Series, 36. Oxford: Oxford University Press, 1981.

Lassner, Jacob. *The Shaping of ʿAbbasid Rule*. Princeton, N.J.: Princeton University Press, 1980.

Lazard, Gilbert. "Deux poèmes persans de tradition pehlevie." In *Mémorial Jean de Ménasce*, edited by Ph. Gignoux and A. Tafazzoli, pp. 433–40. Fondation Culturelle Iranienne, 185. Louvain: 1974.

———. "The Rise of the New Persian Language." In *CHI*, 4:595–632.

Lecomte, Gustave. *Ibn Qutayba, l'homme, son oeuvre et ses idées*. Damascus, 1965.

Lescot, Roger. "Essai d'une chronologie de l'oeuvre de Hāfiz." *BEO* 19 (1944), 57–100.

Levy, Reuben. *The Persian Language*. London: Hutchinson University Library, 1951.

Lewis, C. S. *The Allegory of Love: A Study in Medieval Tradition*. London: Oxford University Press, 1936.

Lomba Fuentes, Joaquin. "La beauté objective chez Ibn Ḥazm." *CCM* 7 (1964), 1–18, 161–78.

MacCaffrey, Isabel G. *Spenser's Allegory: The Anatomy of Imagination*. Princeton: Princeton University Press, 1976.

Maḥjūb, Muḥammad Jaʿfar. "Maṯnavī-sarāʾī dar zabān-i Fārsī tā pāyān-i qarn-i panjum-i Hijrī." *Nashrīyah-i Dānishkadah-i Adabīyāt-i Tabrīz* 15 (1342/1963), 188–213, 261–85.

Manzalaoui, Mahmoud. "The Pseudo-Aristotelian *Kitāb Sirr al-Asrār*: Facts and Problems." *Oriens* 23–24 (1974), 147–257.

Massignon, Louis. "La 'Futuwwa,' ou 'pacte d'honneur artisanal' entre les travailleurs musulmans au Moyen Age." *La Nouvelle Clio* 4 (1952), 171–98.

———. "Les methodes de réalisation artistique des peuples de l'Islam." In *Opera Minora*, edited by Y. Moubarac, 3:11–24. Beirut: Dar al-Maaref, 1963.

al-Masʿūdī. *Les prairies d'or*. Edited and translated by Barbier de Meynard and Pavet de Courteille. 9 vols. Paris: Imprimerie Nationale, 1861–77.

Meisami, Julie S. "Allegorical Gardens in the Persian Poetic Tradition: Neẓāmī, Rūmī, Ḥāfeẓ." *IJMES* 17 (1985), 229–60.

———. "Allegorical Techniques in the *Ghazals* of Hafez." *Edebiyat* 4 (1979), 1–40.

———. "The Analogical Structure of a Persian Courtly Lyric: Hafiz's 81st Ghazal." Paper presented at the Nineteenth International Congress on Medieval Studies, Kalamazoo, Michigan, May 1984.

———. "Fitnah or Āzādah? Niẓāmī's Ethical Poetic" (forthcoming).

———. "Medieval Persian Courtly Poetry: Allegories of Love and Justice." In *Love Lyrics in the Mediterranean Tradition: Studies in Memoriam Samuel M. Stern*, edited by James Monroe (forthcoming).

———. "Norms and Conventions of the Classical Persian Lyric: A Comparative Approach to the Ghazal." In *Proceedings of the Nineteenth Congress of the International Comparative Literature Association, Innsbruck 1979, 1: Classical Models in Literature*,

203–207. Innsbrucker Beitrage zur kulturwissenschaft, 49. Innsbruck: 1981.

———. "The Uses of the *Qaṣīda*: Thematic and Structural Patterns in a Poem of Bashshār." *JAL* 16 (1985), 40–60.

———. "The World's Pleasance: Ḥāfiẓ's Allegorical Gardens." *Comparative Criticism* 5 (1983), 153–85.

Melikian-Chirvani, Assadullah Souren. "L'évocation littéraire du bouddhisme dans l'Iran musulman." In *Le monde iranien et l'Islam: sociétés et cultures*, 2:1–72. Hautes études islamiques et orientales d'histoire comparée, 6. Geneva: Droz, 1974.

Mélikoff, I. "La fleur de la souffrance: recherche sur le sens symbolique de *lâle* dans la poésie mystique turco-iranienne." *JA* 25 (1967), 341–60.

Mez, Adam. *The Renaissance of Islam.* Translated by Salahuddin Khuda Bukhsh and D. S. Margoliouth. Beirut: United Publishers, 1973.

Miner, Earl. "The Grounds of Mimetic and Nonmimetic Art: The Western Sister Arts in a Japanese Mirror." In *Articulate Images: The Sister Arts From Hogarth to Tennyson*, edited by Richard Wendorf, pp. 70–97. Minneapolis: University of Minnesota Press, 1983.

———. "On the Genesis and Development of Literary Systems." *Critical Inquiry*, 5 (1978–1979), 339–53, 553–68.

Minorsky, Vladimir. "*Vīs u Rāmīn*: A Parthian Romance." *BSOAS* 11 (1943–46), 741–63; 12 (1947–48), 20–35; 16 (1954), 91–92; 25 (1962), 275–86.

Mitchell, W.J.T. "Spatial Form in Literature: Toward a General Theory." In *The Language of Images*, edited by W.J.T. Mitchell, pp. 271–99. Chicago: University of Chicago Press, 1974.

Mokri, Mohammad. "La lumière en Iran ancien et l'Islam." In *Le thème de la lumière dans le Judaïsme, le Christianisme et l'Islam*, pp. 325–430. Paris: Berg International, 1976.

Molé, Marijan. *Culte, mythe et cosmologie dans l'Iran ancien: Le problème zoroastrien et la tradition mazdéenne.* Annales du Musée Guimet, Bibliothèque d'Etudes, 69. Paris: Presses Universitaires de France, 1963.

———. "Daēnā, le pont Činvāt et l'initiation dans le Mazdéisme." *Revue de l'histoire des religions* 67 (1960), 155–85.

———. "L'epopée iranienne après Firdōsī." *La Nouvelle Clio* 5 (1953), 377–93.

Molé, Marijan. "Le jugement des morts dans l'Iran pré-Islamique." In *Sources Orientales*, 4: *Le jugement des morts*, pp. 143–75. Paris, Eds. du Seuil, 1961.

———. " 'Vīs u Rāmīn' et l'histoire Seldjoukide." *AION* 8 (1958), 1–20.

Monroe, James T. *The Art of Badīʿ az-Zamān al-Hamadhānī as Picaresque Narrative*. Papers of the Center for Arab and Middle East Studies, 2. Beirut: American University of Beirut, 1983.

Montgomery, Robert L. *The Reader's Eye: Studies in Didactic Literary Theory from Dante to Tasso*. Berkeley: University of California Press, 1979.

Morony, Michael G. *Iraq After the Muslim Conquest*. Princeton, N.J.: Princeton University Press, 1984.

Morris, Colin. *The Discovery of the Individual, 1050–1200*. London: SPCK, 1972.

Morrison, George. "Flowers and Witchcraft in the 'Vīs o Rāmīn' of Fakhr ud-Dīn Gurgānī." *Acta Iranica* 3 (1974), 249–59.

Myers, Henry A. "The Concept of Kingship in the 'Book of Emperors' ('Kaiserchronik')." *Traditio* 27 (1971), 205–30.

Naim, C. M. "The Theme of Homosexual (Pederastic) Love in Pre-Modern Urdu Poetry." In *Studies in the Urdu Gazal and Prose Fiction*, edited by M. U. Memon, pp. 120–41. University of Wisconsin, South Asian Studies Publication Series, 5. Madison: 1979.

Naṣīr al-Dīn Ṭūsī. *The Nasirean Ethics*. Translated by G. M. Wickens. London: Allen & Unwin, 1964.

Nasr, Seyyed Hossein. *An Introduction to Islamic Cosmological Doctrines*. Cambridge, Mass.: The Belknap Press of Harvard University Press, 1964.

Nelson, Lowry, Jr. "The Rhetoric of Ineffability: Toward a Definition of Mystical Poetry." *Comparative Literature* 8 (1956), 323–36.

Newman, F. X., ed. *The Meaning of Courtly Love*. Albany: University of New York Press, 1968.

Niẓām al-Mulk. *The Book of Government or Rules for Kings (The Siyāsat-nāma or Siyar al-Mulūk)*. Translated by Hubert Darke. New Haven, Conn.: Yale University Press, 1960.

Niẓāmī ʿArūẓī. *The Chahár Maqála ("Four Discourses")*. Translated by E. G. Browne. Hertford, Herts., 1899.

Nwyia, Paul. *Exégèse coranique et langage mystique*. Recherches de l'Institut de Lettres Orientales de Beyrouth, 49. Beirut: Dar el-Machreq, 1970.

Ollier, Marie-Louise. "The Author in the Text: The Prologues of

Chrétien de Troyes." In *Approaches to Medieval Romance*, edited by Peter Haidu, pp. 26–41. Yale French Studies, 51. New Haven, Conn.: Yale University Press, 1974.

———. "Demande sociale et constitution d'un 'genre': la situation dans la France du XIIe siècle." *Mosaic* 8:4 (1965), 207–16.

Pantke, Mechthild. *Der Arabische Bahrām-Roman: Untersuchungen zur Quellen- und Stoffgeschichte*. Studien zur Sprache, Geschichte und Kultur des Islamischen Oriens, n.f., 6. Berlin: Walter de Gruyter, 1974.

Papadopoulo, Alexandre. *Islam and Muslim Art*. Translated by Robert Erich Wolff. New York: Harry N. Abrams, 1979.

Parshall, Linda. *The Art of Narration in Wolfram's Parzival and Albrecht's Jüngerer Titurel*. Cambridge: Cambridge University Press, 1981.

Pedersen, Johannes. "The Islamic Preacher: *wāʿiẓ, mudhakkir, qāṣṣ*." In *Ignace Goldziher Memorial Volume*, edited by Samuel Löwinger and Joseph Somogyi, 1:226–51. Budapest: 1948.

Peterson, R. G. "Critical Calculations: Measure and Symmetry in Literature." *PMLA* 91 (1976), 376–75.

Pingree, David. "Mashā'allāh: Some Sassanian and Syriac Sources." In *Essays on Islamic Philosophy and Science*, edited by George F. Hourani, pp. 5–14. Albany: SUNY Press, 1975.

Poirion, Daniel. *Le poète et le prince: L'évolution du lyrisme courtois de Guillaume de Machaut à Charles d'Orléans*. Université de Grenoble, Publications de la Faculté des Lettres et Sciences Humaines, 35. Paris: Presses Universitaires de France, 1965.

Rastgār, Gītī Fallāḥ. "Ādāb u rusūm u tashrīfāt-i darbār-i Ghaznah az khilāl-i *Tārīkh-i Bayhaqī*." In *Yādnāmah-i Abū al-Faẓl Bayhaqī*, pp. 412–67. Mashhad: 1971.

Rehder, Robert. "Persian Poets and Modern Critics." *Edebiyat* 2 (1977), 91–117.

———. "The Unity of the Ghazals of Ḥāfiẓ." *Der Islam* 52 (1974), 55–96.

Reinert, B. "Probleme der vormongolischen arabisch-persischen Poesiegemeinschaft und ihr Reflex in der Poetik." In *Arabic Poetry: Theory and Development*, edited by G. E. von Grunebaum, pp. 71–105. Wiesbaden: Otto Harrassowitz, 1973.

Ritter, Hellmut. *Uber die bildersprache Niẓāmīs*. Studien zur Geschichte und Kultur des islamischen Orients, 5. Berlin: Walter de Gruyter, 1927.

Rosenthal, Franz. "Plotinus in Islam: The Power of Anonymity." *Quaderno dell'Accademia Nazionale dei Lincei* 198 (1974), 437–46.

Roth, Norman. " 'Deal gently with the young man': Love of Boys in Medieval Hebrew Poetry of Spain." *Speculum* 57 (1982), 20–51.

Ryan, W. F., and Charles B. Schmitt, eds. *Pseudo-Aristotle, The Secret of Secrets: Sources and Influences.* Warburg Institute Surveys, 9. London: The Warburg Institute, University of London, 1982.

Rypka, Jan. *History of Iranian Literature.* Dordrecht: D. Reidel, 1968.

———. "Poets and Prose Writers of the Late Saljuq and Mongol Periods." In *CHI*, 5:550–625.

———. "Les sept princesses de Nizhami." In *L'âme de l'Iran*, pp. 101–25. Paris: Albin Michel, 1951.

Savage-Smith, Emilie, and Marion B. Smith. *Islamic Geomancy and a Thirteenth-Century Divinatory Device.* Malibu, Calif.: Undena Publications, 1980.

Schimmel, Annemarie. "Ḥāfiẓ and His Critics." *Studies in Islam* 16 (1979), 1–33.

———. *Mystical Dimensions in Islam.* Chapel Hill: University of North Carolina Press, 1975.

———. "Turk and Hindu: A Literary Symbol." *Acta Iranica* 3 (1974), 243–48.

Schirmann, J. "The Ephebe in Medieval Hebrew Poetry." *Sefarad* 16 (1955), 55–68.

Shafīʿī Kadkanī, M. R. *Ṣuvar-i khiyāl dar shiʿr-i Fārsī.* Tehran: Nīl, 1350/1971.

Shams-i Qays Rāzī. *Al-Muʿjam fi Maʿáyíri ashʿári 'l-ʿAjam: A Treatise on the Prosody and Poetic Art of the Persians.* Edited by Mirza Muhammad Qazvini. E.J.W. Gibb Memorial Series, 10. Leiden: E. J. Brill; London: Luzac, 1909.

Shihābī, ʿAlī Akbar. *Niẓāmī, shāʿir-i dāstānsarā.* Tehran: Ibn Sīnā, 1334/1956.

Soucek, Priscilla P. "Niẓāmī on Painters and Painting." In *Islamic Art in the Metropolitan Museum of Art*, edited by Richard Ettinghausen, pp. 9–21. New York: Metropolitan Museum of Art, 1972.

Southern, R. W. *The Making of the Middle Ages.* New Haven, Conn.: Yale University Press, 1953.

Sperl, S. M. "Islamic Kingship and Arabic Panegyric Poetry in the Early 9th Century." *JAL* 8 (1979), 20–35.

Spitzer, Leo. *Classical and Christian Ideas of World Harmony: Pro-*

legomena to an Interpretation of the Word "Stimmung." Edited by Anna Granville Hatcher. Baltimore: The Johns Hopkins Press, 1963.

———. "Note on the Poetic and the Empirical 'I' in Medieval Authors." *Traditio* 4 (1946), 414–22.

Sprengling, M. "From Persian to Arabic." *AJSLL* 56 (1939), 174–224, 325–36.

Steadman, John M. " 'Courtly Love' as a Problem of Style." In *Chaucer und seine Zeit*, edited by A. Esch, pp. 1–33. Tübingen: Max Niemayer, 1968.

Stetkevych, Jaroslav. "Arabic Poetry and Assorted Poetics." In *Islamic Studies: A Tradition and Its Problems*, edited by Malcolm Kerr, pp. 103–23. Malibu, Calif.: Undena Publications, 1980.

Stetkevych, Suzanne P. "Toward a Redefinition of 'Badīʿ' Poetry." *JAL* 12 (1981), 1–29.

Stevens, Martin. "The Performing Self in Twelfth-Century Culture." *Viator* 9 (1978), 193–212.

Sūdī Busnavī. *Sharḥ-i Sūdī bar Ḥāfiẓ*. Trans. by ʿIṣmat Sattārzādah. 3d printing. 4 vols. Tehran: Dihkhudā, 1978.

Tavadia, J. C. "Iranistic and 'Islamic' Studies." In *Indo-Iranian Studies*, 1:43–50. Visva-Bharati Studies, 10. Santiniketan: Visva-Bharati, 1950.

Thiébaux, Marcelle. *The Stag of Love: The Chase in Medieval Literature*. Ithaca, N.Y.: Cornell University Press, 1974.

Thompson, Charlotte. 'Cosmic Allegory and Cosmic Error in the Frame of the *Canterbury Tales*." *Pacific Coast Philology* 18:1–2 (November 1983), 77–83.

Tomiche, Nada. "Réflexions sur la poésie de ʿAbbās b. al-Aḥnaf." *Arabica* 27 (1980), 275–99.

Trabulsi, Amjad. *La critique poétique des arabes*. Damascus: 1955.

Vadet, Jean-Claude. *L'Esprit courtois en Orient dans les cinq premiers siècles de l'Hégire*. Paris: G.-P. Maisonneuve, 1968.

———. "Quelques remarques sur la racine *ftn* dans le Coran et la plus ancienne littérature musulmane." *REI* 37 (1969), 81–101.

van Ess, Josef. "The Logical Structure of Islamic Theology." In *Logic in Classical Islamic Culture*, edited by G. E. von Grunebaum, pp. 21-50. Wiesbaden: Otto Harrassowitz, 1970.

van Gelder, G.J.H. *Beyond the Line: Classical Arabic Literary Critics on the Coherence and Unity of the Poem*. Studies in Arabic Literature, 8. Leiden: E. J. Brill, 1982.

Vinaver, Eugene. "Landmarks in Arthurian Romance." In *The Expansion and Transformations of Courtly Literature*, edited by N. B. Smith and J. T. Snow, pp. 17–31. Athens: University of Georgia Press, 1980.

———. *The Rise of Romance*. Oxford: Clarendon Press, 1971.

Von Grunebaum, G. E. "The Aesthetic Foundation of Arabic Literature." *Comparative Literature* 4 (1952), 323–40.

———. "Aspects of Arabic Urban Literature Mostly in Ninth and Tenth Centuries." *Islamic Studies* 8 (1969), 281–300.

———. "The Concept of Plagiarism in Arabic Theory." *JNES* 3 (1944), 243–53.

———. "The Hero in Medieval Arabic Prose." In *Concepts of the Hero in the Middle Ages and the Renaissance*, edited by Norman T. Burns and Christopher Regan, pp. 83–100. Albany: SUNY Press, 1975.

———. "Literature in the Context of Islamic Civilization." *Oriens* 20 (1968), 1–14.

Wade, David. *Pattern in Islamic Art*. Woodstock, N.Y.: The Overlook Press, 1976.

Waldman, Marilyn Robinson. *Toward a Theory of Historical Narrative: A Case Study in Perso-Islamicate Historiography*. Columbus: Ohio State University Press, 1980.

Wansbrough, John. "Arabic Rhetoric and Qur'anic Exegesis." *BSOAS* 31 (1968), 469–85.

———. "Majāz al-Qur'ān: Periphrastic Exegesis." *BSOAS* 33 (1970), 247–66.

———. "A Note on Arabic Rhetoric." In *Lebende Antike; Symposion fur Rudolf Suhnel*, edited by Horst Meller and Hans-Joachim Zimmerman, pp. 55–63. Berlin: Erich Schmidt, 1967.

al-Washshā', Muḥammad ibn Isḥāq. *Kitāb al-Muwaššá*. Edited by Rudolph E. Brunnow. Leiden: E. J. Brill, 1886.

Wensinck, A. J. "The Semitic New Year and the Origin of Eschatology." *Acta Orientalia* 1 (1922), 158–99.

Wickens, G. M. "The Frozen Periphery of Allusion in Classical Persian Literature." *Literature East and West* 18:2–4 (1974), 171–90.

———. "Persian Literature: An Affirmation of Identity." In *Introduction to Islamic Civilization*, edited by R. M. Savory, pp. 71–7. Cambridge: Cambridge University Press, 1976.

Yar-Shater, Ehsan. "The Theme of Wine and Wine-Drinking and the Concept of the Beloved in Early Persian Poetry." *Studia Islamica* 13 (1960), 43–53.

Zarrīnkūb, ʿAbd al-Ḥusayn. *Az kūchah-i rindān: dar bārah-i zindagī u andīshah-i Ḥāfiẓ*. 3d ed. Tehran: Amīr Kabīr, 1978.

Zink, Michel. "Remarques sur les conditions de l'anonymité dans la poésie lyrique française du moyen âge." In *Mélanges de langue et de littérature françaises du Moyen Age et de la Renaissance offerts à Charles Foulon*, 1:421–7. Rennes: Université de Haute-Bretagne, Institut de Français, 1980.

Zumthor, Paul. "De la circularité du chant (à propos des trouvères des XIIe et XIIIe siècles)." *Poétique* 2 (1970), 129–40.

———. "Le *je* de la chanson et le moi du poète." In *Langue, texte, énigme*, pp. 181–96. Paris: Eds. du Seuil, 1975.

Index

Library of Congress Cataloging-in-Publication Data

Meisami, Julie Scott, 1937–
Medieval Persian court poetry.

Bibliography: p.
Includes index.
1. Persian poetry—747–1500—History and criticism. I. Title.

PK6416.M45 1987 891.55'11'09 87-1743
ISBN 0-691-06598-5 (alk. paper)

Julie Scott Meisami is Lecturer in Persian
at The Oriental Institute, Oxford University.
This is her first book.